World War II
Front Line Nurse

By

Mildred A. MacGregor

(ex. Lieutenant Mildred A. Radawiec, Army Nurse Corp.)

Dedication

This book is dedicated to those who gave their lives in World War II, believing that it was a war to end wars, and that humanity could solve world problems without sacrificing their finest generation of youth.

And also, it is dedicated to my family: My husband, Dr. Robert K. MacGregor, our daughter, Elizabeth Irene York, and our sons, Robert K. MacGregor, Jr. and John R. MacGregor.

ISBN: 978-1-4243-4328-7

Communication with the author can be made at frontlinenurse@WW2nurse.com

Foreword:
War and the Single Girl

War is too big for the ordinary mind to encompass. As soon as one manages to grasp the abstraction, one has lost the reality of it. And the reality, after all, is what one can see and hear and touch—and imagine in the privacy of one's own head.

Imagine, for example, a young woman, having chosen a career of helping others, of relieving suffering, of tending the hurt and damaged; imagine her thrust into an enterprise in which hurting and damaging people is the whole point of endeavor, of magnifying the suffering to a degree that everything else becomes secondary. Mildred Radawiec, a nurse, a single woman approaching her thirtieth birthday, volunteers to go help in a war that threatens to overwhelm her world. Her fiancé is certain to be called up for military duty the moment he finishes his college work, so they postpone their plans to embark on what they hope to be their life together. Their reality of daily life becomes subsumed in a global adventure in which individuals, with their wants and hurts and imaginations, become grains of sand on a beach, leaves caught in a winter gale.

Life goes on, as they say. No matter the scale of the storm, the scale of life is the personal. This young soldier, bleeding to death on a battlefield, thinks not about the grand objectives of the war, but of home and family. This young nurse, when she's not called to do her utmost to save the young soldier, basks on a warm beach, being what she is, a woman in the prime of her life. When the grinding demands of war are momentarily distant, she dances in the arms of young men to the music of home—the reality of her imagination. Into the battlefields she carries, along with her steel helmet, a silver lamé evening gown, an impulse purchase as she embarked on this incredibly monstrous adventure.

War changes all the rules of life, they say. Well, perhaps, for the moment. Holding the hand of a frightened, dying boy, one faces the truth of all of us, and rages against the horror of it. Holding the hand of an attentive man over a glass of *vin blanc* on the coast of Algeria, with a warm sea breeze wafting the scent of bougainvillea, momentarily hides the fear that tomorrow he may not return but instead die in the flames of war, beyond her help, beyond her hope.

War is momentous, but the moments are personal. Fear and pain and suffering come and go, along with pleasure and joy, but their effects linger. Here is the story of the moments in the life of one young woman, altogether less than three years of such moments, a fraction of her life. Yet those three years still color her world. Forty years later, she began the effort to collect the records and memories of her moments in the war and to make sense of it all. After sixty years, she continues the task, not wanting to forget—or to be forgotten.

As all personal stories do, hers lived in a context. Is the context the real meaning, or is the personal experience? We seek, sometimes, that which is before us, in this moment. A journal, a uniform, and a silver lamé gown.

Donald Skiff
October 3, 2006 (D-Day plus 22,764)

Preface

Mildred A. Radawiec, R.N., Retired Lieutenant, served in the Army Nurse Corp (ANC) and was a member of the Third Auxiliary Surgical Group in World War II. This is her story.

The experiences of several other members of the Third Auxiliary Surgical Group also appear in these pages. Their stories first appeared in *Front Line Surgeons*, authored by Clifford L. Graves, M.D., and are used here with permission:

Major Darrell A. Campbell page 230

Captain Abraham Horvitz page 231

Major James J. Whitsitt page 242

Major Albert J. Crandall page 245

Captain Frank J. Lavieri page 249

Captain Charles O. Van Gorder page 250

Nurse Lieutenant Frances Slanger page 322

Private Jimmie Polite page 348

Captain Claude M. Warren page 355

Nurse Lieutenant Mabel Jessop page 362

Major Charles A. Serbst page 367

Captain Harry Fisher page 376

Additional material originally appearing in *Front Line Surgeons* has been included to provide continuity and context.

Lt. Mildred A. Radawiec, R.N., 1942

Contents

Prologue:
In The Beginning

The events that preceded my going to war had begun a year before, on December 7, 1941, when we were shocked to hear, broadcast over the radio: "JAPS BOMB PEARL HARBOR!" Headlines on the extra editions of the newspapers that were printed immediately after that extraordinary event read: "JAPS BOMB OUR PACIFIC FLEET AT PEARL HARBOR." Men with bundles of newspapers clutched under their arms dashed up and down city streets shouting, "Extra! Extra! Read all about it. Japs Attack Pearl Harbor!" The extra edition cost a dime, five times the price of the two-cent daily newspaper.

The United States of America and Britain declared war on Japan on December 8, 1941. Japan invaded the Philippines on December 22, 1941, and America began fighting Japan on the islands of the Pacific Ocean. The question was: could America alone fight a war in the Far East? England's army and navy in the Far East were already occupied in protecting her colonies, now that Japan was her enemy as well. On December 10, Japan's air force had sunk England's newest and mightiest battleship afloat, the 35,000 ton *Prince of Wales*, and the 32,000 ton cruiser *Repulse*, off the Malay Peninsula. Since the ships did not blow up, British aircraft and destroyers were able to rescue 2000 men from the sea. Eight hundred and forty were lost.

America struggled to send planes and ships to fight Japan, but distance and the loss of most of her Pacific Fleet, along with our being unprepared for war, led to disaster after disaster as Americans were taken prisoner in the Philippines, and casualties on the islands mounted. Our armed forces, faced with war on two fronts and separated by oceans thousands of miles wide, had to weigh their priorities. We were torn between the Atlantic and the Pacific theaters and not prepared militarily to fight in either one.

America decided the war in Europe would take precedence in manpower and supplies over the Pacific war, as it mobilized its industrial resources to create the mightiest navy, air force and army that the world had ever seen.

Hitler was elated when he heard news of the Pearl Harbor bombing. On December 11, Germany and Italy, along with Japan in a tripartite pact, declared war on America. By that time, German troops were retreating from Rostov and from other areas in Russia, where the temperature had dropped to minus forty degrees in bitter winter weather, recalling Napoleon's war with Russia a hundred and fifty years before.

When America had gone to England's aid after the fall of France in June, 1940, Hitler was stunned. The United States had for months been sending aid to keep England alive, and the U.S. Navy had orders to fire on German and Italian warships in the Atlantic shipping lanes.

England, along with the occupied countries, now looked to America for support.

Unrest in Europe had begun with the annexation of Austria by Germany on March 13, 1938. In Vienna, thousands of persons committed suicide rather than be dominated by the Nazis. Germany next occupied the Sudetenland on September 30, 1938.

Isolationists in our country sent a "Peace Ship" overseas in an attempt to forestall war. England's Prime Minister, Neville Chamberlain, attempted reconciliation, but this effort only allowed Hitler time to prepare for his next invasion. The Western world was disturbed by the occupations. We sympathized with Czechoslovakia when on March 17, 1939 their leaders, faced with threats of annihilation, were forced to capitulate.

Hitler's tanks rolled across Poland's border on September 1, 1939, triggering a threatened declaration of war by England on September 3. Finally France, alarmed once again by her neighbor's aggression, joined England and declared war on Germany. On April 9, 1940, Hitler invaded Denmark and Norway, in spite of those nations reaffirming their neutrality earlier, on the 20th of January. Belgium, Holland, and Luxembourg fell when Nazi tanks and air attacks smashed through their borders on May 10, 1940. German bombers began heavy bombing of England's southern ports in May 1940.

Americans were disturbed as they saw news flashes in the movie theaters and pictures in the newspapers of bomb damage and saw the British digging themselves out of the debris. Scenes of children boarding trains, being separated from families and sent to the countryside for safety, saddened us. We read about thousands of casualties throughout Europe and were concerned and anxious for the entire world, but we hesitated sending American young men to fight again as they did in World War I, what had been hoped to be "The War to End All Wars." Newspapers printed large headlines as one country after another surrendered to invasion by Hitler's Panzer Divisions.

Germany had attacked Russia on June 21, 1941 over a dispute about Rumania. Operation Barbarossa, the largest invasion in history, began. Three German army groups, a force of over four million men, advanced rapidly deep into the Soviet Union, destroying almost the entire western Soviet army.

The entire world was now in conflict. Our young men were sent "Over There" once again to save Europe from German domination.

In the United States on February 16, 1942, all men between the ages of eighteen and sixty-five, under the terms of the Selective Service Act, had to register for the draft. The SSA had been established on September

14, 1940, and was the first compulsory military training law in the history of our country. College students near completion of degrees were allowed to graduate, but all men except those in vital positions and considered indispensable to the war effort would be assigned to some branch of the services. Those who volunteered could join the service of their choice; the draftees were inducted into the Army, Navy, Marines, or Air Force, wherever the need was greatest. Most ended up in the infantry.

The war led everyone into a contemplative mood regarding its significance and how it would affect their lives. We no longer had control of our lives. A dark cloud hung over the entire world.

"Let's get married, to hell with the war," was the byword of many young couples. Bob and I faced a difficult dilemma—should we? Or should we not marry? We would be apart no matter what the decision. Would marriage under such circumstances work out, or would separation create unseen problems? If our love was real, it would survive the war. The war might be shortened once the Americans joined the Allies. We decided we would wait until hostilities ended and peace returned to the world.

At the University of Michigan Hospital where I was on duty at the time, doctors, realizing they would be called into service, decided to organize a Michigan Hospital Unit intended for overseas duty. My work as a private duty nurse with many of the leading surgeons at the hospital had provided me with the confidence and experience to perform in most surgical and medical areas. Realizing that I had to make a decision about my future, since my fiancé would be going to war, I attended discussions about forming an army general hospital. The speaker, a retired colonel, told about his experience in World War I. He made us aware of the needs, the sacrifices, and the honor of service. He did not spare the gore, the maggots and high mortality of war. Listening to him stirred my interest when he said, "It will be the most unforgettable experience you will ever have. You will never want to go through it again, but you would not want to have missed it for anything in the world."

He then added, "It won't be the same this time, as there have been great advances in scientific, technological, strategic and mechanical areas of warfare. You won't be able to take much with you, only what you can carry. But do take along something that will lift your spirits when you get lonely or downhearted. There will be times for camaraderie and for relief from the tensions of war, a time for rest, for frivolity, even parties, as men do get periods away from the pressures of war for respite and relaxation."

I began filling out army application forms in quintuplicate and became part of the 298th General Hospital, as the University of Michigan Hospital was called. Ten days later, while I was in Tucson, Arizona, where I had escorted a tubercular patient to a sanatorium, I received an urgent telegram from the United States Army, stating:

Report at once to the Davies Mountain Air Base/ Tucson Air Flight priority to Detroit/ Report to New York Port of Embarkation ten days.

I was surprised that the army was able to trace me so far away. It made me feel indispensable, but it also meant drastic changes in my plans for the future. Diverse thoughts raced through my mind. Hurriedly, I said good-bye to my patient, leaving him in the care of the sanatorium. There was far more important work for me now, as I became frantically involved in the war effort. Airports, bus and train stations were jammed with men in uniform. I was given first priority to travel, while civilians were left stranded in airports. The army sent soldiers to the Atlantic or the Pacific Coast to join various units where they were most needed. I had ten days to clear out my apartment, dispose of all my possessions, settle my personal affairs, and worst of all, part with my sweetheart.

It was with much apprehension that I boarded the train ten days later and watched him, his arm half raised with a last kiss blown my way. The train curved around a bend and he was gone. I was alone, alone in a crowded train. A sinking feeling overcame me. How could I live without him? It was because I knew that he would have to go to war that I had joined the army, but it was I who was leaving!

Chapter 1:
The Troopship Queen Mary

7 December 1942

I struggled up the gangplank of the *Queen Mary* with my heavy suitcase in one hand, a small make-up case in the other, a gas mask and musette bag crisscrossed over my chest, my brown purse hung from my right shoulder plus a canteen filled with water, and a flashlight attached to the wide web belt around my waist. As we filed past a ship's officer, he handed each of us nurses a card with the number of the cabin we would occupy. A crewman led us up the many flights of stairs to our assigned cabins on the main deck. I was surprised to see the cabin filled with rows of bunks lined up in tiers of four, nearly touching the ceiling, with just enough aisle space to pass between the rows. There were twelve bunks in my cabin. Anxious to loosen the attachments that had weighted us down all day we dropped our gear on the bunks and settled after shoving the suitcases under the lower bunks to clear a pathway. There would be no supper tonight, since the ship's halls were crowded with fifteen thousand troops treading the twelve decks to their assigned area. I was hungry, and remembered the sandwich that we got at Camp Kilmer for the road. I climbed to the upper bunk in the semi-darkness with my life preserver, fumbled for my flashlight and started reminiscing about the events of the past few weeks.

I wondered what my sweetheart was doing tonight and how this separation would affect our lives. I missed the companionship and devotion we had shared and wondered if our love would survive the war. I remembered the last kiss when we said goodbye and his wave just as we rounded the bend. Thoughts raced through my mind. Was it a mistake to have joined the Army? I was filled with misgivings about what lay ahead. How long was

Nurses Asselin, Radawiec, Keyes and Huntington, at
Leon & Eddie's, New York, before sailing

this separation going to last? Bob and I had been very close with plans to spend the rest of our lives together. Surely our love would last no matter how long we would be apart.

My mind wandered back to the Roosevelt Hotel in New York where I had stayed a week with seven nurses while we were being inducted. We rode the subway to the Port of Embarkation each morning for physical examination, orientation, and injections against typhoid, malaria, cholera, and tetanus. Then there was the tedious chore of filling out army forms in quintuplicate.

We spent our evenings mesmerized by the bright lights of Broadway, Times Square, and Rockefeller Center. We ate at the famous Leon and Eddy's and other night clubs. On stage we saw Helen Hayes in "Arsenic and Old Lace," Frank Fay in "Harvey" and the "Rockettes" at the Rockefeller Center. We were anxious to see everything we could in New York before the war took us away.

Bob telephoned frequently. He wanted to come to

New York to be with me, in spite of final examinations that were soon due in Medical school. I was gone all day, but most of all I dreaded another parting. I was now in the army "for the duration plus six months." I thought the six months was a long time. I was sure the war would be over as soon as the Americans landed "Over There".

About the time our uniforms were issued and our shots and orientation completed, we were ordered to report to Fort Dix, in New Jersey. There I heard that the University of Michigan Unit, the reason I had joined the army, had sailed without us. We felt betrayed! Inducted into the army under false expectation! We also realized that since we had taken the "Oath", there was not much we could do about the situation. I was now Second Lieutenant, N731714 ANC, Army Nurse Corp. We were placed into a pool to be assigned to any group that needed nurses.

In the meantime, we were assigned to temporary duty at Fort Dix. At the Fort we took care of not very sick GIs who played poker a good part of the day. Our primary responsibility, it seemed to me, was to prevent gambling. Our evenings were spent in the officers' club playing bridge, dancing at weekend parties or driving to the nightclubs in Wrightstown with the newly commissioned infantry lieutenants we had met at the camp and who were expecting to go overseas, as were we.

The Third Auxiliary Surgical Group

On December 5, 1942, we seven Michigan nurses who had missed sailing to war with the Michigan Hospital, now called the 298th General, were assigned to the Third Auxiliary Surgical Group, along with 105 nurses from Camp Kilmer. We heard that this group would operate near the front line to save the lives of seriously wounded soldiers who might not otherwise survive. The Surgical Group consisted of 216 officer surgeons, anesthetists, dentists and 227 enlisted men, and now 112 nurses. We represented every state in the Union, a group of strangers with whom our lives would be intermingled for the duration of the war, "plus six months."

Camp Kilmer was a staging area camouflaged to match the mud where rows of drab wooden barracks were separated by rows of soggy paths. The overcast gray sky and snow flurries with intermittent rain made it a dismal site. Inside, canvas cots lined the huge barn-like quarters as far as one could see in the semi darkness. These dismal quarters were barely lighted by bulbs dangling on an electric cord hung high in the rafters.

Our day started with roll call at seven. I guessed that this was to be sure no one had gone AWOL, as well as a testing period to weed out timid souls. The dining room, with its rows of rough wooden tables and benches, was bedlam when hundreds of women gathered for meals. The din of chatter, the background noise of pots and pans, dishes rattling, and the stomping of boots as we shook off mud and snow upon entering the huge mess hall was enormous. Nurses wore various conglomerations of army and civilian clothes, creating a disheveled appearance. The food was unappetizing; the coffee unpalatable. After a late lunch one day, I watched a GI use the tall galvanized coffee pot as a basin to wash the rough wood table with a muddy looking rag. Small wonder the coffee tasted so bad.

On December 7, 1942, one year after the bombing of Pearl Harbor, we got orders to pack. We were excited and anxious to leave this dismal camp; anyplace else would be a welcome change. We rushed from one barracks to another through the mud and snow to mail our last letters, sign last wills and testaments and powers-of-attorney. We rolled up our bed rolls, packed our suitcases and metal lockers, crammed the last minute PX purchases into our musette bags and made ready to leave the staging area at Camp Kilmer. Then we stood around and waited for hours. When the two-and-a-half-ton trucks arrived we marched toward the rear where a GI handed us a sandwich in a brown paper sack. I tucked mine into my musette bag and was boosted into the truck with the helping hand of another GI who steadied us as we climbed on to the high tailgate step and settled down on the benches that lined both sides of the truck. We were on our way at last!

At the station we formed into a long queue and waited our turn to board the train. As we settled in our seats, we were surprised to hear the strains of "From the Halls of Montezuma." Looking out the window I saw snowflakes gently covering a small band alongside the tracks. A thought flashed through my mind! Is that where we were going or was there no significance to the words of the song, "to the shores of Tripoli?" With a shrill whistle and the screeching sound of steel on steel, the wheels of the train began to turn, and we were off to war!

We left the staging area at Camp Kilmer at eight o'clock p.m., and arrived at the blacked-out port in Weehawken where we boarded a ferry silhouetted against the foggy winter sky. Lights were dimmed and conversation muffled as we settled on cold benches with our paraphernalia at our feet. It took two hours to travel from Weehawken to Manhattan where the *Queen Mary*, the largest, fastest and most luxurious liner in the world

The Queen Mary, before donning her wartime coat of grey paint

was anchored at Pier 90.

It was the *Queen's* first voyage since October 2, when she had collided with the British cruiser *Curacao*. She had the right of way, and the cruiser was in her lane of traffic. Although the cruiser was cut in half, with the loss of 338 lives, the *Queen* continued on with part of her bow torn away. Had she stopped to rescue survivors she might have been sunk by the U-boats that stalked ships in the Atlantic. She had lain in Boston Harbor's dry-dock for the next two months while the damage was repaired.

The *Queen* had been stripped of all the luxurious embellishment that had attracted royalty and wealthy travelers when she crossed the Atlantic in four and a half days, and had been converted to accommodate an entire army division plus a crew of 2000, totaling 17,000. Her precious oil paintings, thick rugs, furnishings, draperies, and crystal chandeliers had all been removed. In spite of her war-time coat of grey paint, however, she breathed affluence and splendor.

In the distance, the silhouette of the Statue of Liberty loomed against the dark sky. Battleships and destroyers on either side of the *Queen* kept watch over her as planes circled overhead. It was known that Hitler had posted a $250,000 reward to anyone who would sink her. The *Queen* was the largest ship ever built and was easily identified by her three smoke stacks.

Now, lying on a top bunk on the crowded *Queen Mary* with my diary and pencil in hand, I remembered that I had been too distracted at ten o'clock to concentrate on my fiancé, as we had pledged to do. Our minds were to transcend time and space, to be together in spirit, wherever we were. I wondered if he remembered. Was he as lonesome for me as I was for him, despite my being surrounded by thousands of people? I tucked the flashlight under my pillow and closed my eyes. Tired after all the activity, I fell asleep quickly in spite of the chatter in the surrounding bunks below me and on both sides. I tossed from side to side on the narrow bunk. Finally I covered my head with my pillow to stifle the sound of marching feet past our cabin door and above me as the troops loaded throughout the night.

The vibration of the ship's engines awakened me at six-thirty the following morning, and as the ship began to get under way its seams creaked with all its weight. At seven, we descended many flights of stairs to the dining room for breakfast. Meals were being served around the clock in shifts. After a delicious breakfast of bacon and eggs, juice and coffee, we nurses went topside, where we could see a vast array of vessels as far as the horizon. I heard that the enlisted men, because of limited hammock space, slept in relays, rotating every eight hours. The rest of the time they spent in boredom in the hold of the ship.

Destroyers on either side of the Queen kept watch over her. A blimp hovered overhead, and planes circled over the entire fleet. Battleships surrounded other merchant vessels loaded with thousands of troops. As we sailed, I saw ships changing position at a given flag signal. The maneuvering was to reduce the risk of getting hit by a torpedo. Nazi U-boats plied the oceans and had sunk many Allied merchant ships close to our shores. These were dangerous waters. Planes checked on the fleet from a distance. Later in the day when I went on deck I discovered that the *Queen* had left the convoy and was traveling alone, as she would be easily identified among the other ships and was zigzagging every eight minutes to avoid being struck by a German submarine, as it took that long for a submarine to get into a firing position.

When transporting luxury travelers before the war, her commander, Sir James Bissett, had broken all records for crossing the Atlantic eastbound—three days, twenty-three hours, and fifty-seven minutes. The *Queen* had carried millions of passengers on round trips commercially prior to the war and would transport 810,000 troops during World War II. We had heard that

Hitler had already announced the sinking of the *Queen Mary* to the German nation. German prisoners aboard the *Queen* en route to internment camps in Canada did not believe they were aboard the *Queen* despite seeing her name on the bulwark. They said the nameplate was subterfuge, that Hitler had declared that she had been sunk. It was probably because she had lain in dock for the two months it took to repair her hull after she had rammed the British cruiser *Curacoa*. We were her first passengers after she was seaworthy again.

Nurses and Red Cross women were assigned cabins on the main deck, fifty feet above water. Our first abandon ship drill was called by the blast of the klaxon. We formed into queues and quickly climbed the many flights of stairs to an assigned place on the deck where, in the past, passengers had played tennis. There were several lifeboats suspended on davits above the deck. When a crewman overheard someone refer to the *Queen* as a "boat," he promptly announced: "The *Queen* is not a boat; she is a ship." He then pointed to the life boats suspended above, "Those are boats. I might as well tell you now that the boats will accommodate only twenty five percent of the ships passengers. The rest of you will rely on rafts or May Wests. In December, survival in the North Atlantic is about seven minutes before freezing numbness sets in. You must carry your life preservers at all times along with your water-filled canteens attached to your canvas belt."

We were also warned that should anyone fall overboard, the *Queen* would not stop to look for them. A British officer crewman told us the fifty-foot drop from the main deck would result in a concussion and would break one's neck. The sun deck where I spent most of the day was a hundred feet above the sea.

A meeting for all Third Auxiliary Surgical Group officers was called at two o'clock. This included nurses, since we were officers in the Army Nurse Corps. We were told to meet in the small lounge where the troop commander issued the following orders: "There will be absolutely no smoking on deck at blackout. Positively no flashlights are to be used outside of the enclosed areas. If anyone has a radio in his possession it will be confiscated for the duration of this voyage."

He repeated what we had heard earlier: "Should any of you fall overboard, this ship will not turn back for any reason. You should also be aware that Hitler has placed a high prize to any of his seagoing vessels for sinking the *Queen Mary*. I remind you again that you must have your life preserver, your canteen full of water and your survivor rations on you at all times. Boat drills will be called by the klaxon at any time of day, and you must go to your designated areas as quickly as you can, short of running. You will never know when it is the real thing. No one is excused from participating. Thank you for your cooperation."

When the troop commander finished, Lieutenant Colonel Fred J. Blatt, the commanding officer of the Third Auxiliary Surgical Group, stepped forward to address us. He explained that our organization was an "experiment in this war." We would be closer to the front line than any hospitals in previous wars and would endeavor to save the lives of the severely wounded soldiers, those who would not survive any delay. We would operate as soon as the wounded were carried from the battalion aid station to the field hospitals close to the Front.

This was the first time we got a good view of our Commanding Officer. Lieutenant Colonel Blatt was of medium height, handsome, heavyset, with clean-cut features. His husky build made him look strong, his chin determined. I guessed him to be about forty-five years old. His dark brown eyes greeted us with an expression of reserve, almost shyness. This was the first time we were together in an area where we could all look each other over. At Camp Kilmer we had met only a few of the executive officers in the dark barracks, lighted by a dangling bulb hanging from the rafter, when we had to fill out forms or get instructions. I looked about me and wondered what alliances lay ahead in this conglomeration of strangers. I knew that it would not involve me, since my affections were for my fiancé to whom I would be true.

Colonel Blatt then introduced Major Clifford Graves who stepped forward to greet us with a broad smile. He expanded on the goals of the "Third Aux," as he abbreviated the title of our organization. The major appeared slim in comparison to the colonel, and younger, possibly in his late thirties. His light brown hair receded above a high, wide forehead. His square jaw and expressive face commanded our attention as he spoke with clarity, enunciating words as an English professor might. His eyes searched over the sea of faces before him with confidence in a relaxed manner. He also told us that it would be our duty to staff the ship's infirmary. That meant we would be working while traveling.

Next, Officer Frasier, one of the *Queen's* crew, added a few reminders: Nothing was to be thrown overboard— papers, cigarettes, anything—that could leave a trail of the ship's passing. Garbage was disposed of during the night so that by daylight the current would have dispersed it and the ship would be far away. The exits from the interior of the ship were hidden by double tarpaulin passageways to avoid any light showing outside the ship. We were advised to go through them carefully to avoid light exposure. We were to be in complete blackout. Portholes were covered and bolted shut.

As I looked out to sea a fellow passenger greeted me with a friendly smile. "Hello, see anything interesting? I'm Ed Donnely, from Detroit."

It was instant camaraderie, as one feels when traveling and meeting someone from near home. "I have watched you as you look out to sea so intensely. Are you part of the crew in disguise or a fellow passenger like myself?"

Looking up at his chuckling face and flashing blue eyes, I could see that he was teasing. "Yes, one might think I was part of the crew, with all the time I spend on deck searching the sky and sea. I guess I'm doing it because I'm curious, and I don't want to miss anything."

We looked up at the anti-aircraft guns on swiveling bases located above us, and noted the precautions the ships were using. Navy gunners on duty in the gun nests were constantly searching the skies for enemy planes, ships or submarines in the horizon. As we strolled along the deck we discovered a large cannon on the main deck, pointed out to sea. When the cannon fired, to make sure it was in working order, the entire ship vibrated. Captain Donnely said it was an eight-inch gun. Others were three inch and the anti-aircraft were 20mm and 50 caliber. Torpedoes rested on a lower ledge on both sides astern of the ship, just above the water line. Somewhere below there were depth charge bombs that would be discharged if a submarine were sighted.

We spotted one lone plane in the distance, checking on us from afar, we figured. A fellow passenger said that we had planes based in Iceland. A short time later, I saw a tiny moving object sweeping down out of the sun, and stared at it, fascinated. Suddenly, all the anti-aircraft guns opened fire in the direction of the sun. The puffs of anti-aircraft gave the appearance of more planes in the distance. The *Queen*, with 17,000 people aboard, would shoot down any plane that came within range of her guns.

Donnely and I spent much of our time leaning on the ships rail, exchanging bits of news with fellow passengers as we kept watch and passed the time away from our crowded dark cabins. At night the phosphorescence in the ship's wake fascinated me as we watched it churn. Looking up into the dark moon-less sky filled with sparkling bright stars, we searched for familiar constellations: the Dippers, the North Star, and a few more distant ones we could barely identify. At ten o'clock, Donnely escorted me to my cabin, and as we parted said, "I'll be looking for you tomorrow."

The *Queen*, traveling between thirty-two and thirty-four knots, began to creak from the stress of swinging from side to side and changing her course every few minutes, or when she fell forward into a trough as the waves of a developing storm slapped against her hull. She raced through the waves and rough sea as if someone were pursuing her. I almost fell off my bunk in the night, but fortunately was awakened by the blast of the big cannon and caught myself just in time. In the morning we were told they fired the gun to test and clean it. I wondered why they did it at night, awakening us.

I gathered information from various sources: a fellow passenger who joined me at the rail, a friendly crewman who was knowledgeable since he had sailed this ship for years, or someone who seemed to have an inside track on what was happening. I jotted these things in my diary at the end of the day, but some information came through the rumor route, often exaggerated. I tried to sort it out as I wrote.

The weather turned mild on the third day at sea because the ship had altered her course, and we were now sailing a southerly route to elude the U-boats that continuously prowled the North Atlantic. The *Queen's* radio was silent but she received coded messages by radio if she was in danger. Her route had been planned so that her exact position was known at every turn.

While eating dinner I heard and felt the ship shudder and the muffled boom of an explosion. I gulped down what was in my mouth, and looked at the women seated around me at the table. Everyone put down her fork and looked at one another. "Was this it? Was our ship hit?" Alarmed, we began putting on the May Wests that hung on the back of our chairs. Later, we heard from passengers who had been on deck at the time of the explosion, who said they saw oil on the surface of the sea. We also had heard that if the *Queen's* sonar instruments detected a submarine, a depth charge bomb dropped in the vicinity would destroy the underwater vessel. The explosion we heard was that of a depth charge. Afterwards, there was a skirmish of activity as the ship's crew made a surprise search of our cabins and staterooms searching for a radio. None were allowed to use a radio. It could send off electronic beams that the enemy could detect.

We practiced abandon-ship drills each time the klaxon sounded and wore our May Wests at all times, along with a canteen of water, as we familiarized ourselves with the route to abandon this behemoth just short of running, then stood beside our assigned life boat until the clatter of the klaxon dismissed us with an "all clear."

In the afternoon an English film was shown in the lobby. It was a warning titled, "Too Much Talk."

"A dreadful catastrophe will occur lest one is mum. The enemy is listening."

It was a reminder for us to be wary of the enemy at all times.

By now many of the women had paired off with officers. There were British, New Zealanders, Aussies, Royal Navy men, and merchant seamen returning home from torpedoed ships. Poles, Scandinavians, Fighting Free Frenchmen, newspaper correspondents, Canadian Nurses, ATSs, Wrens, WAVEs, WAACs and Red Cross workers added to the variety of uniformed personnel. I was getting acquainted with people in my organization as we gathered in the lounge to learn more about what was in store for us in this experiment we were to undertake. A concert was scheduled in the lounge after supper to lend some levity to the long evenings.

Colonel Blatt, who was Regular Army, joined me on deck afterward, and we leaned on the rail and exchanged bits of news. He asked me what I thought about being in the army, and commented on my being on deck a great deal of the time.

I replied, "Well, so far, it's been a great adventure. I am enjoying the experience, and I hope it will continue to interest me. As for being on deck, I prefer that to lying on the bunk in the semi-dark crowded cabin listening to the retching."

I guessed he knew I was a civilian, as were most of the nurses. We felt fortunate in having a commanding officer who seemed to be accepted by the entire group with considerable rapport. Since it was teatime, he asked me to join him in the lounge where many of us gathered in the English tradition of "tea at four o'clock." It provided an opportunity to get acquainted in a friendly atmosphere.

On the fourth day at sea the ship began pitching as a squall started to develop. Undaunted, the *Queen* kept speeding ahead despite the huge waves that sent her up to the crest of a wave then dropped her into a trough where she trembled in every joint as the waves receded. She began to roll from side to side as she strained to regain her equilibrium while zigzagging. The howling wind made eerie sounds through the cables and superstructure as the sea tossed her about like a cork.

The squall developed into a hurricane. Waves encountered waves from the opposite direction and crashed at their height. The ocean churned white, frothed in anger with the wind.

On the fifth day the howling wind raged with such force that the ship shook and creaked in all its seams. It tore at the life boats, swinging them precariously while we drilled. The fierce gale bent cables and tore at the superstructure. Waves sprayed so high they washed over the top deck, a hundred feet above water. The ship tilted forty degrees. (A crewman said nearly forty-three degrees, as the foaming sea fought the gale force wind and rain.) In the dining room, chairs slid across the floor, dishes crashed to the floor, people were tossed about and injured. Port holes were smashed, and water flooded the cabins.

The transport commander swaggered into the dining area and jokingly announced, "The best way to keep your balance is to hang on to the floor with the balls of your

*The Queen Mary nearly capsizes in the storm on December 11
(From Pierre Mion painting, published in Smithsonian
Magazine, February 1978—used with permission of the artist)*
feet."

As he sat down to his breakfast, his chair suddenly slid out from under him and he went rolling across the room, followed by his two poached eggs. He sported a black eye the rest of the journey.

Many people fell. The ship's hospital began to fill with the injured as well as the seasick. Our medical officers, those still on their feet, were busy taking care of the injured. Nurses went on duty around the clock in the infirmary.

While on the top tennis deck, I watched nurse Birdie Mayes, Major Thomas, and several male officers sitting on a bench go sailing across the deck when the bench broke loose from its bolts as the ship rolled precariously. Fortunately, it rammed into a metal guard fence on the opposite side; otherwise they would have continued into the foamy sea. During the night the ship continued to lurch and many passengers fell off their bunks.

A porthole blew open in Lieutenant Tella's cabin while the men slept. Although they were forty feet above water level, the huge waves gushed into the cabin, frightening its occupants. The lieutenant was sure the ship was sinking. Alarmed, he woke his bunkmates and instructed them to put on their life belts.

"We've been torpedoed!" he said, keeping his voice as calm as possible.

"Shall I take my gas mask?" asked one of the sleepy men.

"To hell with your mask! You won't need it in the middle of the ocean!" The water was ankle-deep as Tella led his men out, prepared to abandon ship. But, instead of seeing the decks awash, he was greeted by a perfectly dry alleyway with an MP looking on as if nothing had happened.

"Which way do we go?" Tella inquired.

"Go where?" asked the puzzled MP.

"To the boats, of course." Tella did not have to ask further. The expression on the MP's face was enough. Sheepishly, the men went back to mop the floor.

The *Queen* battled the fierce storm for three days. At times the ship lifted so high on a wave her huge propeller blades were exposed. Several British seamen manning the crow's nest high over the deck were swept away. The *Queen* came within inches of capsizing in the raging sea.

Despite the storm, the passengers who were still on their feet promenaded the deck. They were forced outside by the retching of seasick passengers in the cabins. Patients were admitted to sick bay by the dozen. Some were so dehydrated that it was necessary to hospitalize and revive them with intravenous solutions. Time dragged endlessly for those lying on their bunks retching each time the ship hesitated on the crest of a ten-story wave then plunge forward into a void. Storage walls crashed, spilling fixtures into the aisles. We were in that most ferocious area of the Atlantic known as the "Devils Bowl."

To top it off, Captain Ralph Coffey was faced with having to operate on a fellow traveler with acute appendicitis. Basins containing antiseptic solutions splashed, trays with instruments slid about, surgeons' feet tried hard to cling to the rolling deck. Ether splashed over the gauze-covered cone, and when the anesthetist gave the sign, Captain Coffey picked up the scalpel, and holding firmly onto the operating table, proceeded with the surgery as the ship rocked. Miraculously the patient survived.

On duty at sickbay, Nurse Evelyn Hanley remarked to the doctor making rounds that one of her patients had symptoms that she attributed to meningitis. He promptly admonished her for having the audacity to make a diagnosis and denied that it was meningitis. The patient was buried at sea three days later. It would not do to have the *Queen* quarantined for weeks.

I overslept on the sixth morning, because the ship's rolling and creaking had kept me awake most of the night, and missed breakfast. The swaying sideways and dropping into troughs made me feel queasy for the first time. Since we slept fully dressed it did not take me long to splash water on my face and dash up the many flights of stairs to the tennis deck. Refreshed by the gale and the spray against my face, I felt better.

We heard that we would be aboard an extra day because the *Queen* had been diverted far to the south yesterday because of the danger from U-boats.

Sunday, December 13
Captain Donnely joined me at church services in the big lounge. We were the hardy ones, still on our feet. The lounge seemed almost empty since many sick passengers were confined to their cabins. There was more space to roam, to gather in groups and play bridge, poker, cribbage or solitaire. We walked the decks and found shelter from the cold spray on the stern of the main deck under the huge cannon.

Donnely lighted a cigarette then, pointing to my diamond ring, asked, "Does that mean what I think?"

"Yes, I'm engaged. My fiancé is in school. He'll have

to join up as soon as he gets his degree. What about yourself?" I asked.

"As for myself," he said, "I am a widower. I have two little girls, nine and thirteen. They are being cared for by their grandmother and a maiden aunt while I'm away. Of course I miss them, but they are in good hands. I was just thinking that we might plan on meeting again, somewhere."

I was unsure about what to say, but finally replied with a non-committal, "Oh, that would be very nice."

His casual repartee during our week of friendship had amused me as we promenaded about the decks and stopped to scan the horizon whenever an object caught our attention. Everyone was on alert for periscopes, particularly at dusk when they were hard to detect. We walked the deck at night searching the sky identifying familiar constellations and discovering new ones, then went to the stern and leaned over the rail to watch the ship's wake as she sped across the ocean.

On the 14th, the storm began to subside. Sea gulls circled the ship, indicating that we were nearing land. As the *Queen* approached the Firth of Clyde, planes approached in the far sky, then battleships crossed the horizon, followed by destroyers, minesweepers, and converted yachts. The planes wagged their wings in greeting.

The convoy that had been sent out to escort the *Queen* into the harbor had had difficulty in locating her, causing them considerable anxiety. We were two days off schedule. They guided us through the submarine net into the estuary where we were greeted by blasting horns and raised flags. There were minesweepers, aircraft carriers, submarines, sleek destroyers, battleships, the troopship *Empress of China* and many smaller craft jammed into the harbor. The *Queen* raised the Union Jack as guns roared. She had survived one of the worst storms in her career.

Later, we were told by Englishmen that the ninety-mile gale was the worst storm in living memory. We also learned that German submarines did spot the *Queen*, and one even launched a torpedo, but the distance was too great, and the torpedo exploded some five hundred feet short of the mark.

On the port side, through the hazy atmosphere I saw Scotland, and to starboard, the Hebrides. It was a beautiful sight.

The sun peeked out from behind the dark clouds for a short time, as if to join in the celebration, and then disappeared. We remained aboard for another night, since it was too late in the day to debark. In mid-December the sun sets soon after four o'clock in that part of the world. The following morning, weary, pale-faced young men staggered from the bowels of the ship, seven decks below main deck, where they had eaten little in the past eight days and had lain in cramped, foul-smelling surroundings where in one moment the ship's floor was where it should be, and then the ship listed until the wall became the floor and the floor the wall.

Captain Donnely came to my cabin to say good-bye before he debarked with his Infantry Company. He had been teaching me French phrases such as, *"bon jour,"* *"au revoir,"* *"comment telle vous,"* *"je vous seime,"* along with the card game called Patience. He said, "Perhaps we can meet in London or Paris eventually." He would write when he had an address. Nobody knew where we were going from here. He took my current APO number.

After four o'clock tea I gathered my belongings and struggled to jam the accumulation I had bought in the NAAFI (English for PX) into my already-full suitcase. I heaved into line with the other nurses weighted down by various bags and body attachments, gas mask, musette bag, web belt with mess kit, and canteen with cup attached, spotlight, purse, make-up bag and bulging suitcase. I staggered down the many stairs, and boarded the lighter that transported us to the dock in Scotland. We had been at sea eight days.

Chapter 2:
England

15 December 1942

In Gourock, the ferry and train station were under the same roof. The old unpainted wooden structure and wide floorboard planks creaked as if they might collapse under the weight of the heavily loaded passengers that now descended on them. It was a long, dismal old building, with a leaking roof. Regrettably, the restaurant had just run out of food. There would be no supper tonight. Tired and disconsolate, we sat on our suitcases, opened our first K rations and ate musty crackers, a chunk of acrid cheese, and a hard square of indigestible chocolate. We were pleasantly surprised when several Scottish lassies appeared from the shadows and poured hot tea into our metal cups at the station. Its warmth spread throughout our chilled bodies and helped down the dry food.

When we heard the high pitched whistle of a train in the distance, we finished our tea, then gathered up our belongings and queued up at the tracks. The train screeched to a stop, we marched to our section and struggled up the steps of the train, hanging on to all our possessions. The small compartments that opened off a narrow companionway along the one side of the train were a novelty. The officers, maneuvering their bulging Val Packs, barely squeezed through. A shrill whistle pierced the air as the train pulled out of Gourock and headed south in the black, drizzling night.

We were jammed together uncomfortably in our heavy coats in the unheated darkened coach. I tried to look out the window, but the steady rain made it impossible to see anything in the blackout. There was little sleep in the fast moving train as it whistled past stations without stopping. Towards morning I wiggled out of my tight space and tried lying on the Val Packs in the baggage area to catch some sleep, but the jarring of the train threatened to bury me under the precarious load.

At daybreak we arrived at Leicestershire for a stretch, where more Scottish lassies handed us a package containing a square of chocolate, a meat pie and two wafers. I noticed the conductor's eyes pop when he saw the chocolate. I gave it to him along with the packet. I was not hungry, despite the fact that we had not eaten a hot meal in a day and a half. One of our officers said the meat pie was filled with sawdust and horsemeat. We stretched our bodies and climbed back on the train where a rumor was circulating that we were bound for Oxford. There were no names at the stations as the train raced past. We learned that they did not want the German parachutists to know where they were when they landed on English soil. We arrived at an undisclosed station where large old busses, their windows blacked out, were waiting beside the tracks.

Oxford

As we climbed into the bus, someone asked the driver, "Is this Oxford?" He pretended not to hear. Several of our officers had recognized it as they boarded the bus, but we did not see the city nor the historic campus as we rode on. At one-thirty in the afternoon the bus stopped beside a row of wooden barracks called Slade Camp, and we were glad to find a safe haven at last. Inside, the barracks were bare except for beds and a small tin stove located in the middle of a large room. At the far end of the room behind a partition were a toilet and a washbasin with one spigot. The atmosphere was dismal, damp and cold, as the intermittent rain continued to fall.

My first thought was to find paper and kindling and build a fire to remove the dampness and cold, but there wasn't a scrap of paper to be found anywhere, much less kindling. A bucket half filled with coal stood beside the stove, but how to ignite it? Instead, we unpacked and settled in our new home. I lay down on my bed, and soon was asleep, the first sleep on a stationary bed in ten days.

Colonel Blatt sent a truck out for rations, and by seven o'clock we queued up for our first hot food in two days. The ATS (Auxiliary Territorial Service) the Women's Auxiliary to the British army, was assigned to cook in the nurses' mess hall. Rejuvenated after supper, we decided to explore our new surroundings and discovered the NAAFI, a British officers club, about halfway between Slade Camp and Cowley Barracks where our officers were lodged. The club was a large room with tables and chairs for groups of four, and a most welcome sight: a large pot bellied stove that radiated much appreciated warmth. Our men had already discovered it and were sitting around it drying their damp shoes. We decided this would be a favorite haunt; at least we would be warm.

I joined a threesome looking for a fourth to play a game of bridge with Nurse Bunetta Bixby, Captains Jacob J. Longacre and Walter W. King, surgeons in our group, but there was so much distraction, conversation, telling jokes, singing, throwing darts by the English and their exuberance about the score that it was impossible to concentrate. We had our first taste of ginger beer, a flat and pale amber liquid. Someone said something about pouring it back into the horse. Another got the bright idea that if you heated the poker in the ashes of the hot coals, and put it in the beer, the beer would froth up and at least look palatable. The beer ran relentlessly through one's body in no time flat—a good diuretic, but that was about all. Lights out at the NAAFI was at ten o'clock. Our officers walked us to our barracks in the pitch dark as overcast skies obscured the moon and stars. We walked warily, unfamiliar with the territory, fearful of stepping into a hole.

We often heard airplane engines in the distance and presumed they were the German Luftwaffe. England was being bombed nightly, just as we had read in the newspapers in the States.

After a good nights rest at Slade Camp, the nurses, always hygienically inclined, decided to clean our barracks. We were not comfortable with anyone else's idea of cleanliness. All flat surfaces in the barracks were layered with coal dust. We washed the window sills and scrubbed the floor on our hands and knees with hard brushes. Then we gathered scraps of paper wherever we could find them and learned how to build as good a fire as any Boy Scout. At night we banked the fire with ashes, hoping to keep it going, but there was never enough coal to keep the fire going all night long. The struggle started over again each morning with fanning a feeble flame until the coals caught. As for paper, there was none except for the newspaper that the fish fries we occasionally bought were wrapped in. It was saved for starting a fire from scratch.

We shampooed our hair with Lux Flakes© to remove the seawater and the stickiness of coal dust. No other soap would suds up sufficiently to remove saltwater from the ocean showers aboard ship, and now the coal dust. The warmest area beyond the barracks was a drying room that seemed to be heated by some mysterious force. It was filled with rows of slats spaced horizontally to the floor at waist height, and it was here that we draped our laundry between the slats to dry after washing it by hand. Because the climate in England is always damp, it was an indispensable room. Our shoes were damp all of the time even though we placed them near the stove overnight. Coal was rationed and the embers never held over to morning. The metal footlockers containing our galoshes, issued to us before we left the States, had been lost

Nurses Johnson, Harper and McDonald

37

somewhere at the dock in Scotland.

After we got everything tidy in the barracks, my roommates and I decided to explore the countryside. We were especially curious about Oxford, its antiquity and its historical background. It was a long walk to the bus stop where, on our walks around the rural area, we had noticed people boarding. We wore our Class A's (dress uniforms), as always when away from camp, and we looked quite sharp. We were conspicuously different from the rest of the passengers, but as we boarded the bus no one seemed to notice us. Our headquarters had exchanged our dollars for English money. The ticket girl who took our shillings said, "Hold Tight," and the driver pulled away. No one else spoke. It was as if we were in New York.

We got off at High Street, a curving thoroughfare lined with many quaint small shops and peeked into the windows to see if they were open, for they were not lighted. Rarely did we see customers inside. After walking for some distance we came to a shop with a sign "Mitre Tea Shop." We were delighted. It would be good to rest and have a cup of tea. We were beginning to like tea as the English made it with furiously boiling water, and it took the permanent chill out of our bodies. We were also getting accustomed to the English tradition of everything stopping at four o'clock for tea.

Afterwards we stopped at Mowbry's bookshop, where I bought *A Guide to Oxford* because I wanted to be sure I would see everything worth seeing while in the vicinity. I also bought *Lawrence of Arabia* since I still thought we might be going in that direction, as well as a Nuttall dictionary because I was sure it would be useful.

The American invasion of North Africa had already taken place on November 8, 1942 under General Patton's command. I wanted to learn something about that part of the world where the English were fighting in the desert and where Americans might be joining them.The clerk who waited on us at Mowbry's told us that he had been a resident of Paris for thirty years, up to the time Hitler invaded France in 1940. He had escaped from Paris on his bicycle and had traveled three hundred miles to the English Channel where he discovered that boats were very scarce. He explained that it took fourteen days for him to reach his home in London, a trip that normally took seven hours. The family home was demolished in an air raid a few days after he arrived, killing his sister. He was a friendly man eager to talk. Most English we encountered in public places were not talkative; some did not seem to notice our presence, and in some instances, as on the bus, they seemed unaware of us.

One of our officers told us the reason the *Queen* changed her course on our second day out of New York, was that a Nazi spy caught in South America had information on her route. The *Queen* was warned by coded radio message to change her course. That was the night I was awakened by the roar of her canon and almost fell off my bunk due to the jolting of the ship. We also heard that on that same night the *Queen* was trailed by a submarine. As she raced and zigzagged, many passengers fell from their bunks and were injured. We recalled that a depth charge was dropped that same night. Passengers said there was an oil slick on the water the following day.

Nurses Merl Harper, Edyth McDonald and I decided to meet at the mess hall to see what the ATS women were doing to the coffee. Since it was our own coffee supply, and water is water, we wanted to know why it looked and tasted so bad. We discovered that they steeped it, just as they did tea. It was no wonder the coffee was cloudy and full of grounds. We asked them to boil it for only a few minutes. That settled the coffee problem, but our breakfasts were a continuous aggravation; stewed tomatoes on bread! The only food that resembled anything from our past was hot oatmeal, and we all relished it even if we had disliked it before. We were already getting weary of brussel sprouts, cabbage and carrots. They all seemed to have the same flavor, probably because they had been consistently grown in the same soil. The mutton was tough old sheep that we simply could not get down.

The English officers we met at the NAAFI introduced us to darts, a pastime popular with the English. The dart games were visible in many English pubs and gathering places. They enjoyed what we thought were trivial games, and laughed hilariously during vaudeville performances that we did not think humorous. Their slow reaction to American humor at the USO productions resulted in many Americans saying, "They'll get it tomorrow." At any rate it made us realize the many differences in our perspectives, our customs and our backgrounds.

Our officers began to organize classes to train the enlisted men in the work that they would be expected to do as surgical technicians. Nurses became involved in teaching them to set up instrument tables and trays using a sterile technique, since this would be their responsibility in the operating room. Nurses would supervise and supply the various needs that might develop as surgeons operated, along with administering injections when needed.

Officers were housed at Cowley Barracks, about a mile from Slade Camp, where they shivered in their dungeon-like cells. Old Cowley Barracks with its towers, mullion windows, and crumbling limestone walls once housed the Oxfordshire and Buckinghamshire Light Infantry, the King's most illustrious regiments. The men shivered in the damp stone cells with tiny fireplaces that held only a few handfuls of coal at a time. Even so, after a few weeks when a British inspector came by and found the coal pile half gone, he exclaimed, "My God, that coal is supposed to last you until next spring!"

It was no wonder the officers spent so much time at the NAAFI when it was open. It was the only warm place in camp, with a pot-bellied stove much larger than ours and the added warmth of many bodies crowded into the building.

It wasn't long before invitations began to arrive from certain Oxford residents. They had formed a hospitality committee to welcome us to tea parties, socials, musicals, lectures, and community affairs. We were invited into their homes and enjoyed their genial hospitality. An English home in Oxford was a pleasant contrast to our sparse barracks. In spite of rationing they were generous with sharing what they called cakes (actually these were cookies) with tea. After we became aware that these foods were rationed, we took sugar and butter along on our visits since the English were very short of these two items.

One day I had the pleasure of being invited to tea with a Mrs. H.H.Turner and her daughter, Ruth Turner, M.D., at their mansion on Cornmarket Street. The beautiful china, the lovely oil paintings and oriental rugs held me spellbound, a sharp contrast to our bleak surroundings at camp. Mrs. Turner's husband had taught astronomy for thirty-seven years before he died in 1930 at the age of sixty-nine. A plaque with his name hung in the Cloisters, and his portrait hung in the Commons room of New College. Mrs. Turner asked me to invite a group of friends and to return the following day, because she wanted to take us through New College, where her husband had taught.

The next day after another strange breakfast of bread dipped in something we could not identify, Major Graves and several other officers and I drove to the Turner home, where our hostess greeted us exuberantly. She was a middle-aged woman, bubbling with energy and radiating enthusiasm and friendliness. Her dark wavy hair was pinned in a small bun at the back of her head. Her cheeks were pink, as so many English seemed blessed with. She spoke with enthusiasm as she shook hands, greeting each guest with, "So glad you are here," her speech clipped in the typical English accent. Then, reaching for her coat in the foyer and slipping her arms into the sleeves, she said, "We must be off before the noon hour." We climbed into the reconnaissance car, and our driver headed toward the campus.

New College was not new. William of Wykeham, Bishop of Worcester, built it in 1379. Magnificent is the best word to describe its architecture, replete with high-ceiling halls. A six-foot-wide crystal chandelier hung in the large dining hall. Stone reredos of biblical figures decorated the walls. Huge cauldrons in the kitchen, that had fed hungry students for many generations, hung from the ceiling. The motto above the entrance gate, fashioned from iron fretwork, read, "Manners Makyth Man." I snapped a picture of the motto with my Argus camera (made in my home town of Ann Arbor, Michigan) that my fiancé had given me when I left home.

A portion of the old city wall, well over a thousand years old, still stood because, Mrs. Turner informed us, when the school bought the property the contract called to have it cared for in perpetuity. As we wandered through the dark chambers, she pointed out interesting objects and recalled anecdotes her husband had told her during his teaching years. We invited Mrs. Turner to join us for lunch at the King's Cafeteria at noon. She charmed us with stories of the school's long history. After lunch we split into different groups as we wandered about the city. On the way home I saw a Christmas tree, which I bought for our camp. It was about four feet tall and cost five shillings. I carried it home on the city bus. When I arrived at camp, Colonel Blatt asked, "Where are the decorations?"

The next morning we had a drilling session. The regular army nurses were familiar with drill, but since I had been going to Oxford every chance I got, and had been away the past few days and missed these sessions, I was at a complete loss. I had never drilled before, nor was I familiar with any army routine procedures. I tried to coordinate my feet to the commands shouted by the officer: "Hut, two three four, by the left flank, march!"

I ended up heading in the wrong direction, but I was not alone. There were some slow learners going off into the field with me. I snickered when I found myself detached. Major Harry P. Harper, our instructor, had a hard time keeping a straight face. Because I had been going to Oxford every chance I had, I had missed the previous drills.

In the afternoon I asked Nurse Janice Shimp if she would like to help me pick some red berries that I had seen in the woods adjoining our camp. They looked like cranberries and would make nice swags for the Christmas tree. It was late afternoon, just before sundown—a beautiful sundown, and almost our last. We walked along the leaf-strewn path, chatting, stooping, and picking the berries that made a resounding clang as they bounced in our tin coal buckets. Suddenly we heard someone shout, "Halt! Halt!"

We stopped and looked in the direction of the shout. A soldier was approaching us, his rifle pointed menacingly in our direction. We were terrified. As he came close, he realized that we were young women, dressed in fatigues just like the GIs wore. He began to tremble, realizing that he had almost pulled the trigger. He said, "I figured you were German spies that are being dropped by airplanes to do sabotage. Boy, was I scared."

At 4:30 it was getting dark and visibility in the woods was poor. He warned us that no one was to be in the woods at dusk.

The following day, Sunday, I overslept and missed breakfast. I had been up many times during the night attempting to keep the fire going so it would be warm when we got up in the morning. The dampness and cold in the morning were always hard to face. I had intended to go to the service at Christ Church, but now it was too late. Instead, at two o'clock four of us nurses went to Oxford, where an elderly man at the door of a building gave us tickets to attend a community Christmas sing at Tower Hall.

We entered the hall and saw the Lord Mayor Maud White, dressed in a red velvet robe trimmed in white ermine, surrounded by her elders, presiding at the ceremony. She spoke about England's war effort and ended with the joys of the Christmas season. We joined in singing Christmas carols, after which a collection plate was passed down the rows that were interspersed with the Fellow Americans. The fellow church members around us greeted us. Shortly after the collection the Lord Mayor happily announced that seventy-five pounds had been collected. As she passed us she commented on the generosity of the Americans; it was an unprecedented amount. It had been the spirit of Christmas that stirred the Americans (besides, some had not yet learned the difference between a pound, a half-pound or a shilling). Moreover, there was nothing to spend money on in England, as the shelves in the shops were bare.

When we got home, Janice and several other nurses joined us in threading the berries that had almost cost us our lives. We carried them to the mess hall and looped them around the tree. One of the ATS girls gave me some mistletoe to hang in the entrance. Several men who were playing cards at one of the tables applauded when we finished hanging the swags. The bright red berries contrasted with the green of the spruce and lent a spirit of Christmas to the dining room. We were surprised and pleased, since we were not aware that they had noticed what we were doing.

On Monday our metal locker chests finally caught up with us. I was glad to have my galoshes to protect my oxfords, which never dried out in spite of my placing them near the potbelly stove overnight. It was a chore to worm my cold feet into damp shoes every morning. We also wore leggings (canvas spats) that covered our pant legs up to our knees. We drilled every day, and marched to the bark of, "hut, two three four!" then, "by the left flank, march!" in which case we changed direction abruptly. Major Harper, who led us, was very patient with those of us who didn't know their left flank from their right. It was, however, a means of keeping in top physical condition for the war!

Lectures were also a part of our daily schedule,

conducted by Oxford College Dons. They came to our camp and spoke on a variety of subjects. We learned about England's glorious history and her great achievements in the past. We were reminded of the world's great concern that England had come very close to being invaded and that her future could well be obliterated. At Dunkirk thousands of lives had been lost as the Germans closed in on the escaping British and French troops following Belgium's surrender. Britain had lost all its war material, machinery, supplies and fighting material, along with hospital equipment and instruments that they had sent across the Channel to help France stop Hitler's invasion.

Britain had been fighting Germany and Italy in the desert in Egypt and Libya since 1940. It was from these officers that we heard of the decisions we would face later in the war. They told us that during periods of overwhelming backlog of wounded, surgeons would have to decide to operate on those who stood a better chance for recovery, as against spending hours of precious time on those least expected to survive. Many of us had difficulty dealing with this alternative, but we had not yet experienced war.

We continued to explore the twenty-one colleges at Oxford University. Our guide told us that Balliol and Merton were founded in the middle of the thirteenth century. We visited the Tom Tower of Christ Church and saw the reredos of All Souls College, the Bodleian Library and its collection of curios and ancient manuscripts. We continued on to St. John's, All Souls, Magdalen with its beautiful gardens, and the Ashmolean Museum. The Museum, the oldest in the country, contained drawings by Michelangelo and Raphael and watercolors by Turner, along with rare articles such as the first *Queen* Elizabeth's watch and Guy Fawkes' lantern, and countless other ancient objects.

I spent many evenings in front of the fireplace of the Mitre Tea Shop on High street in the company of Cliff Graves and other officers exchanging current news, rumors, and opinions.

The local citizens began inviting troops to their homes. I was invited for tea with a group of our officers to Mr. and Mrs. Gabra's home at 16 Norham Garden. Mr. Gabra, a government official, and his teen-aged children, Isis and Victor, entertained us while Mrs. Gabra prepared tea and biscuits. Isis played the piano while we gathered around her and sang familiar tunes. Mr. Gabra either anticipated or someone had told him that we might be leaving soon for Africa. He gave me a letter of introduction to his brother, Professor S.G. Gabra, at the University of Cairo, asking him to show me some of the interesting places in Cairo. When we got back to camp, a rumor was whispered that we might be leaving England in the very near future.

An invitation to a party at the Churchill Hospital was announced at suppertime, and as usual the two-and-a-half-ton truck was waiting for us nurses beside our barracks. When we arrived at the gathering, I saw our officers standing around the table where there was food and punch. I noticed Captain McTamaney raising his cup, finishing his punch, and then coming toward me, "Glad to see you, Rad," he said, "looks like everyone is here. Won't you join me?"

I was surprised to hear him call me Rad. However, we had all begun to call each other by whatever names we preferred as we got acquainted. Last names were most commonly used. Since my name was Radawiec, and my hair red, I began to be called either Rad or Red. As most of us were new to army protocol, there wasn't much formality among ourselves at camp.

He took my arm and we headed toward the table, where he ladled a glass of punch for me and another for himself. I could tell it was spiked after the first sip, and when he asked me to dance, I set it down on a side table.

I had noticed him before and came to the conclusion that he was shy. He seemed to be alone most of the time. I got the impression he was having difficulty acclimating to army life, the hodgepodge of hundreds of strangers thrown together, some friendly, others reserved, some audacious or egocentric and a few timid souls, as I thought him to be. It took a bit of adjusting to this new way of life. After the second cup of punch, however, he became quite jovial.

Our group was a mix of people from every state in the union, each with their own peculiarities.

There was much exchanging of partners as we danced and were tagged all evening. When the party was over, he asked to escort me to camp. We rode back in the truck singing the current popular songs, as was the custom. He walked with me from the road to the barracks in the blackout, and at the door shyly kissed me on the cheek saying, "This has been a very delightful evening. Thank you for helping to make it so pleasant."

I knew he was homesick, like many of us, particularly as the Christmas season approached.

On Christmas day we nurses gathered in the mess hall around the Christmas tree and exchanged gifts as we waited for the truck that would drive us to Cowley Barracks where we would have dinner with our officers. Since there was nothing we could purchase in the local shops, we each parted with a personal trinket. I put some Nescafe into a small glass container and wrapped it in a colored paper to give away. I got a small satin fragrant sachet. Everyone seemed surprised and pleased with their gifts.

In the evening at the officers' barracks our dinner was roast turkey, dressing, potato, gravy, salad and a pudding for dessert. It was the best food we'd had since leaving home. They had a GI cook and they ate regular army rations, except the turkey, which was special for Christmas. We had the ATS cooking for us and it was very different from anything we had ever eaten. The officers also had a Christmas tree, but theirs was not decorated. After dinner we sang Christmas carols and the current sentimental favorites, one of which was "I'm Dreaming of a White Christmas." I noticed more than a few moist eyes. We were remembering past Christmases and missing our loved ones.

I had dropped out of drill and marching to give my blistered heels time to heal and to rest my tender feet. A number of our nurses and men were suffering from severe colds and respiratory infections and were convalescing at the Churchill Hospital. When transportation was available, I visited Rita Ryant and Natalie Davis, both of whom had been sick for almost a week. They said that Hollywood stars Carol Landis and Kay Francis, who had entertained troops in the area with the USO, had been patients there recently.

The Gabras, my friends in Oxford, asked me to invite six officers to a New Year's party they were planning. I asked Major Graves to select them. He included Major Snow, Captains Jones, Williams, Hudson and Ferraro. Mr. Gabra had considerable difficulty in getting something to drink for the group, but finally persuaded the New College supply person to give him twelve bottles of ale, ginger wine, and cider. Mrs. Gabra served hors d'oeuvres, while Isis, their teenage daughter, did a ballet performance. She then played the piano to accompany us as we sang, ending with "Auld Lange Syne." Pleasant, casual conversation seemed a natural gift with the English. Just before midnight we dropped in at a party at some friends of the Gabras for a drink and a toast to the New Year before we started back to camp. The Gabras made my stay in Oxford interesting and memorable.

Headquarters organized a trip for those who wished to go to London the first weekend in January. Our driver had overslept and we were late, so we were surprised when we arrived at the station to find the train waiting for us. In London our group had difficulty finding a place to lodge. Major Graves had planned to get rooms at the Park Lane Hotel as he had on a previous trip, but it was full. Our group split up, and everyone was on his own. A taxi was flagged, and the driver took us to a hotel he thought might have a vacancy. We were lucky to find lodging at the Piccadilly. After registering, we went up to our rooms, dropped our bags, and went back down, anxious to explore the world-famous city.

We recalled the nursery rhyme, "London Bridge is Falling Down," as we approached it near the famous London Tower. Then we walked up Petticoat Lane, and on to St. Paul's Cathedral. The Cathedral had been damaged by bombs near the crucifix and the left nave. After riding the underground, we visited Madame Tussard's Wax Museum, where we saw life-size images of famous people in wax. My companions and I walked toward Hyde Park where we joined a small crowd and stopped to listen to a soapbox orator. At Hyde Park people can speak on any subject they care to discuss or debate. Crowds gather and object or agree, with ayes or nays as the orator moves them.

We saw many bomb craters throughout London. Entire blocks had been bombed and many shells of buildings were roped off for fear of collapse. Our group returned to the Piccadilly for tea, biscuits, and relaxation. After a short rest we were off again, anxious to pack in all the sights. We stopped at the Captain's Cabin for a hot rum, and later at the Criterion for another, for it was characteristically cold and damp in January. All hotels and bars were packed with military personnel with the same thought: "Take the chill off." As the fog settled and the blackout obscured any further adventure, we hurried back to our hotel for dinner, cold and hungry.

We were too late! They had run out of food. The doorman said, "There's a war on, you know."

"Yes, we know," we responded, "We came a long distance to try to help your country survive."

But we didn't miss much. The food was always pretty much the same: mutton, potatoes, brussel sprouts or carrots, and a starchy pudding of some sort. We heard that food and gasoline were being rationed in the States. Meat and sugar were hard to get, and apparently all the cigarettes were being shipped to the armed forces all over the world.

In the morning we continued our tour. We were anxious to see as much as we could in London: first to Westminster Abbey, then to the Parliament Building, where Major Sir Joscelyn Lucas, a member of the House of Commons whom I had met earlier, took us through the buildings. Later, we went to St. Stephen's Crypt, where we looked at beautiful paintings and murals. We saw exquisite bas-reliefs of Sir Galahad and the Knights of the Round Table.

Afterwards there was a climb up three hundred and forty steps to the top of Big Ben, where I autographed the Thames side of the clock. As I wrote, the huge bell began tolling twelve o'clock. The vibration made me tremble, and the din was ear splitting. Next stop was the London Tower, where our guide told about Sir Walter Raleigh's twelve-year imprisonment, during which time he wrote the *History of the World*.

The old city wall, built in 50 B.C., still stood. At the British Museum, paintings and murals of the Battle of Waterloo and the Death of Nelson interested us. Walking up Bond Street, we saw much bomb damage. A horseshoe bomb crater encircled St. Paul's Cathedral.

After a full day of sightseeing we raced back to the hotel to pick up our bags then hailed a taxi to take us to Paddington station in time for the six o'clock train. We arrived at Slade Camp at nine-thirty, very tired after a full day.

The next day after lunch, several of us nurses took the bus to the city, where we visited Merton College, the oldest building on the campus, and were fascinated by the beautiful leaded windows. Then on to Exeter College where our Major Graves had attended the Boar's Head ceremony, a tradition that has been performed on New Year's Eve for hundreds of years. Graves told us about his experience as a guest at the ceremony.

The ritual began in 1397 when the Headmaster of

the College, a scholarly but impractical man, had gone for a walk in the woods unarmed except for a copy of Aristotle's "Contemplation." Engrossed in the book, the good professor wandered farther and farther from home. Suddenly a wild boar crossed his path. The beast charged. Escape was impossible. Then just as the ugly fangs were bearing down on him, the professor stuffed his book down the boar's throat, and the animal suffocated on the spot! In gratitude, the faculty of the college each year offers a thanksgiving dinner. It was an elaborate ceremony that included the carrying of a huge boar's head on a tray so large that it took four men to carry it high over their heads.

The faculty at Rhodes House invited our nurses to a party the following Saturday night. At first sight I thought I was back home, because the building closely resembled the Michigan Women's League in Ann Arbor, where I had often dined. Rhodes House had been established in 1902 upon the death of Cecil Rhodes, who had made his fortune in South African diamonds. It provided Oxford students a place to assemble. The sponsors of the ball were the Honorable Mr. and Mrs. Allen. We danced all evening with the distinguished citizens and academicians of Oxford. Blisters and sore feet were forgotten.

On January 9, 1943, my three roommates and I got a twenty-four-hour pass to visit London again. We stayed at the Red Cross Club on Charles Street this time and ate at the officers' mess nearby. In the evening we visited the Piccadilly, and later the Park Lane, where most Americans congregated, and danced in a roped-off area to music played by a GI Jazz band. There were always many more men than women, and since we were all Americans far from home, we enjoyed instant camaraderie with officers who were on leave or located at Air Force bases in or near London.

In the morning we went to the church service at Westminster Abbey. Westminster is French Gothic architecture with many tall pillars. It is the most famous church in the world and the most beautiful structure in England. All the kings of England have been crowned here except Edwards V and VIII. Burial here is the greatest honor England can bestow. Kings, queens, statesmen, poets and other great men have been so honored. Edward the Confessor first built a church on this site in the years between 1050 and 1065, and parts of its old walls still stand.

There was much to be seen in London, but our visits were always too short, despite our hurried pace, because of the short daylight hours in January, the blackout and the fog that settled over the city.

The sad wailing of the air-raid siren alerted us just as we entered the Red Cross building where we were billeted. The mournful sound made us aware of the agony the English endured almost every night. In minutes we heard the sound of aircraft engines in the distance. We did not go to the air raid shelter; instead we decided that since the Red Cross building was solid stone, we would be safe enough. We peeked out the window of our darkened room to watch the colored flares of the anti-aircraft in the sky and were alarmed when we saw a light in a window a short distance away. We wondered if it was deliberate sabotage. Soon we heard rumblings in the distance as bombs exploded. Later the sad wailing of the "all clear" sounded the end of the raid.

The train back to camp was so slow that we missed the last bus and had to walk the four and a half miles to Slade Camp in the dark. Perhaps they had to mend the railroad after the bombing. We were getting accustomed to a great deal of walking. Even on weekends when we were free from drill and marching, we were continually on our feet exploring London.

On January 13, 1943, we got our first mail. I could hardly hold still to open the envelopes without tearing them. I sat down and immediately replied to everyone. Bob, my fiancé, said he was very lonely and thinking of me not only at ten o'clock, as we had pledged, but much of the time. I too thought of him, but with so many people around all the time I did not have time for quiet contemplation, and being continually on the go, I usually fell asleep as soon as I lay down.

I had lived alone in a small apartment before I joined the army and it took a bit of adjusting to acclimate to dormitory living. Besides, I had to get up early to build a fire before going to breakfast so that the barracks would warm up by the time we got back. The package of Nescafe instant coffee that I had requested in a letter to my sister Kate, had arrived, and we began a ritual of boiling water in a tin can on top of the stove and enjoyed the taste of coffee as we remembered it in the past.

Lectures continued daily. British Brigadier General Parrot talked to us about desert warfare in Egypt, where England had fought in the past and was now at war with the Italians and Germans in that part of the world. A rumor began spreading almost immediately: We would probably go to Africa. In the afternoon we watched a demonstration on plaster cast application by Major Hatte. We were kept busy all day. Besides, there were always the laundry, bathing, putting our hair up in curlers and for me the constant daily battle with keeping an eye on the stove that I had inherited. It seemed no one else had any success in building a fire.

In the evening Major Cliff Graves and I took in a play in Oxford. Between acts, tea was served in the auditorium to those who wished to buy it at their seats. It was quite a trick to pass the cup and saucer of hot tea to the middle of the row of seats, then to hand the shillings from person to person to pay for it. The performance was well done, but we found we had difficulty in understanding English humor. They laughed when we saw nothing funny.

Afterwards, Cliff and I stopped at the Randolph for more tea, but after waiting a half hour for service, we had to leave in order to catch the last bus. It was not unusual to be ignored in shops or to wait a long time for service. This attitude of indifference looked to Cliff and me like the beginning of Socialism.

The bus went into the garage for the night when it reached its station, and we had to walk four and a half miles in the rain and blackout. Once, we stopped an English couple to inquire directions to Cowley Barracks because we thought we were lost, but they had no idea where it was. The English did not seem to have any curiosity about their surroundings, or perhaps they suspected us of being spies. We ran into several of our people who were familiar with the route and arrived safely.

We were off to London on weekends every chance we had and as usual we were faced with the problem of getting rooms at the Piccadilly or Park Lane Hotel where we preferred staying. "What shall we do?" Cliff asked the desk clerk at the Park Lane.

"Oh, you will probably have no problem at the Fleming. It's just down the street: take a right at the end of this street, then left at the bank. Oh, you can't miss it. It's next to the park."

We took a right and a left and missed it. After stopping several people to inquire, we found the park, and next to it the Fleming Hotel.

My room overlooked the courtyard. Dropping my purse and bag on the bed, I went into the lavatory, washed my face, sprinkled some cologne about my neck, applied fresh make-up, and combed my hair. Our uniforms solved the problem of what to wear. I had one class A, and was wearing it. It was a dark navy wool jacket with a marine blue skirt, and white blouse with black tie. A navy blue wool belted coat with a matching blue garrison cap completed my attire. Hurriedly, I glanced about the room, picked up my purse, and took the down elevator. There was so much I wanted to see and do in London.

Cliff was in the lobby waiting. He stood tall, his shoulders broad for a man rather slightly built. He wore his pinks, the pants creased straight down the middle, the Sam Brown belt snug against his trim waist. With a broad smile, he greeted me. "Well, that was short. You look beautiful, is there anything special that you would like to do first?"

"Why don't we just wander around the surrounding area? Everything in London interests me. The lecturers at camp have stirred up my interest in English history."

We dropped our keys at the desk, walked outside and up the street, ready for a day of adventure. Our first stop was at Trafalgar Square, which was built in memory of Admiral Horatio Nelson. The Square has an imposing granite column, two fountains and several statues. As we continued our walk, we came to the Royal Albert Hall and stopped to read a placard on a wall: "The Harold Holt Sunday Concert presents the London Philharmonic Orchestra, conductor Leslie Heward, soloist Francis Cassel." Cliff picked up two tickets for the next day's matinee.

Since the long walk stimulated our appetites, we stopped for lunch in the Soho district, and to our surprise found filet mignon with mushrooms on the menu. That was a treat, since we usually got bully beef, or mutton that tasted like goat. Brussel sprouts, carrots, boiled potatoes, and cabbage were always part of a meal. We never saw salads.

In the evening we went to the Haymarket Theater, where we saw Vivian Leigh performing in "The Doctor's Dilemma." She was slim and very beautiful. Her vivacious expressions, flirtatious eyes and pert mouth that turned from a pout to a smile instantaneously charmed everyone. Her fair skin, contrasting with dark wavy hair, made her appear fragile. However, we felt that her performance on stage lacked depth. We had both seen her on the screen in "Gone With The Wind," Cliff in San Diego, I with my fiancé in Detroit. It seemed a long time ago.

In the evenings it was always difficult to find any place to eat. At each hotel it was: "Sorry, we have just run out of food, we are closing the dining room." Wandering around Piccadilly Square in the blackout, we came upon a long queue in the dark and took our place in the line.

In the army one was always queuing up for something, and it was a natural thing to just fall in. Just as we were about to enter the dining room the waiter closing the door announced, "Sorry, it's nine o'clock, the dining room closes at nine. Come back tomorrow. You know."

We replied with our usual, "Yes, we know there's a war on. We are a lot farther from home than you are."

We soon realized why food was not served after certain hours. Besides the scarcity of food, the proprietors needed to allow the cooks and waiters time to get home before the air raids started. We went to the Red Cross Hotel on Jermyn Street to munch on rations that we had learned to carry with us on trips. We mixed water with the lemon powder that was included in the package. While there I addressed several post cards that I had purchased. They were scenes of London, with short messages to Bob and to my family. We were not allowed to use local post boxes; besides, we had no access to stamps. Our mail was handled through the Army Post Office. Since it was censored, we could not say much. About all we wrote was: "We are well, don't worry, we aren't getting shot at, at least not by the enemy."

It had been a busy day as usual, and the bed looked inviting as I entered my room at the hotel. Since the water was only tepid and the room chilly, I skipped the bath, washed hurriedly, and jumped into bed to get warm. There were plenty of blankets. We were at the Fleming Hotel on Half Moon Street, a half-block from St. James Park, which surrounds Buckingham Palace. In the morning, when I looked out my window facing the courtyard I saw a huge bomb crater. When Cliff called for me on the way to breakfast I said, a bit anxiously, "Cliff, look out that window! No wonder we were so lucky to get accommodations. It looks like this is target area for the Luftwaffe."

"Well, I'll be darned!" he responded. "That's a good sized crater. Thank goodness we are leaving tonight, but it's been a lovely place to stay, hasn't it? It's just as well we didn't know this until now."

After breakfast we walked around St. James Park and stopped to watch, through the drifting fog, the changing of the guard at Buckingham Palace. The sun trying to shine through the fog only managed to look like the moon on a hazy night. We continued on until we reached the beautiful Byzantine Cathedral, modeled after the Saint Sophia in Constantinople. The marble pillars, magnificent mosaics, gilt ceiling, and paintings were spectacular. I thought it the most beautiful of all the cathedrals I had seen.

Cliff and I enjoyed scanning the bookstores on Tottenham Court Road and walked up Mayfair, Fleet Street, and through Hyde Park. At two o'clock we went to the concert at Albert Hall. Everyone was dressed for the occasion, women in long dresses, men in black suits, ties and white shirts. It was an elegant affair. Cliff, a pianist and familiar with classical music, was enthralled. There was much applause and several encores. It was a most delightful experience. Afterwards, we went to the National Art Gallery and saw many famous sculptures and paintings.

At the end of a busy day, enroute to Paddington Station in the blackout, I tripped and sprained my ankle. Cliff had to hold my arm to support me as I hobbled to the train. We hung on to our bags and bumped up the steps of the train.

In the morning I slept in because of the tender ankle and missed breakfast. Two lectures were the morning's session, one on psychiatry, the other dermatology. I found both interesting and enlightening. I took notes on most of the lectures, and felt I was getting a thorough education on a variety of subjects that would be useful to me in the near future.

It had been raining almost continually since our arrival in England. The dampness penetrated our bones. At least a dozen of our people were sick. Many had severe colds with hacking, moist coughs, with accompanying bronchitis, and several had a touch of pneumonia. They were at Churchill Hospital, where I visited them almost every day.

Several of us girls went to the Carfax Theater to see Tyrone Power in the movie *Son of Fury*. When we went to the rest room after the movie, we discovered that there was no toilet paper. After that we made it a point to carry tissue paper with us at all times.

I received a note from a nurse in the 298th General Hospital stationed in Bristol, inviting me to visit. This was the University of Michigan Hospital from Ann Arbor, the group I thought I would be part of when I volunteered to join the army.

I had to catch the 12:45 train, which meant I would miss lunch. Luckily, I got the second section of the train even though the first section had already departed by the time I arrived. I had to change trains at three stations, and arrived at Bristol a half hour late, to find Bob's cousin, Major Harry Towsley, Captain Farrier and Lieutenant Coley waiting for me at the station. They invited me to join them at the officers' club for a drink at four o'clock after I got settled in the nurses' quarters with Joanne Gregoire, who had invited me. We exchanged news from home and our opinions of life in the army. I saw many friends with whom I had worked at the University Hospital, including Doctor E. Thurston Thieme, a surgeon I had worked with at St. Joseph Mercy Hospital, where I had received my R.N. degree. I was delighted to see familiar faces and acquaintance. It seemed like home. I also enjoyed the first good-tasting drink since I left the States, a Tom Collins. I always liked the taste of the mix better than the liquor.

The following day I made hospital rounds on the wards with several doctors I had worked with back home. The patients were our young men who had been wounded in North Africa. They had been transported via air and sea from evacuation hospitals in that theater of war. Almost all of the soldiers were incased in plaster casts or splints for easier transportation. They were in good spirits, happy to get out of the war alive. Many would be sent back after they had recuperated.

I was surprised to see Italian POW's happily working on the wards and caring for the wounded. They had reason to be jovial; they were out of the conflict that was raging in Africa. The 298th was comfortably settled, with many conveniences that we at Slade camp did not have. My outfit, the Third Auxiliary Surgical Group, was living austerely by comparison.

I took the late afternoon train to Slade Camp carrying a cherry pie that Major Harry Towsley had his pastry chef bake for me. When I got back, after all the transfers, I stopped at the mess hall and shared it with the GIs. They said it tasted like home cooking.

Aircraft had been flying low over our camp area lately. They were practicing bombing with duds. Since we were in open country, it wasn't dangerous. In the evenings the usual diversion was playing bridge, poker and of course darts, since the English officers were always present at the NAAFI.

Our headquarters had arranged for us to visit Stratford-on-Avon the next day. The two-and-a-half-ton trucks were waiting outside our barracks in the morning. The kitchen crew supplied us with sandwiches, since no restaurant could accommodate an unexpected party of fifty people. It was raining as usual, so we took our blankets for warmth and protection from the rain. We had neither raincoats nor umbrellas for the long trip.

Our first stop was Shakespeare's home, where I sat in the chair where Shakespeare supposedly did much of his writing. We walked a short distance down the road to a thatched-roofed cottage where Ann Hathaway had lived and where Shakespeare courted her under her parents (supposed) watchful eyes. Our guide winked as he told us that they married when their first-born was two years old. At Trinity Church, we saw the beautiful stained glass windows where Shakespeare, his wife Ann, their daughter Susanna and her husband are buried.

*Surgeons Cameron, Serbst, Williams and Boyden enroute
from Oxford to Stratford-On-Avon*

The Shakespeare Memorial Theater, where his plays were performed during festival periods, was an ultra modern building that contrasted with the quaint surroundings. The Avon River alongside the theater winds around the green hills, valleys, and meadows, despite it being winter, occasionally with snow covering the ground. The weather is temperate due to the flow of the Gulf Stream along England's coast.

There was no ice when we were there, but it was always damp due to the constant rain. We stopped for lunch at the Red Cross Club, a comfortable large room, with overhead beams and many windows with small rectangular leaded panes. A glowing fire in the hearth invited us up close to feel its warmth. We ordered tea and ate the sandwiches we had brought.

Another day, our group went to Sulgrave Manor. The name didn't mean much to us, but we were always ready to leave Slade camp, given any opportunity. It was a surprise to many of us that this was George Washington's ancestral home.

There were fifteen nurses in our group, and as we jumped off the back of the truck we were besieged by photographers and movie cameras. *Pathe News*, *Life* magazine, *The New York Times*, *The Associated Press*, and Special Army Relations photographers were there in anticipation of Washington 's Birthday celebration on February 22. They were taking pictures for the home front theaters and newspapers. English enlisted men, along with American GIs from Fairford, drilled on the grounds for the cameras. The English Tommies drilled with terrific precision and clicked their metal-capped heels in tune to the Fairford band while cameras clicked.

When we reached camp late in the afternoon we heard that half of our Surgical Group would go to Africa, where England had been at war with Germany along the central area of West Africa. I was excited and curious about who was going, and hoped that I'd be included. At supper, a surprise party was announced for tonight, urging all to attend. While I danced with Cliff Graves, whose company I had enjoyed these past months, he brought up the subject of Africa. "You are among the lucky ones Rad; you have the choice of going or staying. What do you wish to do?"

"Oh, I want to go," I replied without hesitation. I was afraid of being left behind. Cliff's face was turned away as we continued dancing.

None of the girls knew who would be going up to this time, as far as I knew. Perhaps all those chosen were being approached in this same manner tonight. The party lasted until after two-thirty a.m., and was one of the nicest since we'd been together. The next morning I awoke with a headache to hear that we had to hurry and pack as we were leaving that afternoon.

"Oh cruel fate!" I thought as my head throbbed. But I certainly wanted to go. Heck with the fire. There was too much to do.

I packed everything that I would need into my bedding

roll. Except for several books, I mailed the souvenirs I had purchased in Oxford and London to my family back home. Supper was served early, our last brussel sprouts, cabbage, and bully beef—we hoped.

Major Graves was appointed to take charge of the half that would remain in England. I was sorry to learn that he would not be going with us. He gave a farewell speech at supper:

"To you who are now coming face to face with the enemy, we who stay behind give our fond farewell. We know that you will do yourselves proud. May our reunion take place under happier circumstances."

Cliff and I embraced. We had shared many pleasurable adventures in England. I would miss his companionship. "Good-bye Cliff, until we meet again."

"Good-bye Rad, it was great being with you. Take care."

Our C.O., Colonel Blatt, was in charge of those leaving. He was Regular Army, and had the rank to do as he wished. Major Graves, a civilian volunteer surgeon, probably had no choice in the matter.

Six two-and-a-half-ton trucks were parked beside the barracks to take us to the train station. We said good-bye to the lovely moss-covered campus at Oxford as we drove past on wet, shining High Street. At the station we boarded the dimly lit train with our usual trappings. I found a seat and detached the trappings, as this would be an all-night journey.

Our mood was gay as in the spirit of a holiday. This became a pattern as we traveled. Everyone was speculating about what the future held. After playing card games, story telling, and singing we settled down for the night. I seemed to have lost my seat while playing cards, so I slipped into the luggage area and found a spot to lie down on. I did not sleep as the train rumbled, jostling the luggage about, and the wheels reverberated a repetitive sound. At five a.m. Colonel Blatt walked up the isle of the train with a long tin of spam, and a sharp knife, hacking off chunks.

"Where's the bread?" Someone asked.

"No bread, just meat," the Colonel responded.

Daylight found us back at a familiar place. We were in Gourock where the *Queen Mary* had deposited us just two months ago. Someone joked about the barrage balloons flying above that were supposed to protect England from attack by enemy planes. It looked more like the balloons were keeping the island afloat. Americans in uniform and endless crates of war supplies were stacked on the dock and for miles around. We descended from the train clumsily, after a sleepless night of jostling, to wait on the dismal dock for the ferry that would take us to our ship. I saw a sign on the wall:

"Loose Lips Sink Ships."

Chapter 3:
The Troopship Windsor Castle

We boarded the ferry precariously hanging on to our numerous possessions, and sat on benches along the bulkhead as she sailed up the Firth of Clyde to a two-funneled ship farther out to sea. Arriving at its side, the captain of the ferry was told to return to the dock, because our ship had snapped a cable and lost her anchor when winds of hurricane force had caused the ships in the harbor to drift. After several hours, with full packs bogging us down, we again walked up the gangplank to the ferry, and this time boarded the *Windsor Castle*. While drifting, the ship had collided with another vessel that gashed a hole in her bow. We explored the ship while men worked day and night mixing cement to seal the gap. She was a two-funneled ship of twenty thousand tons with the graceful lines of a yacht. There were 2,500 troops aboard, much more intimate than the awesome *Queen Mary*.

A steward pointed out where a torpedo had landed in the lounge on her previous trip, and smashed into the woodwork. He said the ship continued with the unexploded torpedo lying in its nest in the woodwork until they reached port days later. It was defused when they docked.

Our cabins were crowded, but this time with only upper and lower bunks. The ship was armed with gunners' nests mounted on port, starboard, bow and stern. I had not slept the previous night, so after a good breakfast I lay on my bunk and slept for three hours in spite of the noise of loading troops, and slept through lunch. Supper was delicious: lamb cutlet, creamed potato, peas, salad and canned pears for desert. Coffee was served demitasse!

Charlotte, our chief nurse, called a meeting in the ship's lounge after supper and I, along with several other nurses, were assigned to duty in the ship's infirmary after we lifted anchor. I wandered around the deck and stopped to watch the sunset against Scotland's snow capped mountains in the distance. The sky varied in shades of blue, green and turquoise, interspersed with streaks of pinks and mauves that blended into the dark blue ocean in the horizon. I was filled with a spirit of expectancy and adventure as I leaned on the ships rail and watched the sun disappear below the horizon.

In the morning the steward awakened us at seven with the aroma of coffee as he placed the cup on the bedside table. Breakfast followed at eight-thirty with eggs, our first since the *Queen Mary*. Abandon ship drill was called by klaxon at nine-thirty. When we reached the top deck, we were counted off into groups of ten, and assigned a lifeboat. Mine was number nine, the only one with a cabin and a motor. I felt lucky. A second drill was called after lunch, at which time we inspected our lifeboat and met the crew that would be in charge. At three-thirty church services were conducted, and communion was offered to the Catholics. It sounded foreboding.

After supper, on my way to the lounge I crossed paths with Lieutenant James, one of the group assigned to my lifeboat. He greeted me with a smile just as we were walking past a small table where a Cribbage board caught our attention.

"Do you know how to play Cribbage?" he asked.

"Yes, I've played it before." It was a familiar game that my sweetheart and I often played in my apartment back home. We sat down and he began dealing the cards. "Fifteen two, fifteen four," in between counting, we inquired about where we came from, where we'd been. The usual getting-acquainted conversation. I noticed crossed rifles on his jacket lapels indicating he was in the Infantry. He seemed a bit shy at first when our eyes met, but as the evening progressed we found we shared many interests. He was rather short in stature, huskily built, with deep blue eyes fringed with thick long dark lashes. After several games, we decided to walk the deck before I turned into my cabin. His binoculars hung from a leather strap over his shoulder, and I was curious to see what was on the horizon. He lifted them to my eyes, and I was surprised to see how close everything within range appeared. Since I spent much of my time scanning the sky and sea, the binoculars would serve me well. I wished I had a pair. I knew they were a vital part of an Infantryman's equipment when he would be facing the enemy. We parted at my cabin door at nine. He said, "I'll probably see you at abandon ship drill in the morning, since we're having them so often."

I spent the rest of the evening writing in my diary and letters to my fiancé, my family, and some friends. I had no idea when they would be mailed. At ten o'clock I tried to reach Robert by transcendental meditation. I realized the timing was wrong since this time zone was probably four or more hours ahead of Michigan's.

The next morning, the 8th of February, the *Windsor Castle* lifted anchor and sailed out of the firth escorted by destroyers, battleships, aircraft carriers, and planes. I reported on duty to the infirmary, but there wasn't much to do except pass a few medications and change several dressings, one on an infected foot of a young crewmember, another with a burn on his arm. I took the temperatures of those with headaches or other complaints, and did the usual bedside care and charting.

Later in the day when I went on deck, I was surprised to see that we were traveling alone without an escort. Just as when we were on the *Queen Mary*. It was windy and cold. As I searched the sea for any signs of ships, two British officers joined me at the rail. The younger, a liaison officer said. "Pardon Miss, I would like to present Captain Brown to you, he is the Captain of our ship." He nodded toward the man beside him, then he added, "I am Lieutenant Charles Hayes."

"I am pleased to meet you. I'm Lieutenant Mildred Radawiec."

We stood chatting about the changing weather, when Captain Brown asked where I had been recently, and what I thought of the English people I had encountered. When I told him I had enjoyed many new friends in Oxford along with the tours of London, he said, "We are living rather austerely today. You must come back when the war finishes, and I pray we will be back to normal once more."

Later that afternoon I got a note from Captain Brown, delivered to my cabin by the same British officer. In a blue envelope, it said:

Lieutenant Radawiec Nursing Sister
American Expeditionary Force
Captain's Cabin 2 p.m.

Dear Miss Radawiec:
If you care to come here and see me this afternoon directly the Boat Drill is over, I shall be very pleased to have a chat with you about the things of God. There is no topic of conversation so good. Also should you wish to bring along any others please do so; only in this later case I would be glad if you would kindly let me know beforehand how many I may expect so that I could arrange seating accommodations. Just please feel free to do whatever you wish.

Yours Sincerely,
John C. Brown

I asked my friend Betty to join me because I was a bit timid about going alone. The British officer called for us at four o'clock to guide us to the captain's quarters. Captain Brown received us with a nod and a slight bow. "Good afternoon. I hope you young ladies are comfortable in your cabins. It is too bad we have to crowd you, but that can't be helped."

Before us stood a man perhaps in his early fifties, dressed immaculately in a dark navy blue uniform with gold stripes on his cuffs and epaulets; a white starched shirt set off his black tie. His thinning brown hair, meticulously combed back, glistened like antique gold, and his finely chiseled nose and sternly set chin made me aware that here was an invincible person. His firm lips spoke with the preciseness of the British as he bowed and said, "Please come in, ladies."

Looking straight at him, I said, "Captain Brown, I would like you to meet my friend, Lieutenant Asselin."

He reached out to her hand saying, "I am very happy that you wanted to come with Miss Radawiec." He then led us to a table set with teacups, saucers and a tray with biscuits.

I noticed him bowing his head in prayer as his cabin boy came in with a tray, set it on the table then poured the tea. Then, raising his head, he addressed Betty. "Where in the States is your home, Miss?"

"Michigan," she replied. "We both are from Michigan. In fact we attended the same nursing school at St. Joseph Mercy Hospital in the city of Ann Arbor."

He then asked, "What do you parents feel about your being so far away and perhaps in danger?"

I replied, "We have lived away from home for several years so they are accustomed to our being away. They probably do not feel we are in any danger so long as we have been in England; well, except for the air raids that they read about."

We sipped tea and ate biscuits while answering queries. A Bible lying on the far edge of the table caught my eye and I remembered his note saying something about God. I wondered when he would bring up the subject. This was one of the reasons I had hesitated about coming by myself and chose Betty, a practicing Catholic, for support. I was aware that he was a religious man from his invitation, and now he spoke of his faith and trust in God. I realized that as a person sailing these treacherous mined and submarine-plagued waters, his faith had to be boundless. We continued to sip tea, nibbled at the biscuits, and chatted for about a half hour, when he reached for the Bible saying, "I have great faith in the Lord providing us a safe journey. May I read you one of

my favorite Psalms? It is from the Old Testament, Psalm
46. He began to read:

God is our refuge and strength, a very present help in trouble.
Therefore we will not fear though the earth should change,
Though the mountains shake in the heart of the sea;
Though its waters roar and foam,
Though the mountains tremble with its tumult.
There is a river whose streams make glad the city of God,
The holy habitation of the Most High.
God is in the midst of her, she shall not be moved;
God will help her right early.
The nations rage, the kingdoms totter;
He utters his voice, the earth melts.
The Lord of hosts is with us;
The God of Jacob is our refuge.
Come, behold the works of the Lord,
How he has wrought desolation in the earth.
He makes wars cease to the end of the earth;
He breaks the bow, and shatters the spear,
He burns the chariots with fire!
Be still and know that I am God.
I am exalted among the nations,
I am exalted in the earth!
The Lord of hosts is with us;
The God of Jacob is our refuge.

Captain Brown closed the Bible, and laid it aside.
"That is a very appropriate Psalm for these times,
Captain Brown, thank you for sharing it." We rose from
our chairs as Betty added,
"Thank you, Sir, for inviting us to the tea party. It's
been a pleasure."
Captain Brown bowed his head as he opened the
cabin door and said, "I hope you will come again." Betty
and I were honored at being the Captain's first guests.
The Engineers and Infantry invited us to a dance
in the evening. I had a date with Chief Engineer Jensen
after dinner, but I couldn't remember on which deck we
were to meet. At the dance he seemed upset because he

thought that I had stood him up, but we soon cleared up the misunderstanding. After dancing all evening, I began to feel tired and my stomach was bit queasy as the ship started to roll and pitch. Jensen suggested going on deck to get over the queasy feeling. The misty spray of the sea on my face quickly rid the feeling of nausea as we leaned on the ship's rail and looked up into the sky trying to identify stars until it was time to turn into my cabin.

The next day three destroyers appeared in the horizon to escort us along with of five troopships that joined the convoy. I saw two planes, a Catalina and Sunderland flying a short distance away through Lieutenant James's binoculars that he had loaned me while he was on duty down in the hull of the ship with his men.

About noon I saw the east coast of Ireland as we were sailing via the Irish Sea and south through St. George's Channel. This was the first time this passage was being ventured because in the past two years these waters were considered too dangerous, not only due to being heavily mined by the enemy but also because of the U-boats and submarines that patrolled there. Mine sweepers ahead of us were clearing our path all day long. Through James's binoculars I saw the bows of several sunken ships pointed skyward in the distance. The guns on all the ships in the convoy were tested at dusk. It made our ship shudder, and the noise reverberated across the sea. I spent most of my free time on deck because our quarters were crowded and there was nothing to do but lie on the bunk. I watched the ships in the convoy and searched for submarines on the horizon.

After dinner a British officer and Lieutenant Victor Echevoirri, Chief Gunner on the ship, stopped beside me on deck, and we talked. They told of rescuing the passengers from the *U.S.S. Helena* in the South Pacific when Japanese torpedoes sank it. Tonight the sky was unusually beautiful, with just a sliver of a new moon and many sparkling bright stars in the black sky as we three chatted. The British officer and the gunner had apparently struck up a friendship earlier as had many passengers.

The next morning while on deck, I saw all the ships throwing out a smoke screen and heard the blasting of many horns. Suddenly all ships changed their course toward the west. A low flying, four-engine Sunderland flew overhead from the East. Sea gulls in the distance indicated we were near land, perhaps Lands End, on the southern tip of England. The plane was probably warning the ships of enemy submarines in the vicinity.

At noon I received another note from Captain Brown inviting me to visit him again. I went alone this time and enjoyed a pleasant half hour listening to his adventures. I gathered that his life at sea was very lonely, and in these treacherous waters he seemed to need diversion. Our meeting was casual as before; the English are amiable conversationalists without revealing intimate details. I enjoyed the tradition of tea and biscuits that the captain's cabin boy served us. Captain Brown was a very gracious man, and I felt privileged to be his guest once more.

Our chief nurse had previously spoken to me about wearing my gray woolen slacks and gray blouse. I brought them along because they were my most recent purchases before I committed myself to the army. Since other nurses had donned "civies," civilian clothes, on occasion, I followed along. I thought she was picking on me, then decided that she probably had spoken to the others as well. The many men on board were showering us with attention. Most of the girls were escorted and promenading the deck or sat in the lounge and played card games.

I had a date with Lieutenant James in the evening, but we didn't go to the dance that was held in the small lounge. I didn't know whether he had no dancing skills, or was simply tired after being on duty all day. Instead, we sat on deck and watched the clouds as they raced in front of the moon and stars as though playing hide and seek. I enjoyed being with Lieutenant James, because he impressed me as being a genuine fellow. I had not seen him the past two days and missed him but assumed that because he was a mere lieutenant, he probably had duties that kept him busy with his men below deck.

The weather was warming as we headed south, and I counted eight ships sailing in our convoy now: three troopships beside ours along with one freighter and three battle cruisers. A B-17 Fortress flew close by today as we approached the Azores. Without any warning, an officer and a crewmember inspected all cabins just as had happened on the *Queen Mary*; they were looking for a wireless or radio. I thought to myself, "It's probably the same nut that did it before."

I spent the afternoon in the ship's infirmary again. The patients were mostly in for diagnostic reasons, along with a number of severely seasick GIs. We nurses took turns working in shifts around the clock. I assumed that it permitted the ship's medical personnel to work in some other capacity aboard ship while our services were available.

Tonight I had my first date with an Englishman, the Chief Gunner Lieutenant Victor Echevarri, whom I had met earlier. I had heard that he wrote poetry and thought that he might be interesting. He seemed very lonesome and as we sat down on the deck beneath his gun nest, I waited to hear some spontaneous verse. I was disappointed when he didn't recite any poetry that I might have enjoyed and discovered that he was more than just lonesome. Instead, he wanted to start necking almost as soon as we sat down. I was perfectly safe, since there was no privacy on deck and decided he'd been at sea too long! I thought to myself: "Men are all alike, except that the English are in a bigger hurry. It must be the war. Give me the American lieutenant!'

While sitting on E deck in the morning, a sergeant leaning on the rail noticed what looked like a periscope on the far horizon. It stirred up a bit of excitement as it approached and looked like a submarine. After a considerable amount of signaling, it turned out to be a destroyer that was joining our convoy. Now we were nine.

Later in the day one of the destroyer's anti-aircraft guns shot at what appeared to be an unidentified plane in the distance. All the gunners were alerted to be on watch. We were aware of the constant presence of German U-boats in the Atlantic. Our cabins were searched again because it was feared there was a wireless aboard ship that was revealing our position. At night the moon reflected on the calm sea with just enough light to silhouette the ships that had joined our convoy as we sailed.

We had been at sea seven days, and today, February 12, 1943 was the first warm, sunny day in months. Because I was so happy to see the sun after all the drab cold days, I basked in the warm glow all day, forgetting that with the reflection from the water I got a double dose, resulting in sunburn and freckles that popped out almost instantly. At bedtime my face was flushed and hot. I figured that since we were going to Africa it was just as well to get accustomed to the sun. Besides, I still preferred the deck to the crowded cabin where some of the girls were feeling nauseated, others quite seasick and the rest just lying on their bunks. I was too interested in what was going on outside.

I saw several huge whales off to starboard in the afternoon, swooping up out of the water. They seemed curious about the many ships and wanted to see above the water line. Our anti-aircraft gunners opened fire at an unidentified plane again today. There were more planes off in the distance and we saw another destroyer advancing toward our convoy. There were now five destroyers. Our convoy was maneuvering and retracing in the Atlantic, for there were known Wolf Packs of submarines in the area as we edged eastward around the bend off Portugal toward the southern coast of Spain. Our convoy entered the Strait of Gibraltar, a passage between Spain and Africa eight mile wide at its narrowest point between the continents, and connecting the Atlantic and the Mediterranean. We made little headway because of the dangerous mined sea and the suspected U-boats.

At dark we were surprised to see the bright lights of a city off starboard and were told it was the neutral territory of Tangiers. It was the first time we had seen lights since leaving New York. At 10:30 the huge Rock of Gibraltar loomed up on our port side as we sailed along southern Spain. We had entered the Mediterranean Sea, the graveyard of many ships that had been sunk by the German U-boats.

This expedition was opening new vistas that intrigued me, and in spite of some of the hazards, I was finding it very interesting. I planned to get up to see the sun rise in the morning but didn't realize that I should have set my watch ahead again. I ended up waiting an hour for the sun to rise from the mist, leaning on the ship's rail along with others who could not sleep. I watched the florescence off the stern as the ship churned the sea in the dark. We now were six hours ahead of Michigan time, and I was confused about the time I should have spent trying to meditate on thoughts of my fiancé. I was being faithful, but the time changes had made it impossible to keep track, and I was afraid I was not successful. Besides, it was almost impossible to concentrate with so much chatter in my cabin at bedtime, and there had been no mail delivery since December when we were at Slade Camp in England.

At last the sun peeked in the horizon where the gray sky and shimmering sea were one. The sun edged up unevenly as the ship rose and fell with the waves. Finally, it loomed above the horizon, a huge red ball. Another day had dawned. Both the sun and moon appeared larger in this part of the world. Several passengers joined me at the rail, and we marveled as the sky changed into brilliant shades of pink, blue, and turquoise, while the sun rose from the now azure Mediterranean Sea.

Chapter 4:
Africa

Oran

14 February 1943

We were sailing past the coast of Spain on our port side, with Morocco to starboard. At three in the afternoon, I could see Oran in the distance. At first sight it looked desolate, with the Atlas Mountains rising high above the sea. As we approached land, I saw white stone forms that turned into modern buildings arising on the face of the cliffs as we approached the harbor. Someone pointed out Mount Christo overlooking the city, and on a high cliff stood a picture postcard fort, partially obscured by clouds. The port was bustling with ships of every of every description as we sailed on to Mers El Kebir three miles down the coast.

There were many more ships tied up to cement-embedded hawsers. Two huge battleships, the British Nelson and the Rodney, docked side by side along with torpedo boats, destroyers, merchant ships, and many other vessels. Our ship weaved its way through the submarine net to a vacant berth along the mole (breakwater), and we felt safe. It was too late to debark however, and we were compelled to remain on board ship one more night. Lieutenant James and I played gin rummy, and after dark went out on deck to look at the stars.

The next day while elbowing the ship's rail, I was fascinated by the activity in the harbor. Arabs dressed in white burnoose and pointed goatskin slippers that had no heel support were scurrying about, shouting orders, waving arms, directing other barefoot Arabs dressed in dark, ragged, hooded burnoose. They were helping the soldiers unload crates from the ship. Other troops on the dock, when they saw nurses leaning on the ship's rail, began to whistle and wave as they marched off the dock toward the beach.

An army chaplain on the main deck conducted church services at six-thirty the next morning. Captain Brown added, "Thanks be to God," and a prayer of gratitude to the Lord for the safe journey. He had a close relationship with his Creator. (Months later we heard that the *Windsor Castle* was sunk off the coast of St. Nazaire on its next voyage. That was the same route we had taken.)

The *Windsor Castle* now began to unload her passengers at the harbor at Mers el Kabir. Lieutenant James came to my cabin and helped me close my Hartman suitcase with added straps. The extra purchases from the ships PX made it bulge. He said, "Well, this is good-bye, Rad. Let me have your APO (Army Post Office) number, so I can drop you a line; or better still, if we're in the same area, I can look you up. You've made this trip very pleasant."

"It's been great being with you, James," I said. "Yes, I would like meeting again. Thanks for helping with the straps." I jotted my APO on a scrap of paper and as I handed it to him, he pressed my hand in both of his.

When we lined up and were waiting our turn to debark, I saw him march past with his company of enlisted men. He nodded and winked as he walked past me. He was loaded with equipment: helmet, back pack, duffel bag, binoculars strapped over his shoulders, rifle (probably a carbine) along with musette bag, gas mask, and canteen attached to the canvas belt around his waist.

"Good-bye, it's been nice meeting you, Lieutenant James. Good luck in the war," ran through my mind.

Finally it was our turn to debark, and as we walked up the quay toward the sandy beach, we were faced by a bevy of photographers taking movies of us. They represented various news media correspondents: *Life* Magazine, *The New York Times*, *Pathe News*, and others. We looked bedraggled as we lugged our heavy bags and attachments toward the beach. Would our families have recognized us? I doubted it; we all looked alike. On the beach dark faces from another world surrounded us. Arabs milled around the port; some appeared to be helping with unloading, while others just gawked, chattering and gesturing with their arms. We had landed on a strange continent.

My eyes bulged trying to take in all the sights. The Arabs wore a ragged brown garment that looked like a cape. It hung from their chins to the ground, and was so full of patches that one could hardly identify the original cloth. They wrapped the top of their heads with white cloth, like a turban. Dirty-faced, small boys squatted, hunched under similar rags, and puffed on cigarettes that they had begged, or butts picked up off the ground. They appeared to be no more than ten or twelve years of age, and already their expressions registered boredom with life.

The familiar canvas-covered, two-and-a-half-ton trucks were parked nearby, and GIs, glad to see us girls, helped boost us up the high step with our luggage. They drove us to a French villa at Ein-el-Turck, within sight of the sea. The villa looked inviting. As we entered the large room surrounded by many windows. I quickly walked toward a cot next to a window and dropped my musette bag on it, staking my claim. I was getting used to the ways of the army. If one didn't, one missed out. However, when the skies suddenly clouded and the rain dripped from the ceiling and the wind and rain blew through the cracks in the loosely fitted windows, I regretted my choice of berth.

After the rain stopped, we explored the area and picked up seashells along the water's edge. Our kitchen crew set up in the patio of the villa, and we ate our first meal squatting on the ground with mess kits in our laps. We were becoming like Arabs. Pink roses and bright red geraniums filled the garden, while bougainvillea draped the terrace and blue blossoms climbed the walls of the villa, making it into a fairyland.

A huge full moon rose up from the sea. It was larger than I had ever seen it before and was tinged with a pink double ring around it. Later, I learned what that meant— I was lying on my cot when the deluge came. I wriggled deep into my sleeping bag and wool blankets to keep from getting wet. As the moon slipped over the mountain ridge, it suddenly got dark and left us in complete blackout. There was no electricity.

In the morning Arabs seemed to pop out of the ground in the most unexpected places. They bartered with eggs and wine in exchange for cigarettes and chocolate squares that they called "bon bons," as they wandered around our campgrounds. They became a familiar sight; they were everywhere we went, many squatting on the ground in rags, looking as if they were contemplating the sand.

In the tiny villages Arab men sat in small dark open cafes passing the time of day philosophizing while women, bent in half, scrounged the scrubby land picking up twigs to build fires to cook the millet and unleavened bread that fed their large families. Arab women were burdened with many children, many of whom did not survive the first years of their existence because of malnutrition, poor hygiene, and inadequate medical care. The children had sores on all visible parts of their bodies, and let flies sit in the corners of their reddened eyes without blinking. Women were worn out, looking old in their late thirties as they slaved in the dunghills, eking out an existence on scrubby rocky soil without proper equipment. They lived isolated lives in their hovels, tending children who did not appear to go to school, for I had not seen a building resembling a schoolhouse in the countryside. Arab women were rarely seen in the city. I watched and snapped a picture of their laundry center outside of Oran as I listened to their chatter. It seemed a social event; women knelt along a canal and slapped garments on rocks. It was probably the only time they had an opportunity to gather, and it sounded like a festive occasion.

Chocolate candy, soap and cigarettes were exchanged

for eggs, wine, oranges, a rooster or even sex. French brothels in Oran were frequented by men who could not seem to survive without sex. Our troops learned to communicate with a few French phrases such as, *"bon jour, Madame,"* and *"voules vous promener avec moi?* or simply by smiling and getting what they were after. As the demand increased, the rate of exchange mounted.

The Red Cross Club provided a meeting place where we played ping-pong, badminton and volleyball, or just sat around and enjoyed a sandwich, donuts, and coffee. We played bridge, canasta, solitaire, checkers, and lotto. Any game one could think of was available to us as we gathered with newfound friends at the Club. In the evening we walked along the wide, palm-lined streets of Oran. There were outdoor cafes and restaurants with soft lights, where we began to drink wine with food, since water was not safe to drink off the army post.

Oran was a modern city with many tall white limestone high-rise buildings, and apartments with elevator service and balconies facing the harbor, where the azure blue sea created a picturesque scene. The majority of people were French, with Jews, Spaniards, and Arabs on the fringes. The modern city contrasted with the dilapidated hovels the Arab families lived in on the outskirts with donkeys, chickens, and scrawny, flea-infested dogs. The men, small in comparison to the troops, rode sidesaddle on the matted, bony donkeys along the roads and did not seem to belong to the rest of the society.

We were glad when we heard that we were moving out of the villa with its leaking roof and windows to the Ecole Normale, a French girls' school located several miles east of Oran. Riding in the open truck, we passed two separate horse-drawn Arab funeral processions and heard the Arabs chanting mournful phrases over and over as they followed.

The school was a modern, two-storied limestone, solidly built structure and was unoccupied. We trusted that it would be better protection from the rain than the villa. We dashed up the terrazzo stairs to the second floor where a wide hallway opened into small cubicles. Inside, a thin mattress on a bedspring that humped up a foot high in the middle was the only fixture in the cell. I unrolled my heavy bedroll onto the strange bed and lay down on the raised center, which fortunately flattened under the combined weight. An opening in the outside wall led to a small individual balcony, but there were no doors to shut between the cubicle and the outdoors.

At five o'clock, a GI truck driver arrived at the Ecole Normale with instructions to "hurry" us to the 7th Station Hospital. We had hardly had a chance to settle or freshen up when we were back on the uncovered two-and-a-half-ton truck in which many of us had to stand because there wasn't bench space to seat us all. The driver sped like crazy through the streets while those of us standing teetered and swayed. Some disaster, we thought, must have struck at the 7th Station Hospital to call us back in such a hurry. As the driver accelerated, clouds began to darken the sky, and within minutes torrents of rain came pouring down, drenching us completely. We arrived at the hospital, water pouring down our faces, our hair in strings, and our coats soaked.

"What happened? Where do we go? Where's the emergency?" we asked.

The purpose of the trip was simply to assign us to our areas for duty the next day. We stayed for supper. When we got back to the Ecole, we found that our cells, having no doors to close off the balconies, were flooded. Naturally, it did no harm to the terrazzo floor.

My alarm awoke me at six the next morning, and we were back on the truck by six-thirty. The GI driver greeted us with a big smile, and we were off to breakfast at the Hospital and on duty by seven-thirty. I was assigned to wards 144, 145 and 146, where the patients were sick with various diseases of questionable origin. Among them were mumps, malaria, meningitis, and others not yet diagnosed. I discovered that one of my patients, a blond, good-looking young man, was a trumpeter in the Glen Miller Band. He was suffering from a severe headache, chills, stiffness in the neck, fever, inflamed eyes, and symptoms of paralysis. Meningitis, I thought.

The ward was a large high-ceiling room with cots lined from wall to wall. I took temperatures, rubbed backs, passed medications, and gave steam inhalations with funnels improvised from newspaper attached to the spout of a teakettle of water, heated on an electric hot plate. After a week my assignment was changed to night duty in the huts located some distance from the main hospital, where I visualized having to wallow through the mud from one hutment to another in the dark by myself. I was relieved when a Medical Corpsman was assigned to escort me between the huts.

German officer prisoners filled one of the huts. They were young, most under thirty, tanned from having fought in the desert, blond, proud, and congenial. They appeared contented lying on clean sheets on comfortable beds, warm with good army rations as compared to their comrades who were fighting the English in southern Tunisia and the Americans in the mountains of Algeria. They expressed their gratitude for whatever I did with *"danke schweste."* I was aware of their probing eyes as I took temperatures, pulses, and respirations, and gave medications, treatments, and injections, and wondered what their comments were when I was out of earshot.

Night duty was physically easier than ward work during the day, but it was a twelve-hour shift, and staying awake was my biggest problem as I did the charting. I drank cup after cup of coffee all night long.

Off-duty hours were spent exploring Oran, seeing the sights, and window-shopping on the main streets, but there was nothing one cared to buy. We met officers who escorted us to various haunts where Americans gathered. A favorite place was the American Continental Bar for *vin blanc* or the Red Cross Club for a snack, and often we ended at the Florida Club for dancing. Nightclubs closed

at seven-thirty, and streets were completely emptied by
ten o'clock. Curfew was for everyone, including Arabs.
The MPs, (Military Police) picked up stragglers after that
hour for detention. Curfew was strictly enforced.

I was surprised and pleased one day when Lieutenant
James, my friend aboard ship, appeared at the hospital.
We resumed our friendship and began exploring the
surrounding country at every opportunity. I had my
Argus camera with me and took pictures of Arabs and
local scenes that were a never-ending source of interest,
an entirely different world from anything I had ever seen
before. Lieutenant James often picked me up at four
when I got off duty, and we drove around the outskirts
of Oran. We wanted to see as much of the surroundings
of the city as we could high up in the mountain range.
Occasionally I joined him for supper at the 156th Infantry
Headquarters, where at times French army officers were
also guests. There was a lot of camaraderie in the mess
hall lined with rows of bare wood tables and benches. We
spent evenings at the Red Cross Club in Oran playing
volleyball, ping-pong, bridge, or just sitting and reading
old magazines.

Night duty did not allow any social life, since it was
a seven-to-seven shift. Life was mostly work, sleep, and
self-maintenance. After several weeks I shifted back to
days and began the Red Cross and nightclub routine with
James. We went to the Coco Golden Club to dance, but
the dance floor was so small that there was barely space
for a dozen couples to dance at one time. On one occasion,
our GI driver was not at the parking place where he was
to pick us up before ten. We were afraid the MPs would.
He showed up at ten-fifteen, full of apologies, and said he
had lost his way in the dark, but we knew that was an
alibi.

We enjoyed riding up the mountain to picnic within
sight of the Mediterranean. We built a small fire on the
rocks to boil water for coffee, opened a can of sardines that
James had received in his mail recently, and munched

on my Christmas cookies that had arrived in February (having been mailed in December).

At the hospital, I was back on the ward where McKenna, the trumpeter in the Glen Miller Band, was recovering from meningitis. He got his trumpet out of its case one day and played jazz. It raised quite a few of the sick men onto their elbows to see what was happening. I saw faces light up into smiles. It brought back memories of days past.

I sponge-bathed the sickest with cooling alcohol bed baths to reduce high temperatures, rubbed their backs to relieve back-aches from lying on thin, lumpy mattresses, helped those who could not feed themselves, passed out medications, gave penicillin injections, and did treatments such as steam inhalations, irrigations, hot compresses and soaks where ordered, and of course did the usual charting.

On days off duty, James and I, and his friend Captain Norris, with the latter's girl friend, Nurse Allison, often went exploring. One day we decided to climb the steep mountain to Santa Cruz and the Notre Dame Shrine. The rocky trail was like dried lava and the climb very steep. At a level spot we stopped to rest, built a fire, heated canned rations, and boiled coffee in a tin can.

As we sat and ate, Captain Norris told about his experience the preceding weekend as a guest at a French officer's country estate. He said, "When we got ready to go hunt rabbit I was surprised to see him bring this little ferret along. He let it out of the cage, and that little animal scurried into the field and disappeared. In a minute you should have seen the rabbits skip and hop out of their holes. It took only a few minutes, and the hunt was over. I can't say I enjoyed shooting them, but that ferret sure knew his business. It was the funniest hunt I'd ever experienced. The rabbit to the French is like our chicken dinner."

As the sun began to set, we folded our blankets, gathered our containers, and started down the mountain.

James held my hand as we slid down the steep decline, followed by followed by Nurse Allison and Captain Norris.

Third Auxiliary Surgical Teams Move to the Front

March 1943

Several of our Third Aux Surgical teams were sent to operate near the front at the British 97th General Hospital at Souk El Khemis and the 159th Field Ambulance Casualty Clearing Station, both of which operated similarly to the American Evacuation Hospital. Five teams were sent to Tebessa in March and operated at the 48th Surgical Hospital and the 16th Medical Regiment at Tabarka. Colonel Blatt personally briefed the men before they started: "You are to report to Headquarters II Corps, somewhere in the Tebessa area. Better bone up on your hasty entrenchments. There is a shooting war going on over there."

Captain Bauerle, our Intelligence Officer, delivered the *coup de grace*: "And when you are captured, all you can give out is your name, rank and serial number."

When the men appeared at the airfield for transportation, the Lieutenant at the operations desk at Oran Airfield shook his head. "Yes, we can let you have two C-47's, but we have no Fighter escort, and I don't know how far forward we can take you."

"That's all right," replied Captain Ralph R. Coffey, "just as long as we go in the general direction."

Team member Lieutenant Rocco Tella pointed to the name on the plane as it taxied up. "Cold Turkey sounds bad to me."

Bad omen or not, it was a miserable trip. The pilots sought safety at treetop level and hedgehopped all the way. They clung to every hill, every valley, and every feature of the terrain. Up and down, to the left, to the right, it was like dodging traffic on Broadway. Before long, Third Auxers were sick as dogs. Finally the ordeal was over, and the planes came down.

"Where are we?" asked Coffey.

"Constantine," replied the pilot.

"Constantine? That's a long way from Tebessa, isn't it?"

"Well, it isn't exactly next door, Captain, but we can't take you any farther without fighter escort."

Captain Coffey's blood began to boil. Here he was on his first mission, stymied by a pilot with a faint heart. Drawing himself up to full length, he imperiously addressed himself to the pilot. "Lieutenant, I presume you know your business. I am fully aware that we are running a considerable risk in going to Tebessa, but I also know that at this very moment American soldiers are dying for lack of medical attention. Do you want to deny those soldiers their chance to live?"

The pilots looked at each other sheepishly. "All right, Captain, we'll take you there."

On they went, heading straight for Messerschmitt Lane. Less than an hour later they were down again, this time in the middle of nowhere. The area was completely deserted.

"Where are we now?" asked Coffey.

"About ten miles from Tebessa, and you're lucky to get here. Good-bye."

The pilots gunned their engines, and the planes took off. The Third Auxers looked around. If this was the front, it was a very lonely place indeed—nothing but rolling hills, barren plains, and leaden skies. There was absolutely nothing to indicate human activity, not even so much as a tent. It stared to rain. Soon the men were drenched.

Coffey took his bearings. There were no stars, but he had a keen sense of direction. Taking three men with him, he started out through the trackless waste. Eventually he found a trail, which became a dirt road. The road led to a railroad track, and here in a small shack, Coffey found a detachment of Signal Corps men. "Sergeant, we are looking for Corps Two."

"Sir, the last time I tried to get them it took six hours."

"Better get on that line right away, Sergeant."

Exhausted, the men sprawled on the ground while the sergeant got busy. Corps II was at Youks-les-Bains, about ten miles away. A truck was dispatched. It arrived in the middle of the night, a night that one would not have wished on his worst enemy. Third Auxers rolled up their sleeves and got to work.

Another member of the Third Aux team, Lieutenant Growdon, told of arriving at the 51st Medical Battalion to find a backload of seventy-nine patients. Just behind the French hospital was an ammunition dump. They were told that the dump was a nightly target for Nazi bombers. Sure enough, just as Captain Coffey finished a case, the first bomb dropped. He was getting some plaster ready for Lt. Growdon's case when the concussions rocked the walls. Growdon thought the place was going to blow up, and ducked under the table. When Growdon looked up, there was Coffey standing over him, plaster in one hand and a helmet in the other.

"Which do you want," he asked.

"Helmet."

"Okay," he said. "Come and get it."

Growdon crawled out. He never saw a man as calm as Coffey.

A few days later Lieutenant Maurice Schneider, our anesthetist, became ill, so we sent back to Major Watkins A. Broyle's team for Lieutenant Rocco Tella. Tella thought that Schneider had been killed in action and went to Gafsa expecting the worst.

Casualties kept pouring in, and they decided that they could work two tables if they had an extra anesthetist. So they sent back for yet another man. Lieutenant John M. Serena was picked. Knowing that Schneider had lasted just three days and Tella two, Serena thought: What is this, open season on anesthetists at Gafsa? God forbid! He left his station convinced he was on a suicide errand. Words cannot describe his relief when he learned the true situation.

It was then that we heard about the Kasserine battle that had taken place earlier in the mountains and valleys of Tunis and Algeria, and learned of the heavy loses suffered by the Americans fighting the Germans and Italians.

A rumor reached us on March 23rd that the British in Tunisia had smashed the Axis defenses and had broken through the Mareth Line. The Americans began to progress toward the front again. Our organization received orders that we would soon move eastward.

23 April 1943

More Third Auxiliary Surgical Teams were called to the front. Except for the two Neuro-surgical teams that were sent to operate in the Constantine area in March, no other teams were dispatched until April 24, when seven teams went to join the British 97th General Hospital at Guelma. Six remaining teams went to Souk El Khemis to serve with other British hospitals and the 159 Field Ambulance and the 14th Casualty Clearing Station with the British 8th Army, the equivalent of an American evacuation hospital. Meanwhile the five teams that had flown to Tebessa on the 18th of March finished the campaign partly with the 48th Surgical Hospital and partly with the 16th Medical Regiment at Tabarka. They probed for jagged steel, tied spurting arteries, closed torn chests, repaired lacerated organs, and amputated legs that had been damaged beyond repair due to mines, or just gave a hypo and a word of consolation to those who were beyond help.

There were no facilities for transfusion of whole blood except from military donors, no way of checking blood for malaria or syphilis, no intravenous fluids, no food except C rations. Surgeons never knew whether to hold abdominal cases in the hopes that an ambulance would be along soon or go ahead and operate with the knowledge that the station might have to move the next day. Patients were evacuated as soon as possible, some while still under anesthesia. A fresh postoperative casualty with a belly wound does not travel well. There had been no precedents to establish the mission of forward surgery, or adequate facilities in the combat area. Highly trained surgeons were transferred from one unit to another without explanation or destination or their function. They nursed and prepared food, along with cutting firewood to keep the patients warm in tents.

The task that confronted the men was to create a small mobile self-sufficient first-priority hospital that could be set up alongside the Clearing Station, the so-called Field Hospital. It would be comprised of three platoons. Each unit would have six officers, six nurses, and fifty enlisted men to take care of one hundred post-operatives until they could be transported to an evacuation hospital further to the rear. At the field hospital, the Auxiliary Surgical Teams would do the priority surgery.

Back at headquarters in the vicinity of Oran, we traveled the open roads, sight-seeing whenever we had an opportunity. Our GI drivers or officers lowered and covered the windshield of the jeep to keep the glass reflection from attracting the German Stuka 88s that occasionally made sweeps across the sky. We searched the sky when we heard airplanes, and soon learned to identify the enemy by the sound of their motors.

I was still on duty at the 7th Station Hospital when, on our day off, Nurse Allison, her friend Captain Norris, Lieutenant James, and I decided to drive to the famous French Foreign Legion that we had seen in the movies back home. We got an early start, as it was well over a hundred kilometers from Oran to Sidi-bel-Abbes over mountains and trails.

Norris and James had picked up Allison at the

Hospital in Oran and came for me at the Ecole were I was billeted. Norris was driving a Reconnaissance car. It made us look as if we were on official business. Usually we rode in a jeep or truck. Allison and the Captain were busy chatting away, commenting on the beauty of the countryside, the mountains, the spring flowers, the sea in the distance, billowing puffs of white clouds in the bright blue sky, when suddenly the car hit a muddy spot on the road. It had rained here earlier, and the wet spot sent the car into a skid, spinning it completely around, then straddling it on a cement guardrail alongside the canal.

We managed to climb out of the vehicle onto the road, relieved that we were not apparently hurt, then stood along side the road hoping that some one would come by to help us out of our predicament. Except for my bruised knee and the jarring of the sudden stop, which took our breath away, the rest were unhurt. After a considerable time, a GI truck was sighted coming toward us and came to a stop beside us.

"I see you got a problem, Captain," the GI said as he stepped down from the truck and brought his palm up to his brow in a salute.

Captain Norris responded with a salute, then said, "Yes, I'm afraid so. Since you are heading in the direction we've come from," he said, "I'm directing you to take the Lieutenants back to their camp while you leave your buddy here with me. Lieutenant James will return with a rig to get the car off the rail as soon as he can."

The GI, with a brisk salute, responded, "Yes, Sir."

Allison, James and I climbed into the truck and sat up near the cabin so that James could talk to the driver and guide him to our camp. It was dark before we reached Oran, and we had to ride in blackout the last few miles as the sirens warned of an "alert" because enemy planes were in the area. This was our second alert in the past two days. I arrived at the Ecole glad to be home and safe. As James said goodnight, he added, "Don't lose heart, Rad; we'll try again on your next day off, ok?"

The following week we started out again with high hopes of completing our mission. We packed rations this time for security in case we had trouble. We remembered how hungry we were last week. Sidi-Bel-Abbes is located about seventy miles south of Oran, but the road veers eastward around the mountain and then heads back west. We had no trouble as we drove through the lovely countryside covered with new growth of green and blossoms on the verge of opening into bright yellows and red buds. After several hours over rough country roads we arrived at the modern city, its paved streets lined with cafes and modern buildings along the wide avenue. We stopped at a cafe and sat down at an outdoor round table. At the adjoining table a young man in uniform looked bored as he sipped from a glass and blew cigarette smoke through his pursed lips.

"Is he a Legionnaire?" You could see we all had the same thought as we looked at each other. We were in luck. He said he was on pass and would be pleased if we would join him at his table. All this in French. By this time we had learned some French phases, and between Captain Norris's high school French and his association with the French officers who frequented his unit we managed to reach a good understanding.

The young man began to respond to our questions on his life in the Legion as we sipped *vin blanc* that the elderly waiter had poured then set the bottle on the table. He spoke some English with an accent and started by telling us that the Legion originated in 1831. He said volunteers signed up for a five-year term except for some Germans, Americans, and Britishers who had been known to get out if they changed their mind, but only with the help from diplomatic pressure. He said, "I can escort you, but you can only see the museum."

We were pleased to accept the invitation; wasn't this the sole *raison de etre*? We climbed into the recon car, and as we rode he called our attention to points of interest along the way, such as the square, the various monuments, the courthouse and where the mayor presided.

We learned that the French Foreign Legionnaires were regarded as the most illustrious fighters in the world, that they fought on any side of a conflict that recruited them, and were known to regard death on the battlefield as the highest honor.

He explained that there were men from many nations represented in the Legion. Among them were Germans, Poles, Italians, Spaniards, Arabs and, of course, Frenchmen among the ten thousand members, whose headquarters was here in Sidi-Bel-Abbes.

Life for the Legionnaires was dull, since there was little to stimulate them mentally and since fighting was their main objective. They sat in the outdoor cafes drinking wine for diversion from the barracks monotony. Discipline in the Legion was very strict and punishment harsh. At the end of five years a man got a good conduct certificate if he was lucky. Most of the men were refugees, men without countries, escapees from the law and unhappy homes.

After we entered the grounds, our Legionnaire guided us to the museum where we saw many old relics from wars that had been fought in Crimea, the war in Mexico during the Maximilian Episode, the Franco-German War, and World War I. There were life size wax figures in various uniforms, books of histories of their past conquests, photographs, and a huge variety of weaponry.

Upon leaving, our officers wanted to give the Legionnaire some francs for taking up his free time, but the soldier refused it, saying he was honored to have assisted us. He saluted, clicked his heels and turned in the direction of the barracks.

We climbed into our Recon and drove toward the center of the city and stopped at a cafe where we had the good fortune to get roasted chicken, potato, a salad of greens, and a pastry along with the usual bottle of wine that we had become accustomed to. Our trip to base went without incident. We sang old favorite songs all the way back.

I received twenty-one letters, the first since we left England. Several were from my fiancé, who professed eternal love. I promptly responded to two, one to my fiancé, the other to my family, and mailed them at the 7th Station Hospital in the morning. Since our mail was censored, we were not allowed to name countries, cities, or mention events of the war, or casualties. Such restrictions left me with little to write. I described scenes, mountains, flowers with some innuendo to my fiancé, such as: do you remember the tall vase that you gave me? Well, just replace the `I' with an `O', marked on the bottom of the vase. The vase was from Iran. I inquired about friends and local news. It had been five months since my fiancé and I had parted and I wondered if he was being faithful. There were many young women in the States whose men were overseas, while here there were tens of thousands of lonely men.

Although I dated, I did not feel that I was being unfaithful. Lieutenant James was married, and ours was a platonic relationship. When off duty, we went on sightseeing trips with another couple, seeing the surrounding towns and countryside, but a great deal of our time was spent above the city of Oran in the mountains, the Red Cross Club, and the local cafes. The jeep could climb right up the side of the mountain where there were no roads. We wanted to escape the crowded city and enjoy the tranquility and solitude of nature as we looked on the city below and the sea beyond where we saw warships outlined against the horizon. On these occasions we built a fire with twigs, boiled coffee in a tin can, and ate hard biscuit that was part of K rations that we usually carried when going on trips.

James arranged some time off duty so we could meet again. We drove to Ain-el-Turk via the mountain trail. The view from the top of the Atlas to the sea was breathtaking! The turquoise blue of the Mediterranean blended into the light blue sky, where an occasional white puff of cloud drifted past. He parked the jeep and we sat absorbing the beauty around us. Then James reached for my hand and said. "I'm going to miss you, Rad. You are the only girl that I've ever met who compared with my wife."

"I am flattered," I said. "I guess it's a good thing we are parting, isn't it?" I had not wanted our friendship to go this far.

"And I'm going to be really lonesome without looking forward to being with you," he added, "I wish you'd write me when you get wherever it is you are going."

I took my address book out of my purse, and James wrote his recently changed APO in it. He placed his hand on mine and pressed it for a second, then shifted gears and stepped on the starter. The jeep lurched foreword as we descended around the mountain toward the city below. We made a stop at the Army Service and Supply Headquarters where I wanted to get an OD (olive drab) jacket and a visor cap to protect my eyes from the bright sun. As we passed by the harbor, we watched ships being unloaded of huge crates of war supplies. GIs were directing Arabs, who hung around the port waiting to be reimbursed, mostly with rations or cigarettes. The war was reaching a crescendo in North Africa. Supplies were being rushed to the front along with evacuation hospitals and personnel.

Around the corner, a small cafe with pink blossoms climbing up its wall sent forth a delicate perfume into the air. James said, "I'll always remember you with the fragrance of wisteria, Rad."

I realized that it was best that we were parting as we were growing more than fond of each other and neither of us had intended that. James was a man of strong character and integrity, I discovered as we spent time together, and I admired him for that. He wanted to remain true, just as I did. He drove to the Ecole where we embraced and said good-bye.

The Atlas Mountains

6 April 1943

Up at four the next morning, the Third Auxers were leaving Oran, where we nurses and the rest of our Unit had been on duty at the 7th Station Hospital the past two months. We were heading eastward across the Grand Dorsal Mountains. The Atlas mountain range was intersected by steep gorges on narrow hairpin dusty jagged roads.

Our transportation, General Motors two-and-a-half-ton trucks, were equipped with benches along both sides of its body, that seated seven or eight on each side. As I looked out the back end of the truck, the distant valley below was a myriad of beautiful dew-covered yellow and red wild flowers tinting the rolling hills. We rode past a small Arab village where beside the road in a small-circled enclosure, two bullocks tethered to a central post were plodding around and around, treading grain. It was a picturesque scene turning time back hundreds of years. Arabs herding flocks of sheep in the distance reminded me of pictures of Biblical times. We knew when we were nearing another village miles before we reached it by the fetid odor of open sewage that fouled the air.

Our GI drivers were instructed to speed through the cities even at the risk of hitting pedestrians because of the possibility of mines being placed on the road, grenades tossed at our convoy, or even sniper attacks. They were not to stop on the road for any reason, but to follow the truck ahead in close proximity. We barely got a glimpse of the Arab cities as we sped past.

At night it was hazardous as we drove through the mountain trails with only "cat's eyes" (small round openings in the blacked-out headlights). A small red dot in the taillight was the guide for the trucks that followed in close formation to keep it in sight. The steep grades and hairpin turns were frightening in daylight as we looked over the sheer precipices, but at night they were particularly hazardous. The rear wheels of the preceding truck seemed to touch the edge of the precipice, about to slip over the edge as we watched, holding our breath. We were traveling by the light of a thin rim of a new moon peeking over the Grand Dorsal Mountains.

Everyone sighed with relief when our eighteen-truck convoy pulled into a field below Orleansville for the night where we would bivouac. We were very tired from the strain as well as from the bouncing on the hard wood bench. I jumped off the rear of the truck, stretched stiff muscles, and looked around the barren country.

There was no sign of life, but before our GIs tossed our bedrolls off the truck, Arabs appeared from nowhere, and when supper was ready, we were surrounded. In spite of the walking guard during the night, Arabs were found under trucks, in trucks, and even in the temporary latrines. They had but one purpose: to steal. An Arab could sneak into a tent and steal away without a sound, or lift the side flaps and grasp whatever he could reach.

The next morning after a breakfast of hard tack and coffee at four a.m., we were on the road again. At every rest stop, no matter how deserted the country appeared, Arabs popped out of the ground to barter, and we were eager to exchange our rations or cigarettes for eggs or oranges.

We were still wearing our woolen clothing, since the nights after sunset were very cold in April. Our clothing consisted of olive drab GI long cotton underwear, an undershirt, bra, wool slacks and shirt, sweater, and a navy blue wool coat. We wore blue wool mittens and a knit stocking cap worn to pad and support the double lined iron helmet, along with the usual musette bag, etc.

We took turns lying in the floor of the truck, on top of duffel bags and other paraphernalia, and tried to sleep as we traveled hundreds of miles over mountains on narrow roads better suited for donkeys. Our helmets were useful in several other ways beside protection from injury due to

95

war. As we looked over the precipitous sheer drop into the valley below and jolted on the dangerous trail, several girls retched with nausea.

Every three or four hours all the trucks in our convoy came to a stop for a comfort break, to stretch legs and allow the driver and co-driver to change seats. Everyone jumped off, nurses to one side of the truck, men to the other, not daring to venture much off the edge of the road—we had been warned that the fields were mined. At noon the trucks formed a circle in an open field that had been cleared of mines, and we ate lunch consisting of K rations and hot coffee.

I was always surprised at how quickly our kitchen crew, cooking on gasoline-fired stoves, had hot coffee ready when we came to a stop at mealtime. When I asked Corporal Estel W. Tedder on KP (kitchen police) about that, he said they fired the stoves while traveling because they knew how ravenous everyone would be when we came to a stop. The truck carrying the kitchen supplies was near the front of the convoy, so they had a head start before all the trucks got in position at a bivouac. The coffee burned my lips as I touched the hot aluminum cup to my mouth. Coffee was one item that resembled something of our past and was a favorite with everyone.

Our second overnight stop was near the village of Arba, twenty miles south of Algiers. The environs were hilly and full of rocks. We laid our bedrolls on the ground and retired for the night. When we awakened in the morning several of us were wedged against rocks, having rolled some distance away from where we had placed our bedroll the night before. We slept in the open, fully dressed in fatigues or slacks, as no tentage was put up for clothing changes.

We were aroused by the sounds of the camp stirring at four a.m. I poured water from my canteen into my cupped hand, splashed it on my face and dried it, picked up my mess kit, and joined the procession toward the mess truck where Corporal Tedder was ladling coffee into upheld tin cups. I added powdered milk and sugar, spread the bread with white oleomargarine, and ate standing beside the truck in case I wanted more.

A rectangular tarp had been put up hastily the night before to afford some degree of privacy to a temporary shallow latrine. After hearing that we would be on the road a long time today, we decided to spread our sleeping bags on the benches of the truck to pad them because our bottoms felt bruised and our thigh muscles and backs were strained from the past two days of traveling on the very rough roads. Why hadn't we thought of doing that before?

At dawn, as we got glimpses of the sun between the ridges in the mountains, the valley below seemed to be carpeted in a sea of lavender. "Was it heather?" we all questioned. The scene was breathtaking. "What a beautiful world," I thought, a lovely place to live in if it were not so far from home. Home and loved ones were on our minds, but as we moved farther away, it was getting difficult to transcend the distance and feel in touch.

As the convoy descended into the valley, we saw yellow pennant flags jutting about eighteen inches above ground. On closer examination, we saw black skulls and the word "Achtung Minen" printed on them. The enemy, in their hurried retreat, had failed to remove the mined area markers. Mines by the thousands had been planted to slow the advance of the Allies. Explosions were frequently heard as goats wandering in the fields stepped on them. The Engineer Corps cleared only those mines in the path of the Infantry as they attacked the enemy. Even so, there were casualties after areas had been swept. The Arabs seemed unsure about their allegiance, or perhaps they had been bribed by the retreating Germans to replace mines. These explosive devices posed an ever-present danger.

Every now and then while traveling across Africa we came across a huge sign painted on a wall. "KILROY WAS HERE." We figured that some GI had a keen sense of humor. (Later, when President Roosevelt and Stalin met for a conference and shared a latrine, Stalin, coming out, asked, "Who is this Kilroy?")

We saw snow on the mountain peaks as we continued on, and the hairpin turns became even more precipitous and treacherous. There were detours, washouts, blown-up bridges, and steep passes. At dusk, while still sixty-five miles from our destination, our C.O., Colonel Blatt, decided to continue toward our final destination in spite of the sun's sudden disappearance behind the mountain. Darkness crept in very suddenly just as we entered the most hazardous part of our journey. army signs posted on the road read:

> "TRAVEL AT YOUR OWN RISK.
> YOU HAVE BEEN WARNED!
> THIS ROAD UNSAFE!"

All in large letters! We held our breaths as the trucks rounded narrow precipices with only "cat's eyes," following the small blacked-out tail light of the truck ahead. When we finally pulled into a field in the dark, we discovered that half of our group was not trailing us. Nine trucks were missing!

There was but one explanation: a truck had come too close to the edge of the cliff, and the trucks following the dimmed-out tail light followed it over the precipice. We were deeply concerned, but there was nothing we could do in the black night. Our men scurried about pitching tents, and when ours was up we put our cots together and helped each other lift the heavy bedrolls onto them, and lay down for a long needed rest. This was finally our campsite, after three days and five hundred miles over narrow mountainous trails.

The next day a group of officers retraced the route in search of the lost half of our group. They marveled at how our drivers had been able to follow the narrow winding trail, trestles, and cliffs in the dark. Our fears

*Nurse Lieutenants Stoker, Johnson and MacDonald,
living in tents*

were alleviated, however, when the lost trucks rolled into camp at noon. They had lost us near Constantine and drove around in the blackout all night. A native finally guided them to our camp near Ain M'Lila.

Constantine

The first few days at camp were spent picking stones out of our tents and clearing a pathway so we wouldn't trip in the dark. The ground was uneven and hilly, with a scrubby undergrowth of weeds. We settled down into tent living without tables, chairs, lights, or any place to lay anything down except the bare ground. You either stood up, or you sat on the cot. Outside, you sat on the ground if it was not wet.

The surrounding valley was covered with red, yellow and orange flowers. As usual, the Arabs arrived the next day to barter eggs and oranges. The oranges were most welcome because we had not had any since we arrived in Africa. We feasted on tangerines and oranges traded for cigarettes and chocolate.

After lunch the following day, Captain Robert Coffey asked me if I wanted to take a walk into Ain M'Lila, the nearest village, several miles east of our camp. In Ain M'Lila, an aged, unpainted lean-to shed served as a cafe. There we found five Arabs sitting on a bench at a wooden table, sipping something from small cups and smoking cigarettes that gave off a sweet aroma. They seemed to be discussing a controversial subject as we watched them, waving their arms and shaking their heads. They appeared unsure as first one and then another looked dubiously in our direction, uncertain if they should greet us or not. We were ignored. We were intruders, and the Arabs did not know what to do about our presence.

France had had dominion over North Africa since 1911, but now, because France was occupied and controlled by the Germans and the German army had just fled this territory, the Arabs were confused as to whom they should be loyal. Besides, since the front was changing constantly, the Germans might come back any day.

Captain Coffey and I turned back, because there was nothing in the village except a few dirty urchins with runny noses and flies sitting on festered sores. Captain Coffey said, "Looks like we are in the boondocks. It's going to be a pretty dull existence if this is all there is."

"Perhaps we won't be here very long." I tried to cheer him as we walked back, disappointed with the village.

Back in my tent I got my class A uniform out of my bedroll, smoothed the wrinkles and hung it on a nail I had procured from the car pool and had hammered into the center pole that held the pyramidal tent up. Several of us nurses decided to ride into Constantine, a city some distance away, the next time our truck went there for supplies.

Breakfast in camp consisted of hot cereal, which we enjoyed since it was food we could identify with our past existence. Most meals now consisted of dehydrated eggs, dehydrated potatoes, dehydrated milk, dehydrated onions and lemon powder. The white oleomargarine that replaced butter looked like lard and coated one's mouth so that nothing had much taste thereafter. Artificially flavored powdered lemon was our daily juice, except on some rare occasions when we had canned, very tart, grapefruit juice. This acidic beverage would cut the grease after eating bread spread with oleo. Our meat was canned Spam, served at least once a day for the duration. Everything else was canned, since the army was not using local produce. We were already getting weary of slippery peach halves, our dessert almost every day.

Our gentle and patient cook, Sergeant Joseph E. Montgomery, tried hard to please us. He worked over the hot oven in the heat of the African sun baking plump loaves of white bread that he cut into thick slices. We spread the bread with oleo, and on occasion marmalade when it was available. It reminded me of home when my mother baked bread, and we could hardly wait for it to cool enough to eat.

We nurses felt a tender kinship with our GIs, but our contact with them occurred mostly at meals when they ladled our food into our mess kits as we filed past in the chow line. They would look up to make eye contact and smile or say something just to get a response:

"Do you want more, Lieutenant?" Corporal Tedder, with ladle raised, would ask when there was something special on the menu, if only to get a sign of recognition. We saw them in headquarters, where they handled records, did typing and sorted mail. We were friendly, but the army had rules we had to follow. Dating between enlisted men and women officers was forbidden. The enlisted men's tent area was beyond the officers', which was across from the women's area. The GIs drove us to the evacuation hospitals whenever they were deluged with wounded and needed extra help. We served on detached service at the hospitals until the emergency subsided and then returned to our base camp. Although some may have felt resentment because of the rules regarding the "no dating" between GIs and nurses, most of us realized as time

Caison bearing the body of French General Joseph Edoward Welvert, killed by a road mine in Constantine

passed that it was important to maintain discipline.

15 April 1943

Today Headquarters arranged transportation for as many of us as wanted to attend the funeral of French General Joseph Edward Welvert, of the 19th Corps area in Ousseltia and Kairouan. The General had been killed while traveling on a road that had supposedly been cleared of mines.

A huge crowd had gathered in the city square of Constantine, where we saw General James H. Doolittle, commander of the Northwest African Strategic Air Force, among many other dignitaries from the Fifth Army Headquarters based in Algiers. My attention was drawn to the black riderless horse, with empty saddle that followed the caisson. The horse balked and pranced sideways, then took a step back and lifted his front hooves high into the air, dancing much like a ballerina, nodding his head and tossing his black mane as if bowing. The caisson bearing the French flag-draped catafalque was drawn by Arabian steeds whose foreheads were decorated with crowns of bright colored plumes.

A parade of cavalry on spirited, prancing, high stepping steeds was followed by French soldiers marching in step to the brass band playing the French National anthem, the "Marseillaise." Thousands of natives, Frenchmen, Spaniards, Arabs, Singhalese, British, and Americans crowded the square. In the heat of the blazing sun the stench of unwashed Arabs in dirty patched-up burnoose overwhelmed me as they crowded around us. I took several pictures with my camera that I wore strapped over my shoulder as I traveled.

16 April 1943

I was awakened at 12:30 A.M. by the violent vibrating motion of my cot. My first thought was that an Arab had bumped into it in the dark as he crept under the tent flap to steal, as had happened in the past. My cot rocked from side to side, and I realized I was experiencing my first earthquake. Since we were in open country without any buildings, no damage was done. Neither were there newspapers, so we never heard anything about the tremor. The earth trembled for only a few seconds, but to me it was a revelation of nature's power. Luckily the tent pole and all the Class A uniforms it supported held up.

18 April 1943

Tonight the officers of the 5th Wing Air Force Headquarters invited us nurses to a party. They were stationed about eighty kilometers south of us, and had discovered us when driving past our camp for supplies. As always, we were happy for any diversion from the quiet uneventful evenings in camp. We were glad for a change of scene, for a chance to meet new people, and for any opportunity for excitement. There would be dancing, always a pleasurable activity because you were close to a person who was probably as lonesome as yourself for someone loved and missed. It also was a good way to use up pent-up energy.

The town hall was bustling with many officers and civilians, including the French mayor, his family, and local dignitaries, who greeted us with polite nods and

French phrases. The table along the wall was spread with sandwiches, grapes, wine and canned grapefruit juice that, when combined with alcohol, was a potent mix. We were promptly embraced and were tagged continually, changing dancing partners so frequently we hardly had time to introduce ourselves, or take a bite of food that looked so tempting along the wall. The evening passed swiftly, and before we were aware, it was past midnight and we faced a long drive to camp. We were escorted by some of our dancing partners and sang favorite songs all the way to camp. The songs were: "Home On the Range," "The Beer Barrel Polka," "It's Three O'clock In The Morning," "Let Me Call You Sweetheart," "Paper Doll," and countless others. The following morning we got up early in spite of the short night, because we heard that there would be eggs for breakfast. Our supply officer, Captain Clarence Hudson, had made a deal with an Arab for enough eggs for all of us on this morning.

Time began to drag in the remote area, far from any city with nothing to do to entertain or divert us from the idleness. Occasionally Betty Asselin, Gertie Trainor and I, were lured to the mess tent by the smell of freshly brewed coffee. The GIs told about their trip to a tiny village where they met a French family. As we talked someone asked, "Do you hear a plane?" We stopped talking and listened.

"Yeah, I hear it, it's ours. What the heck is he doing up there in the dark?" Sergeant Nelson asked. "Must be lost, or a straggler coming home after a bomb run."

"If that's a straggler, he sure is lost, probably nearly out of gas by now, too," Corporal Tedder responded.

We all stepped outside the tent to see if we could see anything. "It's too cloudy, but he's one of ours. I can tell by the sound of the engines that it's a Fortress," I added. They awakened me every morning since we arrived here. It was a very dark moonless night. We knew he was lost because planes did not fly in the area of the mountains after dark. In spite of the risk of disclosure of the airfield to the enemy, we watched as searchlights rotated in the dark sky, urging, directing the plane to a safe landing. The sound of the engines faded into the distance as the plane diverted from the lights.

"The crew is afraid of those lights. Probably expect to get shot if they get caught in it," Gertie said.

"That's probably it," someone else added. We were deeply concerned for their safety. The mountains in the area, and the desert only a short distance south of us, were very real hazards in the dark.

"They may have lost radio communication and can't ask for help, or they would follow that light and make a landing," added Corporal Asa Thomas.

"Too bad, nothing we can do. How about some more coffee, Sergeant Nelson?" Betty asked.

Seventeen years later I read a newspaper article about a Liberator bomber, "Lady Be Good." The plane's skeletal remains had been found in the desert. The remains of several of the crew members had been found miles away, in various directions. However, the newspaper dated the disappearance as April 4. When I looked in my diary to check if it was the plane we heard when we were stationed in Ain M'Lila, I found that our hearing the lost plane was dated about the middle of April. However, there were probably other planes that got lost and ran out of fuel in the desert.

We had heard a rumor that the Japanese kamikaze had sunk a hospital ship in the Pacific waters. "The damned pigs," we cursed. There was a lot of hostility felt toward the Japs, as we called them at that time, because of the viciousness of their nature and the atrocities we had heard they were committing on civilian and army POWs.

I had finished reading *Mata Hari*, at last, and at dark tonight we saw the first movie in the field. It was "Andy Hardy Goes to College." Afterward, a group of black soldiers gathered up in front of the crowd with two saxophones, a clarinet and cornet and began playing "The St. Louis Blues." The entire crowd began dancing and stomping to the jazz. It brought back memories of dancing to Duke Ellington's Band in Detroit with my fiancé. Arabs squatting on their haunches on the fringes of the field probably thought we had gone mad. It was a wonderful change from sitting in a dark tent.

19 April 1943

Several of us nurses were invited to supper at the camp near Ain M'Lila, and I happened to sit next to Captain Albert O. Chittenden. His infantry company was among the forces that first waded into French North African soil on November 8, 1942. After we finished eating, we gathered outside his tent where he spread a blanket, and sat on the ground getting acquainted. We had heard that these men were among the first to land in Africa and we were anxious to learn about their experience, since there was very little news in the States about the landing because of secrecy and censorship. And we knew almost nothing about the invasion. Captain Chittenden started by telling about the confusion as soon as they descended from the troop ship into landing craft, then waded towards shore in the face of machine gun and artillery fire.

He started in a slow precise manner saying, "Well, American troops were the first to attempt landing on African soil because of the conviction that the French would welcome us more readily than they would British troops. We were under General Dwight D. Eisenhower's Command, who directed the "Torch" operation from Gibralter. We were supposed to land on the beaches of Morocco, on friendly soil, or so we thought as we waded toward shore holding our guns above our heads to keep them dry. You can imagine how stunned we were when shells began bursting all around us and all hell broke loose. Artillery and machine gun fire opened up, and as we advanced on shore, snipers began to attack us."

"We lost some men who, when wounded, drowned under the weight of their equipment. It was a touch and go affair those first days, since we had to hold fire until fired upon. The Allied Commanding officers had difficulty with French General Giraud, who demanded to be in command of the entire operation in North Africa. However, on the 12th, Admiral Jean Darlan ordered all French troops to cease resistance, and days later he appointed General Giraud commander in chief of the French Forces in Africa."

We later learned that after General de Gaulle, head of the Free French but stationed in England, heard of the invasion, (he had been kept in the dark about it on President Roosevelt's insistence), he was so angry he said, "I hope the French throw them into the sea." However, later in the day he broadcast a message of support to France and its territories through the BBC radio.

French General Giraud, Admiral Darlan and other Frenchmen were afraid to make a commitment that might turn against them if the invasion by the Allies failed. Marshall Philippe Petain, French Chief of State of unoccupied Southern France and a puppet of Hitler's, had ordered African Frenchmen to fight the invasion of the Allies. The Germans had occupied Northern France since France surrendered on June 22, 1940, following the surrender of Norway, Denmark, Holland and Belgium in April and May. It was due to Admiral Darlan's intervention that French troops finally obeyed his order to cease fire on November 12, 1942. He then agreed to command the French troops in the war against the Axis troops now occupying Africa. Other landings made simultaneously in Oran and Algiers, joined by the British, met the same resistance as in Casablanca. Americans were unaware of the state of confusion in France since the Nazi occupation in northern France in 1940.

Captain Chittenden continued, "After four days of fighting the thousands of troops that kept pouring in from the six hundred and fifty ships in the bay, the French Commanders decided to negotiate and finally capitulated. But that's enough about the war. What about some music?"

A soldier began strumming on a Balalaika and we joined in when we recognized the tune, "Home on the Range." We continued with the popular songs of the day, among them "The Beer Barrel Polka," "The Yellow Rose of Texas," etc.

I was impressed with Captain Chittenden's explanation of the confusion of the war in Casablanca. He did not go into detail about the gore or destruction of war but simply into the politics of the French officers who could not decide who should be the man in charge of the French army.

As the evening drew to a close, Captain Chittenden and two other officers drove us back to camp. As we parted he stepped aside with me and asked me if I would care to go to Constantine with him the next afternoon. I was happy for the opportunity to go to the big city and glad to get to know him better.

At noon the following day, he was at the Headquarters tent standing beside his jeep when I looked out of my tent. I picked up my purse and helmet, and joined him at the entrance to our camp.

"Hello, how are you today? I hope we didn't keep you up too late last night. I got off on a tangent. I hope it didn't bore you girls." While he was speaking, he helped me into the jeep, walked around to the driver's side and started the motor.

"No, you didn't bore us," I said. "In fact, it was quite a revelation, since we in the States knew nothing of what was happening during the invasion or since. Everything is censored. You have had quite an experience, and luck to have come through it safely."

As we rode, I saw many varieties of trees and growth alongside the road. He surprised me by calling off their names. I was completely unfamiliar with the flowers we passed in the fields. Oh, I recognized the bougainvillea, but the yucca, eucalyptus, acacia, fig and others were all new to me. I was familiar with the hothouse flowers that were sent to patients at the hospital and a few others that grew in gardens, but my parents grew mostly vegetables to survive during the depression in Detroit. I wondered how Captain Chittenden knew the plants and trees. I was curious about his background. I asked, "Are you into horticulture or forestry?"

"No, I haven't had much time for it, but I did learn about these because they are very different from what we have in the States."

I noticed his eyes shift from the road, not missing anything as he brought my attention to something that I might have missed. An infantry trait, the foot soldier always on the alert, I thought. He seemed a solid kind of fellow who looked out for the welfare of his men, and at camp last night I sensed the respect with which they regarded him. As we rode along, we laughed as we exchanged stories of some of our encounters with the Arabs, of their seeming to pop out of the ground at the most inopportune times.

He parked the jeep beside several others in the central part of town and we began to explore the city, stopping at the edge of a gorge. It dropped hundreds of feet, and I wondered how many had fallen into that abyss. We had heard that if an Arab tired of a wife (he could have four), he could just nudge her over the precipice and no one would ever know what happened to her. I took pictures of the tunnel blasted out of the solid rock that surrounded this ancient city, and other scenes.

When we returned to our jeep, we discovered that it had been tampered with. Items under the seat had been moved and the battery was run down. There were several Arab youngsters a short distance away. We figured they might have had keys that fit it. Chittenden shouted "Ah lay!" to show his displeasure. We had to get pushed when we stopped for any reason, but we got back to his camp before dark. We had supper in his tent, and I heard the balalaika a short distance away. I was delighted with the music and asked, "How could the GI's carry instruments overseas with all the other baggage?"

He replied, "If they could carry it, there were no restrictions; and isn't it great?" I heard later that they tucked them in with the motor pool equipment, in cars and trucks.

Chittenden, after several visits to my camp, commented on how quiet life at our camp seemed in comparison to theirs. On our next date he brought along three enlisted men with their instruments: a guitar, a balalaika, and a violin, along with several other officers that our nurses had been seeing. Sitting on the ground in a circle, we sang along with the music and livened up our camp. Like the Pied Piper, the music drew people out of their tents to join us. Nurses, officers, and enlisted men sat under the stars singing all evening. It cheered the entire area, including Arabs who sat on the fringes of our camp, listening. Our enlisted men enjoyed the evening, as they had so little diversion, and nothing to do after dark.

Captain Chittenden asked me if I would like to invite a couple to come with us to visit Bone the next day. It was the custom to fill a vehicle, jeep or reconnaissance car when going on trips. I asked Esther Laden, one of my four tent mates, and she invited her friend, Major Williams. Early the following day, we gathered up some rations, as was our habit when going away for the day, and started out. It was about two hundred and fifty kilometers over mountainous winding hairpin trails to Bone on the coast of the Mediterranean Sea.

Riding along the mountainous trails and looking down on valleys below, we saw small clusters of abodes below. As we neared the outskirts of a village, the air was filled with the fragrance of orange blossoms. There were cypress, palm, olive, and orange trees, and fields of wild flowers in bright yellows, pinks, and reds.

We had traveled about an hour's distance, chatting and singing, when suddenly the roar of a plane's engine overhead shook the tranquility of the scene. Instinctively, we scrunched low in our seats. Looking upward, we saw an English Spitfire fighter, trailing smoke, pass low over our heads; then we heard a screeching crash as it smashed into the airfield ahead of us.

"For a minute there, I thought we'd had it. That might have been a Stuka; they come in low like that," Chittenden explained.

"Let's hope he got out of that alive. He was already on fire before he crashed," Major Williams added. It was a reminder to us of the speed of the planes and the risk of being on the road.

On the main street of Hammam Meskoutine, we saw what looked like a hotel, and the men decided to investigate because it was nearly time for lunch. Although we had our rations, we were always hungry for real food—meat and vegetables. We were lucky. The French were adept in preparing food without any notice. In short order the cook served us a fluffy egg omelet with cheese, bread, and fruit along with a bottle of wine. We ate on the patio with the scent of orange blossoms permeating the atmosphere.

After lunch we continued on to Bone, a port city that had been a bombing target by both the Allies and the Germans in the past. Shattered buildings and destruction ahead indicated we had reached Bone. Bare walls of multi-story structures lay open with hanging floors and ceilings suspended, ready to fall at the least tremor. Alongside the roads, wrecks of tanks and trucks lay in crazy disarray as we drove by. We stopped at an army base where Chittenden had come on official business. He reached for a folder in the compartment in the Reconnaissance car and said, "Major Williams, why don't you, Rad and Esther wander about the port city while I tend to business. I shouldn't be long here and you might like to stretch. It's safe as long as you stay in the road and don't let anything fall on you. Be back in a half hour." He smiled as he helped me out of the front seat saying, "Watch your step."

"Great, we'll do a little exploring. Let me help you out, Esther," Major Williams replied as he stepped out and went around the car to give Esther a hand.

We started down the road gawking at the ruins of buildings and apartments above. Furnishings exposed on the inner walls stood in place, but on the outside edge, beds and tables hung precariously over the edge of hanging floors and walls that dangled crazily in midair. Tangled mounds of plaster and bricks covered the furnishings that had fallen to the ground. The Germans, as they escaped to the sea, saw that nothing was left in the city that might be of use to the Allies.

As we walked into the business section, we came upon a small cafe that had somehow survived the bombing. Tables and chairs in front of it looked inviting, so we decided to sit down and see what would happen. In a minute an elderly Frenchman carrying a small tray with glasses and a bottle greeted us.

"Bon jour, Mademoiselle's, Monsieur." Then in few words, he asked *"Manger,* wine, beer?"

We decided on beer, as we had not had any since leaving England and wondered how French beer would taste. It was the same ginger beer that the English had imported, with a very small percentage of alcohol, very mild but safer than water, which we did not drink in public places. The cool beer must have been stored in a dark basement or cave, since there was no ice in this part of the world. When we finished, Major Williams put some crumpled paper francs on the tray while the old man bowed and thanked us profusely. We headed back in the direction we had come. I saw Chittenden standing beside the car in the distance. As we came close, he greeted us with, "See anything I should?"

"No, nothing new," the Major replied. "Don't waste your time, Captain, just the usual destruction."

The Major then handed him a bottle of beer that we had bought for him. Chitt fumbled in his back pants pocket and brought out a folded jack knife with five different attachments, yanked the beer cap off and drank the contents in about five seconds.

"Thanks, that was cool," he said. "We had better

head for home, but first let's drive past the port and take a closer look at the sea. Too bad we didn't bring our suits. I should have thought of that; we could take a dip in the wilderness."

Chittenden got behind the wheel and started the motor. We had just started down the main road in Bone when we heard the familiar boom sound of the anti-aircraft guns. We decided not to venture near the port, and instead parked in the shadow of a several trees. Tracers and anti-aircraft pierced the air and we were caught in our first air raid. A dozen bombs exploded in the distance, as a Swastika marked plane roared overhead. We heard the rat-tat-tat of machine gun fire in the distance.

After the noise subsided, the skies opened in a cloudburst, as if the bombs had created the storm. The blankets were unrolled, and we continued on the road. We had traveled but a short distance on the mountain road when we came to an overturned truck just off the edge of the road ahead. Captain Chittenden stepped on the brakes. The car spun completely around on the wet narrow precipice. We headed back in the direction from which we had come until we came to a area wide enough for him to turn around again. The truck, as we passed it, was a bus, but we saw no passengers. We arrived at camp at dusk, tired from the long drive but thankful for surviving two close calls.

Watching him depart in the dark, I saw what a fine young man he was. I remembered the respect with which his men had regarded him when Betty and I visited his camp. We had sat on the ground in the pyramidal tent along with his tentmates, Captains Long and Nelson. A gasoline lamp illuminated the darkness, casting long shadows on the tent wall behind us. Chitt had his GIs bring coffee, bread, Spam and a can of salmon that someone had received from home, as we listened to a German battery-operated radio broadcasting propaganda. When we heard music outside, he turned the radio off, and we listened to the strains of the strings serenading us. He said, "Those guys like to surprise me."

Captain Chittenden had visited almost every day since we met, but today turned out to be our last date, since he was being sent back to the States for rotation. We drove to Constantine and went swimming in the outdoor pool, then sunbathed on the bleachers to dry off. After a sandwich and coffee at the Red Cross Club, we wandered to the market place where we stopped to look at some Arabic rugs that caught his attention.

"What do you think of this one, Rad?" he asked, holding up a beautiful white rug about four by eight feet, striped with a multicolored Arabic design.

"I think it's the most beautiful one in the lot." I thought it would be a nice souvenir to take back to the States. Earlier, Chitt had bought me a corsage with a talisman surrounded by Lily of the Valley, and pinned it on my lapel saying, "You have made Africa a memorable experience for me. I almost wish I didn't have to leave just now." He looked into my eyes, and we both smiled. We knew that going home was what everyone was looking forward to.

We stopped at the small French restaurant, where Chittenden had made reservations earlier. The French woman led us to a table, and then went into the kitchen and brought us a whole baked chicken, potatoes, sliced tomatoes, bread, and fruit. Wine was present at all meals, as usual. We relished the food, and as we were about to finish Chittenden asked, "May I have your address, Rad? I'll send my new one when I write to you." We exchanged APO's. "Tell me what you need or want from the States and I will mail it to you."

"That's very thoughtful of you, Chitt. My folks keep asking me the same thing, but with mail being so long enroute, and sometimes lost, I can't think of a thing. Last Christmas, the cookies they sent traveled for three months and arrived crumbled beyond recognition. Thanks just the same."

The day passed quickly, and we knew we had to start

back to camp before dark. We walked to the parking area where we left the jeep and drove back. The sun was setting behind our mountain, outlining it in a multitude of pinks, mauves and blues that turned into deep purple as we reached camp. At the entrance to my tent he put the lovely rug into my arms.

"This is for you, Rad," he said. Place it at the foot of your cot to keep your feet off the ground."

"But I thought you were buying it for yourself. You must take it home as a souvenir."

"I bought it for you. I want you to have it—please, Rad."

Hesitatingly, I accepted it, as he would not take no for an answer. He then laid the rug beside the tent peg and put his arms about my waist. "Take care of yourself, Rad. It's been great being with you these past weeks."

"Good luck on your next assignment, Chitt," I said, "and a safe trip home. Thank you for the beautiful rug. You shouldn't have done that." We embraced and kissed.

Chitt did not know what his next assignment would be. Perhaps he would teach invasion tactics to troops in the States, since he had experienced the invasion of Africa, or go on to the Pacific Theater of Operations where our men were continually island hopping. Months later Kate, my sister, wrote that my mother had received a dozen red roses from Captain Chittenden after he landed in the States, with a complimentary note about having met her lovely daughter.

25 April 1943

At last! A large bag of mail arrived today, including two most welcome letters from my fiancé. The mail left the States in December in a slow convoy and got stranded in England. From England it was forwarded to North Africa. Since the mail clerks never knew where which half of the Third Aux was (half of our group stayed back in England) they returned it to England and the whole procedure was repeated. It took over four months to get our first mail. I read it over and over. I was happy to learn that my fiancé was thinking of me, especially as we had agreed to try to reach one another in spirit. However, the eight-hour time zone change, night duty and travel had interfered with my being able to keep the pledge. The thousands of miles of separation was hard to transcend. I was glad he still cared.

The next morning, Sunday, a group of us went to church services at the 61st Station Hospital. After lunch I attacked my bedroll. Whenever there was freedom from the pressures of duties, the boredom of tent life was relieved by sorting through one's possessions. I rolled it out of the tent and opened it up to the sun, then rearranged my clothes so that they were more easily accessible when I needed to pull a specific piece out as needed. Sleeping on the clothing was our method of pressing. Sorting became an obsession with some of the girls, and their bedrolls were spread open a great deal of the time. I had been reading *The Sun Is My Undoing*, borrowed from one of our officers. There were very few books available, since they are excess baggage and heavy.

Captain Marion E. Black returned from the fighting near Bizerte, with interesting stories of surgery in tents with electricity furnished by a generator. When enemy planes flew over the generator was switched off, and the operation continued with a corpsman directing a flashlight at the site of operation. Surgeons probed for jagged steel, tied spurting arteries, closed torn chests, repaired lacerated organs, poured sulfadiazine, and injected morphine to those beyond help.

I tried learning a few Arabic phrases when three mangy travelers, carrying a rooster, stopped on the road in front of our camp. The language was difficult to articulate and we had little luck in spite of many gestures in an attempt to understand each other. We got nowhere. It didn't dawn on me until later that they probably wanted to sell the rooster. I never thought of eating a rooster.

At various times of the day we saw Arabs stop

wherever they were, kneel and repeatedly bow their heads toward the earth, while chanting. I heard that they prayed to Mohammed, Prophet of Islam, who was born in Mecca in 570 A.D., and that, orphaned as a child, he tended sheep and camels in the desert near Mecca. His uncle took him along on caravans through Arabia and Syria and to the town hall of Mecca where large fairs and religious meetings were held, and where heathens, Jews and Christians traded and mingled. It was in Mecca that Mohammed heard about pagan idols, about the God of Israel, and about Jesus Christ.

Time began to drag after Chittenden's departure. We could have gone into Constantine in our company truck that drove in for mail or supplies, but that meant getting up early and there was nothing going on in the morning, which resulted in the nurses depending on rides into town with the Air Force men who were camped several miles east of us. We were always ready to leave the boredom of camp life and ride into the only city within the area. Constantine, the ancient city, sat atop a rocky jut of land surrounded by a gorge, accessible only by spans and bridges from the surrounding country. It was named after the Roman Emperor Constantine, (272-337 A D) who, influenced by his mother Helene, in 312 established Christianity as the state religion in that part of the world for the next three hundred years.

We saw the city high on the plateau many miles before reaching it as we drove through the valleys past green fields covered with yellow and red wild flowers. The roads in Constantine on the outer perimeter were tunneled out of mountain rock on which the city was built. The inner roads wound through the city trailing into ancient donkey trails that led us to the market place, the Casbah. It was crowded and noisy, with babbling Arabs waving their arms as they bartered at the rickety stalls. The wood counters were covered with carcasses of lambs; their decapitated heads with staring eyes covered with black flies.

Now and then, we saw an overloaded cart being pulled by a small, matted, scraggly donkey as he tripped and stumbled up the incline on ancient cobblestones, while an Arab sat up front of the two wheeled cart and beat the poor animal with a long whip. It was said, "The French browbeat the Arabs, and they in turn vented their hostility on the poor donkeys."

We purchased grapes, melons, and oranges but dared not eat them until we washed them in chlorinated water when we got back to camp. As usual, we ended up at the casino and sipped *vin blanc* or ginger beer with new acquaintances and watched the panorama as it unfolded before us. Various branches of Allied troops from the armies gathered there for amusement or relaxation. We enjoyed the excitement, the camaraderie, the flirtation, and singing the popular tunes of the time to music played by enlisted men on stringed instruments, banjos and guitars.

Besides the Americans, there were French army officers dressed in bright blue uniforms, their jacket epaulets and visored caps trimmed with gold braid. They were decorated with ribbons and medals. British desert troops in khaki shorts, knee length stockings, and pith helmets, and Arab sheiks in galabiyeh's, their heads wrapped in turbans reminded me of the movie, "Lawrence of Arabia," that I had seen. The Scots wore plaid kilts, knee length stockings and berets. This was the only gathering place for diversion from war within a hundred miles. In spite of it being called a casino, which is associated with gambling, I never saw any gambling there. The Red Cross Club, a short distance from the casino, was a quiet refuge where we could get sandwiches made with spam, donuts, coffee or a lemon drink, and play ping-pong, badminton, darts, or bridge if we could make up a foursome. It represented a change of pace from the casino's fervor.

The babble of many tongues, the commotion and din, the constant comings and goings of people greeting one another, and the camaraderie of all the nationals gathered under one roof was an exciting experience, a marked contrast to lying on the cot under a mosquito bar, reading, writing letters, sweltering in the heat and going to mess to eat the same food day after day.

At camp in the evenings, the officers, including the nurses, often played softball with our enlisted "boys," as we called them. Our C.O., Colonel Blatt, played until he tripped on a tent peg on a dark night and fractured his leg. The men helped him into a two-and-a-half-ton truck so he could hold his leg out straight and drove to the 61st General Hospital where the orthopedist applied a long leg cast. He was back at camp in a few days.

On a visit there we heard that one of their nurses had been killed in a jeep accident.

When the aroma of coffee permeated the air, we joined the kitchen crew in the mess tent to pass the time. Our GIs were kept busy with camp duties but there was not much excitement in their lives. We nurses were friendly with them, but we knew that dating enlisted men was prohibited.

Life became simpler as our needs diminished, and we were acclimating to nomadic living. Like Arabs, we sat on the ground while eating. When it rained we stood balancing the mess kit, eating quickly before the food and we became drenched. When the ground became saturated and the field a quagmire, we resorted to wearing men's boots, as our oxfords sank in the mud, filled with slush and remained submerged when we lifted our feet.

As the climate warmed and the ground became dry, hard and dusty, we changed from our woolen clothing to one-piece fatigues for casual wear at camp or when traveling long distances. Daytime temperatures, as the rains eased, became very warm, but as soon as the sun set it turned quite cold. There was snow in the mountains. We wore flannel pajamas and a sweater when going to bed, and those who had sleeping bags added wool blankets over them to keep warm. The rest improvised by folding blankets so they could wiggle into the pocket to keep the sides sealed

Chairs, tables, electricity, bathtubs, toilets—things we had always taken for granted in the past—were luxuries. There were no boxes or shelves to lay things on. A cup, a clock, eyeglasses, or a book was placed on the ground. A suitcase was opened too often to be of use as a bedside table. Four cots lined against the walls of the pyramidal tent, plus one across the middle on either side of the supporting central post filled it. In the tents, most of our time was spent lying down, since sitting on the cot's edge for any length of time was uncomfortable because the wood slat that held the canvas taut from head to foot pressed hard against the backs of one's thighs.

Our water supply was a lister bag, an olive drab canvas bag about four feet tall, supported by timber in the middle of camp with the sun beating down on it. It provided for all our immediate needs, drinking, bathing and laundry. We sat on the cot in the dark tent with the flaps dropped to bathe from the small amount of water held in our helmet propped on the ground so it would not spill, and brushed our teeth outside the tent. Our wastewater was dumped between the stakes of the tent where it was absorbed quickly in dry weather. If we did not empty it, "Whimpy," the camp pup, always thirsty, came running across the field and drank it. Soap apparently made no difference to this tiny black and white terrier that raced from tent to tent whenever he escaped his leash. Whimpy's master, Estel W. Tedder, was part of the kitchen crew and had procured the pup by bartering (probably coffee) with a French family in the vicinity of Ain M'Lila. The tiny mouse of a dog became the bright spot in our lives and the company mascot.

30 April 1943

As the war in Africa continued into the final weeks, we nurses were sent on detached service to the 38th Evacuation Hospital near Beja, and to the 3rd General

Hospital near Mateur, when they became overwhelmed with casualties. As always when traveling long distances, our convoy stopped for a break every few hours in what appeared to be isolated, uninhabited country for a rest stop. Invariably, Arabs popped out of what seemed a hole in the ground, and we found ourselves stared at as we squatted. Since the one-piece fatigues we wore had no back seat drop, we had to drop it from the neck down exposing all. We wore only a bra and panties underneath. We discovered it was not the best attire for traveling, but we had no choice when summer arrived. We were covered with dust and sand stirred by the fast rolling trucks as we raced to our assignment. Our lips became rimmed with mud when we moistened them with our tongues. As for those who wore eyeglasses, their eyes were encircled with dirt looking like clowns; we chuckled as we stared at each other, because no one could see herself. Make-up applied in the wee hours no longer showed through the accumulation of dust. We were gradually getting accustomed to simple living.

We now worked twelve-hour periods and lightened the work for the nurses at the Evacuation Hospitals, which left little time to get acquainted with the unit personnel. Besides, they had their own circle, and we were temporary outsiders. The wounded soldiers we received were transfers from the fighting in the El Guettar under General Patton's command and had been first treated at the 48th Surgical Hospital, located nearer to the fighting, where our Third Aux Surgeons had operated on them. Many were in leg, arm, or hip casts for ease in transporting them eventually to England or perhaps the States if they were handicapped for future service. Our work was assisting doctors in the operating room, checking wounds, changing dressings, giving injections of Sulfadiazine, medications, and boosting their morale just by being there. As the need for our support lessened we returned to our camp at Ain M'Lila.

We returned to dashing into Constantine or spent time

in self-maintenance, washing our clothes and hanging them on the tent ropes. Our blouses were spread on the bedroll so that they were pressed by our body weight as we slept. There were no electric irons. Our wool skirts didn't need much attention, but when they got soiled, we got gasoline from a current Air Force acquaintance and dry-cleaned them ourselves. Our bedrolls contained all our possessions, and much time was spent looking for things, checking and rearranging it.

As the heat of summer bore down and the afternoon sun blazed hot, we found ourselves spending more time lying on our cots under the mosquito net with tent flaps raised, reading, writing letters, and trying to catch any whiff of moving air. It felt as if a hot oven door had been opened with a fan set behind it, sending forth gusts of hot air. It was too hot to exert any energy, and we began to understand the lethargy of the Arabs. Our small camp was far from any form of entertainment or movies provided by the army, and since we were short of transport, we could not travel the long distances where there was diversion. The USO never came near, and movies were shown only at large camps. However, we discovered that when we were in Constantine, at the casino or the pool, we did not notice the heat as much, so we took every opportunity to ride into the city.

The Air Force, because of necessity for vast open space for airfields, was located a few miles beyond our camp. Pilots, bombardiers, and their crews came calling as soon as they discovered nurses living in the tents alongside the dusty road. We accepted invitations to their camp and were entertained in their improvised clubhouse. They also provided us with transportation into Constantine, and livened camp life as couples paired off and romances blossomed.

Meanwhile, many of our surgeons wasted precious time doing nothing for long periods, waiting for the call to serve. Time dragged heavily for them as the war in Africa was fought a long distance away in the desert, and now across the mountains of Bizerte and Tunis. They were idle and bored for months without diversion because of the nature of warfare in Africa. Too few field hospitals where surgical teams could do surgery had come into existence. The Third Auxiliary Surgical Group was ready and waiting to take part sometime in the future. However we nurses were kept occupied much of the time at the few field hospitals when casualties were heavy and additional help was needed.

6 May 1943

We nurses were called back to the 38th Evacuation Hospital, still near Beja. on detached service. It was about eighty miles northeast of Ain M'Lila, but around the mountains it was a daylong rugged trip in a two-and-a-half-ton truck. The tent I shared with four nurses had short stubby ends of straw strewn over the ground, a change from the crushed stone we had in the tents at Ain M'Lila. The stone was neat, but both were rough on bare feet. The following day a GI electrician installed a light bulb that hung from an insulated wire in the center of the tent. Now I could read in the evenings while lying under the mosquito bar. My skin and freckles had turned a golden tan, some of it perhaps due to the Atabrine pills we had to take to avoid malaria.

The current rumor was that the fighting in Africa would soon be coming to an end. This was welcome news that the wounded brought back from the front. I was on duty in the operating room when the surgeon I assisted removed a bullet from behind a soldier's kneecap but was unsuccessful in removing the bullet in the knee joint. There are a lot of blood vessels in the area of the joint and the spurting of blood made the bullet impossible to find. I hated to see him suture the wound without removing the bullet, as it meant the soldier would have to go through surgery again. But I assumed that the surgeon had good reason for this omission. He also removed a bullet from the soldier's right arm. Surgery at the 38th Evacuation

Hospital now was of general type, removal of bullets and shrapnel, along with road accidents, and now and then appendectomies. The seriously wounded had been operated on by our Third Auxiliary Surgical teams that were attached to the 16th Medical Regiment at Tabarka, a British general hospital and the 159th Field Ambulance and Casualty Clearing Station near Souk El Khemis. When the wounded were able to tolerate being moved they were airlifted to the evacuation hospitals farther to the rear, and from there they were sent to army general hospitals in England.

7 May 1943

The fighting continued as Americans advanced on Bizerte and the British neared Tunis, until both cities fell on the 7th. Two Nazi divisions surrendered unconditionally on the 9th to the Americans in Bizerte. The First Infantry Division deserved much of the credit for having fought courageously in the mountains to clear a pathway for the advance. The 34th Division, after a fierce hand-to-hand battle with the Germans who were entrenched on the hill above them, took Hill 609 on the 1st of May, but were held there, and the 9th Division cleared the enemy in the northern sector of the area. On the 6th of May after a massive artillery and air bombardment by the Allies, what was left of the Panzers was destroyed.

The Axis Surrenders Africa

On May 12, 1943 the Afrika Corps, under General von Arnim, surrendered "unconditionally" as demanded by the big three: Roosevelt, Churchill, and Stalin. All organized Axis resistance ceased. The victory was decisive in the whole area with the American capture of Mateur on the 3rd of May, 1943.

I watched from my tent at the 38th Evacuation Hospital where I had been on detached service, as the German and Italian prisoners rode past our barbed wire enclosure, driving their own box-like trucks and other motor vehicles; some without tires clanging past, and stirring up clouds of dust as they headed west toward the internment camps. Trucks were packed with standing soldiers. Thousands upon thousands were walking, tattered men with dirty, bloodied bandaged heads, arms, and legs shuffling past our barbed wire enclosure. Many appeared relieved that the war was finished and were singing the songs that had primed them for war in their youth. Some of the men occasionally waved and smiled; others appeared haughty and aloof, looking straight ahead. Now and then a German officer stopped at our camp to inquire if this was the prisoners' camp. Little wonder; we were behind barbed wire, and they are out on the road.

Prisoners continued marching past our camp day and night. The rattling trucks, the shuffling of feet, and murmurs kept us awake. I saw a motorcar traveling fast on only three wheels. I supposed it would collapse if it slowed down. Motorcycles with a passenger in a bucket seat attached to its side and two men on the main frame whizzed by. Many thousands were walking, their worn-out shoes wrapped in rags. Some wore straw thongs held together with rags. As the prisoners continued to march, stragglers began to fall by the wayside, and hundreds of wounded were admitted to our hospital. In the operating room I assisted the surgeons in applying plaster casts to arms and legs after debridement of infected wounds to protect them in transit. We cleaned wounds, poured sulfadiazine powder into them and changed dirty bloodied dressings on heads, arms, legs, and bodies. The men looked at us suspiciously until they realized that we were genuinely concerned about their injuries and welfare. The soldiers were covered with dust from the long march, but their good looks, blond hair and blue eyes showed through the dirt. They looked tired after years of hard fighting in the desert. The exodus continued for three days and nights until 250,000, about half of them

Germans and the rest Italians, had passed our enclosure. They stirred up so much dust that the haze obscured the sun. Miles of scorched trucks and damaged tanks were left on the roads in Tunisia as the prisoners marched westward. The 1st Division was responsible for the capture of the thousands of prisoners, but it was the 1st Infantry Division fighting so valiantly in the mountains that cleared the path for the onslaught. Since November 8, 1942, when 30,000 Americans landed at Casablanca, Oran and Algiers, Americans had suffered over 6,500 casualties, killed, wounded, or taken prisoner.

Arabs that had left their homes and fled into the hills to stay out of the path of war began to return in caravans with donkeys pulling heavy loads on two-wheeled carts. Barefoot women, bent over with packs on their backs, trailed behind, followed by straggling, dirty urchins.

I was called back at night to scrub for Captain Robert Augustine who, the nurses warned me, was impossible to please. We amputated a gangrenous right arm on a young American who also had several abdominal wounds and a damaged liver. The young man was in very poor condition, and I wondered if he would make it. It disturbed me to see the havoc wrought on so many young lives. I

Bizerte Harbor in ruins

survived Captain Augustine and never knew why I was selected, but it helped me remember him many years after the war when I read of his accomplishments in a book written by Marguerite Bourke-White, the famous woman photographer in World War II.

Captain Augustine had operated in the Tropics, in the Arctic, in Alaska, and in South America. He demonstrated his ingenuity in planning the layout of the hospital tentage so that the wounded entered at one end, went through admitting, triage, x-ray, surgery, and then into the post-operative tent without leaving coverage. Other units copied this plan, since it protected us from light exposure to enemy planes, and when it rained kept our shoes from sinking in mud.

Our work began tapering off, and the rains kept us inside our tents where I read until my eyes burned. The light bulb was not bright enough to prevent eyestrain. Writing letters and sleeping to catch up on needed rest were our main occupations while on detached service, but when few letters came through, now that they had to be routed from Ain M'Lila as well as the confusion in England, it was difficult to be enthusiastic about writing.

Rumors were whispered about this hospital's next move, now that the war had ended. The question was: will those of us on detached service with the 38th Evacuation Hospital go along with them, or would we go back to our own organization? Most of the Third Aux girls wanted to go back to Ain M'Lila because the evacuation hospital had many ridiculous rules and restrictions. We thought that was the reason we saw so much frustration and more imbibing than we had at our camp. One moment we heard we were to move with the evacuation hospital; the next day we were to return to our own organization. It didn't make much difference to me, but I was amused as I watched the girls getting anxious about returning to their romantic attachments at our camp.

Now that we were idle once more, we began to

get invitations to tour the surroundings with new acquaintances. Russ Nixon, a member of the Red Cross stationed at Constantine, arrived at camp and invited me to join him and his friend to see the Roman ruins at Timgad. I was delighted and asked Madalyn Andreko to join us. Russ often stopped at camp without notice, and if I was there, I joined him on his expeditions. I think that if I had not been there, he would have asked anyone else. He was a dependable, pleasant companion without any romantic notions that I was aware of. He also wore his garrison cap crushed, like the Air Force men did, and was always neatly dressed in class A uniform.

I filled my canteen with water, my blanket, helmet and purse in hand, and stopped at Madalyn's tent. We went to the recreation tent where Russ and his friend were waiting. Russ said it was about a 150 kilometer drive southeast toward the desert, so we would be gone all day. We climbed into the jeep and were off.

Our blankets, always part of our equipment, were used to pad the rock-hard jeep seats or to spread on the ground when we stopped. Russ brought rations along, as we never knew if we would find a place to eat. Helmets, always worn when leaving camp since it was regulation, were usually removed when out of sight because they quivered if not tautly fixed with the chinstrap. Besides, how could one be light hearted with an iron hat weighing one down? As we rode, Russ told us a little about what we might see in Timgad. "You will see how the Romans and Christians lived in Africa during the 4th and 5th Century A.D."

He apparently had access to books about this part of the world that most of us were ignorant about. When something interested me, and I wanted to know more about it, I wrote to my sister Kate, and asked her to look it up. That was a long process and took forever, since we often moved before the answers arrived, and because of the mix-up that put half of our Third Auxiliary Group in Africa while the other half remained in England.

When we reached Timgad and the ruins, an elderly Arab dressed in a white galabiyeh appeared from behind one of the ruins, just as they always seemed to pop out from nowhere. He took it upon himself to guide us, pointing out interesting objects. He spoke just enough English that we could understand what we were seeing. Russ brought our attention to the straight layout of the roads in directions facing due North, South, East, and West. We decided that this Arab had guided many other tourists, since with few words and many gestures he was able to explain what the columns had supported and their purpose.

The Physicians' residence in the center of the Roman square was next door to a house of prostitution. Even in those early days social diseases were recognized and treated. At the arena we tried to visualize gladiators fighting lions and tigers, and the sacrifices made at the Temple. It made me think of the cruelty of men throughout history.

The market place was located near the center of the square, and each stall was identified by the bas-relief motif, etched in stone above it. Our guide pointed out the library, the forum, and the residential section to us, and took pictures of the deep ruts worn in the stone blocks below the Arc de Triomphe, where now only tall stone pillars remained. We were told that Roman soldiers, returning in chariots and carts from distant battles had worn the deep indentations in the stone road.

On top of some of the tall stone columns of the fallen palace and forum, storks had built nests on the high ledge. A long-legged bird, its beak pointed downward, stared at us as we walked below. A beautiful Mosaic Baptistery fountain stood in the Christian area, intact despite the strong earthquakes in the fifth and seventh centuries, along with exquisite turquoise and blue mosaic walls with delicate detailed figures and designs. A Christian cemetery was located at the far side of the city, and a Roman one on the opposite edge.

The excavation of these ruins began in the early

1900s and was far from completion when we visited in the spring of 1943. Timgad was destroyed first by the Barbarians who came down from the mountains in the fifth century and later by the earthquakes. When we completed our tour, Russ paid the Arab with a handful of paper Francs, and with much bowing we parted. On the way back we were lucky to find the Grand Hotel at Batna open. Our expedition ended with a delicious dinner of roast beef, potato, a salad of tomato and onion, bread, butter, and a bowl of fruit and wine. We arrived home before dark, stimulated by the events of the day.

In the next few days I encouraged several groups to visit the ruins, and the old Arab, profiting from my return trips, gave me an old worn coin. The face bore the profile of a Roman wearing a helmet, an image that was barely visible after the eons of time. I took many pictures of the ruins. Archaeology opened new interests in me that have stayed with me ever since.

Betty and I had a date with several Infantry officers who asked if we would like to go to Tunis. They had a munitions carrier, and we drove on roads marked with yellow flags, indicating that the fields had not been cleared of mines.

As we approached Medjes-el-Bab, we saw American light tanks scattered in the field, along with damaged assault cars, jeeps, trucks, and an occasional German tiger tank. A putrid stench filled the air. Instinctively, we pressed our fingers on our nostrils and covered our mouths, holding our breath as Lieutenant Avery explained, "It's the bodies in those Sherman tanks."

The field was so heavily mined that no attempt had been made to remove them. No one spoke for some time. My heart ached for those poor boys entombed in steel in that desolate place.

A huge aqueduct appeared in the horizon as we neared the outskirts of Tunis. We were surprised to see many tall modern buildings intact and shops open for business. We had been only in destroyed cities in the past months. However, when we reached the Port of Tunis, it was total destruction. The Allied Air Force had bombed it while the Germans held it, and the Germans put the finishing touches by demolishing the rest of it as they escaped. The entire area was leveled, and the harbor was filled with sunken German and Italian ships. Hulls protruded skyward, smoke stacks, superstructure and wreckage cluttered the bay. I took some pictures of the harbor as we walked past.

Driving past the Luftwaffe airfield, we saw many damaged Junker 88s and ME-109s scattered over the field where our B-26s (Marauders) caught them on the ground. Towards evening we rode to Carthage and saw the beautiful Byzantine Cathedral which, we were told, was the second oldest in the world. As darkness fell, the white dome illuminated by the huge full moon created an unforgettable picture. There was so much we would like to have seen, but the sudden darkness forced us to head back to camp over treacherous roads, with mines on both shoulders.

We drove past Mateur, the city the Americans had captured. It had been bombed and so heavily fought over by Mark IV and Mark V tanks that when we visited the following week there was nothing left but rubble. Our driver stayed on the narrow road, and continued on to Ferryville where we were surprised to see buildings standing in a beautiful city. We were stopped by several "Limy's" (British enlisted men) and told that it was "off limits" to Americans. Americans were permitted to visit only those cities that we had captured and these were Mateur and Bizerte, which were almost completely demolished. We grumbled about it until we realized that perhaps they were entitled to the spoils of war, since they had been fighting in the desert for nearly three years. However, everyone knew that without the American forces and our tremendous ability to build war materials and deliver them here, this campaign would not have been over now and quite likely might have been lost.

On our way back to the camp, Betty and I looked backward when we heard a strange sounding motor and saw a couple of GIs on the road behind us. They were riding merrily along on a captured German motorcycle, when they suddenly realized that we were girls and attempted to pass us to get a better look. At the same instant a two-and-a-half-ton truck appeared around the bend from the opposite direction on the narrow road and crashed into the motorcycle. Hearing the thud, and seeing the boys tossed into the air, was a sickening experience. We used the rifles that the men in the truck carried to splint both legs of one, and the arm and leg of the other, who had a compound fracture of the left leg. They were driven to our hospital. We were upset with the end of what had been an adventurous day. I checked on the boys later and found their legs and arm encased in plaster casts. They were recovering. Youth can withstand much affliction. I remembered one of the boy's names because it was so unusual. It was "Vooch;" he said he was from Mississippi.

Captain Rivere sat next to me at supper the next evening and asked me to go for a walk afterward. Because we had so little transportation, our officers spent much of their time in boredom playing poker, bridge, sorting through the bedroll and bartering for eggs with the wandering Arabs. Rivere, a surgeon, as most all our officers were, was slim with finely chiseled features, clean-shaven, and short-cropped hair. He was always neat in appearance and was quick in responding to any challenges, and seemed to command the respect of his peers.

I assumed he was married, as the majority of our officers were, and could sympathize with their being lonesome. Rivere had not paired off with anyone, to my knowledge; quite a few twosomes had formed by then. I could not help but wonder what the future held for some of these women. With so many single men in the army, I could not see the logic of getting involved with a married man in what might be a long-term relationship. However, most of the twosomes included the more mature nurses and not the younger girls, who hung together or dated the transient flyer groups. Perhaps the older nurses were not comfortable with the young Air Force men who came calling, most of whom were in their mid-twenties.

Captain Rivere and I walked to the hilly edge of camp, where he brushed away some stones so we could sit down. After discussing the day's events, we began talking about personal topics and home life. He was forthright. "Yes, I'm married," he said, "and I have two children." He had noticed my ring before so he knew I was engaged. It placed us almost on the same basis, that of being lonesome for a loved one far away.

"You know, Rad"—he had heard my name being called across camp, yet it perplexed me to hear it from him. I would not have called him Dan, at least not right off. "I got the surprise of my life when I unpacked my bag back in England to find that my wife had tucked in several packs of French Safes, that she would understand my need for companionship and even for intimacy. I was so surprised to find them that it made me wonder what was happening in the States."

I began to feel uneasy with the drift of the conversation, and when I did not respond and he sensed my shifting away from the close proximity of our sitting position, he quickly changed the course of the conversation. I was also glad when the sun began to set beyond the mountain, for the sudden darkness to conceal my embarrassment. I stood up, saying, "We'd better head back before the guard makes his rounds and stumbles over us here in the dark."

I had enjoyed being with him in group gatherings in the past, enjoyed his humor and versatility, but I had not encouraged him nor anyone in our group to get involved with me romantically. I wanted to be free of any close relationship, since it looked as though we were going to be living a communal type of existence for the duration of the war. It strengthened my determination to be free of any entanglements that might cause future heartbreak.

Chief Nurse Charlotte, after breakfast, announced that the navy officers at the storage post near Telergma had invited us all to a party. It was always called a party when we gathered with men from another unit. As we finished eating supper, two trucks arrived at headquarters with a navy officer stepping out of each one. The young men helped us up the steep step in the rear of the vehicle, while commenting on how pleased they were to meet American girls. The officers sat in the cab up front with the driver. I guessed one officer was afraid to sit with so many women, even though one of our own officers came along to be sure we all got back safely.

As soon as we arrived at the storage post, a small band started to play and a group of men gathered at the trucks to help us off and escort us into the building. The fellows were determined not to allow anyone to monopolize any girl for more than a few minutes, resulting in our dancing continually with little opportunity to get acquainted with anyone in particular. The drink was canned grapefruit juice, which was our morning juice throughout the war, but spiked at parties. Canned tart grapefruit juice was difficult enough to swallow by itself. It sent a shiver down my spine every morning at breakfast. Since navy ships had refrigeration, they had access to foods other than rations, and we were served ham and meat sandwiches other than Spam, along with a variety of fresh vegetables, lettuce, tomatoes and fruits that were a real treat. We ate heartily between dances and when the band took a break.

Upon returning to our post after midnight, our enlisted men on guard duty said that some Arabs had been stealing from our tents during our absence. A number of our people had commented earlier on having lost some items in the past days. The guards said, "Them A-rabs just creep among the tents while we're on the other end of camp, lift a tent flap, and grab whatever is in reach."

134

We knew the Arabs treasured our white mattress covers, as they would serve as a summer garment and reflect the heat of the sun. Since we had no mattresses, the covers were surplus, and some of our forces had exchanged them for chickens, eggs or for French francs. The Arabs also fancied our winter long john underwear as well, since the nights were very cold.

Now and then the French police raided the Arab hovels and returned the mattress covers and underwear and whatever else the Arabs had bought or stolen. We felt sorry for them, but it didn't stop the practice. We were not supposed to sell, and they were accused of stealing whatever the police found that was army equipment.

Our bedrolls containing all of our possessions lay on our canvas cots, with the shoe pockets hanging over the foot of the cots easy to reach from the tent flap. A mosquito net was suspended overhead on four bars with the bottom of the net tucked under the bedroll to prevent mosquitoes from entering and our getting malaria. Bulky items, makeup, toiletries, and frequently needed items were kept in our suitcases that served as an end table beside the head of our cot. We hung our dress uniforms on hangers on a nail on the central tent post. There were other items such as shoes, musette bag and loose items that were tucked under the cot on the ground, that a stealthy Arab could pilfer by simply lifting the tent flap. One of our nurses woke up one morning to find a void where her suitcase had been the night before. It was one of the occasions when the French police brought back a lot of mattress covers and long GI underwear to our camp. Of course no one at our camp claimed the items. "Must have belonged to the Air Force."

Nurse Eleanor Bernick and her lieutenant friend asked me to join them, along with Lieutenant W. Thomas Woodward on a trip to Batna. Lieutenant Woodward was with the 84th Engineer Battalion. When I heard that he had taught art at Wayne University in Detroit, we were friends almost immediately. We began mentioning familiar restaurants, theaters, and entertainment clubs as we reminisced together.

We packed spamwiches and lemonade, and bought oranges at an Arab village on the way. We traveled past hills and valleys and fields covered with wild red and purple flowers as far as one could see. When Lieutenant Woodward commented on the beauty of the country, I couldn't resist saying, "Yes, but I wish it wasn't so far from home."

At noon we stopped at a level spot in a field, spread a blanket on the ground and began eating our sandwiches. Between bites, Lieutenant Woodward reached into his musette bag and brought out a sketchpad and charcoal pencil and began sketching as we ate. In just minutes he sketched a front view and profile of Eleanor and me, accentuating our nose and chin in caricature. It amused us because they were very good likenesses in spite of the exaggeration.

Conversation was easy, even with new acquaintances, as we related news from letters from wherever one called home. Both men were scheduled to go to Oran in the next few days, and probably would return to the States.

As we ate, a P-38 (twin-engine Lightning) traveling at terrific speed buzzed over us. Fighter planes always flew very fast but this one was unusually low. A P-38 pilot was romancing one of our nurses, Isobel Johnson, and we joked about it being her friend, checking on her. We continued on to Batna after lunch, and since all towns were similar; that is, the usual Arab abode, squalor and sand, we did not stay long. We got home before dark, as it was not safe on the roads after dark. No one would ever know what became of you in this vast country.

I reported for duty at the dispensary tent the next morning and gave typhoid shots to our personnel as they came straggling in most of the morning. I gave myself one also. They always left my arm sore, discolored, and swollen. At four-thirty in the afternoon, without any warning, the skies burst open and rain came pouring down in torrents. It came so suddenly that we hardly had time to drop the tent flaps and lace the entrance to keep it from blowing inside. The rain came down in a deluge, with big drops plopping on the tent as though it would never stop.

As my tent mates and I sat on our cots in the dark tent, we heard the sudden gushing of water through our tent. It entered the upper corner of the tent, surged between cots and continued through the other end of the tent, spreading wider as it raced and gained momentum. We grabbed at our possessions on the ground to prevent them from being carried away with the flood. Thunder and lightning flashes filled the air as the storm turned our tent into a sea of mud.

The rain stopped as suddenly as it had started. When I got up off the cot my oxfords stuck in the mud as I raised my feet. There was no place we could go, so we stayed on our cots with our possessions taking much of the space. There was one redeeming feature after the rain had stopped, and I opened the flap. In the horizon I saw the most brilliantly colored rainbow that I had ever seen, with both ends in full view, but there was no pot of gold at either end.

The following day was spent cleaning up after the storm. I found a batch of baby mice in the shoe pocket of my sleeping bag. They were tiny pink nude babies with long tails. I turned them out into the adjoining field trusting that mother mouse would collect them and find them a hole in the ground. They would grow up and come back, I thought, but I didn't have the heart to do anything else.

I looked out of the tent and saw an Arab roaming past our camp carrying a bag. I knew by his slow pace that he had something he wanted to sell. I went to the road and saw it was potatoes. I began to barter with him, and we soon arrived at an acceptable price. My tent mates were excited about real potatoes for a change from the dehydrated ones we always had. After getting some lard and a pan from Sergeant Montgomery, we peeled, washed, and sliced them, then fried them on the kerosene stove one of the girls had borrowed from an officer. We fried them just outside our tent, and the aroma floated over the entire area. I had to balance the pan over the fire while they fried. We saved some to have the next day.

When there was nothing else to do we spent time layering our clothes on the cot beneath the sleeping bag to press them. After hanging my wool blankets on the tent ropes to air, I found the heat so intolerable that I had to lie down. I tried to read, but even that seemed tiring. It was no wonder the Arabs had so little ambition when the temperature hovered in the 120-degree range. Later, when I stopped at the headquarters tent to see if I had any mail, Colonel Blatt was standing at the entrance and pointing to a chair. "How are you, Lieutenant?" he asked. "Have a seat, let's talk."

I sat down on the folding chair and realized how good it felt to sit in a chair for a change.

He continued, "Is your mail coming through O.K.? Is your family worried about your being in the war?"

"I don't know if all my mail is getting here, or if there is ever such a thing as getting enough. I think my mother has some qualms about my being in the war, but I have lived away from home for several years, so she is used to my absence. Getting mail is the most exciting part of our life, don't you think?"

"Yes, I'm sure that's true. It's good to hear what our families are doing. The problems they have with food stamps and shortages of meat and gasoline are difficult, but maybe the war won't last too long, and we will be returning home."

I knew that he was regular army, married, and had a teenage son. I supposed he was missing his wife and wondering how a teenager was getting along without his father. He was handsome, with a muscular, thickset body. He looked at me rather quizzically as we chatted, and I realized that he was lonesome and shy. However, I also knew him to be assertive when he made decisions.

He didn't usually pay much attention to our comings and goings, which was very convenient for us. We were free to do and to go as we pleased when not on duty. He probably realized that it would be quite difficult to try to control a mature group of professional men and women who only recently were civilians. I had observed, when on detached service at hospitals, the firm control over the personnel, with rules and restrictions that we had a hard time abiding. Perhaps it was necessary in the larger organizations, but we, in the Third Auxiliary were free to come and go as we pleased.

The Air Force Arrives

28 May 1943

The 321st Bomb Group, 446 Squadron, moved in several miles beyond us and promptly invited us to a gathering. We were surprised on entering a house instead of a tent, a room cleared of furnishings except for a Victrola funnel atop a cabinet in the corner, and men gathered in groups. Immediately I recognized the tune, "Smoke Gets In Your Eyes," as a man approached me asking, "May I have this dance?" Others followed suit, and the floor filled with couples huddled close, heads snuggled, humming, and getting acquainted.

My partner swayed me across the floor to the music, his lips close to my ear he whispered, "Sure is nice to be with an American girl. I'm Bailey. Maryland's my home. What's your name, and where are you from?"

I'm "Rad—that's short for Radawiec. It's what my friends call me. Michigan's my home. It's great to be in a house for a change. How did you manage that, and dancing on a slick wooden floor, Lieutenant?"

"Just call me Bailey. As for this place, well, you know how the army works. We 'procured' it for this dance. Can't dance on dirt, and we wanted to throw a party as soon as we discovered you girls down the road. It took a good bit of scrounging to slick the floor. It was a bit tacky in spots."

Then another officer tagged Bailey and I was dancing and getting acquainted with a new fellow.

I learned that Lieutenant Bailey piloted a B-25, a Mitchell Bomber, and they had been on a bombing mission on one of the islands in the Mediterranean earlier today, and that one of their buddies had just returned after making an emergency landing in Tunis. They were happy that he made it back, because when they last saw him, he was in trouble with an enemy fighter on his tail. They also saw buddies bail out of a burning plane spiraling to the ground after being hit by anti-aircraft, and were concerned for the crews that failed to return from the mission. Bailey came back after another partner tagged him, and we continued to get acquainted and being interrupted.

I mentioned to him having recently being near Beja on detached service with the 38th Evacuation Hospital. Bailey said he knew the area, since they flew over it almost every day to bomb the Islands of Sardinia and Sicily in the Mediterranean Sea.

Laughing, he said, "You know, we began accumulating extra rations and planning a party as soon as we saw laundry hanging on tent ropes when passing your camp. I guess girls like to suds thing out more than men do." Holding my hand as the record was changed, he added, "That's a beautiful ring you're wearing. Does it mean what it looks like?"

"Yes, I'm engaged to a fellow back home."

"That makes us even. I'm also engaged. A girl I met in Florida, where I trained."

Other fellows tagged, and I danced with captains and majors, but Bailey tagged back without any trepidation on account of rank, and asked to drive me back instead of my riding in the truck that had brought us. My friend Betty and her Lieutenant rode along with us in the jeep.

Our friendship began on even ground. I preferred this kind of relationship. It was safe. The next afternoon a plane marked "Buzz Wagon" passed low over my tent. It was Bailey's signal that he would be over, as we had agreed at parting last night. He and Lieutenant Van Arsdale, who had just recovered from having been shot down three weeks earlier, were at our camp within an hour. Lieutenants often had difficulty getting transportation, as they were out-ranked, but Bailey said he would come even if they had to hitch a ride on any army vehicle passing by. They were lucky; they got a jeep. Betty and Van Arsdale, her friend of last night, joined us, and we were on our way to the pool in Constantine. We sunned at the pool's edge, drank lemonade from our canteens, and talked. I liked swimming, but diving had been my specialty since high school swimming events. As I lay alongside the pool, I studied the high diving board that no one was using. I said, "I'm going to try that board."

As I got up from the bleacher and headed for the board, Bailey warned, "Better be careful. It looks pretty high."

I walked toward the ladder and began to climb it. It was a long climb, and when I finally reached the diving platform and looked down to the distant water, I hesitated. I had never attempted to dive from such a great height before.

What should I do? I couldn't climb back down that ladder with all those eyes watching me. I simply had to dive; there was no alternative. I took the measured steps to the edge of the diving board, jumped up a couple of times to test the spring, then turned around with a prayer and jumped into the air doing a back jack knife, my favorite dive. The interval before I slapped my lower back on the surface, submerged, and then came up, seemed like an eternity. The crowd in the bleachers clapped their hands and whistled when my head finally popped out of the water. As I shook the water out of my eyes, I saw Bailey standing at the poolside ready to jump in case I wasn't coming up, saying, "Wow! That was some dive! You didn't tell me you were an Olympic star."

He reached out to help me out of the pool, and we stretched on the bleachers to sunbathe. He lay on his back, I on my abdomen since my back felt tender from the slap on the water.

When we had sunned enough, Betty and I got dressed in the small co-ed cubicle, separated from the men's by only a slatted door that was hung about eighteen inches above the floor. We walked the short distance to the Casino where we joined several of Bailey's comrades and sipped weak ginger beer or *vin blanc* that some preferred. My back was tender for days from that impact on the water. Thereafter, I confined my diving to the medium board, with the rest of the crowd.

As we headed up the narrow street toward our jeep, the French boy who had been guarding it asked if we wanted to "*manger?*" Of course we did. We were always hungry. He led us down a narrow side street, into a small house where a French woman prepared a chicken dinner for us while we chatted and sipped *vin blanc*. The food included the usual salad of cucumbers, tomato, and sliced onion. French bread with butter and watermelon completed our dinner.

Afterwards, we went to the Red Cross Club, played several rubbers of bridge, ate donuts, drank coffee, and then headed home.

Bailey and his crew became regular callers at our camp. We played cards in the evenings and when he did not have to fly, we went to Constantine where there was always plenty of excitement. One day as we sat in the Casino listening to the music he asked, "How about flying with me one of these days?"

"On a Bombing mission?" I asked incredulously.

"No, never that. Just over the surrounding area—that mountain." He pointed toward the range of mountains across the road.

"Oh, I'd love that." I was thrilled for a chance to go

up in a plane.

"We fly out early tomorrow. How about after I get back from the mission?"

"That will be great. I'll be waiting." I had flown as a passenger in commercial planes in the States, but this was a B-25 bomber.

The next afternoon about three o'clock, Bailey picked me up and we drove to the airfield where the "Buzz Wagon" stood. I smiled as I read the big letters. He had named it well. A row of bombs stenciled on its fuselage indicated the number of bomb runs completed. I didn't count them, but knew that he was close to going home, and that might be about forty-five missions.

Bailey helped me up through the hatch in the belly of the ship, and I worked my way past machine guns, parachutes and other flying paraphernalia into the cockpit, and sat next to him in the co-pilot's seat. The motors roared as we taxied up the runway. As we lifted into the sky, the propellers stirred up the desert sand. While flying over a lake, Bailey jettisoned several bombs. I guessed it was for our safety in case of an accident.

We flew toward the Atlas Mountains and saw openings into caves at close range. Bailey pulled the plane up sharply to clear the mountain ridge. Flying over Constantine, I could see the gorge in its entirety surrounding the city and the trestles connecting it to the adjoining land. It was a spectacular scene. As we headed back toward the airfield, Bailey let me take the controls for a brief moment over a level area.

Bailey and a member of his crew came over about three times a week and, with Gertie or Betty, we made up a foursome for bridge or drove into the city for entertainment. When exploring the Casbah, located beyond Constantine, Bailey put his arm around me to keep the crowds, carts and donkeys from brushing against me in the narrow passages. We pitied the poor overburdened beasts, as their Arab masters beat them with whips when the mangy animals stumbled over old, uneven stone paths.

On parting at the end of an evening we embraced and parted with a kiss. I had no guilt feelings or felt disloyalty to my lover. Bailey's life was at risk on every mission that he flew. The day before, a squadron member was hit by a 20-millimeter shell that damaged his plane so severely that he had to make a crash landing. He suffered lacerations to his face, arms, and legs, but was lucky to land at a safe base.

A caring friend, affection and intimacy were of the utmost importance when life was lived on the edge.

The roar of the B-25 engines awakened us almost every day at dawn. I would raise the flap of my tent and count them as they passed overhead on a bombing mission. They formed into a V pattern soaring over the mountain range toward a distant target. Hours later, when we heard the distant roar of engines, we counted again. We saw feathered propellers, holes in fuselages and wings, and stragglers trailing smoke, and we prayed that they would make a safe landing. Missing planes always concerned us.

The B-25 Group planned a celebration on the 30th of May, and invited all of our nurses to the party. It was to have been a farewell party, as they were going to move to an airfield at Souk el Arba, about two hundred miles northeast of us. However, Colonel Pearson, returning from a mission, crashed, and all six crewmembers were killed.

Bailey came over in the evening and, as we sat on our blankets on the ground, told us what had happened. "It's a sad day at camp," he said. "Those were all great guys."

After a few moments he said, "We all hate leaving this place, and most of all it means I'm not going to be able to come over very often. I'm going to miss you, Rad. Being with you these past weeks has made a big a difference in my life. I'll always remember the night when we met."

I nodded. "That was a lovely evening. We had a lot of fun dancing in that sparse room to the phonograph. Was it corn starch that made the floor so slick?"

"Yes, we stole the cook's entire supply; but he never knew what happened to it. He had to requisition some more so he could thicken the gravy and make pudding."

"I remember you're being the first to cross the room to ask me to dance; and how quickly the other men got up courage and followed."

"That didn't take courage, honey. The minute I saw you, I knew I'd have to hurry across, or the other guys would beat me to you. You know how it is in the army. If you're polite and stand back, you miss out. You end up with the cot in the darkest corner, and they have just run out of meat as you hold out your mess kit in the chow line."

I recalled having to learn that lesson as a civilian entering the army. I learned that you had better get into the queue early, whenever it was formed for whatever reason to get your share of whatever it was, or else you lost out.

"I'm going to miss you too, Bailey. It's going to be very dull around here when you leave. I wish you would do something for me. Please don't try any heroics on the missions; just do what you have to. And do come over when you can." In my mind I knew that this would be good-bye, since he would soon complete his fifty missions and would return to the States.

"I'll write you as soon as we settle, and fly back the first chance I get." He put his arms around my waist and holding me close to his side, we walked toward my tent. At the entrance we stopped, and pressing me close, he kissed my forehead. Our lips met in a long kiss, our first.

"Good-bye, Rad," he whispered. "With any luck, I'll be back soon."

"Good-bye, dear. Good luck." I watched as he disappeared into the night.

I had grown very fond of Bailey. He was a gentle, thoughtful, loving young man. We had had instant rapport from the first meeting. I also knew he was engaged and would be gone soon. Perhaps that was how he had got engaged in Florida. Many short acquaintances resulted in marriages as men left for war. That was one of the reasons that I didn't marry my sweetheart. I was unsure whether our marriage would survive the separation. We knew that he would have to go into the service as soon as he got his degree.

Partings and farewells! There had been many in the past few months. We were like the nomadic Arabs that we passed on the road as the climate drove them to another territory. Monotony descended over the camp for those who had become friendly with the Air Force boys and now were separated by hundreds of miles.

There were a number of nurses and officers who had paired off within our organization who were not affected by the partings. They were together every day, sat next to each other three times a day at mess, and spent evenings together, day after day. I had deliberately avoided this kind of relationship, as I wanted to be free. Besides, I knew that many of these men would be going home to wives or sweethearts after the war. But on the whole, there was a lot of camaraderie within the entire group: officers, enlisted men, and nurses in our communal life as the time passed.

I was on duty at the dispensary when the B-25s flew over us the next morning. I looked up and waved as the Buzz Wagon tilted its wings. The night before, Bailey had given me his APO address along with his home address in Bel Air, Maryland.

Several other nurses were feeling the loss when the day of their departure arrived. We would miss them and the familiar sound of the B-25 engines. Time began to drag almost immediately.

I returned to reading while lying on my cot under the mosquito bar. But one cannot lie on a cot indefinitely without getting a backache. There were no chairs. The ground was hard and covered with stones.

After Bailey was gone I got up early and rode the mail truck into town with Betty and Kay. In Constantine we made reservations for lunch at a French restaurant. We wandered about during the morning, stopped at the Casino for an hour and at noon went to lunch. Before we were seated, two infantry officers sitting at another table promptly got up and invited us to join them.

In the army we were all kindred spirits, at least those of us far from home. We were one large family united by a fellowship, a kinship that bound us together. We joined the officers and were soon telling each other where we were from, how long we'd been away, etc.

Before long the French woman brought wine and plates filled with food. There was no menu. You got what they had. It was rabbit. Although we would not normally select rabbit, it was a change from the chicken that we usually ate in public places, and anything was better than Spam and dehydrated potatoes.

The woman put a plate of roasted corn on the cob on the table. We all reached for it eagerly, and began buttering and salting it. At the first bite, looks of disappointment were exchanged as our teeth sank into the dry, tough kernels. It was not what we had expected.

Our friends explained that it was field corn, the kind that was fed to animals in the States, and not the cultivated kind we had anticipated, the soft sweet moist fresh corn. However, we continued to eat the dry kernels, spreading more butter and salt. The French had heard that Americans liked corn, so the woman prepared what she had, not realizing there was a difference. A salad of sliced tomatoes, and grapes for desert, completed our luncheon.

When we returned to the Casino after lunch, I saw the Arab sheik sitting in his same booth. He was there each time that I was, and had begun to nod a greeting of recognition as I passed his booth. His complexion was not as dark as the natives that we saw, but his eyes were seductively black. He was an attractive young

147

man, apparently of some distinction, and was always in the company of French officers in a booth apparently reserved for them. Since the Casino was crowded with troops, American and Allied, he didn't stand a chance of meeting or even attempting to approach an American girl. He reminded me of Rudolph Valentino, in the movie "The Sheik."

After a ginger beer, our group left the crowded Casino and went to the Red Cross Club where we played cards and listened to the record player. When we said we ought to get back before dark, our luncheon friends offered to drive us back to camp, as was the custom. We invited them to stay for supper, and heard about their experience when they landed in Morocco on the 8th of November 1942, not knowing if they would be greeted or shot. The French greeted them with cannon and machine gun fire. They told of fighting the German Afrika Corps in the nearby desert, at the Kasserine Pass, and in the djebels. There was no place for protection, as the ground was so hard that foxholes, if dug, were shallow. Of freezing at night and wallowing in mud when it rained as they ducked the 88's that sixty-ton Tiger tanks spewed from a distance of three thousand yards. And tanks crushing men in shallow foxholes as the heavy tracks rolled over them. And the fierce battle up the sides of mountains with the Germans dropping grenades and firing at our soldiers as they fought their way up. These young officers were on R & R, rest and recuperation, and would be returning to their company soon to fight in Sicily.

I was on duty at the Dispensary the following day, but there was not much to do except for a few typhoid shots administered to GIs, those who had been on detached service and had missed them. I dispensed Atabrine pills that we took twice a week to avoid malaria. In the afternoon I went to Ain M'Lila with Betty and bought potatoes, carrots, cherries, tomatoes, lemon, and two eggs at the market. The groceries cost 255 Francs, or $5.10 American dollars.

Mail call brought me letters from Major Graves, in England, Lieutenant James, in Oran, and a note carried by nurse Eleanor Bernick from Lieutenant Bailey, where she had visited her boy friend near Beja. These were all welcome letters, and I was glad to hear from Bailey, who said he missed me and would come over first chance he got. But I missed letters from home, from my fiancé in particular. After supper we rode to the 61st General Hospital for showers, and perhaps a movie if we were lucky. We sometimes attended church service at the 61st General Hospital when transportation was available.

While idling at the Red Cross Club one afternoon, a local French artist, Leon Rumel, asked if I would allow him to paint my portrait. With nothing more to do I sat and sipped tea while he painted in watercolors. I must have looked rather somber because that is how the portrait turned out. It was true. I was leading a rather dull existence since Lieutenant Bailey left.

Going out with a group of girls was not my bent, and hadn't been since nurses' training days when life was strictly all femme. I had spent three years in a convent-like atmosphere while in nurses' training in a Catholic Hospital. Growing up with brothers as playmates, I preferred male companionship.

At camp my time was spent reading whatever I could borrow and lying in the sun alongside my tent on hard ground, acquiring a tan. Since I spent more time at camp, I now discovered that we drilled and did exercises daily. We did our laundry in our helmets and hung it on the tent ropes at a forty-five degree angle.

After the Air Force's B-25s moved to Souk el Arba, our lives had become very dull. We spent the afternoons rearranging our clothes in the bedding roll and airing out our blankets. The heat was becoming unbearable, so my tent mates and I spent the rest of the afternoons lying on our cots. It was exhausting to move around, as the temperature stayed near 120 degrees, and I was beginning to be less critical and more understanding at the lethargy of the Arabs.

As I walked past the headquarters tent after supper to pick up my mail, Colonel Blatt invited me inside. We talked about current events—rumors mostly, since we knew little about the war, because there were no newspapers or radios. His dark hair, olive complexion with deep brown eyes that faced me rather shyly made me aware of how handsome he was. He was of medium height, with an athletic frame much like a football player. We felt lucky in having him as our commanding officer, since he did not restrict us. We chatted for a few minutes and I realized he was lonely and probably talked with many other nurses just as he did with me.

I picked up my one letter, said goodnight to the colonel, and opened it. It was from Lieutenant Bailey, inviting me to a party that the 25th Bomb Group was planning. He had flown several more bombing missions since leaving Telergma, and I knew he would soon be flying back to the States. He asked, "Will you make every effort to come because I am anxious to see you again." He would arrange a flight to pick up others who might like to come as well, and ended the letter "With Love."

I wondered if it would be wise to go. I was just getting accustomed to the separation. Besides, he would be leaving Africa very soon. Back in my tent after dark, I replied to Bailey's questions by flashlight: No, I didn't think I could go to the gathering, even by plane. I wrote that I missed his visits, and going into Constantine was not the same pleasure without him. And yes, I would be pleased to have him come to visit me.

Much later I heard of an incident when some Red Cross women flew to a party from Naples and crashed into the sea and were lost!

Several days later the Buzz Wagon buzzed over my tent, landed at Telergma, and in a short time Bailey was at the reception tent calling out my name. I realized how much I had missed him and how glad I was to see him again as he greeted me. His dark blue eyes, visible under the tan pith helmet, made him look like a movie star, a tall, slender, handsome young man. He put his arms around me and we kissed.

We went to an early supper at the same French home where we had eaten many times before, and where he made arrangements when he landed. The French woman served us roasted chicken along with potatoes, a salad of sliced tomato, French bread and melon for dessert. We ate in a small room by candlelight, holding hands across the table while chatting about recent developments and the bombing missions. I felt his hand tighten when he told about the loss of friends when their plane was hit by anti-aircraft while flying over Sicily.

He said, "I may not be able to come this way again, Rad, since I have nearly completed my missions and am now waiting for my Captaincy to come through before I leave for the States."

"Oh, I'm glad for your promotion; congratulations! And I'm happy that you are almost finished with those dangerous missions, but I'm going to miss you very much."

"I'm sorry to be leaving you, Rad. You have made this place so much more pleasant, especially when I was flying on the bomb runs, when I would look forward to being with you, to be able to talk with you, to unwind. Knowing you has made it more tolerable."

"You have made life much more exciting for me, Merle." I often called him by his first name when we were alone. "When you get Stateside, have a great celebration and drop me a line about where the army plans to send you next." We knew that he had to return before dark, so thanking and paying the French woman, we said, "Au revoir," and drove to my camp.

As we drove up to my camp, Colonel Blatt stepped out of the headquarters tent at the entrance of the barbed wire enclosure and greeted us. He knew Bailey because he had seen us together and he had eaten at our mess occasionally. They saluted one another. Then Colonel

Blatt said, "Bailey, I need to go to Bizerte soon. Is there a chance you could fly me there?"

I thought to myself, "Our poor Third Aux, always begging transportation."

Hesitatingly, Bailey replied, "Well, I'll see what I can do. You know I've about completed my missions, but I will talk with my commanding officer. Of course, I want to come here every chance I get."

Traveling over the mountains, it was a long tortuous ride to Bizerte. By plane it was a mere jaunt. Now Bailey had to leave in a hurry. He walked me to my tent, held me close in his arms and we kissed a warm tender kiss. "Good-bye, Rad, I'll try to get back real soon if I can arrange a ride for your C.O." He was off in a cloud of dust.

Saying good-bye, parting with pals, friends and lovers was a continual process in war. It began with Lieutenant James Lytle, a fellow I met at Fort Dix when the University of Michigan Hospital Unit 298 sailed without me and six other Michigan nurses.

Nursing at Fort Dix was similar to any hospital in the States except that the patients were young men who were up and about soon after their operative procedures and recovered quickly after treatment. They were in good physical condition, having recently been inducted into the army. My work consisted of distributing bed linen after breakfast trays were collected, passing medications, changing dressings on wounds, making rounds with doctors, and supervising the ward, and seeing that there was no gambling among the poker players.

I met Lieutenant James Lytle at the weekly dances that the Fort sponsored for its personnel. Lytle and I attended camp movies, and on weekend evenings, with another couple, drove into Wrightstown to dance at the various nightclubs. Within a few weeks Lytle was shipped overseas, and our contact thereafter consisted of letters spaced at long intervals, then stopped.

Lytle's outfit was Company B, 81st Armored Reconnaissance Battalion. Lieutenant Lytle was wounded on a reconnaissance mission, near Bizerte, while fighting the Germans and Italians in early 1943. I found out about him when I encountered the 81st Armored and met his comrades, who informed me that he had tried to get a pass earlier to visit me when they were in a nearby area but was unsuccessful. His comrades, wounded in the same campaign, were recuperating at the 38th Evacuation Hospital, where I was on detached service. Lytle was shipped to England and perhaps the States due to extensive wounds. I never heard from him again. A soldier's personal possessions often got separated in the confusion when transferring from hospital to hospital. His comrades never heard from him either.

The Sahara

Several friends stopped at camp one morning on their way to the Sahara and asked if I would join them, and if so, would I invite another nurse. As always, I was ready for adventure and said, I asked Madalyn Andreko to come. She was congenial, and often joined me on double dates. Russ Nixon, a Red Cross officer, and his companion, John Temple were on their way to Biskra, an oasis town in the Aures Mountains on the edge of the Sahara about two hundred kilometers south and due west of Ain M'Lila, the small village near our camp. We took our blankets, boxes of rations and filled our canteens with water, as we always did when going on a long trip. The day was bright and sunny as usual. It wasn't long before we were in barren, uninhabited country, except for an occasional Arab hovel far off the road, surrounded by a low wall that blended into the scenery. Russ entertained us by telling about his various trips in the surroundings and arranging trips for idle or recuperating troops. We exchanged rumors that always dominated our conversation. Russ, being stationed in the city, had more news about the war, about the stalemates, and the losses suffered by our infantry who were fighting experienced German troops.

As we neared Biskra, we saw from a distance a quaint

Arab transportation in the Sahara

settlement of mud huts clustered alongside the road, and as we advanced we discovered Arabs covered from head to toe in burnooses, squatting against the low wall that fronted the mud huts. They were apathetic, probably having a noonday siesta, and completely ignored us. We continued on into Biskra and stopped to admire a tall building, covered in pastel colors of mosaic, surrounded by flowering shrubs and tall palm trees in deep contrast to the hovels nearby. Bright red and pink flowers in bloom covered the grounds, and the wall of the building was covered with climbing pink Bougainvillea.

Palm trees lined the pathway to the entrance to the building where a French Officer standing at the gate greeted us as we approached. After a brief exchange in French with Russ, the officer offered to guide us. We drove through the tiny town's main street past several buildings and the town hall, and then continued south into the Sahara, a vast expanse of sand stretching to the horizon. After many miles, we arrived at an oasis with a clump of palm trees among head-high mud-built walls through which the road twisted. Lethargic Arabs watched as we drove by them. Russ slowed down when we came upon many small mounds in divergent patterns on the ground. Suddenly he pressed his foot on the accelerator as a whiff of breeze sent a putrid odor in our direction. Our guide told us it was the local cemetery. The dead were simply laid on the ground and covered with a layer of sand. We raced past trying not to breathe the foul air.

We continued on the sand-covered dirt road until we approached a tall wrought-iron fence surrounding a building. In the iron fretwork at the entrance above the gate were the words, "Hotel Atlantique." The building looked inviting, and we were pleased when our guide led us into the garden. Bright red, yellow and blue flowers were planted along the walkway leading to the entrance where Bougainvillea climbed along the lower walls of the four-storied tile building. It was here that the Frenchman said Marlene Dietrich and Charles Boyer stayed while "The Garden of Allah" was filmed. We posed in front of the entrance and the Frenchman snapped a picture with my Argus camera.

The surrounding territory had been the Twelfth Air Force Base for the 97th, the 301st, and P-38s in the Mediterranean Theater of Operation in December 1942 and early 1943. The desert stretching into eternity was a natural airfield that could accommodate all the planes in the world. We returned along the main road in Biskra, an oasis town on the northern edge of the Sahara, with hopes of finding a place to eat. The Frenchman knew of a place and led us to a home where he introduced us to a French woman who greeted us pleasantly then and led us to a small room. After we were seated at a table, she poured *vin blanc* into four wine glasses and, leaving the bottle on the table, she excused herself and disappeared, while we sipped and waited. The time passed quickly, although it was over and hour before we were served chicken, whole potatoes, a salad of tomato and onion slices, bread, butter and cantaloupe for desert. As we ate, Russ, nodding his head knowingly while squinting his eyes, said, "You know what? That guide has something going for the two of them. I bet ten Francs this is his house, and he picks up trade by standing at the gate in front of the hotel."

Madalyn's escort, Captain Temple, added," And he's probably been doing it ever since Dietrich was here. At any rate he is an Ally. It could have been an Arab and we'd still be bartering about the price. It was well worth it. We saw the Sahara, an oasis, and best of all we were in the company of two lovely young ladies for a day."

We finished eating, and after many thanks, Russ paid the woman. We climbed into our vehicle and headed north. We had traveled several miles when two vehicles blocked the road before us. Our companions got out of the car to investigate. It was an accident, and two Frenchmen had been injured when their car collided with an American truck driven by two GIs. They were waiting for a vehicle that would take the men to a nearby French hospital. The GIs were not injured, and their truck was not disabled. We continued on when we saw that there was nothing we needed to do.

The Flying Fortresses (B-17 Bombers)

June 1943

We were awakened at dawn by the thundering roar of engines overhead across the same path that the B- 25s had flown until recently. I lifted the tent flap, raised the mosquito net and stretched my body to get a look, and saw huge four-engine Fortresses in formation heading north, probably toward Sicily, Sardinia, or Pantelleria, the islands in the Mediterranean that the enemy occupied. Before the Fortresses it had been the B 25s, twin-engine medium bombers better known as the "Mitchells" that we had counted. As I watched, I wished them good luck on the target and safe return. Later in the day when we heard the roar of engines, we dashed out of the tents and watched as B-17s with shattered wings, feathered propellers, and jagged holes in fuselages limped home, and we said a prayer for their safe landing. The habit of counting planes would continue to be part of our daily life again.

We had heard about the hazards our previous neighbors, the B-25 pilots, faced on bomb runs, about losing buddies and searching the sky for parachutes, and if lucky the parachutists might land safely, even if in enemy territory. Now and then we were thrilled when we saw a plane with a feathered engine or holes in the fuselage fly home hours later. And we worried about the plane we heard in the dark in the mountains, perhaps with damaged instruments, crashing or flying into the Sahara.

Two Air Force officers stopped at headquarters the following day to invite several nurses to their camp for supper, to get acquainted. The following day those nurses who had been with them announced that the Fortress squadron was planning to have a party in the next few days and all the nurses would be invited. We were glad as time hung heavily since the Mitchell B-25s moved away. Our only diversion since then had been the Casino, whenever we could get transportation to enjoy the excitement that went on there. There was a conglomeration of Allied troops from different areas of fighting in Africa in various types of uniforms. The local sheiks wore caftans and turbans in varied striped colors wound around their heads. Outside the casino, Arabs in patched dirty hooded burnoose squatted on the ground to pass the time away.

In the Casino, the booths were wide enough to seat four to six if it was crowded. The booths lined the entire room except for space for the four-piece band that played on occasions. Here we drank weak English ginger beer, *vin blanc* or hot tea, flirted with new acquaintances, listened to a string quartet or just watched the panorama unfold. We often brought our swimsuits along and swam in the outdoor pool a short distance from the Casino and cooled off from the hot afternoon sun on the bleachers.

The rule was to get back to camp before dark.

19 June 1943

At breakfast this morning our chief nurse announced that we were invited to a party that evening. We never needed much notice, since most of us were willing on a moment's notice to go whenever an opportunity presented itself, anything to relieve the monotony of lying on the cot during the hot days and dull evenings in a dark tent.

The invitation came from the 20th Bomb Squadron (H), 2nd Bomb Group Air Force. The B-17 Fortresses had taken over the airfield at Telergma after our friends, the B-25 Mitchell men, departed to an airfield near Beja. Our Colonel explained that two Air Force officers had stopped by to invite all the girls to join them for a party that the French Mayor of Chateaudun had arranged. They would send several trucks to pick up all who wanted to go at five o'clock.

We learned that the Mayor wanted to celebrate the end of the war in Africa and to honor the 12th Air Force Group at the same time. Several French families were sponsoring the celebration. Flags decorated the town hall in the city square, the ballroom was decorated with colorful festoons, and refreshments were served. It was just what we needed to recover from longing for the lost companionship of the B-25 men who had moved away. By some strange coincidence showers were available to us that same day. A mobile unit happened to drive by our arid camp and stopped to see who we were. It was the first time we had a warm shower out in the open. We shampooed and scrubbed in the warm spray of water coming from above instead of bending over a helmet on the ground. We were shielded by a squared-off tarpaulin. The girls got their Class A uniforms out of their bedrolls. In rummaging through mine, I came across the silver lamé formal dress that I had purchased at Sax Fifth Avenue during my stay in New York. I recalled the old army colonel's advice back in the States when he told us of his experiences in the WW I. He had said, "There will be occasions for celebrations, so take something along, something special that will make life a bit more exciting."

Wasn't this such an occasion? The end of the war in Africa? I lifted it off the bedding roll and shook off the wrinkles. The skirt was a bouffant two-layered silver

The Dress

gray tulle net laid over a gray satin underskirt. The silver lamé sleeveless bodice fitted snugly at my waist. It had a long-stemmed pink velvet rose with green velvet leaves attached to the waist. I had acquired a golden tan lying in the sun at the pool and lying beside my tent. I draped the dress in front of me and looked in my steel mirror. The contrast between my red hair with the silver lamé of the gown was striking. It was a beautiful formal dress, although out of place riding in the back of a truck. The other nurses wore Class As. Some of the girls looked a bit envious, but that did not deter me. The old Colonel had said it was O.K. Silver sandals along with long white kid gloves completed my attire. The fifty-mile ride was rough, as were all roads in the country distant from the cities in Africa. When we arrived, the GI drivers held out their arms to support us as we jumped off the rear of the truck. When the driver helped me, he asked, "Are you a Hollywood star?"

Nurses Van Straten, Nace, Bernick, Kirschling and Radawiec,
ready for a party

Entering the foyer of the hall, I headed for the large oblong mirror to smooth my windblown hair. As I patted it down, I noticed a tall blond officer's reflection in the mirror as he approached from behind. Our eyes met in the mirror. His were the dark blue that the Mediterranean turns into at dusk. In the background the strains of my favorite song, "Begin the Beguine," began to be played by the band.

"Hello. You're very pretty, Red, may I have this dance?" A smile revealed even white teeth against suntanned features and a firm chin.

Chuckling, I turned to face him. I knew the dress captivated him. "Hello, Lieutenant. They're playing one of my favorite tunes. Yes, let's dance."

He put his arm around my waist as we entered the ballroom, and holding me close, we glided into the rhythm of the "Beguine." His hand-crafted pointed boots glided over the floor in unison with my silver sandals. Pressing his lips close to my ear, he whispered. "If anyone cuts in, I'll refuse to give you up. I'm Brunson. What's your name, and where did you come from, honey?" with a Texan drawl so thick you could slice it with a knife.

"My name's Radawiec. I came with the girls on the truck y'all sent." I tried to mimic his southern drawl.

He pressed me close to his body as we glided across the floor to the fox trot, when a Captain approached us and tagged him. He was outranked!

"I'll be back," he said, as he walked to the side of the hall. I saw him dancing with Nurse Bernick as he passed nearby. After several dances he was back.

"Wow!" he said. "I thought I'd never get tagged so I could get back to you, Rad. That's what the girl I danced with told me you were called. You certainly had a lot of partners. By the way, that torpedo juice is pretty awful stuff. Let's you and I go outside, I've got some bourbon stashed in the truck that's much smoother."

Torpedo juice was just what was being served. The Air Force had "procured" it from a Navy installation by draining powerful 180-proof alcohol from a torpedo and diluting it with canned grapefruit juice.

We went out into the black night, where he climbed into the back of the truck parked next to the building. He got the bourbon out of its hiding place and, jumping off the back of the truck, he opened the bottle and offered it to me. I took a sip, and cringed. I had never liked the taste of liquor. Brunson gulped a swallow and replaced the bottle in the truck. The brilliance of the stars against the black sky absorbed our attention as he held my hand and guided me in the blackout. We finally stopped to try to identify familiar constellations. Being a flyer, he was more familiar than I with the stars in this hemisphere at this time of the year. I could not identify any.

Then turning to face me, and holding both my hands he said, "You know Rad, you are the most beautiful girl I have ever seen. Tell me about yourself. Where have you been all my life?"

Smiling, I replied, "Thanks, Lieutenant. You have been too long away from the States. It's my dress, Brunson. It is pretty, isn't it? I fell for it when I saw it in a shop window in New York. I'm from the Midwest—Michigan, but come, let us dance. You dance divinely."

"No, I mean it, you are like an apparition, a fairy princess." He put his arm around my waist, guiding me in the dark into the building. Pressing me close to his body, we fell in step to the rhythm of the music. It was wonderful to be held close. I had almost forgotten the feeling. But it was only for a minute, or so it seemed. He was tagged before we got halfway across the dance floor. I heard him mutter something under his breath as my new partner led me into a fox trot. It sounded like, "I'll get even with you, damn it." His buddies were ganging up on him.

He stood on the sideline. I sensed his eyes following me as my partner and I danced. He was waiting for someone else to tag me so he could come right back. My dancing partner was asking questions, the usual ones. I responded with my name and organization and caught a glimpce of Brunson at every turn and felt his eyes following, turning, as I danced past. He stood alone, handsome in his pinks with a Sam Brown belt snug against his waist. His deep blue eyes looked anxiously about as his hands fidgeted in his pants pockets. As soon as my partner was tagged, he headed my way, whirling me as if reclaiming a possession. His strong arms held me close. I floated along on air.

I was impressed by his manners, his determination. My other dancing partners were great, but it was Brunson who seemed in rhythm with me as we danced. When the evening came to a close, he asked if he could take me back to my camp along with another officer who had a jeep. I told Major Brown, one of our several surgeons who had come to the party and assumed a kind of responsibility for us girls, that I would ride back with Brunson.

Major Brown approached Brunson, and as I introduced them, he asked, "Are you sure Lieutenant Radawiec will be safe with you? You know how dangerous it is at night on these donkey trails."

Brunson answered with complete composure. "I will be most cautious. You don't need to worry, Major."

Betty and Captain Hedrick drove back with us in the black night. The trucks followed with the rest of the party. It was a jolting ride, worse in the jeep than in the two-and-a-half-ton truck. Brunson wrapped the blanket around us as we huddled together in the back seat of the jeep. The night air was always chilly in the mountains. He kidded about girls from the North being cold, insinuating that southern girls were not. As always, we sang as we rode along. The girls in the truck behind us were singing too. We could just barely hear them as we went around a bend in the road.

Singing originated in our group when we began traveling in trucks back in England. We knew every popular song from the Thirties up to the most recent ones heard when new people came from the States with a recent hit. Betty and Captain Hedrick joined us as we sang, "Home on the Range," "The Yellow Rose of Texas," "The Beer Barrel Polka," and ending with "Let Me Call You Sweetheart." We arrived at our camp long past midnight, and as they walked with us toward our tents, Lieutenant Brunson, his arm around my waist asked, "May I see you tomorrow, Rad?

"Yes, I'll be here," I replied.

"I think I'll be free about three. We can decide what to do then."

"That will be fine. You're a marvelous dancer, Lieutenant Brunson. I'll see you tomorrow."

I turned, reached for the tent flap and was about to enter my tent when he said, "Wait a minute, what's the hurry?"

He held onto my arm, bringing me close to him, embracing me, his lips meeting mine, and saying, "Tonight has been the greatest! Goodnight, Rad, I'll see you tomorrow."

The party was the loveliest one I had experienced since our arrival in Africa. There had been other parties, dances, casual gatherings, and meeting new people, but tonight seemed different. Perhaps it was that "special event," the silver dress that made it so. I washed my face in the cool water in my helmet, hung the dress on the nail on the supporting tent pole, and then crawled under my mosquito bar and under the wool blankets to put on my flannel pajamas. It had been an exhilarating evening. I felt like Cinderella.

Lieutenants Brunson and Wolfe arrived at camp the next afternoon just as Edythe MacDonald and I were walking toward the rec tent to be there to greet them. They had joined in requesting transportation, making it easier to get a jeep. Lieutenant Wolfe and Edythe met last night at the dance, and now the four of us climbed into the jeep and headed toward Constantine.

It was the beginning of many foursome gatherings spent on trips, picnics, swimming parties in the

Mediterranean off the coast of Bone, fun at the Air Force Club, playing poker or bridge, candle lit chicken dinners at the French home at Ain M'Lila, and relaxing evenings lying at the base of our mountain not far from our camp.

The moon in Africa, when full, hung low in the sky, and as billowy clouds whisked past its face, it seemed to be playing hide-and-seek with us as we sat close. Brunson told about the bomb run that day, the near hits of the anti-aircraft, the enemy fighters they encountered. He mentioned some of the tricks the guys pulled when they wanted to get out of a mission that they felt might be more risky than usual, and turning back from a mission. They would say the engines sounded out-of-order, missing. We talked about the current rumors that were constantly in the air and laughed about the Arab antics. When Brunson asked, "What about that ring? I said it was what it looked like, a commitment. He simply nodded his head.

They were flying on a distant mission in the morning and had to be in by nine o'clock tonight. He said they would fly out very early, long before sunrise. There would be the usual flak to dodge and probably more than the usual fighter planes to outwit. I knew that every mission was a challenge with death.

The roar of the B-17 engines, the Flying Fortresses, as they were called, awakened me almost daily as they flew over our camp on their bomb runs toward Sardinia, Sicily and now Italy. I lifted the flap of my tent, stretched my body off the edge of my cot and counted as they flew overhead. We were again losing new acquaintances as we heard the flying boys tell about the planes they watched spiraling down on bomb runs. If they were intercepted by the Luftwaffe fighter planes before they reached their target, they were lucky if their parachutes opened, but even then many of them floated into enemy territory and were taken prisoner or were lost at sea.

Now as I counted them flying out I wished them safe return. Hours later, when their engines roared overhead, I counted again and was troubled about the missing planes, and prayed that those with shattered wings and feathered propellers would land safely.

The Flying boys often stopped at camp and offered us a ride into Constantine where Allied troops gathered at the Casino: the British on leave from the desert war in Libya where they had been fighting since 1940, the Scots, and French officers. The gathering created a kind of pandemonium in the packed building as we sat and watched the panorama and chatted with our new friends.

The swimming pool provided a pleasant diversion, and we often took our swimsuits and towels when we went to Constantine just in case someone would suggest a swim. It was always crowded on hot afternoons when the sun beat down and the temperature reached 115 degrees. After a swim, playing in the water and diving, we would lie on the bleachers acquiring a tan over our entire bodies. Often we would walk the short distance to the Red Cross Club for donuts and coffee and play cards. It was easy to get up a foursome for a game of bridge. We tried to get back to camp for supper and always before dark after having had a bad experience of getting lost in the blackout and running out of gasoline.

The Air Force boys were flying missions almost daily since the rainy season had finished. They were awakened in the dark, dressed in their flight suits over woolen GI underwear, boots, and flight caps. They then went to the mess tent where hot coffee, scrambled powdered eggs, toast spread with yellow-colored lard, jam, and very tart canned grapefruit juice were available.

With the sound of truck motors, and clanging tailgates being dropped, they downed a final cup of coffee to jar them awake and boarded the two-and-a-half-ton tucks that drove them to the briefing tent. A large map on the wall disclosed the target, along with the route that the planes would follow. It might be an oil field, some vital bridge, an armament building, an installation or railroad terminal. They got their directions, synchronized their watches, and were driven to the field to their bombers.

Because of a shortage of fighter planes to escort our bombers in 1943, our Fortresses, loaded with four tons of bombs, often encountered Messerschmitt fighter planes long before they reached the target. The enemy fighters dove from above and came from below the heavily loaded slow-flying Forts, which had to maintain their position in the squadron and continue dutifully toward the target, while their turret and tail gunners tried to ward off the lightning speed of enemy Messerschmitt gunfire. In the Fortresses, the gunners were frequently wounded in their exposed positions in the plexiglas bubbles in the tail and above the fuselage. As the enemy fighters dispersed, anti-aircraft gun crews on the ground took over the attack as the Forts continued toward the target. When a Fortress was hit and spiraled downward, the succeeding plane filled its place in the squadron, and they continued in tight formation toward the target. The crews watched for parachutes until the plane spiraled from sight and they felt the vibration of the explosion as it crashed to earth.

Our friends, the B-17 officers, were now frequent callers at our camp, and about six of us nurses were going steady with them. They invited us to their club, a tent they had improvised, where we danced to record music, played cards or just chatted. We sang and often were accompanied by a GI strumming on a banjo or guitar. One of the songs Brunson's group often sang, and that he wrote down for me was:

SQUADRON OF PINEAPPLE PETE

We searched this town all upside down,
For a glass of beer, we're gonna drink it down,
We came in here for a glass of beer,
And we want it now.
How 'bout service, how 'bout service,
Gotta have a glass of beer,
How 'bout service makin' us nervous
Why'n the hell did we come here?

Sooner or later there'll come a waiter
That for sure we know damn well,
Where'n the hell's the God damn waiter,
Gotta have a glass of beer.
My comrades dear, I gravely fear
That we will never get service here,
But here we'll stay, 'til judgment day,
You'll find us growing quite old and gray.
Here comes the beer, here comes the beer
Bubbling and foaming, so let's give a cheer.
Give a cheer, give a cheer,
For the boys who drink the beer,
In the Squad of Pineapple Pete.
We are brave, we are bold,
For the liquor we can hold
Is a story that never grows old,
So we'll guzzle and we'll guzzle,
While it trickles down our muzzle,
So we'll cheer boys and never go dry,
With a rip and a roar,
With the M Ps at the door of
The Squadron of Pineapple Pete.

We went to Constantine whenever we had a chance, as it was the only place with a building that could accommodate a large number of troops. Now and then a small band supplied us with music, and we danced on the little space cleared in the center of the room, or we joined in group singing. It was exhilarating to be with troops from different countries, listening to the variety of languages: French, British, Scot and Arab, as well as American from different parts of our own country, speaking in various dialects. The diversion of tall stories and witty remarks created a feeling of complete abandon, allowing us for the moment to forget the war.

I was surprised when Lieutenants Brunson and Yeager arrived, to see them wearing revolvers strapped around their hips. They were going to take us to the 61st Station Hospital where the movie, "Virginia City," was being shown. We had heard rumors about the Arabs being agitated and might possibly cause trouble, but we hadn't given it much thought at our camp. However, since the Air Force took it seriously, we realized that it might be a real threat. I didn't think the Arabs could accomplish much, but they could have had weapons, or mines, and perhaps even bombs stashed in the hills. It raised considerable apprehension, so that guards were doubled at all the camps.

As we sat on the ground after the movie, the boys told about losing a Fortress over Naples that day. I had wondered why they seemed unusually solemn tonight. Yeager added that the flak was so thick one could have walked on it. They were more serious than I had ever seen them. Losing comrades was beginning to affect them.

After breakfast the next day Bruns and Headrick dashed over, full of enthusiasm. I heard the familiar, "Hey Rad!" while fumbling through my bed roll looking for something I needed. Sticking my head out of the tent I waved a greeting and said, "In a minute." I picked up my brush and facing my steel mirror, I brushed my hair, applied a bit of lipstick, pressed my lips together to stretch it, smoothed my slacks, and went out to greet them. They were excited as Bruns asked, "Would you like to fly to Algiers with us today—now?"

Seeing the exhilaration at my acceptance, Headrick added, "See if Betty Asselin and Gerty Trainor would like to come too."

I dashed toward their tent, but they already had seen Headrick and Brunson, and they knew something was up. "We'll be ready in five minutes," they replied.

We were always eager to go, anywhere, anytime, rather than swelter in the hot tent. We dressed in minutes and were off to the Telergma airfield. They helped us into the huge belly of the Fortress, and we took off with the roar of the four engines. Headrick piloted with Brunson in the co-pilot's seat.

Before we knew it, we were over Mostaganem, not realizing they had had a tail wind and had over-flown

Algiers by an hour. Turning back toward Algiers, we saw below us a fifty-ship convoy on the Mediterranean heading toward the Harbor. We landed on the airfield at Algiers at 4:15. Hurriedly, we boarded a Bus into the city and shopped for souvenirs. As we passed a flower shop, Brunson insisted we go inside, and he bought a corsage made up of roses and lilies of the valley and pinned it on my suit jacket.

With his eyes focused on mine, he whispered. "Do you know what I'm thinking at this moment?" Then pointing to a bouquet of gladioli and lavender, he asked the shopkeeper to wrap it. I felt like a bride as we entered the officer's mess in Algiers, with the bouquet in my arm and the corsage on my lapel. After supper we hurried back to the airfield to get home before dark.

We were delayed in take-off because the brandy, the apparent reason for the trip, had not yet been delivered. While in the air we saw the northern lights. We landed in Telergma after dark—without landing lights! The Arab uprising was still imminent, and we heard that several Arabs had been shot.

25 June 1943

The Fortresses raided Messina today and got shot up very badly. Brunson said a Messerschmitt fighter plane suddenly appeared in their midst and was shot by Lieutenant Hershey's Fortress crew. Unfortunately, the fighter pilot lost control and crashed into a Fortress loaded with bombs, exploding both planes in mid-air. The explosion sent a second Fortress into a tailspin. A third Fortress, they thought, possibly fell into the sea. Thirty men were lost, along with three Fortresses! Bruns's plane returned full of holes. I was thankful that Brunson was safe, but at camp we were all very saddened at the loss of so many young men.

26 June 1943

The Air Force Group invited us to a party tonight. We wondered why a party after yesterday's terrible losses. Headquarters probably wanted to lift the spirits of the men whose buddies' cots were empty last night. Champagne on ice was a rare treat, since there was no refrigeration anywhere in Constantine. We also had the brandy that had been issued at Algiers the day before yesterday. We danced every dance as all the officers were tagging us. Brunson held me close as if defying anyone to tag him, while whispering, "What a lucky guy I am, to be here, and you in my arms in this faraway desert."

It was an exciting evening. Bruns drank a bit more than I'd seen him drink before, and was very amusing and relaxed. When Major Dorner, our Third Auxiliary officer—one usually came along to chaperon the girls—asked if I had a ride back to camp, Brunson replied, "Course shee haas," with that terrific southern Texan drawl. Headrick drove Betty, Brunson, and me back to camp. We huddled under the blanket and sang all the way back. Among our favorites were: "The yellow Rose of Texas," "Let Me Call You Sweetheart," "You Are My Sunshine," and many other favorites.

4 July 1943

Fifty-six Forts flew out at 8:00 this morning, and fifty-two returned at 3:00. Several had landed at Malta. Lieutenant Yeager, in plane 607, the plane Bruns usually flew, was hit. It was on fire as it went into a tailspin, Brunson said. They counted six parachutes. Not much hope for Yeager. Bruns was very upset at seeing his friends shot down. He called for me after mess, and we spent the evening at their club at the base of the mountain, with Captain Evans and Margie Bruce. I tried to take Bruns's mind off the loss by telling about the antics of our new puppy that one of the GIs had acquired, but it was a melancholy evening. We ate hard-cooked eggs and drank some wine that they had brought in their canteens.

5 July 1943

Brunson's Group flew out at 11:30, after the Chateaudun Group flew out at 8:00 a.m. When Bruns and Wolfe came over after supper, Wolfe told about how Brunson caught seventy-six planes on the ground in Sicily on a satellite field, after they had been moved from another field where the Chateaudun Group had hit them earlier in the day. He dropped fragmentation bombs, and damaged most of the planes. We were in the rec tent with Edythe McDonald, when Wolfe reveled about Bruns's accuracy in the bombing today. I was proud and glad, since I had heard from the other fellows about Brunson's expertise on the bomb runs. As usual, they had to get back at nine o'clock because they were scheduled to fly very early the next day.

6 July 1943

The noise of a plane alerted me just in time to see the Buzz Wagon thunder low over our area, and at 1:30 Lieutenant Bailey arrived with Van Arsdale, who had just been let out of the hospital after having been shot down three weeks ago. We were happy to see our friends again, for they had not been over in weeks. As we sat on the ground in the rec tent, they told of their recent raids over the islands. Bailey told about Lieutenant Axen's plane being hit on the bomb run and surviving a crash landing in Tunis. His face, arms, and leg were badly lacerated.

Andreko and Kay inquired about their former boyfriends, and Bailey handed them each an envelope. He said," Mail between short distances never seemed to clear the APO without going to base sorting areas, and possibly back to the States." He added, "Life at Souk-el-Arba after Ain M'Lila sure is a boring existence."

Looking into my eyes he said softly, "I sure miss those times we spent together, Rad."

"Perhaps things work out for our good." He knew what I meant. We did miss them. It was a lonely time for all those who dated the fellows. I thought the others felt much the same way. These young men would be returning to the States soon, since they were near completing the fifty missions required. I knew someone was waiting for Bailey back home. He was a fine gentleman, and I have enjoyed knowing him.

8 July 1943

Most of our surgical teams were leaving camp, preparing for the invasion of Sicily, while Third Aux headquarters, nurses and the enlisted men not assigned on surgical teams remained at our base in Constantine. The surgeons had to carry eighty pounds of equipment on their backs as they marched the two miles to the dock at the Bay of Bizerte. They spent a sleepless night on the hard ground before boarding an LST whose bow dropped open to permit large army vehicles, tanks and ammunition to be loaded. The sea was calm as the armada of ships stretched far out to the horizon. Destroyers churned the outer perimeter, and planes patrolled the skies as troops loaded.

Captain R.W. Adams told of stuffing himself with navy food that we in the army hadn't seen since landing in Africa. There was no refrigeration in the field, therefore no fresh meat or iced drinks, all of which were available on board ship. As the armada began to sail, a north wind blew up waves that began to roll and pitch the shallow-draft ships. Their food did not stay with the men long, and buckets began to be passed out as the worst sea in months took hold.

During the storm that night, a large crate of explosives broke loose from its shackles on the LST. The boatswain's mate, whose leg had been wounded in an earlier raid but who was too valuable to leave behind, limped out cursing his luck because he had to shore it up before it blew up and everyone else with it. It was a formidable task to tackle in the blackout.

10 July 1943

Operation Husky, the code name for the invasion of Sicily began on this day. American C-47 planes dropped parachutists on Sicily on the 9th and 10th prior to the landing of American troops. On the second day after the landing of our troops, German planes suddenly appeared and began strafing and bombing the southern coast of Sicily. American anti-aircraft aboard ships and others on shore opened fire, forcing the enemy to abandon their attack.

Soon after the enemy attack, a flight of C-47 planes flew overhead and dropped parachutists within the correct drop zone. However, when a second group of C-47s made their approach to the drop zone, an over-zealous machine gunner on the ground opened fire and was immediately joined by other anti-aircraft crews, along with allied ships at sea. The low flying planes were easy targets as they plunged into the sea, with the paratroopers trapped inside. Brigadier General Charles L. Keerans, who went along as an observer, was among the 318 casualties, killed or wounded.

On the ground, fighting progressed under General George S. Patton, Seventh Army Commander. Americans approached Sicily from the south and began fighting their way up the western coast, as cruisers with heavy armament lobbed missiles toward targets on shore on the second night at sea. At dawn, enemy planes, flying high above the ships, dropped bombs that resulted in huge waterspouts rising amidst the ships. Anti-aircraft aboard ships opened fire, filling the sky with puffs of smoke.

At daybreak the hilly shores of Sicily were visible from a long distance away, as minesweepers, barges, and small craft shuttled about. Captain Adams relates that just as the crew was about to guide his ship to shore, the chain that controlled the bow door snapped and they were unable to debark. Since their LST was to be the first to land, it was not long before an escort vessel pulled up alongside and a hoarse voice through a megaphone shouted, "Get on that goddam beach, you stinkers!"

"We can't," answered the LST captain, and then began a long conversation back and forth, the details of which made no sense to Adams as the ship wallowed in the combers.

Finally, repairs were made and our surgeons stepped out onto the pontoon bridgeway dropped by the LST, remaining aboard until they could step off into the shallows and wade to shore. They went past a concrete pillbox and a disabled gun, and met a soldier who told them that when the Americans came forward, Italians opened fire from the pillbox, resulting in many casualties. A brave American then sneaked around the back with a Bangalore torpedo, and that finished the argument.

Our surgeons began operating at clearing stations set up near the beach as men unloaded from ships and proceeded to the fighting. A German bomber flew over and bombed an LST, sending huge clouds of black smoke into the sky. The battalion set up a first aid station as our men dashed to the beach, to help with the casualties that were being carried on litters and placed on the ground. They injected plasma and did first aid, fixing the men in transportable condition so they could be moved to the clearing station, where they could operate.

The unloading continued all morning until suddenly pandemonium broke loose, as a Messerschmitt sped over and strafed the roadway, then disappeared faster than the anti-aircraft batteries could turn their guns. The sound of a plane was a signal for wild firing from a dozen spots, as fingers were itchy and nerves taut. Flak fell everywhere. The struggle continued as infantry climbed rugged hills and descended into valleys, fighting for every bridge crossing. The hilly island was difficult to assault and easy to defend from the high ground, just as in the mountains and djebels during the fighting in North Africa.

14 July 1943

The rest of our organization, mostly headquarters

and supply officers, remained in Africa while the fighting progressed in Sicily. July 14th was Bastille Day, a day celebrated in France since 1789, when revolutionists stormed the infamous prison in Paris and set the prisoners free. Since France ruled North Africa, there would be parades and celebrations in Constantine because of the national holiday.

Lieutenant Brunson and I decided to celebrate by killing the five chickens that we had bartered for with an Arab a few days before. They had their legs tied together with a piece of hemp, and I felt sorry for them, hanging upside down like that.

Arabs enjoyed bartering. It was a game played before reaching what they considered a fair price, and they were disappointed if you did not participate. We paid for the chickens with cigarettes and francs.

Brunson had been feeding the chickens at his camp. I was amused when visiting there to see him wet the bread, squeeze it in his hands, break it up, and calling out in a high pitched voice, "Hee, cheek, cheek, cheek, cheek, cheek!" while tossing the bread out.

"These are Arab chickens Bruns," I said, "they don't understand Texas talk,"

"Just you watch how fast they come."

Of course they scrambled like crazy toward the bread. They were small chickens, just a bit larger than a bantam, and scrawny.

I asked Shorty, our C.O.'s orderly, to cook them for us after Brunson had their heads chopped off. We were going to have fried chicken and a watermelon that we had bought at the Casbah in Constantine. Shorty had guarded the watermelon and chicken in the mess tent for us.

Brunson decided to invite Captain Triggs, his C.O., to join us.

We had hoped to be on our way before noon. At 3:30 there was no sign of Brunson or Triggs, so the picnic was off. But that was not unusual since Brunson, a mere lieutenant, was never sure about being able to carry out his plans.

At 7:30 I heard the familiar call, "Hey, Rad!" coming from the rec tent. Bruns was full of apologies. He had started out three times, and each time was waylaid. He had to see about having the nose of a new B-17 armored. That took until 5:00. Afterward, the enlisted men asked him to pitch in the baseball game, and finally he had to go over batteries for tomorrow's target with Captain Triggs.

Instead of a picnic we picked up the chickens and watermelon and drove to his camp and ate sitting on the ground in Captain Triggs's tent. Captain Headrick, a pilot with whom Bruns sometimes flew, stuck his head into the tent, so we asked him to grab a leg, a very small leg. He said he smelled the chicken and couldn't resist tracking it down.

Brunson drove me back to camp soon after we ate, because they would be briefed very early the next day and gone at dawn. As we were parting at my tent, he said, "I should be back by 4:00 tomorrow, honey. I'll try to be here about forty-five minutes after we return and do interrogation. Shall I make reservations with the French woman for supper at Ain M'Lila? Would you like that?"

"Yes, that will be great. I'll be looking for you, Bruns, and do be careful."

He held me close as we parted with a kiss. We were always hungry.

Lieutenants Brunson, Headrick, Betty and I planned a picnic a few days later. We asked the mess sergeant if we could make a few spam sandwiches. We wrapped them in a towel and placed them in our helmets, and with blankets under our arms, sat in our tent waiting for the jeep and the familiar "Hey Rad," or "Hey, Betty."

There was no one on duty at the reception tent to announce visitors and it was not necessary, since there were very few callers. We greeted our guests with a wave from our tent, crossed the field and joined them. We were always willing to go anywhere, to get away from the monotony of camp life.

We drove to the base of the mountain, spread our blankets on the hard ground, and sat down. It gave our dates an opportunity to unwind, tell about the day's mission, perhaps even to relieve some the pressure they had been under. There were always losses, planes downed.

Being with Brunson lifted my spirits. I felt enchanted, safe as if I had known him a long time. I had been away from home nearly a year, and home seemed very far away. We had become a twosome, dating almost daily or as often as we could get away from our duties. We played bridge, exchanged rumors, went on picnics with our spamwiches and powdered lemonade. We climbed the mountains and did target shooting. I thoroughly enjoyed being with him, and found myself depending on him entirely for companionship. This was the situation at a time when we were idle at camp, isolated in a dry barren field with temperatures ranging at 110 degrees.

Incoming mail was slow reaching us. The APO and the mailmen were still confused as to which half of our organization was in England and which in Africa. It resulted in our mail sailing back and forth between Africa and England for long periods, with no word from loved ones.

The seven-thousand-mile separation was hard to transcend, to feel the closeness of a lover far away. I wondered if my fiancé was being tempted as I was. Was he being faithful? I thought about him and responded promptly to the few letters that reached me, and at ten o'clock when at camp, I tried to span the distance and reach out to make a spiritual contact, but it was not working. I had some guilt feelings about Bunsen. I still loved Bob, and was true, but the long periods without mail made me wonder. Ships were being sunk by German U-boats by the hundreds. Were his letters being sunk? Had he stopped writing? Had someone else taken my place?

To love and to be loved was—is—paramount to life.

After supper Brunson and Wolfe were at the rec tent calling out as usual in the direction of our tents. They had been on a distant bomb run today. We heard the engines roar overhead while it was still dark, and watched as they returned after four in the afternoon. Since I couldn't count them in the dark as they went out, I didn't know how many had gone on the mission. On their return we saw many damaged Fortresses with shattered wings, parts of tails missing, and a number with one or two propellers propped (not whirling), I was both thrilled and chilled as I watched and counted when they thundered overhead, and prayed that they would land safely.

Now Brunson and Wolfe were at the rec tent calling our names. I stuck my head out of the tent entrance and said, "Just a minute," then quickly added some mascara and lipstick, and ran a comb through my hair. Clutching blankets and helmets, Edythe and I joined them, climbed into the jeep, and headed toward our mountain, where the boys spread them within a few feet of each other. Wolfe and Bruns talked about the twelve-hour bomb run over northern Italy. Wolfe remarked about Brun's superior hit on the bomb run today.

Brunson added, "I felt a terrific jolt above me in the bomb bay and expected to be blown away. Probably the concussion of that explosion."

Bruns used the secret Nordon bomb sight, a mechanical computer utilized in high-altitude bombing. He was personally responsible for carrying it on and off the Fortress. Bruns also had the privilege of choosing the pilot he preferred to fly with. I was surprised when I overheard one of his comrades mention that. I knew he flew with various pilots, but never thought to question why.

They made comments about the guys that parachuted when their Fortress was hit by flak, as if it was part of a day's work, nothing unusual, a routine occurrence. Wolfe, who is a pilot added, "One guy came damn near tangling with the propeller on my number four engine after he ejected."

Bruns and Wolfe made some caustic comments about the guys that chickened out, who turned back from a run if the engines made any out-of-the-ordinary sounds. Edythe and I knew this was getting it off their chests. Tough talk. Underneath, they were concerned about when it would happen to them.

The billowy clouds seemed to play peek-a-boo with the bright moon and cast shadows as Bruns and I lay side-by-side looking at the stars. I had never before seen a moon so large, so brilliant, and so hypnotic when the clouds disappeared. I thought that if I could climb just a short distance up the mountain that I could touch it.

Bruns and I were oblivious to our companions just a few feet away when, leaning on his elbow facing me, he said, "You know, I'm beginning to feel sorry for your guy back home, Rad." Then he added, as if an afterthought, "Do you have to wear that damn ring all the time?"

He had mentioned the ring before and knew it was a touchy subject. I always felt safe wearing it.

"O.K., don't answer. But it does bother me." He turned on his back and looked up at the stars.

Our conversation shifted to idle talk: the book I was reading, happenings of the day, Brunson about continuing his education after the war, his experience at Texas University, planning for the future.

Then he said, "You know, Rad, I was thinking about going into psychology before the war. I had some experience in counseling boys who had had adjustment problems, to find if that was what I would like to continue doing in the future. After I got my degree, I had to join, as did everybody. I chose the Air Corps, and came all the way to Africa to find the solution to my future. It is you. Nothing else matters as long as I am near you. Just love me half as much as I love you."

"But I do. You are very precious to me, Brunson. I'm just not able to plan anything different right now. The dangerous bomb runs worry me, and yet . . ."

Bruns interrupted, "I know, my dear, and I can understand that reasoning, but I want you to know that I love you, love you more than anything in this world."

We embraced. The clouds conveniently hid the moon as we pressed close and kissed. We could hear Lieutenant Wolf and Edythe saying it was time to get back. We got up, picked up our blanket, and headed toward the jeep and camp. They were to fly out early in the morning as usual.

"Goodnight, my love," he said. "I'll come over as soon as I finish playing baseball. I'm the pitcher for the enlisted guys. Will that be O.K. with you?"

"Goodnight Bruns. I'll be waiting."

I heard the planes roar out early the next day and lifted the flap of my tent, but it was too dark to count. I said a prayer as I wriggled back into my sleeping bag. I knew that Brunson often pitched for the GIs in his squadron. There were occasions when he came over quite late because of a tied score, and stayed only a very short time since they had to rise so very early on bomb runs.

His flight crew and the ground crew enlisted men needed the companionship of their officers to get to know and depend on each other. Bruns took his responsibilities seriously, and that was what I admired about him.

12 July 1943

Today our B-17's flew over Messina. They bombed two railroad bridges on the enemy's chief supply line. Brunson's bombs hit the target, a fifty-foot wide bridge. The crew took a lot of flak, and a 20-millimeter shell hit Brunson's Fortress wing. He said, "I thought they were out to get me when the plane shuddered and tilted from the impact of the explosion. It seemed like instant revenge."

We celebrated that evening and had supper at Ain M'Lila with Betty and Richard Headrick, the airman with whom Bruns often flew. The French woman fried a chicken, fixed a tomato and cucumber salad, with bread and butter, and melon for desert. After the boys paid the women with wrinkled French Francs, we rode to our mountain, not far from our camp, and spread our blankets at the base. It was our special spot where we felt we could be alone. Brunson and I were seeing each other a lot as the days passed. Often he would dash over with a comrade for just an hour. They had to be back by nine or ten because of the early morning flights.

As we sat close, Brunson turned to face me, and putting his arms on my shoulders, his eyes looking into mine, said, "You know, Rad, I'm falling in love with you, hard. I want to be with you every chance I get. You are what keeps me straight when things get rough. I don't know how I got on before we met."

I looked into his eyes, then lowering mine, I said, "Bruns, you are very dear to me. I always look forward to your coming. You are the highlight of my day." I was beginning to be very fond of him. I remembered how jealous I felt early in our friendship, when I heard Nurse Bernie say to him, "But you *promised,* Bruns," and my resentment of her being in the rec tent when she knew I expected him. He was a little embarrassed, but it was probably due to our original meeting at the Chateaudun Ball when we all met for the first time.

However, there was something in Brunson's casualness and make-up that made me feel that he was testing me, teasing and making me jealous. I tried to ignore it and pretended it didn't bother me. It was unusual for me to feel the emotion that I thought I had guarded against up to now. As he leaned toward me, and kissed me, I repeated, "You are very dear to me, Bruns. I watch when I hear you fly out in the morning, and pray for your safe return. You are on my mind all the time you are on the bomb run. I care a great deal for you."

"O.K, but I want you to more than 'care,' honey. I love you—very much."

We embraced. He held me close, looking into my eyes,

waiting for the words I could not say.

Captain Headrick and Betty began to get up and fold their blanket. Headrick said, "Time to go Brunson. We don't want to get in late. The major will give us hell."

Brunson pressed me closer to his body. Our lips met as he whispered, "I hate like the devil leaving you, Rad."

We kissed again as he extended his hand to help me up. We headed toward the jeep. When we reached camp and my tent, he said, "I'll be over tomorrow as soon as I can get away, my sweet."

The next day, Sunday, Lieutenants Brunson, Webber, and Godeki, excited about having a day off, arrived in a recon car and called to me as I stood in the entrance of my tent. They asked if I could get Celia Kirschling and Betty to join us for a picnic and a swim at Phillipville. We had no problem getting the girls to accept, since we had no other plans. We decided to put our swimsuits on under our slacks and shirts, took towels, helmets and blankets in hand, and climbed into the recon. I sat in the front seat with Godeki and Bruns. It was a long ride, but with Brunson next to me and the camaraderie of the group, the time passed quickly.

The azure Mediterranean, its whitecaps sparkling in the sun as we neared the sea, was a beautiful sight after the rugged dusty roads and sparse, dingy Arab villages.

We girls undressed on one side of the recon, while the men tossed their clothes off on the other side. We raced to the sandy beach and into the sea, splashing each other as we ran. The men brought inflated tubes for floating, and a large ball that we tossed to each other. We got sunburned, since the day was bright and the reflection of the sun on the water gave us a double dose. The men fooled around, racing one another and ducking each other under the water. When we got winded we rested on the beach and ate watermelon that they brought and had covered with sand on the waters edge, and drank canned grapefruit juice and water from our canteens. I took some pictures as we sat. We had a wonderful, carefree time.

On the way home we stopped at a small café, hoping to get something to eat. The elderly Frenchman who greeted us had his wife stir up an omelet while he placed wine glasses on the table and poured cool *vin blanc* into each. Then he brought out a long loaf of French bread sliced thick, butter, tomatoes, and a bowl of fresh fruit for each person. It was a very satisfying lunch. On our way home as dark descended, we took a wrong turn and headed for Guelma. Having wasted gasoline, we corrected our direction at an army post and ran out of fuel just as we reached the edge of our camp.

Tomorrow's target was top secret, as were all targets, but tension in the unit made them aware that it was going to be a very important mission. As usual, it would not be divulged until the pilots' briefing in the morning. However, rumor had it tagged as a very perilous mission. Someone mentioned, "Maybe oil fields." If that was correct, they would be exposed to a great deal of flak. However, it would bring the war to an end sooner if the Nazis were deprived of fuel.

The fast Messerschmitt ME-109s flew circles around, above and below the slow B-17's as they flew in formation en route to the designated target. When attacked by an enemy fighter plane, the bombers continued onward while their machine gunners fought the enemy plane, or they exploded and spiraled to earth. The enemy fighters were always there, intercepting them before they reached the target area, at which time the ground anti-aircraft crew took over while the fighters refueled and fought the Fortresses on the return trip to base.

When I mentioned my apprehension to Brunson on the bomb runs, his reply was, "Honey, don't you worry, my number's not up. I'll be over as soon as I can get away after I'm debriefed."

We both knew better than that. In war, numbers didn't matter. Wolfe told me that Brunson had been recommended for the Distinguished Flying Cross for performance over and beyond the call of duty. It was when his plane was hit before they had reached the target and several of his crew were wounded. They continued in formation, while Brunson attended the wounded then returned to the bomb bay and dropped the load on the target for a direct hit. I knew he was a good shot because we occasionally did some target practice against the foot of the mountain, and he picked off a bird flying high above, without blinking an eye. I felt sorry for the bird, since we saw so few.

I was among a group of nurses assigned to duty at the 61st General Hospital. However, Dorothy Henry wanted to go in my place, so I stayed back. Brunson came over at five, and I was glad I had remained at camp. We rode back to his camp for supper and afterward played gin rummy with Betty and Hedrick. They served thick slices of watermelon. We overheard talk that tomorrow's target was to be a very vital one, and the bombardiers had been warned that anyone who misfired would be court-martialed.

19 July 1943

Eighty Fortresses roared over our tents at 7:30 this morning. At eight o'clock in the evening when Bruns came over, I greeted him in the rec tent, and anxiously asked, "How did the mission go?"

"There were a thousand planes over Rome today!" he exclaimed. "Our group bombed factories, railroads, bridges, vital centers and other strategic areas. At briefing this morning the major warned us to stay clear of the Vatican, the Cathedrals, and the City itself. We met no resistance. Their fighters were caught on the ground and bombed. There was some flak, but it wasn't very accurate. We saw mobs of people on the streets. They were lucky we had been warned not to bomb the city and the architecture. Now tell me what did you do today, my dear?"

"I did the usual when time hangs heavily. I sorted through my bed roll and you know what that means:

185

shaking out, folding, rearranging, then mess three times, read a little, sunbathed, but most of all, I thought about you. I prayed you would be safe."

"Thanks for the prayers, we sure need them. Let's take a ride over to my place."

I went back to my tent, got my helmet and blanket, and we rode to his camp where we joined his tent mates at a watermelon feast.

22 July 1943

I counted only eighteen ships returning from the raid at 4:00, and when there was no sign of Brunson at 6:00, I knew something was wrong. In the meantime, my friend, Lieutenant Bailey and three of his crew: Lieutenants Vink, Axen, and Taylor, flew in from Souk el Arba where the 321st Bomb Group, 446th Squadron, had moved a month ago. Bailey made sure I knew he was coming by buzzing very low over our camp. I could read "BUZZ WAGON" on the fuselage as the B-25 roared over my tent. Bailey had forty-some missions to his credit and would soon be flying back to the States. They are a handsome group of fellows, and we were happy to see them again. Their visits were rare, since they had few opportunities to fly for pleasure. There were only a few American girls in their new territory and they were lonesome. Betty Asselin, Gert Trainor and Marge Bruce were glad to see their boy friends again, and since it was time for mess, they joined us for supper.

Many of our officers knew them from the time when they had been stationed near us, and welcomed them as well. After supper Bailey and I walked over to the rec tent along with Betty, Gert and their Lieutenants. They had to hurry back, since this was an unscheduled stop, and they had to land their plane before dark. Bailey was expecting a promotion before leaving for the States. He said he was lonesome since he left Ain M'Lila and missed our jaunts into Constantine. They stayed a short time, since it got dark as soon as the sun set behind the mountain. I was glad to see Bailey once more before he left for the States.

In the meantime, I was concerned about Brunson's failure to come over. At 7:30 Captain Headrick came over to tell me that Brunson had just arrived after having made an emergency landing at Bizerte. He said that his tail gunner had his arm shot off, that his plane had fifteen good-sized holes and looked like a sieve, that Brunson was covered with blood when he landed, and that they were sure he had been wounded. Headrick said the plane was a mess. One area three feet in diameter had 200 holes.

Headrick asked me to come to the "Country Club," a spot at the base of a mountain where we often met with Betty, his girl. He said that Brunson would join us after he was interrogated. When Bruns arrived a short time later, I could sense the tension he had been through. His eyes were somber and dark. He was not the smiling, self-assured person I was accustomed to. His jaw was set as he embraced me. We sat down on the blanket he helped me spread on the ground, then said, "We were attacked three different times, a direct hit before we reached the target at Naples, and two direct hits afterwards. A big piece of shrapnel came within an inch of my head. That's a bit of a shock when I'm just above the bomb load."

I leaned close to him and touched his cheek. I could feel his jaw twitch. He was under a lot of pressure, and his nerves were on edge. I tried to distract him with trivial incidents at camp. I told him about the tiny black and white puppy the GIs had acquired and how he romped through our tents drinking wash water from our helmets, and raced from tent to tent to greet us.

Bruns held me close as he whispered tender words of love. In the back of both of our minds ran a similar thought: "How long does one's luck hold out?"

Since Headrick had to fly in the morning, they had to be back to their camp by ten o'clock. Brunson pressed me close to him, and whispered. "You, my darling, are what keeps me sane. I don't know how I could go on without looking forward to being with you." Our lips met in a kiss.

"You are very dear to me, Brunson. I always pray for your safety, my dear when you are up in the sky."

We got into his jeep and drove to my camp where we parted with a quick embrace and kiss, since Headrick was waiting at the entrance.

At 5:00 the next morning, everyone at my camp except headquarters personnel departed for the seashore at Dji Djelli, northwest of our camp by several hundred kilometers. Since I couldn't go swimming, I stayed back. Instead, I went into town and got a permanent wave. My hair always took a very tight curl, and in spite of my warning the French beauty operator about it, I got a very tight curl, leaving my hair bronzed and quite frizzy. Afterward, I had lunch with Madame Delores Simon, a French woman I had met at a headquarters gathering earlier in the week. We shopped at the Casbah where I saw decapitated heads of lambs displayed on wood counters, their eyes opened wide, as if staring at me. Flies were buzzing over all the raw meat.

I bought several woven reed shallow bowls and a vase, souvenirs that I would send home. There was a rumor spreading that we would soon be moving. We could mail packages back to the States without any problems, because there were many ships returning to the States with their hulls empty after unloading war supplies on these shores.

30 July 1943

While on my cot with the tent flap raised to get some light, I was reading the book *Mata Hari*, when I suddenly heard a plane at a very high altitude. We were familiar with different engine sounds and were able to identify most planes. This plane hovered over our area at an unusual height, almost beyond sight for several minutes, it seemed. Suddenly it screeched into a whistling nose-dive. All personnel at camp dashed out of their tents to see debris falling as the plane came plummeting and disintegrating in the air. An explosion shook the earth as it hit the ground just beyond our camp. Flames engulfed the entire plane. We dashed toward the wreckage, thinking we could pull the occupants out, but the explosion of ammunition, and the fire would not permit us to get close to the blazing plane. We had no water; our lister bag hanging in the center of camp was but a drop.

Running up the incline in the heat and suddenly coming to the inferno, my stomach tightened and cramped. I felt sick. I looked up and saw "Buzz Wagon" through the flames. Bailey's plane! I searched the sky looking for parachutes, wishfully consoling myself that they had baled out, out of sight, perhaps just beyond the next djebel.

Later that day we heard that Lieutenant Merle Bailey, in the 321st Bomb Group, 442nd Squadron was testing two new engines on the Buzz Wagon when the plane caught fire and fell. Several guards were posted at the smoldering plane's site overnight.

The next day Colonel Napp and Major Pinger gathered up the remains of Lieutenant Merle Bailey, his crew, Noel Coffee, Sergeant Neffer, and two enlisted men and took them to Constantine for burial. Lieutenants Vink, Breach, and Tommy Williams came over and gave me several snapshots that Bailey had taken during our friendship. I asked Vink to destroy the pictures that Bailey had of myself when he sent his things home. Bailey had completed 47 missions. It was a sad day at camp. The men had endeared themselves to many of our personnel.

I felt sorry for his family, for his sister he affectionately referred to as "Bunny." He often mentioned her when we were together and I surmised they had a close relationship. I knew it would be shocking news to his fiancée. It bothered me that they would get only the brief message: KIA, (killed in action.)

I thought about writing to his family for several days. After mulling it over, my conscience compelled me to write. In the letter I told them of meeting their son and

The B-25 "Buzz Wagon" and crew.
Lieutenant Bailey is third from left.

about seeing his plane crash. This letter probably would not have got past the censor if it had been checked, but I felt better for having written it. I would have wanted to know what happened to someone dear to me, to hear everything I could about their last days. It would be comforting. At least that was my feeling. The Bailey family and their friends replied to express their great sorrow, and gratitude for my letter. His mother and sister corresponded with me for many years after the war.

Several days later I had the opportunity to go to the cemetery at Constantine with our GI driver Sergeant Robert B. James. When we got there we were told that Bailey and his crew had been buried at the new cemetery at E.B.S., (Eastern Base Section.) We continued on and found the burial site, although Bailey's cross was not yet in place. James put one up temporarily. Then placing a bouquet of flowers on his grave I took a picture of the site to send to his family. As we bowed our heads in prayer I wished my dear friend eternal peace and remembrance. It was sad parting with such fine young men.

31 July 1943

I got my monthly army pay today. After the allotment, rent (tent) and food were deducted it left me with $38.70 American, that we exchanged into francs. I lay in the sun alongside my tent in my two piece bathing suit and thought about Bailey and his crew, and what a shock their families had in store.

Towards evening Brunson, Headrick and Evans arrived to ask a group of us out to eat. They had made reservations at the French woman's house. She could only fix omelets for such a large group, instead of the usual chicken, along with French bread, salad, melon, and wine. There were eleven of us altogether with an extra man. We had a hilarious time each trying to outdo the other in telling stories and jokes, embellishing all. After supper one of the men stood up and began swaying his body and shuffling into a dance. Instantly, we all joined into a Conga Line holding on to the hips of the person ahead while singing and dancing to the rhythm of: 1, 2, 3, kick! We shuffled and twisted, dancing around the dining room table, into the grimy kitchen that reeked of sheep, and back to the dining room again. The French woman stood aghast, her hand on her cheek, her eyes following our every turn. She probably thought we'd all gone mad.

Captain Evans and Marge, Bruns and I rode to our Club at the foot of the mountain afterwards and spread our blankets. We were in high spirits; the evening had been hilariously exciting. We laughed, sang and romanced as we sat on the ground. Brunson, fumbling with his shirt collar, removed his silver wings, and while pinning them on my blouse recited with much fanfare:

> "While air raids and shrapnel burst about
> Drown my promise of eternal love
> And Arabs emerge like spooks in shrouds
> I pin my wings close to your heart
> Pledging my love and faith to never part."

I was thrilled as he pressed me close to his body, and

said, "I will treasure your wings always Brunson."

He held me close saying, "I'll love you forever, Rad." When we heard Marge and Evans rising, and Captain Evans saying, "Time to get back, Brunson," he got up and held his hand out to me We climbed into the front seat of the jeep and Brunson drove back to camp.

As we parted, I sensed a bond between us, with his wings pinned on my shirt pocket. Holding me close as we kissed, he said, "I will always love you, Rad. Goodnight sweetheart."

The next evening I got a message that Brunson would be delayed because he had to pitch for the GIs in a baseball game against the officers. He would pick me up afterward to see the movie "White Cargo" that was to be shown at his camp. This would be a treat, since movies rarely came near our area.

As we sat on the ground looking at the screen, we saw Arab men around the perimeter of the field. They were seeing an entirely different world, and we wondered what they thought as they watched the movie. Brunson said, "It's probably the greatest entertainment they've ever experienced. By the way I'm going into Constantine in the morning. I'd like to have you come along. Can you get away?"

"I'll get away all right." We were doing nothing but sweltering in the tents with the temperature up to 115 degrees while we waited for our next move. Going to Constantine got us out of the heat, at least, and took our minds off the boredom of lying on a cot under the mosquito net to keep from getting malaria.

He arrived at the rec tent at nine, before I had completed my morning minutiae. I hurriedly combed my hair and applied my make-up, peering in the metal mirror. It was unbreakable and not very reflective, but better than nothing. Then, picking up my helmet and purse, I dashed across the field to the rec tent where he greeted me with a hug and a kiss on my cheek. There was never anybody in the rec this early in the day unless they were expecting a guest.

We headed toward the jeep parked at the barbed wire entrance beyond our headquarters tent. Bruns spread the blanket on the front seat and helped me into the jeep, then walked around and climbed behind the wheel, and we were off. The Macadam roads were becoming very rough from pot holes due to heavy army traffic. Our blankets served to pad the hard seats, and kept us warm after the sun set when the weather cooled.

We parked in the usual parking area in Constantine, close to the Casino, then walked to the Casbah where I bought a pair of white goatskin pointed slippers that had the heel crushed down, the same as the natives wore. It took a bit of bartering, a tradition with the Arabs that we learned to play, before reaching a fair price. As was our custom when in town, we ate lunch at the French restaurant. Today we had roasted chicken, along with legumes, bread and wine. We were surprised to get ice cream for dessert, our first since arriving in Africa. It was probably not safe to eat, but we were so surprised, we ate it without thinking. Normally we would not eat food that had not been cooked or peeled when we ate in public places.

After lunch we went to the Casino. It was crowded as always. We listened to the record player, exchanged rumors, and enjoyed the camaraderie of the people gathered there. In the army we were all part of the same entity, at least it seemed so overseas. The majority of us were volunteers who had joined the army after the declaration of war. On meeting new people, the first questions anybody asked was: "Where are you from?" We were forever looking for someone from home or at least from our home state.

Brunson was anxious to drive back to the Casbah, where he bought five watermelons and a block of ice. This was the reason for his coming to town in the first place, I realized. After we picked up two of his comrades who needed a ride, by the time we arrived at my camp the ice was practically melted.

In the evening the 96th Air Force Squadron gave a party and invited all the nurses from our camp. We were presented with lovely corsages upon arriving and were treated royally the entire evening. Delicious hamburgers were served along with alcoholic drinks. I wondered where they got the meat, unless they had flown to a port and got it from the Navy. It was probably the entire reason for the party, celebrating fresh meat, I thought. A small band played the current popular tunes as we danced far into the night. Brunson got tagged by his fellow officers too often to suit him. Colonel Thomas tagged me a number of times along with Captain Kelly, Bruns' lead man. We, that is, Lieutenant Wolfe, Edythe, Bruns and I, didn't get back to our camp until 2:30! However, we were not the last ones. The group was not scheduled to fly the next day and this could have been another reason for the celebration.

However, on parting, when Brunson said that they were moving toward Tunis the next day, I was stunned. I'd had no indication of a move up to this moment. Everything was secret in the army. Brunson's leaving made me wonder about his giving me his silver wings last week. Now we knew, and perhaps he knew all along, that we would be parting.

"I'll write as soon as we settle, and come as soon as I can find a way," Brunson said, as he held me in his arms and we kissed good-bye. "Please know that I hate like the devil leaving you. That I love you dearly and will return the first chance I find."

"I will miss you Brunson, I love you very much. Goodbye, and do take care."

In spite of invitations and new acquaintances, the days began to drag monotonously. I began reading the book "Arrowsmith" and spent days on my cot under the mosquito bar.

Ploesti Oil Fields Bombed

1 August 1943

One hundred and seventy-seven American B-24 bombers, Liberators, under Lieutenant General Lewis Hyde Brereton's Ninth Air Force Command based south of us roared across the Mediterranean today. They flew over the mountains of Albania, Yugoslavia and the Danube River before enemy fighter planes in Bulgaria intercepted them. Fighting their way through the enemy fighter planes, then through thick antiaircraft fire, they finally reached Rumania. The bombers began their run on the Ploesti oil fields and refineries at a 500-foot altitude. The first flight of Liberators dropped their bombs as planned, but as the following low-flying planes flew toward the target at the low level prescribed, they exploded from the detonations of the bombs dropped by the preceding bombers before they had a chance to drop their own bomb loads

Of the one hundred and seventy-seven Liberator bombers, fifty did not return. Forty-one were shot down. Four hundred and forty-six of the seventeen hundred and thirty-three men who started out were killed or parachuted from the crippled planes and taken prisoner or were missing in action. The flames from the exploding oil fields sent fires raging high up into the sky as the bombs of the first flights exploded. Of the hundred and seventy-seven planes that flew out that day, only thirty-three were fit to fly the following day. It was the deadliest day for the Air Force up to then.

The Air Force determined that the disaster resulted from the low level of flight of the heavyweight planes.

Farewell To Ain M'lila

12 August 1943

We rolled up our bedrolls, packed our suitcases and

folded our cots as the GIs collapsed the tents, folded them and tossed them into the two-and-a-half-ton trucks. We, the remaining personnel left behind while our surgical teams fought in Sicily, were leaving our campsite of four months. Our surgeons and their enlisted team members had been operating in clearing stations and evacuation hospitals in Sicily since "Husky," the code name for the invasion that began on July 10, 1943.

We spent the first night in a granary, but the cats meowing kept us awake most of the night. I had never seen a cat in Africa before, and was surprised there were some here. At 3:30 a.m., we were awakened. Since we slept in our cloths we were ready after a cup of black coffee and a thick slice of bread spread with oleomargarine. We were back on the truck heading towards the Harbor.

Whimpy, our small dog, riding in my lap, was car sick, as were many of the nurses as we rode over narrow mountain trails. However, the nurses used their helmets, whereas Whimpy vomited on my lap.

The roads were jammed with trucks filled with prisoners, all heading toward the coast. We traveled all day, with stops every four hours for a break. On one occasion we stopped at Souk el Arba, Bailey's last camp. It was still difficult to believe that he was gone.

The following day we nurses were assigned to duty at the 3rd General Hospital near Matuer and began taking care of the casualties from the Sicilian campaign. They were being transported from Sicily on the Seminole, a hospital ship, along with other ships until such time as evacuation and other hospitals were able to be established on the island.

A few days later I got a message from one of Brunson's buddies that he would come over about seven. I was late getting off duty and by the time I washed and changed, we had lost a half hour of precious time together. I noticed a change in Brunson the minute I neared the rec tent. He was pacing in front of it. I discerned a strained expression on what used to be a happy-go-lucky smiling countenance. I had begun to notice a change even before the move, as time passed and I got to know him more intimately. He was becoming tense as he neared the fifty-mission mark.

He greeted me with open arms and held me close to him as our lips met in a long tender kiss. "I have missed you, Rad. Time has dragged interminably since we parted. Tell me, darling, how have you been?"

"I have been very lonely without you, Bruns. My life isn't the same since you went away. It has become dull and meaningless without your presence."

We went into the tent and sat on the chairs around the card table. Bruns told about his comrades who had not returned from bombing missions, fellows I knew when they were stationed near us at Ain M'Lila.

"You know, Rad, I'm no longer as concerned about that damn shell marked 'Brunson' as I am about all those unmarked strays that zap all around me in the air."

The pressure of the missions and concern for comrades shot down was beginning to demoralize him. I began to wonder how much longer the flying men could tolerate the stress before they broke down. Time with Brunson always raced by before we were ready to part. Holding me close, he said, "I'll try to come earlier the next time so we can go exploring. O.K. with you?"

"You know it will be O.K." I looked into his eyes and his met mine as he pressed me close to his body and we kissed. "I'll be looking for you, Bruns. I'm so happy that we are able to get together again. You are very precious to me and I've missed you terribly. Please come whenever you can, my dear."

We kissed again and he said, "I hate like the devil leaving you, Rad." We walked toward the jeep and parted. As he drove off in a cloud of dust I wondered when I would see him again.

A week later Brunson and I walked along the coast of the Mediterranean where the enemy had made their last ditch stand in Bizerte and discovered huge caves, fox holes, and trenches dug in what looked like solid rock. The caves facing the sea had concealed enemy artillery from our bomber planes as they approached from the sea or from above, and had kept our warships from advancing toward the harbor. Communication wires strewn over the ground indicated the speed with which the Germans escaped from North Africa. We were careful not to step on the wires for fear of setting off mines.

We met Major Evans and his date, and drove to the sea where we shed our shoes and stockings and waded in the cool water. Bruns was accumulating missions and I knew it would not be much longer before he would leave, but he did not bring up the subject. The day passed quickly and we were back at the hospital for supper. They had to check in early as always, because planes did not fly at night. Parting was, as always, difficult, since we never knew when we would meet again.

With their defeat in Africa, after the Americans captured Bizerte and the British took Tunis, the Luftwaffe continued bombing Allied ships and docks that were being stockpiled to continue the war in Sicily, and their route was over our camp.

Even before we heard the sound of plane engines, the night sky would suddenly become illuminated with white and green flares, and searchlights scanned the dark for the enemy planes. Once the anti-aircraft crew caught the enemy in the searchlight beam, tracer bullets in rapid succession, followed by ack-ack shells, exploded the plane if it had not yet dropped its bombs, and it plummeted to earth in a ball of fire.

At times we wondered why our anti-aircraft did not open fire on the enemy when we knew they were above, and discovered that damage to us from falling shrapnel would far exceed the damage the German plane could inflict on its target in the harbor. We trusted that the pilot did not want to waste his bombs on us. We were familiar with the whining whistle and thud of shrapnel as it fell to earth.

The 3rd General Hospital had been a German Hospital prior to the victory in Africa. It was a one-storied set up in permanent buildings that they had left intact, probably because they had to leave in a hurry. My work was demanding since I had the responsibility for the entire ward. Air raids by the enemy were frequent occurrences, and our sleep was disrupted. A German plane exploded in the sky one night as we watched the air raid. One of my patients, Sergeant Urquhart, a twenty-year old Air Force boy, related his experience on the bombing flight over the Ploesti oil fields. His head, face and upper part of his body were completely encased with bandages because of severe burns received when his plane caught fire in that raid. He was on one of the fortunate few planes that made it back to Africa. He talked as I took care of him and while feeding him, since his arms and hands were encased in bulky bandages. He was glad to have survived, but I wondered what his reaction would be when his dressing would be removed from his face, and head. He was transferred to England for recuperation. I never saw his face.

We were receiving wounded soldiers by ship and by air. The work was physically exhausting as casualties mounted. We worked long hours, and got little rest due to the bombings in the night. Another ME plane crashed near our hospital tonight. We heard the terrific explosion and watched as it burned.

15 August 1943
Whenever Brunson and Wolfe came over, our first conversation was on catching up on the current rumors. Then Edythe or I inquired about their recent targets and the results. I told of the experiences the wounded boys talked about in the wards, of leaving wounded behind when the German Tiger tanks blasted our Shermans into burning shells as they overtook them. The infantry had fought a tough, experienced enemy for six months and paid a high price in casualties. We had been sitting next

to Edythe and Wolfe when Brunson stood up, and holding his hand out to me said,

"Let's go for a walk Rad." We sauntered off on the road, and with his hand still clasping mine we walked a short distance before he spoke. As he turned toward me, I noticed a solemn look on his face as he started to say, "After this damned war is finished I hope to go back to the University and get a degree in psychology, Rad. What do you think about that as a career?"

Psychology was a subject I'd had some exposure to as a nurse, but without a doctorate it was considered by the doctors of psychiatry as infringing on their field. The subject would probably come to the forefront at the end of the war when veterans returned home, and would very likely be a good field to work in.

We also talked about family history, heredity, inherited diseases, syphilis, and insanity. I wondered what he was thinking, what he had in mind. Was he delving into my background in case our love affair would lead to serious ties? My state of health in case of intimacy?

I said, "Yes, Bruns, psychology might be a career wide open in readjustment to civilian life when the war is finished. I expect there will be a great demand for it."

"I wanted to know your feelings about my choosing that type of career, what you thought about it."

"I think it has great possibilities, Bruns, and you should do well as a psychologist from my point of view, knowing you as I do."

"I'm glad you feel it's a good choice, Rad. Your opinion is very important to me."

We walked back to our companions, and as the sun descended over the mountain and darkness closed in, we lay down to watch the stars and the moon as it peeked out from behind a cloud. Bruns and Wolfe talked about the bomb runs, the close calls, and the many holes the Fortress could withstand and still fly. About the parachutes getting tangled in the planes' propellers as their buddies bailed out. Edythe and I realized that they needed to talk, to get it off their chests, to be able to face tomorrow, when they would again be flying over enemy territory. I'd seen the effect on their camp when they returned from a raid after seeing planes veer off out of formation and spiral down.

Captain Wolfe, lying a short distance from us, called out, "By the way Rad, has Bruns told you he's been recommended for the DFC (Distinguished Flying Cross) and the Silver Star?"

"Oh? Bruns, congratulations, honey! What did you do this time?" I knew he had been recommended once before.

"It was nothing that anyone else would not have done. All in a day's work."

I looked into his blue eyes, eyes that looked like the sky where he spent each day, fringed with thick dark gold lashes. They met mine. I bent toward him, and in a low voice asked, "You trying to set some kind of record Brunson?"

He turned toward me and held me close. "No, it's all part of a day's work. What is important is that I'd do anything in the world for you Rad. I wish I could convince you . . ." he looked at the diamond ring on the third finger of my left hand. "Won't you take it off so I can love you without feeling guilty?"

I didn't answer. I was torn between loyalty to the past and the lover in my arms. Letters from home when they did arrive continued with pledges of love and loneliness, but that was far away.

My fiancé was the kind of man that women made a play for. He was tall with dark brown slightly wavy hair, deep blue eyes, and a cleft in his firm chin, but it was his demeanor, his gentleness, his being that I had fallen in love with. He was a thoughtful, considerate, loving person. I compared him and his manners to Herbert Marshall, my Hollywood idol. I wondered what was happening on the other side of the world. Was he having the same problem? Would he be there when the war was finished? It was impossible to transcend space and feel in close communion. There was an interval of four months when no mail arrived for any of our group. Was he writing?

I relied on Brunson for affection. I did not want to live a barren existence without love. Bob had aroused that in me. Now I was captivated by Brunson's tenderness and devotion. Life without love was meaningless. I was still being true, but it was getting to be a challenge. Besides, I knew Brunson would be leaving soon, as he was nearing the fifty missions required before returning to the States, and that was another reason for my remaining faithful. Watching the swiftly moving billowing clouds as they passed in front of the bright moon and stars, neither of us spoke. I knew Bruns was both anxious to get the missions over with and concerned about our parting. Wolfe's joking and chuckling with Edythe roused us from our thoughts. Wolfe loved to tease Edythe.

Brunson turned toward me. Leaning on his elbow, he looked at me as if reading my thoughts.

"I've been having a lot of mixed feelings, Rad. I'll sure be glad when that fiftieth mission is finished, but I will hate like the devil leaving you. I want to be with you every minute, every chance I get. You are my inspiration. Knowing you has kept my hopes up when things get rough. You must know that I love you, how much I need you."

"My dearest, you are the bright spot in my life. I, too, am anxious for the end of these hazardous missions, and wonder how I will survive after you are gone. I look forward to your coming each day and am miserable when you can't make it. Time drags interminably, and life is empty without you. All that is left is work and sleep. I pray for your safety every night and when you are out on missions. You are very precious to me, Brunson."

I began to sense a developing tension in Brunson as time passed and missions accumulated. He was becoming more restless, pensive, as time between our meetings became less frequent. He put his arms around my waist and pressed me close to his body. As we lay close, the sentimental music of an accordion drifted across the river. We recognized the tune since we had been singing all the popular songs of that period throughout our travels and gatherings at parties. It was a favorite one:

TELL ME WHEN YOU'LL BE MINE
You are a joy beyond compare
I can't wait a moment more
Each day is a life away
Let me show you the way
To joy beyond compare
My darling tell me when . . ."

Out in the dark sky the sound of a plane disturbed the magic of the moment as its searching beam lingered on the four of us as it flew overhead. We burst into laughter as the light held on us. We were never alone! If it was not a jeep's headlight, it was someone stepping on us in the dark, or an Arab popping out of the ground. But an airplane's beam—that was a first!

Edythe, a Texan, laughingly exclaimed, "Must be one of your buddies telling ya'll, it's time to call it a night!"

As we rode in the blackout, beams of searchlights began scanning the sky as enemy planes streaked overhead. Bizerte was being bombed again. Brunson and I got out of the jeep and stood beside the road and watched the anti-aircraft fire. The raid began at 11:25 and continued until 12:15 midnight. One plane, caught in the light, was like a fly in a spider's web, struggling in vain to escape. It turned into a ball of fire in the midst of streaks of colored lights, which arched skyward, and we heard the thud and thundering rumble of explosions in the distance.

The raid over, we continued toward camp. At the nurses' tent area, with his arms around my waist, Brunson guided me in the dark. Lieutenant Wolfe and Edyth trailed behind us. Parting was always difficult, since we never were sure about when we would be together again. Brunson pressed me close, saying, "Good night, my love. I always hate leaving you."

"I don't like seeing you go either, my dear. Please take care of yourself and come when you can. Good-bye, my dear."

We kissed and I watched him until he disappeared in the dark. I heard the jeep rumble past on the dirt road.

17 August 1943

It was officially confirmed that Sicily had surrendered today. It took thirty-eight days to defeat the Italian and German Armies. British General Alexander had said it might take three months. General Patton's Seventh Army invaded on the western side of Sicily, while the British Eighth attacked from the east. The Americans reached Messina two hours ahead of General Alexander's Eighth Army. Unfortunately, 40,000 German and 62,000 Italians crossed the Messina Straight into Italy along with large quantities of supplies, guns and tanks. They lost about 10,000 men killed or captured. The Americans and British suffered about 7000 killed and 15,000 wounded. Over 100,000 Italians were taken prisoner.

We heard through rumor that our Fortresses bombed Marseilles today, the 17th of August. Our B-17 friends, along with Brunson, who was now stationed in Tunis, executed the raid. I later heard that he flew in the lead plane of his squadron.

18 August 1943

Air raids in the vast emptiness of Africa did not seem as alarming as they did when I was in London in the old stone buildings that might collapse and bury the occupants. As Bruns and I walked across our camp near Matuer, we recognized the sound of enemy planes in the distance. Almost instantly, tracers were making patterns in the black sky searching for them above us. We heard thunder in the distance as bombs exploded. The bursts of ack-ack (antiaircraft canon) resounded as the gun crews searched the black sky.

We stopped to watch the air raid. Brunson put his arm around my waist and held me close as we looked up into the sky, fascinated by the tiny plane high above heading eastward.

"It looks like a bird from here," I commented. "How can they hit such a small object from the ground?" I asked.

"It's not difficult when they spray all that flak around him when he's caught in the beam. Just being there the cannon will get him."

The plane was corkscrewing downward and then flew straight up, turned sideways, desperately trying to get out of the beam and the flak that was bursting around it. "I feel for the poor devil," he said. Brunson could well sympathize. He knew what the pilot suffering at the moment.

"I'm just glad you are here, Bruns, instead of up there. I do wish you were done with those darn missions."

We were oblivious to the danger of falling shrapnel as we watched, fascinated by the plane caught by the searchlight, then watched as it streaked to the ground. We heard the exclamations and hurrahs and the clapping of hands in the dark as people applauded. It was as if someone had scored a touchdown. Perhaps we had all lost perspective.

"That's one less you need to worry about, Bruns. I can't say I mind his going down if it means an end to the war and your getting out."

He pressed me close to his side. "That poor devil didn't stand a chance. Once he was caught in that search light, he was trapped, blinded."

Brunson could identify with that pilot. He was anxious to go back to the States, and I was both glad and sad, glad that he would be out of danger when he completed his missions, sad because I would miss him when he was gone. He held me close as we silently pondered about what lay ahead for us. The time raced by and because the bomb runs were daily affairs, I knew he had to leave. We could not linger.

"I never know when I can get back to be with you, Rad. It's always so uncertain. But I'll come first chance. You know that, darling. I love you very much."

"I'll be watching the sky and waiting for you, my love. Take care." He pressed me close as our lips met in a passionate kiss.

We parted at my tent, and I watched him until he blended into the night and waited until I heard the motor of the jeep start up. Then I opened the tent flap, and except for the breathing of my tent mates, all was quiet.

The news that greeted us first thing the next morning was that the APO was bombed last night, along with the icehouse. I wondered if our mail was destroyed. As for the ice, I didn't know there was any in our area.

Our sleep was continually disrupted as the Luftwaffe made desperate attempts to cause as much damage as they could at the Ports of Bizerte and Tunis. At ten-thirty one night my tent mates and I were awakened by the lightning speed and screeching of enemy planes. We stood in the dark and watched the anti-aircraft fire. I counted two armor piercing, two incendiaries, and every fifth shell a tracer. They filled the sky with an array of color.

When a plane was caught in the beam of the search-light, it squirmed, flipped, turned, twisted and dove in its attempt to evade the searchlight. I felt sorry for the pilot when a 20-millimeter shell caught it, and watched the lightning effect as its bombs exploded. The plane parts plummeted to the ground trailing a tail of fire as it plunged to earth and exploded again. We felt the vibration when it hit the ground. The Luftwaffe were bombing the supply ships that were moored at the port. We heard the explosions of bombs and planes as they fell on Bizerte and in the morning we heard that between five and seven planes had been shot down during the night. Two may have fallen into the sea.

I arose at six thirty the next morning, late and cold. My tent-mates were gone. I must have slept hard not to hear them; besides I have never liked getting up early. I dressed hurriedly. We were now wearing seersucker dresses on duty instead of fatigues. I splashed water from my helmet onto my face, brushed my teeth outside the tent with water from my canteen, and put on my make-up peering into my metal mir-

Front row: Nurses Aird, Kirschling, and Andreko. Back row: Nurses Bleau, Harper, MacDonald, Radwwiec and Bernick

ror. I then dashed over the stones to the mess tent while suppressing a deep yawn with one hand and clutching my helmet in the other. I gulped the hot coffee from my metal cup, spread some marmalade on the thick slice of white bread, and ate as I rushed across the field to my ward.

I found the ward responsibilities very taxing. There was so much I needed to do, but I had so little help. My corpsman had all he could do with emptying urinals and bedpans for the thirty patients, not to mention passing food trays, taking temperatures, and physically assisting the men out of bed. And then there were the ward inspections. Officers expected every bed, patients' shoes and belongings lined up, all utility items to be spick and span, office equipment in order, charting completed and in their files when they made rounds. It wasn't this stringent at Fort Dix before the war, I grumbled.

20 August 1943

All the same exhaustive work, day after day. It was very hot during the daytime, often 115 degrees. I spent hours at bedside care and did treatments such as changing dressings, irrigations and inhalations, and passed out

207

medications. Then I charted everything, and copied new doctors' orders on to treatment and medication cards, and discarded cards of orders changed or discontinued. We always kept narcotics locked, and checked them coming on and going off duty to be sure they were accounted for. The work was tedious and I wished I were home.

27 August 1943

I had a half-day off for a change. Brunson was over soon after lunch with Lieutenant Godecki, who was trying to locate a friend, a P-38 pilot who had been shot down over Sicily in July. We found him at the 94th Station Hospital. He told us that he was shot down, wounded, and taken prisoner by the Germans when they controlled Sicily. While hospitalized in a German facility he was bombed by our B-17s and bombed again while in transit to the Gerbini Airfield. He had had some very close calls. He also told us that he had downed four German planes. Godecki stayed with his friend while Brunson and I drove to the Mediterranean and sat on the beach and watched the sparkling turquoise waves as they washed into the sand and ebbed back slowly into the sea. We went to the officers club in Bizerte for supper, and I was home by 10 p.m.

As we parted, Bruns said, "I'll be over the first chance I have, honey, and please don't you work so hard." His lips met mine as he pressed me close to his body. "I love you." I slipped into the dark tent. Everyone was asleep.

29 August 1943

As I was crossing the field toward the nurses' area on my half-day off, I heard a plane high above and saw it tilt its wings. Since I was expecting Brunson, I knew that it was he. Knowing that he could spot a target from 20,000 feet I felt sure that he saw me as I waved. After he arrived a half-hour later, he and I drove back to the airfield with Lieutenants Headrick and Godecki.

We flew south over Massicault, la Goulette, Carthage and the Golfe De Tunis. Flying over the Tunis Harbor we saw many sunken ships and hulls protruding skyward. Smoke stacks of still others and superstructures and wreckage cluttered the bay. We landed at la Goulette were we met several other nurses who had arranged to arrive earlier. As we walked along the waters edge at la Goulette, one of the men told us about Lieutenant Newcomber, whom some of us knew who, while floating in a one-man rubber life raft had fallen asleep, and that a terrific wind and sand storm took him out to sea. Airplanes were out searching for him, just as did our plane when we circled the Golfe De Tunis, although we did not know it at the time.

We all gathered at the Officers Club and were surprised to find a wood floor in the tent. The men had also torched designs into the bar, trimmed the wall behind it with raffia, and used bomb racks for high stools. We drank canned grapefruit juice and ate spam sandwiches at the bar. Brunson was attentive and affectionate as always, but I sensed something about him was different. He was not the confident, jovial person I was accustomed to. I decided he must be suffering from flight fatigue, since it was a common affliction as missions increased in distance and became more hazardous.

Towards evening we drove to Carthage where at the Cathedral a Catholic Mass was in progress. Bruns and I slipped into a row and stayed for the service. It was conducted in Latin. I prayed that he would complete his missions safely. It was a solemn occasion. He said when we were outside, "Do you want to know what I prayed for?" As I looked into his eyes and nodded, he added, "I prayed that we would always be together."

29 August 1943

I got a letter from my fiancé, the first in two months. His father had suffered a stroke. I was very saddened by this news. I knew and liked his father, a Scotsman who had through hard work and initiative had become a successful businessman and had inspired all four of his children to get degrees from the University of Michigan. He had wanted Bob and me to marry before I joined the army. I knew this was a difficult time for Bob and his mother, who was active in the community affairs and in their church functions. I also got letters from my brother John and sister Julia. They wanted to know what they could send to me. They said that they got very little news about the progress of the war in Africa and Sicily and were being rationed sugar, gasoline, oil and cigarettes, but were glad to sacrifice everything if it would help our cause.

The wind and sand storm at la Goulette yesterday was blowing sand throughout our area today. We were evacuating our sickest long-term patients to England or the States, depending on whether they would be able to return to duty. As our work lessened, the 3rd General Hospital planned a celebration. Brunson was to come to the party if he didn't fly late or wasn't briefed too early the next day. He didn't come. I was very concerned about him and hoped he would hold up through the few more missions he had to complete. I spent the evening writing letters home.

4 September 1943

Saturday. Inspection on the ward, as usual. I worked like fury tucking mosquito nets on all the patients' beds and straightening the ward before the officers arrived. The days were long and empty without having seen or heard from Brunson all week. I was afraid something had happened to him. Was he ill, or had he perhaps crashed? Would someone at his base contact me?

Work took up all my time, and left me too tired to do my laundry or want to write letters or even read, although that was difficult after dark anyway. Sleep continued to be disrupted by the nightly air raids. The enemy dropped flares close to our installation tonight, but an alert anti-aircraft crew fortunately caught it in its glare, and we watched it spin to earth where it crashed and burned for hours. I went back to my tent, got my camera and snapped the burning hulk. We heard later that Bizerte, Tunis and Ferryville were also bombed.

8 September 1943

General Eisenhower and Marshal Pietro Badoglio, who had replaced Benito Mussolini on The 25th of July, when King Victor Emmanuel demanded Mussolini's resignation, announced the surrender of Italy.

9 September 1943

The American Fifth Army commanded by General Mark W. Clark, supported by 700 Allied ships, invaded Salerno, in Italy. They suffered severe losses due to General Clark's decision not to use heavy supporting bombardment. The Third Auxiliary Surgeons remained in Sicily with the Seventh Army.

My work in Mateur began easing up somewhat since our sickest men had been evacuated. The ward was livelier as men discussed how the war should be fought. Those from the South were still disagreeing with the Yankees about the Civil War.

I was about to go to bed at 9:00 when, "Hey, Rad!" issued forth from the rec tent. I looked out and there stood Brunson, after a week and a half absence! I hurried toward him, thrilled to be in his arms again. He said he had been extremely busy and could not get away. He had been in the lead ship as bombardier that dropped bombs on the Brenner Pass, a main roadway between Italy and Germany since Roman days. The Pass was in the lowest valley of the Tyrol Alps.

He said, "Eighteen ships started on the mission but four turned back, for various reasons. We flew over Italian soil for two and a half hours without fighter escort, and encountered enemy fighters all the way to and from the target. We made a direct hit on the Brenner Pass, the primary target, and on another unscheduled bridge over a stream. On another run we made a direct hit on a double train track supply line into Germany through the Alps."

"Oh, Bruns, I am so proud of you. But why did so many Forts turn back? It's not fair for only fourteen to stake their lives when so many dropped out."

"Oh, they had to do some fast talking to get out of being court-marshaled."

I was delighted to be with him again. We went to the movie on the post, but the projector broke down halfway through, so we sat in the field along with many other couples from the hospital. We chatted and embraced in the dark, as Brunson pledged his love.

He said as we got up to go back to the tent area, "I have missed you terribly these past ten days Rad, but there was nothing I could do about it. We are constantly on alert. There have been so many guys wasted, since we now are flying deeper into Europe and have fighter escort only now and then, and that for only short distances. The Ju-88's fly circles around us as we maintain formation, while our gunners try to zoom in on them."

I was happy to be with him as always, but deeply concerned about the pressure that I sensed when he talked about so many guys being wasted. He had used the term "wasted" before, and I had thought about it later. Yes, it was apropos; so many of our finest youth sacrificed, lost forever, and so many hearts broken. The Air Forces along the Mediterranean had been flying a thousand sorties a day for the past two weeks, concentrating on airfields and communication targets in Italy. It was no wonder the men were suffering from fatigue.

The following day when Captain Bradford Evans and Brunson came over, Evans told me that Bruns was again recommended for a DFC for the direct hit on the Brenner Pass. He added that Bruns was unhappy because he has forty-nine missions and has been grounded until his promotion to Captaincy came through. They had come over to invite the nurses to a party that the 20th and 29th Squadrons arranged. They needed to relax after the strenuous missions, and to get over the losses of comrades. Their morale needed a boost.

Dinner was served at 7:00 p.m. on the fourth floor of an old building in Tunis. We had delicious beef for the first time since we had been in Africa. Afterward, we meandered between the 20th and 29th Squadron Clubs. They were housed permanently in tents with wood floors that had been blow torched and oiled. We danced, sang the current favorite tunes, and romanced. Brunson looked solemn as he stood on the sidelines after being tagged. He was tired and disgusted with his C.O. for grounding him. He was definitely suffering flight fatigue. I was very concerned.

10 September 1943

It was a long day. I spent it lying on my cot, since it was sweltering. What a way to spend a day off! It was too hot to even go to mess until supper. Brunson didn't come. He said he would if he could get transportation. My consolation was mail from Bob, my fiancé, from Captain Donnely from the *Queen Mary*, and Lieutenant Bailey's family along with their friends in Bel Air, Maryland. His parents and sister were heartbroken. What sorrow for families, wives, and sweethearts! I continued to get mail from them now and then, as they seemed to get solace from keeping in touch with the last person to have been in touch with their son. For us, getting mail was our connection with the real world thousands of miles away, a reminder of another time and place.

12 September 1943

We still had many casualties from the Sicilian campaign, as well as those coming by ship from the invasion of Salerno in Italy. I enjoyed caring for our wounded; they were grateful for our being there. We reminded them of home, their families, sweethearts, wives. My only criticism was that we who were on Detached Service (D.S.) got no recognition for work done. We were outsiders, assigned to areas where the workload was the heaviest. The Evac personnel probably needed a rest and justifiably so in the campaigns fought in Africa. However we were too busy and tired at the end of these periods to remember to comment on the fact that others got credit and perhaps promotions, but we who filled in during the peak periods when casualties were at their worst, were forgotten. We were on our feet endless hours, and I was thoroughly convinced that the world was round, for I was continually climbing up hills.

18 September 1943

I had a half-day off and no plans, since I had not heard from Lieutenant Brunson in eight days. I slapped at flies and sweltered all afternoon. Toward evening I got enough energy to open my bedroll, sort through it and hung my dress-up blues on the tent pole after shaking out the wrinkles and dust. Time dragged interminably without any diversion from work.

24 September 1943

I had to move my possessions into another pyramidal tent because mine was going to be filled with new cut wheat. While I was in the process—perspiring, dusty from the wind and blown wheat, and dragging my bedroll—who should turn up but Brunson. He had just returned from R&R, (rest and recuperation) in Cairo. What a surprise after two weeks of loneliness. He stood at the rec tent while I washed and changed into my blues and joined him. He opened his musette bag filled with packages. He lifted out a very small box and as I opened it, said, "I remember your mentioning that Scarabs meant good luck. I hope this ring will bring us luck. Major Stone accompanied me and had friends in Cairo who helped us shop. The jeweler said it is very old and precious. It's the real McCoy. I hope you like it."

"Oh, Bruns, it's beautiful. I love it." It was a green petrified beetle with inscriptions in Hieroglyphs on its underside. He brought Channel No. 5, Xmas Night, and Omar Khayam perfumes, all wonderful fragrances. Also a gold U.S. insignia for my visor cap, a bottle of Coca-Cola and an Egyptian cake called Grappis, and a beautiful picture of himself and Major Stone on horseback in front of the Pyramids.

Major Stone and Captain Brunson,
on R&R in Egypt

Best of all, Brunson was his old self again. We got into the jeep and drove to Bizerte where we ate supper at the E.B.S. (Eastern Base Section.) Afterwards, he asked if he could put the Scarab on my left hand, third finger. I removed my diamond ring, placed it on my right hand finger, and he put the Scarab in its place. We embraced as he said, "That's the way I feel about you Rad. I love you and always will."

I was thrilled to be with him again. "I've missed you terribly, my dear. I never realized before how dependent I am on your being with me. I love you very much."

After we finished eating, we joined some couples who were walking along the beach of the very blue Mediterranean. During the sunset we sat on the beach and watched the whitecaps crash into waves that rolled unto the beach. We were together. Nothing else mattered.

My diary had many blank pages after that night, since each day was a repetition of the day before, and I was too tired at night to write. On my half-day off, I hemmed the seersucker uniforms that had been issued for hot weather. Until recently we had been wearing heavy twill fatigues. The only diversion was that the 105th Hospital nurses had joined us on Detached Service here at the 3rd General, as we kept receiving many more wounded GIs.

1 October 1943

Naples had fallen to the Fifth Army. I had heard that our Fortresses had been bombing it, although I had not heard from Brunson in more than a week.

2 October 1943

Brunson and Captain Wolfe came over to a dance here at the 3rd General Hospital. Wolfe had been seeing Edythe Mac Donald as long as I had been going with Brunson, but she and I never discussed our dates or the future, since we knew that army controlled everyone's lives. We exchanged partners and while I danced with Wolfe he reminded me that since Brunson had completed the required number of missions, he would be leaving the area soon. Brunson flew his 50th mission yesterday, on my day off. The target was Munich, Germany, but the weather was so heavily overcast they had to turn back even though they were over Germany. Brunson was now on Detached Service in Tunis with the 12th Air Force on Lieutenant General James Doolittle's staff.

4 October 1943

The ward workload was heavy again and I was asleep when nurse Andreko awakened me at nine to say that I should try to get a half-day off tomorrow because Brunson wanted me to come with the nurses that were going to be picked up to go to Tunis. The half-day off was granted and the next day the seven of us who were invited to La Goulette, to the 2nd Bomb Group's villa on the sea, were off. Bruns had asked one of the fellows who came to pick us up to be sure I came along if it was possible. We climbed into the weapons carrier, and after a long rough ride arrived hot and dusty.

I was disappointed to hear that Bruns was not at camp. He finally arrived at seven, full of apologies. He had spent the day looking for the 376th Bomb Squadron, a B-24 outfit that he was to join. He said he was to be on detached service with them if he ever found them. He last heard of them in Cairo.

We spent the day swimming in the sea, and in the evening danced to the record player while others played bridge. Brunson and I had only an hour together before we had to return to Mateur, since Wolfe was going to fly his 50th mission in the morning and they had to be in early. We rode back in the big truck since several of the fellows escorted their dates back to Mateur. Brunson and I sat close holding hands and whispering endearments. We knew that time was running out for us.

As we parted at my tent, he reminded me, "You have

my home address (he had printed it in my address book long ago), so you can reach me there as I have no idea where I will be assigned. I will write as soon as I know where I will be stationed. You know that I love you with all my heart." He held me close to his body as we kissed.

"Take care of yourself Brunson, I will miss you terribly. You have been the light of my life. It will be a long war without you near me."

6 October 1943

The rainy season had begun and we were wallowing in the mud again. I was on the ward alone, and was very busy, since Nurse Wagner, who had been assigned to help on the ward was off duty because she had been tossed out of a weapons carrier when it hit a deep rut in the road while riding last night. She was not seriously hurt, but would be off duty for a while.

10 October 1943

In the evening Wolfe and Brunson came over. I was surprised and happy to see Brunson once more. Edythe joined us and we went to the enlisted men's service club and had doughnuts and coffee, then went for a drive. We four always had a lot of fun, as Wolfe was such a clown. Edythe, too, was facing a parting now that Wolfe had flown his 50th mission. I was happy to be in Brunson's arms again, but parting was always difficult.

15 October 1943

I drove to Tunis with a group at noon, and heard that Brunson was gone. He had flown to Algiers, enroute to the States. I was stunned, yet we had been expecting it from day to day. We ate two suppers tonight, one at La Faloque, another later at the Tunisian Palace with an ordnance group, friends of the nurses I was with. They drove us back to Mateur afterwards.

18 October 1943

Today, we nurses from the Third Aux who had been on D.S. at the 3rd General Hospital were alerted to return to home camp at Bizerte at once. In the army, orders called for immediate action. Perhaps it was to confuse the enemy from discovering any move. I hurriedly rolled up my bedroll, packed my suitcase and we were on the road in two hours. We arrived at camp just as the sun was setting, and had a late supper. We were surprised to find no tents set up, and were told that we would sleep on the ground in the field tonight. We opened our bedrolls in the dark and, looking up at the stars and tired from the long ride, my eyes closed and I was asleep.

In the morning I awoke with aching muscles due to the rocks on the ground and bumps in the bedroll. We broke camp at three in the afternoon and were on our way to the Port at Bizerte where the Seminole, a Hospital ship, lay at anchor. I took many pictures, the last ones of Africa. It had been a great adventure. Africa was completely unlike the rest of the world.

The Company Dog

19 October 1943

As we prepared to leave Bizerte, several nurses decided to make certain that Whimpy, our GIs' dog, would be able to come with us. I had procured a small shoe bag to carry him in, but because of the long waiting period at the port, we had to let him out to stretch his legs. Just as we were about to depart the ferry that had brought us alongside the Hospital Ship Seminole, nurse Leonore Keyes decided she could charm the captain of the ship and simply carry Whimpy in her arms. As we filed past the captain of the ship, we heard him say in an inflexible loud voice, "Dogs are not allowed on board ship!"

Fortunately Gladys Snyder's chaplain friend, who was seeing us off, said he would take Whimpy back with him. We were sorry to lose our dear organizational mascot, and angry that we had listened to Keyes. Whimpy looked bewildered as the chaplain, a stranger to him, took him from Keyes. The dog balked when the chaplain tried to lead him on his leash toward the ferry. We heard him bay as the ferry began to return to port. We knew he would be heartbroken at losing all his friends, and we were fearful that he might stray and get lost in Bizerte. It was no place for a small dog to be stranded. We felt very anxious about him and saddened at the loss of a pet that had brought so much pleasure to camp life during our stay in Africa.

We would miss seeing him run across the campgrounds as he raced from tent to tent visiting his friends, drinking water from helmets that we kept near our cots for washing. He didn't seem to care if it was soapy. Yes, I would miss him, miss stroking his short black and white smooth coat and rubbing his stomach when he rolled over for more attention.

Stormy, another dog that Nurse Betty Ferber had recently adopted, was left behind in Bizerte with her friend in Company A. He was still a pup with reddish hair and large paws, a sign that he would grow into a big dog. I did not feel quite as badly leaving him behind, because I knew the men that took him would care for him.

The rumor whispered about was that we were returning to England to reunite with the half of our Third Auxiliary Group that had remained there while we were in Africa. Every trip was secret and full of speculation. After a wonderfully restful night on the hospital ship and a delicious breakfast of bacon and eggs we were surprised to be debarking at eleven the next morning in Sicily.

Because there was a water shortage in the buildings in the city, we were bivouacked in staging area No.3 in the usual pyramidal tent on low ground with course weeds underfoot. Nearby was Mondello, the resort town with beautiful homes on the beach and a Casino situated on the Sea. Here, General George S. Patton Jr. had established his Seventh Army Headquarters. Unauthorized personnel were not allowed in the vicinity. It was rumored that he had steaks flown in from the States for his staff and the correspondents that covered his army advances.

It was in Sicily that General Patton got in trouble while visiting a hospital. On seeing a young man walking about the ward he asked, "And what are you here for soldier?" The young man was trembling and mumbled something that gave General Patton the impression that he might be malingering. Patton slapped the poor soldier, calling him a coward. One of our Third Aux surgeons who was at the hospital at the time of the incident said that the soldier was suffering from malaria and was having chills.

Third Auxiliary Surgeons played a major roll in the Sicilian campaign, operating first on the beaches, and in the clearing stations. Many wounded were transported to the Field and Evacuation Hospitals in Matuer and Bizerte for treatment and recuperation until territory was gained to set up hospitals on the island. The war in Sicily ended on August 17, after thirty-seven days of fighting, with the Americans and British meeting at the northern coast at Messina.

Two weeks after our arrival in Sicily, we were surprised and delighted to see our Whimpy running as fast as his short legs could carry him toward our camping area, with the chaplain trailing behind. We were elated to have our little dog again. The chaplain had hitched a ride to Palermo on a B-25 bomber with a pilot friend.

Whimpy's master, Corporal Estel W. Tedder, had procured the four-week old tiny terrier from a French family while we were stationed in Constantine. We figured that since Tedder was on duty in the mess tent, he probably bartered with coffee, since the French relished it and it was in short supply, along with cigarettes that all Africans craved. Tedder was on K.P. duty as usual when we led the dog to the mess tent. Whimpy, spotting Tedder from a distance, raced toward him, while his master, surprised at seeing his pet, bent down with arms outstretched. Whimpy, with a flying leap, landed in Tedder's lap, began licking his master's face. It was a sight to watch the reunion between a dog and his master. Whimpy's tail wagged like a windshield wiper at high speed. Tedder just smiled and smiled, happy to have his dog again.

As soon as we found our way around, we began to explore the countryside, and were puzzled at seeing Sicilian women dressed in black, bent over, working in the fields. They were smaller than we, and all looked middle-aged. We surmised that they were in mourning until we discovered that black was the custom.

Our goal was sightseeing. Sicily dates back to the Stone Age, and has been the crossroads of past civilizations that influenced many diverse cultures, including ancient Greeks, Romans, Byzantines, Normans and Arabs. Our first site was the ancient cathedral carved out of rock where a princess had fled for refuge and lived here high on the topmost mountain. We visited the beautiful China house that Lord Nelson had built for Lady Hamilton and where they held their trysts. We explored the Catacombs where ancient skeletons lay displayed on shelves. A trip to another mountain took us to the Cathedral Monreole

Nurses Radawiec and Harper sight seeing in Polermo, Sicily

and its many ancient artifacts.

The 20th Engineers stationed on the island began to entertain us with movies and dancing parties at their club and invited us to join them at the home of a countess whom they had met. She offered us cocktails, our first since we left England, along with tomato sandwiches, ice cream, and coffee served demitasse. Many afternoons were spent sun-bathing on Mondello Beach, wading along the Mediterranean Sea, and now and then stopping at a small Sicilian restaurant for a fish dinner on the beach.

Our new officer acquaintances invited Edythe McDonald and me to attend the wedding of *Nino e Costanza*. The ceremony was conducted at a Catholic Church in Palermo and the reception held in the adjoining church garden. Champagne, wine, and a variety of cakes and pastries were served to the guests and family members. The newly wedded couple asked us to stand with them for the photographer, and within a few days I received a copy of the photo.

Since the war in Sicily was finished, our stay here was simply to wait until the army decided where to send us next. I, along with Merle Harper, Edythe MacDonald, Isobel Johnson, and Eleanor Bernick, managed a ride into Palermo in an army truck. The GI drivers dropped us off in the business sec-tion, where we wandered up and down the main street peering into shop windows to see if there was anything we might be interested in. We found the merchandise was too outdated for our taste, but we still wanted a few souvenirs, so we bought dainty sheer linen embroi-dered handkerchiefs, doi-lies, a leather cigarette case, novelties we hadn't seen in

Sailboating off Sicily
Nurses Bernick, Harper,
Radawiec and MacDonald

a long time.

When it came time to return to camp we hired an open carriage that we saw standing near the square. The Sicilian driver sat up high in the front seat holding onto the reins of two spirited horses that were very nervous because of the crowd that soon surrounded us. The natives had seen very few American women before the war. Because there were five of us, we had to have two carriages, three in one and two in the other. Since the distance to camp was the same for both, the drivers kept signaling to each other with arms raised, fingers indicating how much they should charge us, as the fee ought to be the same no matter how overcharged we would be. The horses gave their drivers a hard time; perhaps they recognized us as enemies. They balked and were very nervous as we neared the camp area. The horses would not go through the gate that opened into the site of our camp. The drivers stopped, and we had to walk the rest of the way. There was the usual haggling about the fare, because both drivers needed to arrive at the same price. It was solved in Italian gibberish, and as expected we probably paid twice the normal price.

I met Captain Frank Bane of the 20th Engineers at a gathering his company had arranged. We danced to the victrola music, and played bridge with Betty and her new friend. Frank was a tall, lean young man with dark brown hair, hazel eyes, and firm clean-cut appearance. He stood erect, his shoulders broad in neat summer khakis. As we chatted, he confided that he was considering making army a career after finishing his education at the University of Virginia. Our friendship of about two weeks was cut short when his company was suddenly quarantined due to an outbreak of diphtheria, and my unit was alerted to leave Sicily.

Chapter 5:
Return To England

11 November 1943

The weather turned cold, and with it came the rain as we wallowed in the mud, confined to our tents speculating as to where we would go next. Would it be Italy, southern France, or perhaps the Pacific theater of war? We were again faced with the problem of getting Whimpy aboard ship as when we departed from Bizerte.

At four a.m. the usual departure time, we were surprised to find a ground meat patty being dropped into our mess kit for breakfast. It was the first time we were served meat in our organization since we left England nine months before. What a break for our Whimpy, I thought. I saved a bit for the dog, and when we got back to our tent, I wrapped the meat around a minute dose of Seconal in a capsule. We would put him to sleep before we got aboard ship this time. I placed the meat on the ground while my tent mates, Marie Miller and Edna Parker, watched anxiously to be sure that he ate it. Unfortunately, the meat crumpled, and the capsule fell out. I bent down to pick it up, but as I reached for it, Whimpy lunged at it, and it was gone.

As usual in the army, it was "hurry up and wait," for hours. I had to let Whimp out of the bag and kept him within a small circle of nurses who were anxious to help get the dog aboard. It was noon before it was our turn to board the ship Monterey. We repeated the Seconal, wrapped this time in a bit of chocolate, and when he got sleepy, I stuffed him into the bag. I walked up the gangplank with my precious bundle without further ado.

He was free in our stateroom except when the ship's mate rapped at the door to come in to clean the bathroom. When we heard the knock, one of us girls grabbed the dog and scurried into the nearest bunk and threw the covers over both herself and the dog. He was never discovered on board ship by any of the crew during the entire two weeks it took to reach our destination. As usual when on board ship, we nurses took over the work in the infirmary, while their staff was assigned other tasks aboard ship. There were the usual accidents, seasickness, and a few wounded to care for. The U-boats were still a threat as they scoured the Mediterranean Sea. I spent my free time on deck searching the horizon for submarines.

On November 26 the Monterey docked at the Firth of Clyde in Scotland, where we repeated the procedure with the sleeper and placed Whimpy in the bag, and had no problem as we debarked. However, our troop train had not arrived, and we were faced with having to wait at the station. We were aware of England's rigid laws about importing dogs and had heard that even General Eisenhower's dog had to be impounded for a long time. We waited anxiously.

While we waited for the train, Whimpy awoke. Confused, tired and cramped, he began to protest by barking furiously. I caught sight of the stationmaster as he began looking for the barker. The girls closed in to conceal the dog while the GIs, alarmed after recognizing the bark and seeing the stationmaster looking about the crowd, began barking to distract him. Other GIs, among the thousands in various other organizations waiting at the station, joined in the barking, harassing the man to give up the search. The troop train pulled in, and we got aboard. Nobody could possibly stop us now. We got off the train in Litchfield where Whimpy was just one more dog on the post.

While walking Whimpy on the campgrounds with Edythe Macdonald and Merle Harper one afternoon, I noticed a large dog running toward us. As he closed in and pounced toward Whimpy, I picked up our small dog high above my head, while the big dog kept jumping up trying to grab his leg. One of the girls finally grabbed the big dog by the collar and led him away while I dashed toward the barracks.

Litchfield was like being back in the States with all the comforts of beds, chairs, tables, showers, a PX, and an officers club. We were back in England, and Whimpy was free to roam the camp again, visiting his friends. I was told that when I was away on detached service, Whimpy spent many hours lying on my bed.

After a month in Litchfield we moved to Bewdley Barracks near the village of Stourport, where we rejoined the other half of the Third Aux that had remained in England under Major Clifford Graves's Command while we were in Africa and Sicily. We settled in wooden barracks and waited for the invasion of the continent. Bewdley camp was barren of trees and shrubs. It spread over a hill with many hutments spaced over a bleak countryside. A large water reservoir just off the walkway between our hutments was a curiosity. We figured it was there to put the fire out in case of an air raid. We could hear the Luftwaffe fly over us on their way to bomb London every night.

Front row: Whimpy, Nurses Radawiec, Ferber, Ryan, Watry and Aird. Back row: Nurses Ford, Bernick, Asselin, Kirschling, Grimes, Jessop, Major Hudson and Nurse Nace

Two surgeons in our group, Major Whitsitt and Captain Black, upon returning from an assignment in Birmingham at blackout, asked directions on how to get to the hutments. They were told to "just follow the walk." As they hurried along

227

on the narrow walk, with Whitsitt well in front, Captain Black trailing behind heard a terrific splash followed by an ominous silence. Captain Black stopped in his tracks, bewildered. What was this, an ambush? Had the camp been seized by German parachutists? Then he called out.

"Whitsitt, where are you, can you hear me?"

No answer. That meant foul play. Drawing his scalpel the only weapon he had, Captain Black advanced slowly ready to snatch his comrade from the enemy. Finally, as he was able to pierce the darkness, he saw Whitsitt's head in the middle of the placid pool. "Why you son of a gun! Why don't you say something?"

"Damn it, Blackie, at least you could do me the pleasure of walking in too!" That was their baptism into Camp Bewdley.

Our days were spent attending lectures on various topics from outside speakers' experiences. Major Graves arranged demonstrations illustrating the practical side of field surgery. Here the veterans of Africa and Sicily showed how to make Tobruk splints, flutter valves, pelvic rests, suction pumps, and many other useful devices. Nurses taught the GIs sterile technique and explained the purpose of the surgical instruments that they would have to become familiar with as well as the technique of hypodermic injections, and Wangensteen therapy: inserting a long thin rubber tube into the nostril then forcing it through the esophagus into the stomach. This procedure created a means of relieving discomfort or distention in abdominal surgery by removing fluid and gas from the stomach and intestines by way of constant mild negative pressure. Of course, the routine bedside care of the sick was always emphasized.

In our spare time we walked to the nearby village for tea in a quaint teashop and took trips to more distant cities by way of the big trucks. We sang our way through many parts of England during our travels. The more adventurous people took off for London on weekend leaves. Christmas in 1943 was celebrated in camp, since traffic into London was prohibited because of limited hotel space. On New Year's Eve we drove to Reading and at midnight joined a group of jovial English folk at the town square. At the stroke of twelve we joined together with arms around each other's shoulders and greeted the New Year singing "Auld Lange Syne."

1 January 1944

We settled into the usual camp routine of lectures, drills, marches, and teaching GIs. We laundered our clothes by hand, and hung them in the warming room on slats. I fought to keep a fire going in the small stove, and scoured the place for newspaper to restart it in the mornings. We walked to the mess hall through melting snow and mud in the bitter cold three times a day, and took the bus to the movies in the nearby small town. We often took the train to London where there was always much entertainment and excitement while we waited for the invasion of the continent.

Operation Tiger: D-Day Rehearsal

Between March 27 and April 22, 1944, twenty Third Auxiliary Surgical teams consisting of four surgeons and four enlisted men on each team departed our camp at Bewdley to join Medical Battalions in the southern part of Devon at Slapton Sands off the coast of the English Channel. Volunteers for the gliders and parachutists were called, with many applicants among the men in our unit. The southern part of England was overrun with men and equipment preparing for the greatest assault in history. The inhabitants were overwhelmed by the giant tanks, monstrous bulldozers, long-toms, armored cars, grotesque DUKWs (boats on wheels,) trucks, and jeeps, all crowding the country lanes that rarely had seen anything larger than a bicycle. Roaring planes, clattering tanks, and trucks filled with soldiers sharing the road with farmers' carts and bicycles made one aware that life would go on in spite of the war.

Several of our teams were assigned to the 29th Division and were sent out to sea to practice landings against an imagined enemy. Doctors felt the maneuvers were more exhausting, more painful and testing than the real thing. The maneuvers were called Tiger, Duck, and Beaver.

Major Darrell A. Campbell, a surgeon, tells his version of the maneuvers in our history of the Third Auxiliary Surgical Group book titled *Front Line Surgeons*, authored by Clifford L. Graves, M.D., a comrade-in-arms. The following is Major Campbell's story:

We left Torquay on open trucks in driving rain. Of course it was midnight. In the army you always move at midnight. We tried to protect ourselves with our raincoats and with the tarpaulins but it was futile. Nothing keeps rain out of an open truck.

From Torquay to the Bristol Channel is only about a hundred miles, just a nice jog when you are out joy riding, but that open truck took five hours over it. Early in the morning, before the sun had made even a dent in the grayness, we got out—cold, wet, and numb. Thank goodness, we're through with that, we thought, and looked around hopefully for a place to warm up. Our place was a nice, cozy DUKW, (duck) but it wasn't warm. We piled in.

A duck is a great invention, but the novelty of riding in one soon wears off. They're not made for comfort. When the water is the least bit rough, you get a constant spray. With us it didn't make much difference because we were wet already. There was a brisk southwestern blowing and the sea got rougher the farther out we got. After we fed the fish with our breakfast of biscuits and cheese, we turned around and came right back to the same spot we started from. Now for a good hot breakfast, we thought. Our C.O. had other plans. "Get up that hill and make it snappy!" he hollered.

The hill was long and sandy and it got pretty steep towards the end. When we got to the top, we were bushed. "Pitch tents," came the order. "And make it snappy." Have you ever tried to pitch a tent when you are sick to your stomach, wet to the bone, panting for breath, and shaking with exertion? Brother, it's no fun.

And then, after all that mad dash, we just sat there for three days. Yes, sir, we just sat there and lived on chocolate bars and stale cheese, not so much as a cup of coffee. From that little trip I learned just one thing: if you survive one maneuver, you're good for ten battles.

Captain Abraham Horvitz's experience was a real battle, a one-sided one. It follows:

It was on the morning of April 27, 1944 that we left Plymouth Harbor. The code name for the maneuver was TIGER. It was a Thursday morning. The sun was warm and bright and was reflected like myriads of dancing diamonds from the water of the Channel. It was a peaceful Channel, and we were all set for a pleasure cruise.

We had embarked a couple of days before and waited in the harbor for the maneuver to begin. The actual maneuver was to take place at Slapton Sands, a number of miles farther up the South Coast of England. It was a practice invasion, dress rehearsal for D-Day. According to the plan, we were supposed to leave for the invasion coast on that morning but not to land on the beach until the morning of the following day.

Our own convoy consisted of seven LST's, each loaded to the gills with implements and personnel for invasion; six hundred men approximately in addition to the crew. Our Company B of the 261st Medical Battalion and its attached two surgical teams were on LST #511, the third from the end in the line of seven as we left Plymouth. As we steamed out, the routine General Quarters alarm was sounded. It means a call to battle stations. Everyone proceeds at once to the position or job he is to occupy in case of battle. It's a rather frightening sound—loud enough to wake the dead. Everyone remains at his station until the signal is given that General Quarters is over. Our team was to take its station in the wardroom. That is the small club and dining room for the officers. It was located in the mid portion of the ship's upper deck level. It all being practice, we just went there when the General Quarters alarm sounded and remained there until it was over.

It was a beautiful morning. The seven ships made an impressive sight outlined against the clear sky. One of the ship's ensigns told me we were scheduled to pass by Slapton Sands some time during the middle of the afternoon but that we would continue on by, moving slowly along the Channel, turn around during the night, and come in to land on the beach at 8:00 the next morning. I asked the ensign if we were to have any protection now that we were moving out into the Channel.

"There's supposed to be a Corvette somewhere," he said.

It was around 3:00 o'clock in the afternoon when we passed Slapton Sands. We could make out some of the activity going on around the beach. The first boats were supposed to have landed and discharged their personnel and materiel at 8:00 o'clock that morning. We could hear some guns. Everything was proceeding according to plan. We continued on moving farther out into the Channel. The coast jutted outward and we lost sight of the beach.

Maurice Schneider and I decided to turn in about midnight. The majors had their quarters on deck level along with the Naval officers. The rest of us slept in bunks in a compartment in the forward part of the ship—the first level below deck. The enlisted men had to sleep anywhere they could make themselves reasonably comfortable.

It was exactly 2:00 A.M. when General Quarters alarm went off. We, thinking it was but practice, were hesitant to get dressed, but that was all decided when one of the crew came rushing through, closing off the steel watertight compartment doors. "This is it, boys," he said. "Ship torpedoed behind us!" We dressed, put on our life belts and helmets and ran up on deck, intending to go on to the wardroom. As we came out on deck, we saw a large orange moon hanging very low on the horizon. It looked as though it was just about to fall into the water. It was cool, and we were shivering a little; maybe it wasn't entirely the cold. What attracted our attention almost immediately was a large fire burning out in the Channel about a mile behind us. It was obviously the last LST in our convoy—burning and going down. U-boats or E-boats? We didn't know that minute.

There was only one LST behind us now. We could make out its outlines readily in the light of the moon. It was coming on about a hundred yards behind us. Suddenly there was a terrific explosion. It had a dull sound, as though a great heavy mass had fallen onto a heavily carpeted floor. The LST right behind us burst into a great mass of flame all at once. The torpedo must have struck her in the powder magazine because she seemed to have disintegrated with that one burst. Things began to happen on our own ship. It wasn't more than a minute, and all hell seemed to break loose all around me. Colored flashes of light filled the sky. For a stunned second I didn't realize what they were. But then I knew—tracer bullets. The yellow and purple ones were coming out of the water from German E-Boats. The pink ones were going into the water from our own anti-aircraft guns.

There was a lot of confusion and shouting on deck. If I knew then what I have learned since, I would have fallen flat on my stomach and stayed there, but I didn't. I ducked my head and ran, and after what seemed an age finally reached the middle portion of the ship, found a doorway and dashed in. I decided I'd better get to the wardroom. As I came down the narrow corridor toward the wardroom, a soldier came running toward me, holding his hands over his belly.

"I've been hit," he cried.

He fell down at my feet. I looked at his clothing, and they appeared to be undamaged. I thought at first that maybe he was hysterical, but when I opened his shirt, there was an abdominal wound where the fragment had entered. I had some soldiers carry him into the wardroom. Now that I had something to do, I felt better. Casualties began to be brought in. We administered first aid and treated shock. There was nothing else that we could do at the time.

While we worked, the shooting on our boat stopped. It hadn't lasted very long, maybe a few minutes, but the show wasn't over. The E-boats sent a torpedo into the LST directly in front of us. Then came some more shooting. The convoy was now breaking up. It was every ship for itself. We headed for nearest land, which was twenty miles away. We couldn't send for help because of radio silence. To use the radio would reveal our positions as well as that of the boats that still remained afloat. Later, I found out that the Captain of our ship had no chart, no idea of the minefields that had been laid down by the British. We never saw the Corvette that was supposed to protect us. Later we learned that it had been sunk.

We sat and waited for the torpedo we knew would come. Our work was done. There was nothing more to do but wait, but the torpedo never came. The only way we could figure it was that they had run out of torpedoes. Nothing else was there to stop them.

At about 6:00 o'clock in the morning in the gray mist we were able to make out land. Columbus himself couldn't have been happier at the sight of land than we were that morning. An hour later, we anchored in the little harbor of Weymouth. The other LST's showed up. Four of us left out of seven. Two behind us had been sunk, the one in front hit but still afloat and later pulled in.

We unloaded our 19 casualties from our LST. These included the captain who had been hit in the leg while standing on the bridge, the executive officer who lost his right eye, and the radioman who was hit in the arm and in the scrotum; he lost one testicle. Fortunately no one on our ship was killed. Ralph Coffey went along with those evacuated to the nearest hospital, the British Naval Hospital at Weymouth. The rest of us remained on board.

Shortly before noon we got under way again. General Quarters alarm was sounded as we were leaving the harbor. I knew it was routine, yet it evoked similar emotions to those I had felt the previous night. It was as though a conditioned reflex had suddenly taken possession of me. This time, as we came out of the harbor, two British destroyers joined us. It was like closing the barn after the horse is gone, but we were very happy to have them. Almost 800 lives were lost in that maneuver. We felt that it had been a rather expensive session. We landed at Slapton Sands at 8:00 o'clock that evening, just twelve hours behind schedule. The earth felt good under our feet.

Our clearing station was set up exactly as it was going to be set up on the invasion beach a month later. I pitched my pup tent for the first time. I fell asleep right away but was awakened by an air raid during the middle of the night. A German plane was shot down just a short distance from our field. As it fell, it sounded as though it was coming right down on my little tent, but that's the way they always sound. Saturday and Sunday were beautiful days and we relaxed in the sun. On Monday, May 1, we packed up and drove back to our camp at Truro. The maneuver was over. We all got drunk that night. Casualty figures often differ in number, and whether these 785 included navy and Englishmen on the Corvette that was sunk was not clear.

When our men returned to camp from the invasion practice, we heard whispers of the many lives lost in the practice run at Slapton Sands. We were shocked and wondered at what lay ahead when the English Channel would have to be crossed. The incident was hushed up. The army did not want the Germans to know about their U-boat successes: the sinking of two LCI's, the damaging to the third LCT that had to be towed into dock and the Corvette with the loss of more than seven hundred men in the Slapton Sands practice run. The disastrous Tiger exercise when nine German E boats discovered in the Channel by chance, was not made public until 1987, when an Englishman found the traces of war sunk off the beach near his tavern in Slapton Sands.

Besides the men on the Tiger exercise, one other Third Auxer came close to losing his life on maneuvers. This was Captain Torp. Torp had asked for his assignment to the Third Aux "so that I could devote myself to professional work." It was on the Duck maneuver that Torp met his Waterloo.

Troops were debarking from LST's into LCI's. The trick was to slide down a rope ladder and make a neat contact with the bobbing, slippery surface below. In calm weather this was easy. In rough weather when both vessels were rocked in uneven rhythm, it was decidedly tricky. When Torp started down, he knew that he was in for trouble. In the first place, he was not used to violent exertions and in the second place, his physical proportions made it difficult for him to see what was going on down below. Halfway down he hesitated. Should he try to reach that treacherous void or should he clamber back towards the safety of the mother vessel? In this extremity he had an open mind.

It so happened that on the other side of the ship a similar debarkation was taking place. A loud-mouthed boatswain with a megaphone was bellowing to one of his men, "Let go, you fathead!" His voice carried to all parts of the ship. To Torp it was the inspiration he had been waiting for. Without a further look he released his hold and obeyed the law of gravity, a most natural thing to do for a man of his dimensions.

At this moment the two vessels were separated about six feet and into this chasm Torp disappeared. Sailors sprung into action. They lowered ropes, threw out life belts, kept the ships from grinding together. A few minutes later Torp was standing on the deck of the LCI, surrounded by his half-snickering, half-solicitous teammates. "A fine outfit this is. Here I expect to do professional work and look how I wind up. I Quit!"

Romance Problems

Romance flourished as GIs and Officers in England waited for the Invasion of the Continent to take place. Although over fifty thousand Americans acquired English wives overseas, the course of true love in those days was not a smooth one. The army, with an eye on the many natural obstacles, had set up an elaborate cooling-off process.

A request to marry had to be passed up the line of command to its ultimate pinnacle, a journey of many weeks. Then, if the decision was favorable, the applicants had to wait sixty days before they could apply for a license. One Third Auxer decided to overcome the hurdle. He filed the papers to wed his girl.

Three weeks went by, four, five, and Joe was now in the staging area with one foot in the Channel water. He investigated at the Medical Battalion Headquarters. No one had even seen Joe's letter. Disgusted, Joe was on his way out the door when a sergeant spoke up. "Wait a minute, Captain. Maybe it's in that pile over there." The sergeant pointed to a stack of papers that had been gathering dust for weeks.

Joe started leafing through. Suddenly he jumped a foot. "Here it is. Permission granted!" But applicants must wait sixty days from date of last endorsement. That was bad news.

With the invasion perhaps only weeks away, Joe was sunk. Nobody had authority to waive the waiting period except army headquarters. Another letter would surely bog down. Joe decided to rewrite the letter and hand carry it. It meant he had to get all the intermediate signatures himself: First, the unit chaplain; next, the commanding officer of the clearing company; next the commanding officer of the medical battalion; then the commanding general of the Engineers Special Brigade; and finally Army Headquarters. Joe learned to present his story with heart-rending fashion after so much practice. Wherever he went, he got at least an encouraging handshake and a sympathetic nod. Then he reached the end of the trail, the office of the Adjutant General.

There he struck a snag. In his ignorance that Army Headquarters still considered the invasion a top secret, Joe blurted out that he wanted to get married "before the invasion."

"What invasion?" inquired the colonel casually.

"Why, the invasion of Europe, of course."

"Did you tell anyone that you were going on an invasion, Captain?" asked the colonel, gradually warming up to such a dangerous possibility.

"Why . . . no sir, not in so many words," said Joe, completely floored by this unexpected twist in the conversation.

"Captain, as far as you and your friends are concerned, you are here for a change and a rest. Now, go away. Don't bother me any more."

As Joe reached the door, the stern man suddenly relented.

"You might see the chaplain though."

The army chaplain was a man whose religion was measured strictly in terms of directives. But there was something in Joe's urgent pleading that made him soften.

"I want to see the girl. If she is all you say, we will give you permission."

Joe was elated. He dashed out the door for the nearest telephone booth. "Get on the train right away, dear. You've got to be here by tomorrow morning. Better get yourself a ring. I won't have time to buy one."

The south coast of England was a restricted area. No civilians could get in or out, except by special pass. Joe's bride-to-be had no pass but she had plenty of pluck. She talked her way past the police and met Joe at the appointed hour. The chaplain was impressed. He not only gave the couple his blessing but he even made the adjutant sign the papers right away. At last things were beginning to move.

Flushed with their success, the couple now went to Torquay. There was no time to lose. Joe's medical battalion had been alerted and would be bottled up tight in a few days. Telegrams went out. Kay's parents and friends were to be in Torquay the next day. Now for a priest. That was easy. The priest listened sympathetically. Yes, he would be delighted but did the affianced have their license? Joe had been so wrapped up in army regulations that he had forgotten completely about the civil procedure. To the county clerk's office he went. The clerk was all smiles. For the small fee of ten shillings he would publish the banns, and Joe could pick up the license three days later.

"Three days from now?" Joe stammered. "Why that's ridiculous. I'll be with my outfit then!"

"Sir, I'm sorry but that's the law, and I have never made an exception in all my forty years in office."

Stymied by a stubborn county clerk! Who was this pip-squeak anyway? Joe would carry his cause to the registrar himself. But the registrar was adamant. Not even the invasion could change English law. Things looked bleak. Another precious day had passed and Joe was no nearer his goal. With hanging head and sagging spirits he returned to Torquay.

The next day started badly. Wedding guests were beginning to arrive. Kay was in a dither. The people in the hotel wanted to know what time the wedding would take place. Joe felt sick. He wanted to get away from it all. Mumbling some feeble excuse, he put on his coat and wandered back to battalion headquarters. Here things were even worse. Orders had arrived. The office was being packed up. Husky GIs were tugging at the desks, the tables, and the safe. Joe sat down. He lit a cigarette and cursed all the county officials in the world.

Suddenly he heard a familiar voice. It was the

adjutant who had let Joe's letter gather dust.

"Well, if it isn't Captain Joe! How are you, Doc.?"

Joe could have killed the fellow but he restrained himself and said something about the weather.

"And what became of your request, Captain? Did it ever come through?"

"Blast it all!" said Joe. "A fellow might as well try flying to the moon. I've seen everybody from a two-bit county clerk to the general and no luck. I think I'll go and hang myself."

"Wait a minute, Captain. The brigade chaplain is a friend of mine. He knows a lot of people. I'll call him right away."

Joe accepted the suggestion with reservation. A few minutes later the adjutant came back.

"The Chaplain wants to see you right away, Captain. He is at headquarters."

The Chaplain listened to Joe as if he were listening to his own son. "We've got to see you through, Captain. I know the monsignor at Eppington. Let's go and see him." The monsignor listened sympathetically but he confessed that he was powerless. No one had authority to tamper with the law of His Majesty's government. There followed a long list of reasons, but Joe wasn't even listening. He was just thinking about all the people at Torquay who were waiting for the wedding. Then the chaplain spoke up.

"Father, would you have any objection if we saw the bishop about this?"

"Impossible. The bishop has just had a serious operation. He is in the hospital at Tavistock. No one is allowed to see him."

The chaplain and Joe went outside. "We're going to Tavistock," said the chaplain.

At Tavistock, the bishop was recuperating from nothing more serious than a tooth extraction, and he listened closely to the two American officers.

"And is there nothing that can be done for this

impetuous officer and his charming fiancée?" was the chaplain's closing question.

"Well, now, let me see. We had a case here during the last war. I believe there is a rule that this provision may be waived for members of the Forces. It's never come up before, but I see no reason why we could not apply the same rule to American servicemen. Wait a minute."

The bishop picked up the phone. A long conversation ensued. Then came the verdict: Joe could get his license right away. The bishop called the monsignor. The monsignor called the priest. The priest called the county clerk. The county clerk opened his office. The guests were notified. The license was issued. The priest came down. Joe and Kay were married. They had a one-day honeymoon and have lived happily ever after.

Bewdley

In Bewdley, while waiting for the invasion, surgeons and nurses continued training the enlisted men for the work ahead. After their experience in Africa and Sicily, the surgeons, now veterans, gave orders with knowledge and authority to the supply officers. Under the surgeons' supervision electricians wired reflectors, batteries, and operating lights. Carpenters built stock tables, sawhorses, and plasterboards. Ordnance mechanics made Mayo stands, intravenous poles, and water taps. Technicians tested autoclaves, basic sets, and medical chests. Nurses sewed laparotomy sheets, glove containers, and muslin wrappers. Buck privates pitched tents, strung wire, and fired stoves. Anesthesia machines and suction machines were obtained at the last moment.

I was sent to the 120th Station Hospital at Tortworth Court, in Gloster, for a six-day course in anesthesia. A month later I went on D.S. to the 305th Station Hospital for three weeks of practical work in anesthesiology by the various methods: ether inhalation, spinal injection of procaine, sodium pentathal by intravenous injection, and the nitrous oxide-oxygen machine. I got quite adept in the spinal block type of anesthetizing the lower half of one's body, and preferred it to all the other types of anesthetic whenever I had a choice. It was a process of injecting a long needle with a procaine solution between the lumbar vertebrae, resulting in numbness to the lower half of the body.

On returning to Bewdley, I saw Whimpy on my bed and was told that he often spent time there while I was on D. S. It was in the middle of May that I missed Whimpy's daily visit to our hut and was concerned about him. Three of us girls went to the headquarters hut to inquire about him and were told that the officer who was in charge while our C.O. was away had sent Whimpy to the local humane shelter. We were very upset and promptly got a ride to the shelter to retrieve him because we felt that that the officer might have taken his authority too seriously. When we arrived and inquired about our Whimpy, the person in charge told us that they had been instructed to euthanize him immediately. We were shocked to hear that our little dog was dead. It was true that with the invasion day approaching, he would present a problem, but it had never occurred to us that this would mean death to our pet. When we told the enlisted men what had happened, they were very distressed. They said that anyone of their English girl friends would have been happy to take Whimpy. Needless to say, the officer who had ordered Whimpy to be put to sleep became the most detested person by those who were attached to the little dog. That dog had won our hearts and cheered us through the Africa and Sicily campaigns.

We continued to drill and march daily to keep in physical condition for what lay ahead. There had been some changes in our personnel as officers and nurses were assigned to evacuation hospitals and our C.O., Colonel Blatt, changed places with Lieutenant Colonel Elmer A. Lodmell from the 44th Evacuation Hospital.

Chapter 6:
Invasion of France

6 June 1944 – D-Day

At midnight, two Third Auxiliary Surgical Teams boarded the Horsa gliders along with paratroopers, in the southern part of England and flew across the Channel to land behind enemy lines beyond Utah Beach. It was D-Day, H minus 4 and 1/2 hours, when Major James J. Whitsitt, who crossed with the 307th Glider-borne Medical Company and landed on French soil at 1:30 a.m. The following is his experience:

They left England shortly after midnight. The glider approached the coast from the west as the clouds broke, and he could see land clearly. Suddenly there was a clatter on the hull of the glider.

"What's that?" Whitsitt asked.

Colonel Eaton, Chief of the Division Staff, pointed to the three jagged tears in the fabric. "Flak!"

Streaks of fire climbed up from the ground. Little balls whizzed past and disappeared in space. They looked like fireworks, but Whitsitt knew better. These were tracer bullets. The glider was down to five hundred feet, and they broke formation. Then all hell broke loose. The Germans were heavily entrenched at Ste. Mere-Eglise and had been warned of the approaching flight. Anti-aircraft batteries opened up, sending balls of fire from a dozen points. Below, a road lined with trees stood out in the glow of shell-bursts. This was the drop zone!

The green light flashed, the rope parted the craft from the plane, and it went into a rapid descent. His eyes fixed on the field ahead, Whitsitt braced himself. They overshot. The glider hit a tree, spun around, and rammed its nose in the ground, spilling the men like matches out of a box. It was H minus 4 ½ hours. (Land troops would invade at 6:30 a.m.)

Whitsitt was stunned. He had been pitched thirty feet. Next to him was Colonel Eaton. Whitsitt crawled over. "Are you hurt, Colonel?"

"I don't think so, but my knee sure hurts, I can't move it."

Whitsitt investigated the glider. The pilot had been killed and the rest of the occupants had scattered. Machine-gun fire raked the field. Whitsitt ducked. In the darkness there was little he could do. All around, paratroopers engaged German patrols in hand-to-hand combat. The first man to give his position away was lost. Whitsitt crawled back to the colonel, who was suffering great pain. He injected him with morphine and dragged him into a ditch as light began to show on the horizon. The wrecked glider made a target for the German mortar crew in the next field. Two shells came close. Then he saw something that made him rub his eyes and look again. A figure was coming down the road, and a most unmilitary figure at that. It was a French boy, leading a donkey cart! Just as if nothing had happened, this boy was on his daily chore of feeding the cattle or whatever he was wont to do at six o'clock in the morning. Whitsitt did not speculate. "Damn it," he said to Colonel Eaton. "If that boy can do it so can we." He rose up and motioned the boy to come forward.

"Bon matin, mon garcon. What about the cart?"

"Mon Dieu! Les Americains!" There followed a torrent of words.

Whitsitt cut the boy short. The situation called for action, not words. He lifted the colonel on the cart, took the donkey by the reins, and mustered his best French:

"Allons!" The little procession moved off.

They had barely gone a hundred yards when the Germans spotted them. Bullets hit the cart and the donkey. Whitsitt dived for the ditch. The boy started to run. He was cut down. Whitsitt gnashed his teeth. "I knew I should never have started this," he said to himself.

A German grenade landed at his feet. He picked it up and threw it back. His aim could not have been more perfect. The explosion killed two Germans and discouraged the others from further interference. Miraculously, Colonel Eaton, still on the cart, escaped injury. Whitsitt remained pinned down for several hours. He knew he could make no progress as long as he tried to transport the colonel at the same time. He helped the colonel to the ditch. "You better stay here, sir. I am going on a reconnaissance."

He had learned his lesson and moved cautiously. There were plenty of dead Germans in his path but no live ones, and he reached Turqueville where he knew there was a first aid post set up in a house. There were a dozen casualties, none of them serious. Whitsitt commandeered a jeep and went back to get the colonel. He was lucky. Within a half hour he was back.

On his return he found the aid post swamped. Turqueville was and island of American troops, and there was sharp fighting. Many of the casualties needed immediate attention. There was no time to be lost. He selected the kitchen as an operating theater. He improvised a table, boiled his instruments, ransacked the bedrooms for linen, and taught the dental officer to give ether. From then on there was no rest.

Towards nightfall small-arms fire came closer and closer. A paratrooper reported that the woods surrounding Turqueville were alive with Germans. This was a sizable body of German troops, that were retreating from the coast towards Ste Mere Eglise. Trapped, they established themselves between Turqueville and Fauville, in the very area where Whitsitt now found himself.

As yet there was no contact with the 4th Division. Everything depended on whether the paratroopers would stand their ground. All night the issue was in doubt. Whitsitt had no time to follow the battle at first hand, but he received periodic reports while he was working at the operating table. A corporal assumed the job of special liaison agent. Triumphantly, this man would stick his head in the doorway and exclaim from time to time: "Major, we just got another one!"

"Good," Whitsitt would reply without stopping. In the morning German bodies littered the woods. But the paratroopers suffered too, and the facilities of the station were totally inadequate. For Whitsitt there was no relief until the next morning, when the 4th Division troops finally entered Turqueville. Their arrival relieved a desperate situation. The house was filled with casualties, whose only chance of survival depended on rapid evacuation to the beach. Colonel Eaton was among the men taken out. He shook hands with Whitsitt, saying, "Major, if it were not for you, I'd be a dead duck."

Still not knowing anything about the rest of his team, Whitsitt proceeded to Hiesville as soon as the last casualty had left Turqueville. At Hiesville he found Major Albert J. Crandall and his men up to their ears in work. Immediately, Whitsitt pitched in. It was not until the next day that he learned where his own clearing station was.

Major Albert J. Crandall and his team were attached to the 326th Glider-borne Medical Company of the 101st Airborne Division. The first wave consisted of 6,600 parachute and glider troops. Crandall and his team followed in the 51 gliders that carried command personnel, anti-tank weapons, and part of the 326th Medical Company. For the first time in history, a complete surgical team was to be glider-landed in enemy territory. He was the surgical spearhead. Take-off was at H minus 5 hours.

There was little talk in Crandall's glider. Everyone thought of what the next hours would bring. After an hour and a half the steady roar of the tow planes was broken by the angry crescendo of a Nazi fighter. It passed directly overhead and disappeared as quickly as it had come. The tow planes scattered; the road was in sight. On the short flight from St. Sauveur to Ste. Mere Eglise, the gliders ran through a heavy anti-aircraft barrage. Crandall tried to orient himself through the din. He had a mental picture of the country and he recognized the inundated area without difficulty. Flak eased up. On went the warning light. This was it.

Another glider shot out of the darkness. It crossed not more than twenty yards away, sheared off a wing, and pancaked heavily. Forewarned, the pilot of Crandall's glider veered away. He skimmed over the trees and came and in for a perfect landing, but was unable to stop before the next row of trees. The sound of splintering wood rent the air. Crandall felt as if he hit a brick wall. He bounced forward, crashed through the hull and catapulted twenty feet. It was H minus 3 and 1/2 hours.

When Crandall scrambled from the wreckage, the first thing he noticed was the deathlike silence. No roar of engines, no bark of guns, no whistle of wind. Just silence. Was he the only survivor? A voice from the middle of the field called, "I'm hurt! Can anybody help me?"

Crandall turned. It was Lieutenant Colonel Murphy, the pilot of the glider that had preceded Crandall's. He was badly hurt, and his passenger, Brigadier General Pratt, the Assistant C.O. of the division, was dead.

Crandall did what he could for Colonel Murphy and

established and aid-station under the wing of the glider. Shortly, he heard that there were four more gliders in the same field, all of them with casualties. The parachutists who had jumped from the gliders before they landed were machine gunned as they dropped from the sky. Some hung in trees, and one, Private John Steele, played dead as he hung for twenty four hours from a church parapet at Ste. Mere Eglise. He watched the massacre that went on above and below, with blood streaming from the sky.

In the middle of these activities, Crandall heard that the other members of his team had landed just two fields away. All had crashed landed, and his teammate, Captain John S. Rodda, had suffered several fractured ribs, but that did not stop Rodda. Within a short time everybody was busy.

"Major, I think this fellow has a broken back!"

"Put him here." Crandall bent over to examine the casualty. Then he became aware of a sound that was later to become very familiar, the sound of an empty bottle tumbling through the air. It was a mortar shell. Everybody ducked. There was a dull thud, then silence.

A paratrooper crawled over to investigate. "It's a dud. The Krauts don't even know how to set a fuse!"

Crandall realized that the Germans had a bead on them. It would be foolhardy to remain here. He gave orders quickly. All the wounded were to be carried to the ditch, the team to gather at the end of the field, and no one was to say a word. The men were getting their baptism of fire.

At dawn, leaving part of his team to care for the causalities, Crandell organized a reconnaissance party. Cautiously they advanced toward Hiesville, but caution was not enough. They ran into a German patrol. Every man was on his own.

As soon as the patrol moved off, Crandall continued. A dog barked. "Where there is a dog, there are people," Crandall said to himself. "I've got to find out where I am." He crossed a field and came to a farmhouse. The house was dark. Crandall knocked, and to his surprise his knock was answered almost immediately. A farmer, fully dressed, stood in the door.

"Entrez, mon capitaine. Votre ami est deja ici."

There followed a long dialogue from which Crandall gathered that another American was in the house. "Un blesse grave, mon capitaine!"

A casualty! Instinctively, Crandall put his hand on his

medical pouch. He followed the farmer to a back room. It was obviously the best room in the house. A fire was roaring in the fireplace, and a bed had been pushed as close as possible to the source of heat. The casualty sat on this bed. His shoes were off and he had one foot in a bucket of steaming water. A good-looking girl busied herself putting hot compresses on the other slightly swollen ankle.

"Hallo sergeant, what's the matter?"

"Nothing much, Major. Just a sprained ankle."

"Can you walk?"

"Not very well."

"I'll send a jeep for you as soon as I can."

"Sir, if it's all the same to you, never mind the jeep, I'll be all right here. This isn't a bad spot." The paratrooper nodded towards the girl.

Crandall turned to the farmer: "Ou est Hiesville?"

"Hiesville? Mais, mon capitaine! C'est la bas!" and the farmer broke into the French equivalent of "You can't miss it."

Crandall struck out. It was lighter now, and he soon ran into members of the first battalion of the 506th Parachute Infantry who were on their way to Hiesville. He selected five paratroopers to take possession of the Chateau Colomblienne. The building stood off by itself, apparently deserted. Crandall led his party towards it.

A shot rang out. It came from the stable. One of the paratroopers slumped to the ground. The men scattered and brought the stable under fire. Two scouts edged forward while the others covered. They reached the courtyard and entered the house. Crandall awaited developments while lying in a ditch. Another shot rang out, and one of his bodyguards collapsed. The chateau was not a healthy place.

A rifle team arrived. Bullets beat a pattern. Reinforcements came up. The house was sprayed. The two paratroopers who had entered found only a French family. There was no further fire. At 8:05 a.m. the building passed into American hands.

The French occupants welcomed Crandell with open arms, but cautioned him that German snipers were in the vicinity. He started assuring them that they need have no fear. In the midst of his conversation there was another shot and a man who had been standing in the courtyard wheeled and fell. This was going too far. While Crandall finished his rounds of the house his paratroopers made a thorough search for the sniper

247

but without success. In spite of all their efforts the courtyard came under intermittent fire during the four days it was in use. The situation was quite typical of Normandy. Snipers were everywhere and it was difficult to dislodge them. The man in the Chateau Colombienne was not silenced until a bomb laid the building in ruins.

Meanwhile the 326th Medical Company began to arrive along with the Third Auxers. Crandall set up an operating room in the milk house, which had a concrete floor, large windows, and a pump with spring water. The living room was converted into a shock ward and the kitchen into a minor operating room. The courtyard became a reception station. The medics improvised litters from window casings, feed troughs, kitchen tables and sawed-off ladders. The Third Aux fired the huge stove, boiled instruments, arranged the tables, and prepared plaster. At H plus 3 hours, Crandell selected the first case. It was Lieutenant Colonel Murphy. He survived and was the first casualty from the 101st Airborne to return to the States. To Crandall's men goes the credit of performing the first surgery on the beachhead. Overland evacuation of casualties started on D-Day plus 1. Crandall and his men never stopped. In a week of fierce fighting the 101st seized the causeways, advanced on Carentan, and effected a junction with the Omaha beachhead. Carentan fell on June 12. The Utah and Omaha beachheads joined on June 14.

On the evening of D-Day plus 3, the operating room was going full blast. There was heavy fighting on the causeways, and ambulances were arriving incessantly. At eleven o'clock Crandall did a hurried triage. There were four casualties with abdominal wounds, three with chest wounds, and several dozen with wounds of the extremities. He quickly assessed the abdominal cases and selected the worst one. There had been no rest for three days, and yet Crandall's hand was steady as he opened the abdomen. This was bad—three holes in the stomach, one in the large intestine, and a lacerated kidney. Start with the kidney, was Crandall's thought. "Large clamp," he said, holding out his hand.

At this instant he paused. A roar of low-flying planes filled the air. They passed directly overhead. Then came the ominous whistle of bombs. The earth shook. The massive building shuddered. A heavy beam came down from the ceiling, carrying bricks and plaster with it. Lights went out, walls caved in, and windows were blown to bits. Everybody in the operating room was knocked down. One entire wing of the building became a sixty-foot crater. The Nazi bombers had found their mark.

Rescue work was virtually impossible. Scores of men were buried under debris, crushed by fallen masonry. Tons of cement settled down and smothered those who were pinned. Men who had talked lightheartedly a moment before were now moaning and praying for deliverance. The Third Auxers were badly shaken but otherwise unhurt. For hours they stumbled through the wreckage trying to tell the living from the dead. Not until daybreak was it possible to make up a score. Of the station personnel, eight were killed and fourteen injured. Among the men who were being cared for at the time, the losses were even heavier. Hiesville was one of the worst catastrophes to befall a medical installation in the war.

After the fall of Carentan and Cherbourg, the 101st Division returned to England. There Crandall and his men found orders directing them to return to the Third Auxiliary Surgical Group in France. However, Major Taylor, the Commanding General of the Division, had other plans. He requested that the team stay. General Kenner gave the men their choice. Every member of the team elected to remain with the 101st. They became an integral part of the 326th Medical Command, shared in its glory later in the Holland operation, and tasted defeat at Bastogne. Such were the men of the Third Aux.

Captain Frank J. Lavieri, a member of Major Whitsitt's team, enplaned the glider later on D-Day.

This was his birthday and he relished the prospects. Ste. Mere Eglise was in American hands, and was easily identifiable. The glider began losing altitude. They were on their own. At an altitude of fifty feet, Lavieri saw something that made him freeze. In the field directly ahead, two Sherman tanks were burning fiercely! He turned to the pilot in a futile effort to point out the danger. The man was dead! Nothing could prevent the glider from settling on the tanks. It grazed a clump of trees, lost a wing and landed squarely on top of the burning tanks. It could not have been done more neatly. Flames enveloped the wooden structure. The men were trapped.

The Horsa glider is built of heavy plywood, so heavy that even a strong man could not break it. Lavieri was not a strong man.

Physically he stood five feet four, weighing less than one hundred and ten pounds. At the time of his induction in the army he had quite an argument with the examining physician. The physician wanted to reject him, but Lavieri pointed out to him that he was an accomplished acrobat, and demonstrated his prowess on the spot. The examiner was impressed. "All right," he said. "We'll take you in, but be careful. Don't try any stunts."

Lavieri's stunt came on the evening of June 6. The nearness of the flame gave him superhuman strength. He crouched low. Then he leaped like a battering ram. The hull gave way and he shouldered his way through. The others followed, not a moment too soon. They were in the midst of German held territory. The German 88's had knocked out the tanks and now the machine guns went into action. They were less than fifty yards away. Singed, dazed and shaken, they dashed into a ditch. Of the eight men, one was hit.

Captain Charles O. Van Gorder, on Crandall's team with the 326th Glider-borne Medical Company, tells his experience when he landed behind the enemy line:

Just as he stepped out of his glider, the following one crash-landed and skidded into his glider. As he looked about, he spotted three German tanks, and quickly dashed into a ditch, where he found the injured troopers that had landed just ahead of him. Going into the damaged glider, he found General Pratt sitting in the front seat, his body slumped over the steering wheel of the jeep that was being transported by the glider. His neck had been broken by the weight of his helmet as the glider crashed into the trees when it landed. General Pratt was the highest ranking General killed in the invasion of France.

In spite of the crash landings of the gliders and fighting the enemy on impact, the glider-landed paratroopers and infantry gathered together and proved themselves an effective fighting force. Casualties on D-Day ran as high as 16,000 when American paratroopers started dropping on France at one a.m., five and a half hours before ground troops came ashore. Scattered paratroopers landed in hedgerows, separating them one from another as the men fought the enemy in small groups far inland from the beaches. Some unfortunately landed next to enemy entrenchments. Many parachutists where killed by anti-aircraft and machine gun fire as they floated down from the sky. Some parachutists, weighted down with 70 pounds of gear, drowned in the marshes of the flooded Meredet. Many who were caught in trees were gunned down or slaughtered with bayonets as they hung. At the close of D-Day, the 82nd Airborne listed 1259 paratroopers killed, wounded, or missing. The 101st Airborne listed 1240, with over 60% of their supplies destroyed, damaged, or in the hands of the Germans.

To this day the French keep a facsimile of a parachutist hanging from the parapet of a church steeple. When I was in France for the 50th Commemorative Anniversary of the invasion of World War II in June 1994, they told me about blood raining and intestines trailing from the sky.

The Invasion[1]

6 June 1944
Clouds hung low over the English Channel with cold rain, high winds, and choppy seas as an armada of over 5000 merchant ships and landing craft crossed the Channel. The naval forces, led by 2 battle ships, 2 monitors, 23 cruisers, 105 destroyers, and over a thousand of other types of warships, including sub-chasers and minesweepers, sailed for the beaches of Normandy. In the air were 3500 heavy bombers, 1700 medium and light bombers, 5500 fighters, and 2400 transport planes, strung over 100 miles. It was the beginning of Operation Overlord, the invasion of Western Europe.

On D-Day, six Third Auxiliary Surgical teams crossed the English Channel in LCIs (landing craft infantry) and landed on Utah Beach, and eight teams landed on Omaha Beach. Nine more teams landed on D-Day plus 1. Casualties in the amphibious landing started before the men stepped off the ramps that lowered them waist deep into the water. On Omaha, the 150-foot cliffs that dominated the beach gave the Germans an unobstructed view. Their artillery shells created havoc on the landing craft while they were still a half-mile from the shore. Mines cut down the infantry of the 29th Division who struggled toward the beach, along with a fusillade of machine gun fire from the cliffs, pillboxes, and mortar pits, and artillery fire. They faced a massive system of gun emplacements surrounded by barbed wire and mine fields. Some infantry companies suffered over ninety percent casualties. Hundreds of infantrymen were killed before they reached the shore. Those who did had to fight for their lives to get past the mines, the barbed wire and metal and concrete obstacles covered over by the tide, in the face of machine gun and artillery fire from the cliffs above. Germans in cement bunkers opened fire on the men as they descended from the LCIs into smaller craft that were to bring them closer to shore. Many, when they stepped into the Channel, went under with their heavy packs.

At the end of D-Day the VIIth Corps Headquarters listed 2,374 killed, wounded or missing. This was Omaha Beach. Offshore on the U.S.S Augusta, General Bradley seriously considered abandoning the Omaha Beach landing and radioed Eisenhower for permission. The message never reached Eisenhower.

Utah Beach landings met little opposition except for some artillery rounds from a distance, and were able to put ashore 20,000 soldiers and 1700 vehicles with few casualties. Further inland, Rommel's "asparagus," metal stakes planted to obstruct allied planes on landing, along with thousands of mines, presented additional problems.

On D-Day, H plus 6 hours, the "Empire Anvil" discharged its remaining Third Auxiliary teams into an LCI. Aboard were Majors John B. Peyton, Robert M. Sutton, and Francis M. Findlay. After circling aimlessly for an hour, the LCI got instructions to attempt a landing. They got as far as the surf when three shells in rapid succession hit them directly off the bow, inflicting heavy damage. Fortunately there were no casualties. Intimidated, the LCI backed away. Two more times in the next hours the LCI made a run for the beach, and each time it was driven away. Finally, at H plus 10 hours, the captain maneuvered his ship through the surf and ran her aground 75 yards from the shore. Clutching their equipment, the men jumped into waist deep water and stumbled to shore. They were on Dog Red beach.

Third Auxer Major Findlay recognized the command party of the Engineers Special Brigade and motioned for his team to follow, when a shell struck. One moment the men were approaching each other; the next moment they were all on the

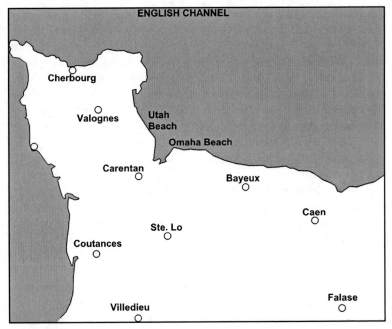

ground. When Major Findlay raised his head, he saw that his teammate, Major Christopher Stahler Jr., had been wounded in the neck. General Hogue was paralyzed from a wound in his spine and his adjutant had been killed instantly.

Major Findlay's team and a team headed by Major Peyton were plunged into a desperate situation five minutes after they hit the shore. It was disheartening for these men to find themselves on the beach with nothing but a few morphine syrettes. They collected the wounded, gave first aid and shielded them from fire. It was here that one of our enlisted men, T-4 Robert J. Smith, distinguished himself for his work, and later was awarded the Silver Star.

While our men were engaged on the beach, the 61st Medical Battalion discovered a blockhouse up on the bluff where casualties could be taken out of harm's way. It had been a German strong point until guns from our destroyers out at sea blasted it. It became the first medical installation on Omaha beach worthy of the name. It lasted but a day. Hauling the wounded up the bluff was a grueling task for the strongest men. As casualties accumulated, they were placed wherever there was room in the primitive shelters, on litters, on blankets, or directly on the cement floor. The majority of the wounded still had their gas-impregnated clothing covering their wounds. Dead and dying lay next to those that might live. Majors Peyton, Findlay and Captain Walter Twarog felt sick at heart. With nothing but morphine, plasma, and dressings, how could they hope to do the job they were supposed to do? How could they treat patients with peritonitis, fractures and deep chest wounds? They examined the casualties, gave plasma, loosened tourniquets, strapped chest wounds, and made up a priority list selecting those that could be evacuated to the beach and sent back to England.

At midnight Major Findlay felt as if his back was broken and his head about to split, when a fresh casualty was put down at the entrance. Findlay heard the rattling respirations and he knew that he had to act quickly. He knelt down and helped the man cough up the fluid that was drowning him. Then he discovered the cause of the trouble: a sucking wound of the chest. He covered the wound with a large battle dressing and taped it closed. Then he inserted a needle into the man's chest and allowed the excess air to escape. He called for plasma, and in the dark it took four men to start it. Two men held the blanket across the exit, the third held the lantern, and the fourth manipulated the bottle. Findlay felt for the patient's veins with perspiration rolling down his back. Slowly he advanced the needle, first one way than another. It was the hardest venapuncture he had ever done. This was another first major surgery done on D-Day.

As the men continued examining, giving first aid, and injecting morphine, they suddenly heard the roar of the peculiar intensity of the German Messerschmitts. They heard two bombs explode at the water's edge. Then the roar became deafening as a bomb exploded almost at the blockhouse opening. Findlay was knocked off his feet as great clouds of sand billowed into the pillbox. The wounded moaned. The medics cursed. Plasma bottles were upset. Sand seeped under dressings. Blankets were blown away. In the deathly darkness of that man-made catacomb, men were sorely tried. Order was not reestablished until dawn. Such was D-Day for Majors Findlay, Peyton and Captain Twarog and the members of their team.

Within twelve hours, over two hundred Third Auxers were operating on the beaches of Omaha, code name for Normandy. They operated in bomb craters, and behind the protection of disabled tanks and trucks that had been damaged by the

German artillery stationed high on the cliffs above the beach. The surgical equipment had not yet caught up with them, due to the barrage of fire the ships encountered in the first landings from enemy artillery, mortars, machine guns, metal obstacles, and mines. Ships and landing craft went under, men drowned or were mowed down by machine gun fire that spattered them as they waded toward the beach among mines strung to objects under water. Equipment and instrument crates went down or were lost in the confusion of the landing. Surgeons operated with what they carried on their backs. It was mostly massive first aid, tying off bleeders and covering wounds with bandages or whatever they could utilize, such as towels and sheets. The wounded were sent back to the ships when the situation at the beach permitted and returned to England for further care.

The beach clearing stations where the wounded were collected were operated by the medical battalions of the Engineers Special Brigade, and it was to these stations that the Third Aux teams were attached during those first hours after landing on the beach. The Division Clearing Station arrived four hours later and set up operations further inland, as ground was gained. When the field hospitals finally arrived days later they relieved the clearing stations of surgery. The clearing stations reverted to giving first aid, sorting the casualties, and sending the seriously wounded to the field hospitals for surgery.

Medical corpsmen, part of the battalion, aided the wounded on the battlefield, giving first aid, applying tourniquets to bleeding arms or legs and dressings and pressure to wounds where needed, and giving morphine if necessary. Litter bearers brought the wounded to the battalion aid station where the medical officer, after giving emergency treatment, sent them to the nearby clearing station where they were sorted. The seriously wounded were sent to the nearby field hospitals for surgery, the others to the rear evacuation hospitals as they became available.

June 18, 1944

Third Auxiliary Surgical Group Headquarters and our remaining surgical teams, along with nurses and enlisted men, departed Camp Bewdley, boarded the trucks, and sang their way to Southampton. The surrounding countryside and roads were bursting with army equipment. Huge bulldozers, tanks, armored cars, long toms, grotesque ducks (boats on wheels), huge trucks loaded with ammunition, and jeeps, were all fighting their way on country lanes that never saw anything heavier than a bicycle before. Yet a few miles north of this indescribable confusion, farmers plowed, mailmen made their rounds, and workers went to the factories. In London the theaters were crowded, and business went on as usual.

We were billeted in a squire's large estate near Southampton. The nurses crowded in several rooms in one section of the residence, with the rest of the group somewhere nearby. Our cots were so crowded together that there was barely room to walk between them. We spent our time lying down, since there was no place to go except to mess. I found an interesting book on the library shelf, *Greyfriars Bobby*, about a Skye terrier famous for keeping a daily vigil at his masters' grave in Edinburgh for fourteen years, along with other stories of devoted animals.

On June 21, we arose in the dark, and after a hasty breakfast were in the trucks and on the road to the port. We spent the day sitting on the dock beside thousands of troops waiting to board ship. Huge barrage balloons shaped like dirigibles floated in the sky above us. They appeared to be holding the island afloat with the millions of tons of war equipment and tens of thousands of army personnel waiting to cross the Channel. The balloons were held by heavy cables, an endeavor to obstruct enemy planes from approaching vital areas. At noon we ate our first C-ration, comprised of hard biscuit, a tin of Spam, a packet of lemon powder and a square of hard chocolate. I poured water from our canteen into my tin cup and added the powder. Lemonade.

Empire Lance LCI

21 June 1944

Late in the afternoon we boarded the Empire Lance, and struggled into the gymnasium where hammocks were hung across the entire expanse of the LCI troopship. The hammocks were hung so close to one another that one could just walk between them, and hung with barely space to raise one's head without bumping the hammock above. Our musette bags lay on the floor below us. In the rest room, toilets lined one side of the room with no privacy between and a few washbowls hung on the sidewall. We slept fully dressed in slacks, and rocked in hammocks as the ship steamed across the English Channel. No meals were served; we ate packaged K-rations. The following afternoon we filed to the opening of the LCI and stepped off the ramp into a landing craft, assisted by a Seabee who stood thigh-deep in the water. The craft shuttled us to a makeshift pier where we were helped up onto a temporary dock by another Seabee standing hip high in water.

Omaha Beach – D-Day plus 16

22 June 1944

We proceeded to the cluttered beach and saw damaged jeeps, weapons carriers, Sherman tanks, trucks, and huge guns tilted on their sides, DUKWs, and bomb craters. In the water, ships like behemoths lay on their sides; others with only their masts protruding from the water. There were many other tangled, unidentifiable obstacles on the beach and in the water.

My eyes followed the rise in the land in the distance and I wondered why the solid mass of vehicles—jeeps, weapons carriers, trucks and every other army vehicle were barely moving up the steep incline. Later I discovered it to be a narrow one-way dirt road. The army had advanced inland only several miles on Omaha Beach. Ahead and high up on the bluff we saw the remnants of German bunkers, where they had a bird's eye view of the Allied ships as they approached the shore. Now and then a Cub plane flew overhead as if watching the unloading and activity below.

When all of the nurses finally reached the shore we stood waiting, as no one seemed to know what to do with us, until we heard an excited officer passing by exclaim, "What in Hell are these women doing on the beach! They're sitting ducks for the Luftwaffe." He sent for a truck, and soon we joined the long line of vehicles that were slowly moving up the steep incline.

At the top of the plateau we found ourselves in a wheat field where a large tent had been set up. It was filled with canvas cots, and here we spent our first night on French soil. We ate our second box of C-rations and slept on the bare canvas cot fully dressed, since our bedrolls had not caught up with us as yet. The roar of the artillery and the rat-tat-tat of machine gun fire were to become a routine part of life, we discovered. The following day we were assigned to various front line field hospitals, where we would be in charge of the surgical unit assisting our Third Auxiliary surgeons in its operation.

In the first days after the landing of troops on the beaches of France, except for their battalion aid stations where first aid was applied, surgeons landed with surgical supplies carried on their backs but could do little more. The wounded were shipped back to England. As territory was gained, clearing stations were established, surgical supplies and tentage became available, and as unloading of ships and some order of sequence of supplies became possible, field hospitals were established.

Until the field hospitals were set up, surgeons performed massive first aid on the beaches and battalion aid stations. Other surgeons, landing behind enemy lines with the paratroops and glider landings, operated in the fields or wherever they found shelter.

Field hospitals were set up a short distance behind the clearing station, where the wounded were first brought from the battalion aid station and sorted. The critically wounded were sent to field hospitals to be operated on, while the lesser wounded were transferred to the rear to be shipped back to England or the evacuation hospitals. With the arrival of the field hospitals and nurses, the surgeons could now turn their attention to surgical procedures, while nurses took over the responsibility of seeing that they had the sterile materials needed for the operations. Up to now, the enlisted men whom we had trained in England had assisted the surgeons.

Field hospitals were made up of three platoons that leap-fogged one another to be close to the front as the Infantry advanced. In placing the tents in the field, four tents were joined together to form a cross. These four tents were the hub: (1) Receiving. (2) Resuscitation which involved transfusions, x-ray, laboratory, cauterization, intubation and everything that modern surgery demanded. (3) Operations tent. (4) Post Operative care. A casualty could be admitted, triaged, resuscitated, and operated on without having to leave tent coverage. The field hospital nurses and the corpsmen were responsible for the post-operative care of the wounded until they could tolerate being moved to the rear, usually to an evacuation hospital, and eventually to England for longer convalescence.

Third Auxiliary Surgeons found that casualties at the field hospitals were of three kinds: (a) about one third were chest wounds, often combined with abdominal injuries; (b) another third had abdominal wounds; (3) the remaining third sustained severe extremity wounds. By and large, most had multiple wounds and usually were in a desperate situation. There was no way of telling what the wounds would show once the bloody blankets and clothes had been removed and the clumsy dressings cut away. It might be a small puncture wound or there might be a hundred jagged lacerations. The one with the tiny perforation might be in profound shock while the next one with his intestines out on the abdomen would nonchalantly ask for a cigarette.

Some incidents stand out as, for example, the mortally wounded sergeant who used his last breath to say, "Please get me back to my platoon Doc. There's nobody knows those boys like me." Or the raw recruit who pleaded, "Doctor, please take my leg off, I know it's no good." Or the burned paratrooper who charged into a flamethrower to bayonet his attacker. Perhaps it was the arrogant German feldwebel who clawed at his splints and spat at the nurse who was caring for him. Or the disciplined grenadier who sat at attention when he was spoken to and keeled over dead two minutes later. The receiving tent showed human nature in the raw.

Third Auxiliary surgical teams performed the surgery on casualties that were delivered to them anywhere from an hour to several days after injury. The average time was four to six hours. The wounded, with grime and dirt from the battlefield still on their faces, rarely made any noise. They were preoccupied with what they were doing when they were wounded. Some muttered about the mine, the grenade or the shell that hit them. Most were in shock. They all felt that since they had reached a hospital they would recover. They had heard that only three percent died. Fortunately, they did not know that the overall mortality did indeed run to about three percent but in the field hospital it was twenty-five percent and often higher due to the severity of their wounds.

With the arrival of the field hospitals the surgeons could now depend on sterile equipment, autoclaved drape sheets, instruments, proper lighting, pre-operative injections, and the doctor anesthetist had the necessary equipment to anesthetize the soldier prior to surgery. Nurses saw that the operative area was in order, monitored the patients' fluid levels, selected the proper instruments for the type of surgery. They checked the surgical procedure, anticipating the surgeons needs, sterilized

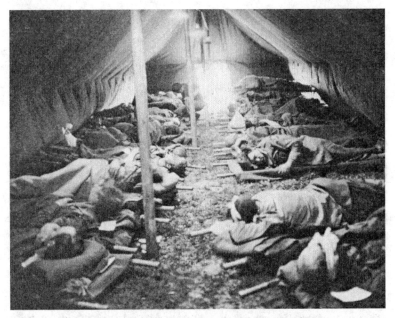

The receiving tent of a field hospital.
These casualties have not yet been triaged.

whatever was called for, and assisted wherever needed. The surgeons could now turn their entire attention to repairing the wounds.

At the field hospitals we operated on those who would not survive unless treated as quickly as possible. These cases were mostly chest and abdominal wounds, where surgeons removed shrapnel and bullets, debrided tissue, repaired and aligned bones, and removed bone splinters. Many included amputations of legs and arms. Those with brain and spinal wounds were transported to the evacuation hospitals, as those units became established on the continent.

Neurosurgery was a specialty not practiced by the general surgeons, and required more time. However, such cases did come through our field hospital for emergency care. My eyes froze on a shell that protruded from the middle of a soldier's forehead as I hurried past him lying on the operating table, while the surgeons stood off to the side trying to decide what they should do. Would the shell

On the fiftieth anniversary of D-Day, Dr. Fred Ireland salutes the grave of enlisted man John H. Malone, who stepped on a mine on D-Day.

explode? I continued on with the task I was preoccupied with at the adjoining table and didn't remember to inquire about what happened to him. The question was, would he tolerate the move to the evacuation hospital where our neurosurgeons, Major Walter G. Haynes, and Captain Donald D. Matson operated?

These men were extremely overworked because of the

great demand for their specialty and the intricacy of the surgery, which took hours to perform. I learned later that on occasion they operated for seventy-hour stretches, and after that were on call for any emergency or problem that arose with their post operatives.

We nurses operated eighteen-hour stretches in the beginning, and I remember one thirty-six hour stretch, after which we stumbled to our tents and collapsed into profound exhaustive sleep. There was no time to think. We became like robots during the next several months except when a nearby explosion jolted us, or something out of the ordinary occurred

In the rectangular, limited space with sloping roof and mud floor, the surgeons did their job. Conditions might be primitive but performance was superb. Two operating tables now filled the space as we became busier. Improvised reflectors cast their beams on the operating table. The teams split up, the leader usually working with the second assistant. The first assistant worked at another table with the technician, while one anesthetist could anesthetize both patients by placing them so that their heads were next to each other.

The operating nurse saw that the soldier had his preoperative atropine, the operation site readied, that the surgical instruments on trays were in place, that sterile drapes were applied, that the surgeons and assistants were masked and gowned, and was alert for anything that the surgeon might call for.

To prevent infection, sulfanilamide, and later penicillin powder, as it became more available, was diluted into solution and poured into open chests and bellies as well as other wounds before suturing. Morphine was used generously for relieving pain and probably gave the wounded a sense of well being in spite of their serious condition. Among the wounded were medics and litter bearers who became casualties when they went to aid the injured on the battlefield. Danger from mine fields was always present.

Front line surgeons:
Capt. Jones, Major Boyden, Capt. Floyd and Capt. Dodds.

Nurses prepared the wounded boys for surgery. Many were only eighteen years old and "boys" was how we referred to them. We checked the wounds, took blood pressure and pulse and gave the preoperative injection. No two wounded were alike. Many were beyond human power to repair the damage done by the machines of war. Casualties from the 5th of June to the 24th numbered 10,943, with 9,386 dead and 1,557 missing (their bodies were never found). Many had drowned in the invasion landing.

It had been raining continuously since we landed, and the fields were seas in mud. Our boots (we wore the same boots and fatigues as the GIs) grew heavy with mud as we walked from our pyramidal tents to the operations tent or to mess. Leather suitcases accumulated green mold; tents were dank and dark. Life consisted of work and little sleep, seven days a week, ever since we landed on the continent. During those first days above Omaha Beach, we were besieged by swarms of bees that hovered over the fields particularly at mealtime. They were angry, bloodthirsty, and hungry. One stung my finger as I held on to my mess kit while standing in the muddy field, hurriedly eating spam, powdered potatoes, and canned green beans. Bees were crawling over my food, falling into the peach juice and buzzing angrily. The sting felt like a burning cigarette had been pressed on my skin. We kept moving, wiggling, shaking, trying to get away, but there was no escaping. They were everywhere by the thousands. I cringed when the thought came to me about where they had been before they sat on my slippery peach half. We ate quickly while flicking them off with the spoon. In those first days the kitchen crew had to feed thousands. There were neither tables nor benches to sit down, nor was there time.

27 June, 1944

The vital Port of Cherbourg fell after massive support from our naval guns, including three battleships, four cruisers and eleven destroyers, to units from three divisions of the VII Corps attacking from the south. However, it would take some time to repair the port, since the enemy had wrecked the port installations, obstructed the harbor, set booby traps and demolished the area before they surrendered. General Schlieben and Admiral Hennecke, the local naval chief, were captured along with 30,000 prisoners.

We were puzzled when the boom of artillery and gunfire, that had been continuous since we landed, suddenly ceased on this day. I stepped out of the operations tent momentarily to see why, and saw a jeep with fluttering white flags drive past, closely followed by two white flagged ambulances, going south. The report was that a temporary truce had been arranged between the American and German armies while our ambulances carried seven German nurses, "schwestas," to the German front line. They had been captured when Cherbourg was surrendered, and the American army felt that the Germans would need their services.

We moved on with First Army as the front advanced through Isigny, Carentan, Periers, Coutances, close behind the 29th Infantry Division, working like automatons, rolling up our bedrolls every three to five days, tearing down the tents, climbing into trucks, riding past leveled villages whose chimneys stood like tomb markers against the sky. Bloated horses, their legs rigor-mortised, lay by the roadside. Cows roamed the fields needing to be milked, approaching anyone carrying a helmet on his arm. We had our first fresh meat when a calf was slaughtered after it had fallen into a foxhole and broke its leg. It had to be eaten promptly since there was no refrigeration. It was a special treat; there had been nothing but K-rations to eat in those first weeks.

1 July 1944

Field Marshall von Rundstedt was sure the war was lost soon after the Allies landed. When General Jodl, who attended Hitler's conferences twice daily and directed all the Nazi campaigns except the Soviet theater of operations, asked him, "What shall we do?" Rundstedt answered saying, "End the war. What else can we do?" Rundstedt was dismissed, and Field Marshall von Kluge took over as Commander in Chief of the West.

3 July 1944

I was awakened by a tremendous bombardment of Artillery bursts and the rat-tat-tat of machine gun fire nearby. I stepped out of the tent to see the world on fire. Raging flames spread across the horizon as far as I could see, and explosions shook the earth in the dark night. A thought flashed through my mind: the American army is celebrating the 4th of July. Actually, it marked the start of a major drive by American forces from the Cotentin Peninsula to breach a line from Coutances to St. Lo. The shells had landed on the German ammunition dump, setting the forest on fire.

As we moved deeper inland, we found the narrow country lanes barriered by centuries-old six- to eight-foot-high hedges that slowed progress, and with the continuous rain our vehicles became mired in mud. Our Sherman tanks could not traverse the hedgerows, and the infantry following the tanks were slaughtered by Germans concealed behind the hedgerows.

We had been operating without letup as the infantry tried to scale the hedgerows in the face of enemy fire, and fell when they stepped on mines planted by the thousands. A young soldier who had lost parts of both legs said, as we were about to anesthetize him, "The Germans are using horses to pull their artillery!"

The surgeons and the rest of us looked at each other, surprised and heartened. Perhaps the war would soon end if they no longer have fuel to run their engines. He then added, "I wonder how my family will feel about my losing my legs."

We heard by rumor that our infantry had come upon a cellar full of calvados, a very potent alcoholic liquor made from the apples that grew in this part of France. They celebrated by getting very drunk, and some men lost their eyesight because wood alcohol had been deliberately added to the calvados by the enemy.

9 July 1944

Troops from the British 1st and Canadian 3rd Divisions, after fighting thirty-three days supported by the battleship Rodney and other naval gunfire shelling the German positions, had finally reached Caen, their 6th of June (D-Day) target. The RAF began the attack by dropping 2500 tons of bombs on the city. Afterwards, all of Caen lay in ashes except for two large beautiful many-spired Norman Abbeys.

12 July 1944

First Army was brought almost to a halt by the

stubborn defense of the enemy as American casualties mounted. It was all the same massive chest and abdominal wounds, often accompanied with amputations. I had to rush to keep both surgical teams supplied with all that was called for, as we tried to keep up with the backlog of wounded.

In July the rains continued as the infantry slogged through the mud following the tanks on the narrow, sunken roads. When our Shermans tanks attempted to mount the hedges they exposed their soft undersides to enemy fire and exploded. It wasn't until an ingenious sergeant, Curtiss G. Cullin Jr. of the 102nd Cavalry Reconnaissance, improvised a device to cut through the hedgerows, that the problem was remedied. Sergeant Cullin made a hedgerow cutter by attaching tusk-like prongs made up from Rommel's beach obstacles and scrap steel welded to the front of the tanks. The "Rhino," as it was called, could now cut into the base of the hedgerow. However, the enemy held fast with Tiger and Panther tanks that were larger and more heavily armed than our Sherman tanks. Machine gun, mortar, and artillery fire caused heavy damage to our infantry and tank crews who were trapped inside the burning tanks.

Progress was slow. Since D-Day, First Army had suffered over 61,000 casualties including 11,300 killed. More men were lost in the Cotentin Peninsula in July than in the initial landings in June. We heard that in England 2750 civilians were killed and 8000 were wounded by Hitler's secret weapon, the pilotless V-1, or Buzz Bombs, as we called them.

German commander Von Kluge soon realized that his troops, despite Herculean efforts, were in serious trouble. He knew that Hitler would never countenance retreat or surrender, and that "The Furher" was in denial about how the war was progressing and about the fate of Germany. Von Kluge had become aware of a resistance group formed by young German staff officers who were opposed to Hitler, but he had not committed himself.

Wounded German prisoners
left behind and operated on by the Third Auxiliary

He now agreed to cooperate with the group if it could assassinate Hitler. Additionally, on July 17, General Erwin Rommel agreed to end the war initiative and to the formation of a new government in place of the Nazis, should the attempt on Hitler's life, planned by Col. Von Stauffenberg, be successful.

20 July 1944

Col. Count Von Stauffenberg, a wounded, decorated officer, entered Hitler's headquarters in Rastenburg, in East Prussia, as part of a war conference. He placed his briefcase (containing a bomb) under the conference table, close to Hitler, then left the room, ostensibly to make a phone call. Unfortunately, the briefcase was moved so that when the bomb went off Hitler, though shaken, suffered only minor injuries. The next day, Stauffenberg and several leading participants in the conspiracy were shot.

The revolt would lead to the execution of more than

5,000 people, including many generals, officers, politicians and their entire families. Von Kluge turned his back on the conspirators inasmuch as he said he would help only if Hitler were dead.

Field Marshall Rommel, famous for having commanded the Afrika Corps, was severely wounded in an allied aircraft attack on July 17. He soon found himself replaced by Von Kluge. Rommel was sent home to recuperate, where he was later visited by an emissary of Hitler with a proposal. He could chose suicide by poison, or be disgraced by being put on trial by the "People's Court," with the threat that his family would join him on trial, on suspicion of being involved in the assassination plot. Rommel chose suicide.

The Bombing of St. Lo

25 July, 1944

We in the second platoon of the 51st Field Hospital stopped on a hill above St. Lo when we heard the roar of approaching planes. Our hospital was to stand by until the infantry, who were below us, made the anticipated advance. The noise was a continuous roar of engines as the sky filled with fighters and bombers flying from the north. "COBRA," the code name for the bombing of St. Lo by our Eighth and Ninth Air Forces based in England, began this morning. I began counting our planes as they appeared in the distance, but soon lost track as they filled the sky. It was a breathtaking sight, and brought back memories of the war in Africa. Fighter planes, P-47 Thunderbolts and P-51 Mustangs, followed by the familiar B-25s, B-26s, B-17s, B-24s and others filled the sky ahead of me. There were hundreds, then thousands, flying in formation. As they dropped their bomb loads the earth began to tremble. Smoke and fire filled the horizon as the din of explosions fill the air. The noise was deafening. I was thrilled as the planes continued on and on. They would surely eliminate the enemy behind the hedgerows towering above them, opening the way for our advance. Our troops had reached a stalemate that kept them locked at a boundary 30 kilometers inland from Omaha Beach where First Army had landed on D-Day, seven weeks ago.

I climbed on top of the water tank to get a better view on the valley below and watched as German anti-aircraft fire exploded in puffs of black smoke in the midst of our B-17s. I saw bomb bay doors open and bombs streak earthward. The earth shook continually as in an earthquake, as explosions and smoke filled the air for what seemed like hours. Enemy anti-aircraft bursts blackened the sky, spitting ack-ack as it reached for our planes, and I watched horrified as three Fortresses flying in formation, one after another tilt to the right, then spiral to the ground. The force of the impact as each one plunged to earth and exploded caused the water tank I was standing on to shake with such force that it jolted me off of it. The sky turned dark as the smoke and dust from the exploding bombs from 3000 bombers filled the horizon.

Within an hour of the bombardment, our 51st Field Hospital was in operation instead of moving with the infantry after the raid as had been planned. Litter bearers began bringing in wounded infantrymen by the score and we were overwhelmed with our own casualties.

A corpsman called me outside of the operating tent to look at a wounded soldier that he brought to the entrance because he was anxious about him. The sun, trying to penetrate the haze of smoke, made me squint as I came out of the dim tent to find many wounded lying on litters on the ground. I looked down at the soldier on the ground before me. I did not have to look close to see the massive belly wound, spilling intestines. I sensed his eyes following mine as I scanned the wound. Then turning to him, his anxious eyes staring from the ashen pallor of his face, I said, "We'll take care of you soldier."

I went back into the tent and fixed a hypodermic with morphine, and injected the needle into his arm and pressed the syringe. I patted his shoulder to reassure him, but I knew he would not last long. He was bled out, and blood was extremely short at this time.

We had been depending on volunteer donors from the service troops of the 29th Division and the Third Armored Division in its first short but costly mission north of St. Lo. There were many who might survive if they were operated as quickly as possible. However, we in the operating room could operate on but one soldier at a time. Though there were two teams operating, it was a time-consuming process to anesthetize, locate fragments of shrapnel, clamp off and tie bleeders, repair torn organs, intestines, muscle and tissue. It was later confirmed that the mangling injuries and blast syndrome cases that arose from the close range bombing were among the worst that the Third Auxiliary Surgeons operating at the 51st Field Hospital handled.

Lt. General Lesley J. McNair, commander of all the United States Army ground forces, among other dignitaries, was observing the bombing of St. Lo, when a bomb landed on his slit trench. It threw his body high in the air, mangling it beyond recognition except for the three stars pinned to his collar. He was buried quietly without fanfare since army did not wish to reveal the incident to the enemy.

St. Lo was pulverized. German soldiers went berserk, and thousands were killed. We heard later that the initial planes dropped their bombs accurately; that the front line was marked by long bright colored strips of cloth on top of tanks and jeeps and other vehicles along with colored smoke to guide the bombers, but smoke from the preceding explosions concealed the markings, as shifting winds blew the black smoke toward our infantry, resulting in the succeeding planes dropping their bombs short, killing 111, and wounding 490 Americans.

The attack by 380 medium bombers and 550 fighter-

Saint Lo, France, following the bombing

bombers, along with 1500 heavy bombers, dropped over 4000 tons of bombs on Panzer Lehr's three battalion command posts, demolishing them along with a regiment of parachute troops. The surviving Germans retreated after suffering a thousand killed, hundreds wounded and many demoralized, incoherent, babbling men. The air attack cleared a path for our Sherman tanks and the infantry, who had fought so desperately among the hedgerows since D-Day.

Later we heard that Cobra had begun the day before, on the 24th, but had been scratched because of heavy cloud cover over the target. However, it was too late to cancel the flight since some 400 bombers had already reached France. Due to the overcast and human error, twenty-five of our infantry were killed and 111 wounded.

The bombing left us dejected not only because of the terrible wounds we saw as we worked at repairing them, but also the physical exhaustion from the continuous long hours of work since we landed in France. We dragged our heavy mud-clodded boots toward our tents to fall into a much-needed sleep, that was disrupted by the thunder of bombs and artillery bursts in the distance.

Our 51st Field Hospital followed the First Army as it

continued southward capturing Avranches, where we saw in the distance the famous Mont St. Michel Cathedral on a rocky isle in the Gulf of St. Malo, an arm of the English Channel. The isle, accessible to land at low tide, is also linked to the mainland by a causeway. Mont St.Michel Cathedral was founded in 708 by St. Aubert, the bishop of Avranches and the Benedictene Abbey. Our Field Hospital bivouacked overnight on the mainland, and in the morning I saw the famous Cathedral in the distance rising from the waters of the Channel.

Since the sixth of June, the Third Auxiliary Surgical Teams, who did all the seriously wounded surgery at the various front line field hospitals, had performed surgery on 1281 casualties in sixty-three days. This averaged 20.3 operations performed during a twenty-four-hour period during this phase of the campaign. A team consisted of two surgeons, a doctor anesthetist, a surgical nurse (writer's part) and four enlisted men.

I recalled that the problem of selecting "who to save" had been discussed in Oxford when British surgeons, veterans of the desert war in Egypt and Libya in 1942 and 1943, had told us of their experience. They had learned that it was better to operate on the wounded men who had a better chance for survival, rather than to spend hours on those who were probably beyond saving. We rejected the idea then, but now we found that we were doing the same. It was heart-rending to know that many men whose wounds were questionable could not be saved due to the limited surgical personnel in the field hospital working intensely trying to save those who stood a better chance of surviving.

We had been following the Big Red 1 (one) and the 28th Divisions since landing in France and only heard news via the rumor route or what the wounded told us. We never saw any top Army officials as we followed the infantry.

Von Kluge, Commander of the German Seventh Army Headquarters, ordered the withdrawal of his command to an area southwest of St. Lo. However, when General Paul Hausser, the first Oberguppenfuhrer SS (who replaced General Dollman, who had a heart attack a few weeks after D-Day), instead ordered his Korps to regroup near Percy, von Kluge burst with anger. There would be no one to guard the coast toward Avranches and the bridge at Pontaubault that led to the main roads into central France. This was not the first time that Hausser had crossed von Kluge. Hausser, however, was a Nazi, Hitler's man.

In the meantime, American General H. E. Dager led his Combat Command B into Avranches, surprisingly without fighting, due to Hausser's decision to go to Percy instead of southwest toward Avranches as von Kluge had directed.

Von Kluge and SS General Hausser got orders from the German high command, Hitler's men who directed the army from East Prussia, to recapture Avranches at all costs. Hitler ordered von Kluge to divide the First and Third Armies, and then drive the Americans into the sea.

The German survivors of the St. Lo bombing, the 5th Parachute Division with the 77th Infantry Division and field artillery commanded by Colonel Rudolf Bacherer, now began their attempt to recapture Avranches. Fierce fighting raged as rain and Allied artillery fell on Dager's men. Then began the house-to-house fighting, with the Americans looking into the sky for the help that had been promised, when suddenly the clouds dispersed and a squadron of P-47s happened to fly over them.

Noting the red ground signal the men had placed marking their zone, the planes strafed and bombed the enemy into submission, as the horses dragging wagons bolted and galloped off with their shafts slamming against their flanks. Dead and wounded littered the roads and fields.

General Dager joined up with Combat A and headed toward Pontaubault, and the following day crossed the bridge that had been bombed repeatedly in the past four years because of its vital route leading to Brest, Nantes, and Alencon. To lose the bridge meant having lost the campaign to the Germans.

Allied planes continued to bomb and strafe the Germans as they tried to hold the Allies from advancing. As the German convoy escaped eastward the roads leading toward Mortain were blocked by debilitated tanks and hundreds of burned trucks. Local civilians were forced by the Germans to push the debris off the roads into ditches.

In the woods, jagged, burned tree trunks stood grotesque, their straggly boughs clinging to fragments of blue and gray uniforms streaked with blood. The forest in Mortain was no longer green. There was no undergrowth of shrubs; bare splintered trunks and stumps of trees were silhouetted against the skies, and the ground, gray with ashes, still smoldered as our field hospital moved forward to set up operation tents. We saw bloated horses with legs outstretched amid the clutter of damaged artillery guns, Swastika-marked Panther and Tiger tanks, box-like trucks, and horseless wagons. Horses were trapped in the wreckage neighing, their eyes bulging with fear and pain. They were mercifully shot in the head by our infantry. Beside the road, German crosses marked the graves of their dead.

Our GI truck drivers raced us nurses past in the newly conquered territory, to avoid possible stray sniper attacks as we dashed to set up the field hospital. Wounded were arriving by ambulances and trucks before we were ready. Wounded were placed in the triage tent to set priority for surgery. Those whose condition was beyond help were made comfortable with morphine. This procedure had been repeated ever since we had arrived in June. Tourniquets on arms and legs of those with other injuries were loosened temporarily to keep tissue alive while we operated on their more serious wounds in chests and bellies. We worked day and night as the fighting grew more fierce.

It surprised me that, as badly wounded as they were, the injured were coherent and told of some of their encounters. One young soldier told about seeing eight dead comrades lined up beside the road who had been emasculated by the desperate enemy as they fled. We were infuriated to think the enemy would resort to this type of savagery.

Hitler demanded his men to fight unto death. They had no choice, for to turn back meant their own SS troops would shoot them. It was death in either direction for the German soldier.

General Patton's Third Army Arrives in France.

1 August 1944

General Troy Middleton's VIIIth Corps, under General George Patton's Command, after a stiff fight at St. Malo forced the enemy to withdraw to the ports of Lorient, St. Nazaire and Brest. Rather than diverting westward toward the peninsula, where the ports were strongly held by the Germans with supplies that would last them for months, General Bradley, after attempting to overwhelm them by land with navel and air support, decided to leave two strong divisions under General Patton to prevent the enemy from breaking out of the peninsula. Leaving the naval units to harass the ports with strong land and air support, the First Army regrouped their forces at Avranches, and poured into Normandy with artillery and armor supporting the infantry, then turned westward.

The German General Ramcke, with 38,000 well-trained troops, held on to Brest until the 19th of September. In the fighting, Middleton's VIIIth Corps in Brittany had suffered 9,831 casualties, killed, wounded, and missing, along with the loss of thousands of tons of ammunition, air power and transport. With the Germans' stubborn hold to a lost cause like Brest, General Bradley wondered what would happen when we reached their homeland

On the 3rd of August, General Omar Bradley decided to swing the First Army eastward toward the Seine instead of the Loire River. North of us, Field Marshal Bernard L. Montgomery, with his Canadian and Polish armies turned toward Villers-Bocage, southwestward, with the Germans caught in the middle, fighting both sides and keeping the rear open for the inevitable retreat. General Clarence R. Huebner's 1st Division occupied Mortain on August 3, without much opposition.

Hitler was furious when he heard of the loss of Mortain, and demanded that von Kluge counterattack, recapture Mortain, continue to Avranches and force the Americans into the Channel. There would be no retreat unless Hitler gave his permission. Germans suffered massive artillery bombing from all directions, followed by infantry attacks and strafing by American fighter bombers. The roads were obstructed by demolished vehicles, burning Panther and Tiger tanks, anti-tank guns, trucks, and wagons attached to bloated dead horses. Blood covered the earth as bodies crushed in the onslaught were overrun. The air filled with the stench of death, decay, and smoldering fire as the Germans fled. Our field hospital followed our troops through the Mortain Forest, now only bare tree limbs and stumps. Strips of German dull-green uniforms, caught in the crotches of limbs, indicated the destructiveness of the war.

Generals Eisenhower, Bradley, and Field Marshall Montgomery had agreed to the encirclement of the enemy at Falaise. Third Army Commander General Patton left Middleton's VIIIth Corps to continue the siege in Brittany in the west, where German General Ramcke held on until September 19. In the meantime, Patton had continued eastward to capture Le Mans, and then headed north toward Alencon and Argentan, in turn, to form a junction with the Canadians between Argentan and Falaise.

Field Marshal Montgomery ordered the First

Canadian and the 2nd British Armies toward Falaise. The First Canadian Army was to capture Falaise, and then continue to Argentan; the Second British Army to head back westward and south to encircle the enemy there. The British were to meet with the Americans in the south at Argentan.

Von Kluge, aware that he would be trapped if he pursued the attack on Mortain, wanted to retreat eastward, but Hitler demanded that he drive the Allies into the sea and continue to attack Mortain. In August when Hitler finally realized that a trap was indeed being set he was too late to save the situation. The Germans were now fighting for their lives as they were attacked from the north, the south and the rear and bombed from above.

At this difficult time, Field Marshal von Kluge was caught in an air raid and lost contact with his headquarters all day. Hitler was suspicious that he was being disloyal and might have surrendered to the Allies. Back at his headquarters that night, von Kluge said that his radio had been damaged by enemy aircraft early that morning and he was unable to stay in contact with his troops. Unconvinced, Hitler replaced von Kluge with a Nazi fanatic, Field Marshal Walter Model.

In the northern sector the British army fought fiercely attempting to reach Falaise and the junction where they were to meet the American army, who had already reached Argentan. Americans, fearful of shelling the British, dared not go beyond the agreed destination, which led to a gap between the Allies, through which the Fifth Panzers and the German Seventh Army began their desperate retreat to the east. Although slowed by the failure of the Canadians to reach Falaise, and the misunderstanding between Montgomery and General Bradley, the British and Americans nevertheless finally did link up at Chambois on August 19, but not before 40,000 or more Germans escaped through the Falaise Gap to fight again. Between 10,000 and 15,000 Germans were killed and 50,000 taken prisoner in the Mortain and Falaise battle.

On August 15, Von Kluge, facing defeat and linked to the attempt on Hitler's life, and now replaced, swallowed a cyanide capsule.

The Germans had suffered 500,000 casualties in France since D-Day. The Allies lost 200,000 killed, wounded and missing, of which 133,300 were Americans. During these severe battles our field hospitals, following close behind the front line, heard bits and pieces of the action and the pitfalls from the infantry as we cared for them. There had been no letup since we landed on Omaha Beach.

As the Nazi army retreated toward Germany, our work eased and we had a chance to look around the countryside. Several of us nurses were walking along the road when a jeep with a Lieutenant at the wheel stopped and asked if we wanted a lift. We were glad for an opportunity to see the surrounding area and joined him.

"I'm Lieutenant Thompson; I'm on the way to check on my artillery crew down the road," he offered. We each called off our names and then I added, "Oh great, I have been curious to see the guns that had been shooting those loud bursts of shells we had heard since the invasion."

I wanted to know how they knew where to direct their shells. We asked a lot of questions, and he was happy for the company. He said, "The artillery crews are stationed miles to the rear of the fighting. They do not see their target, but they receive messages over the field phone line strung by the signal corps at the front, who gives them the information. Or they receive calibrated figures sent from an observation plane indicating a target to be destroyed. They then set their 155mm howitzer gun to those figures; place the missile into the gun, then pull a lanyard that sends the missile toward the target."

When we reached the field where the men were dug in, we were surprised at the size of it. The excavation was large enough for the big gun to be concealed, with enough room for the four men who were in the dugout, along with pivoting room for the huge barrel that protruded outward. The pit and the howitzer were camouflaged with tree branches and tarpaulin. They lived in open country far from contact with other men, waiting for something to happen and bored with their solitary existence. They were amazed to see us as we stood at the pit's edge. Lieutenant Thompson said, "I thought you would be surprised."

Immediately the usual exchange of the standard questions when meeting comrades began with:

"Where are you all from, Lieutenants?" asked one of the boys as he looked up from the pit.

"I'm from Michigan, so is Lieutenant Betty; Edythe hails from Texas.

"What about y'all? Where are y'all from?" Edythe asked in her Texas drawl.

"Kentucky, Virginia, Pennsy, New Jersey," each called his state.

If anyone named your own state you immediately felt a kinship. Home was the thread that tied us together. It meant fellowship and a sense of security, a reminder of things past. These young men in their prime of life were putting in time, waiting for the war to finish, anxious to return to loved ones. We told about some of our recent experiences of the war and how anxious everyone was for it to end, especially now that we had the Germans on the run.

Lieutenant Thompson, not wishing to distract them from their duties any longer than necessary, interrupted by saying, "I brought you men some mail, a couple of old magazines and rations. Any news you want to pass on?"

"We aint got any news worth the telling," one said, "But it sure was good seeing you nurses. Reminds us of home. Come again."

"Keep a good watch, men." Thompson raised his hand to his brow and saluted.

"Good-by y'all," from Edythe and Betty.

"Good hunting, soldiers," I added as we turned to leave. "See you in the victory parade."

"If our luck holds out," one of the men replied. We got into the jeep with the Lieutenant, and with a salute from the GIs we were off.

When we reached camp we were surprised to see thin metallic strips floating down from the sky and our officers standing around looking skyward puzzled. I wondered if they were some mysterious enemy attack. Later we heard that the strips were called "Window", used by our planes to confuse the enemy radar. The wind had floated them back toward us. Earlier we had had a "gas attack" alert when the sound of the Klaxon rattle reached us from afar. It sent everyone scampering to their tents in search of their gas masks. We looked like men from Mars when we ventured outside and saw one another in the masks. It turned out to be a false alarm.

The 51st Field Hospital followed close behind the infantry as they advanced, setting up and tearing down tents every few days. In August the rains began to subside and the sun began to beat down on us. The dirt stirred by the thousands of retreating enemy, followed closely by our infantry, the Shermans, the anti tanks and armor on the narrow roads turned the shrubs and forest gray, and the atmosphere hazy with clouds of dust.

I remember only fragments of things that happened during the chaotic months of June, July and most of August. I do recall one incident when I was jolted awake by a plane as it roared low over our tent, followed by a crash and a claustrophobic stillness. I found myself surrounded by tarpaulin. The velocity and vibration of the plane had caused the tent pole to crash inches above my head on the cot. As the center of the tent collapsed it isolated each of the occupants into a kind of pup tent. When help arrived to rescue us from our enclosure, they explained that a German plane on a reconnaissance flight had flown too low for our antiaircraft to fire at it without causing damage to our people.

This was a period when there was no time or thought of writing or remembering letters received nor memories of many of the happenings. If there was a break, when we did not have to operate immediately upon arriving at a new area, our thoughts turned to food. We were hungry, especially for a change from the monotony of rations. Visions of real eggs or perhaps a chicken filled our mind.

Bartering

Now we had a chance to scour the surrounding countryside to see what we could find to eat. My tent mates, Florence Bestman and Kay Watry, and I decided to go bartering as soon as we arrived at an advanced area. One had to do this promptly upon arriving at a new advance, or the farmer would have run out of eggs or chickens, as there were many others in the army in the same frame of mind. We gathered our hard chocolate squares, soap, and cigarettes and ventured into the woods. Clad in fatigues, we looked much like infantry as we trekked forth.

We hadn't ventured very far when suddenly we saw several figures rising from the bush with rifles pointing in our direction. We stopped in our tracks, and cautiously turning our heads to the right, then left, to discover that we were surrounded. Kay mumbled something, but I don't remember what it was, as I was frightened. She was always quick with a pertinent remark in any situation. As the men closed in, assuming a stealthy bent position with rifles leveled at us, I noticed that they were in plain clothes and one was a black man. When they saw that we were women, they dropped their firearms downward and greeted us in French exclamations of endearment. They were the FFI, the French Forces of the Interior. They were clearing the area of possible stray snipers as the Germans had departed the area only hours before.

We breathed a sigh of relief, and divided our rations among the six men. It wasn't until they were beside us that I recalled that the tall black Senegalese man was an ally who fought with the French army in Africa.

Thoughts of food could lead one into a dangerous situation, but it did not stop us from bartering. On another occasion I was given a pet bantam rooster by a generous farmer. I carried it back in my arms, and when we reached our bivouac area, he perched on the wood frame protrusion of my cot as if he knew it was his home. However, when he crowed with all his might at the first light of dawn and awakened the entire army, I knew that I could not keep him alive for long. I gave the little rooster to the next farmer with whom we bartered.

15 August 1944

Allied Forces landed in southern France under General Alexander M. Patch's Command, known as the Dragoon operation. They advanced thirty miles with little resistance. They were followed by French General de Lattre's French Corps. By the 23rd of August the Allies were 140 miles inland from the Mediterranean.

Enemy Parachutes

The last units to escape through the Falaise Gap were the German Fifth Panzer and the Seventh Army. They passed through the Allied lines around Chambois and St. Lambert during the night of August 20. The building of the German parachutist headquarters was left smoldering, since they had set it on fire, as was the custom when retreating. The embers were still glowing when several of us entered the building. We rescued several parachutes, and I believe this was the first time it dawned on us that they could well have left booby traps or mines behind. Others in our group followed and soon much of our camp area was camouflaged by parachutes as we draped them above from tent to tent.

More souvenir "salvaging" (actually, looting) consisted of going through leveled houses to find something to rescue from the ruins. Since we could not carry any more equipment than we already had, looting limited me to a china cup and saucer, which didn't last long when tossed into the truck with my bedroll. I did pick up an ancient Bible out of the ruins and sat down in the ashes to leaf through it. It was dated in the 16th century, and I knew it was very valuable. I could not take such a precious book, the words of God spoken to prophets thousands of years ago. I placed it on a shelf where it might be safe and came away empty-handed.

There was a great deal of destruction of homes now that we were close to the cities, and what we took was trivial in comparison to the wastage of war. We were warned that the Germans planted mines as they retreated and it was dangerous to wander about.

A Bath Tub

Several of us nurses were invited by two officers, who came to our camp, to their quarters one afternoon. They were housed in an undamaged house, which was a very rare sight. We went from room to room admiring the furniture and beds, all intact. But when we discovered the bathroom, with a tub, we were elated. We asked our new friends if they would not mind if we took a bath. They knew how they felt when they discovered the house and tub. The men had enjoyed the luxury of their first tub bath since leaving England. We each in turn luxuriated in the warm water, and then ventured forth with dripping hair, to rejoin our party. It was too bad to have had to put on the same clothes, but that was a small matter. We spent the afternoon playing card games, along with relating our experiences and telling them the episodes the GIs had told us as we cared for them.

After the German escape through the Gap, our hospital followed southward toward Alencon, bivouacked for a day or two, then headed northeastward and bivouacked on the outskirts of Versailles. Since we were not going to operate immediately, as we had in the past months, Gertie and I decided to explore the surroundings while waiting for the next move. We wandered up the road right after breakfast and had no trouble getting a ride in the first army vehicle going south from our camp. The driver asked, "Where do you want to go?"

"Chartres?" some one ventured.

"Yes, that's where." We had heard of the Chartres Cathedral. Why not? We had seen Cathedrals in England, North Africa, and Sicily; they are the tourist's first priority. We didn't question the distance, never gave it a thought. After about an hour's drive, we noticed a small army medical installation marked with a large red cross as we rode past. About fifteen miles later we were in Chartres. The GIs let us off on the main street, and Gertie and I started rather timidly walking along the winding street. The area was completely deserted. It looked as if all the people had abandoned the city. We stopped to look at a placard tacked on the door of an impressive stone structure. It looked like a menu posted on the door. As I tried to read the French, Gertie pressed the latch on the door. It was locked. We peeked in the window. Nobody was inside.

Turning toward me, Gertie said, "There are two uniformed men coming down the street." We looked at each other apprehensively, and then continued to pretend reading the sign. As they came closer we recognized a British and an American officer with the insignia of the O.S.S., Office of Strategic Service, an intelligence corps.

They greeted us pleasantly, "Yes, the place is closed, you won't find anything open. In fact, the town is quite deserted. Why not come to our place where we can fix a bite?"

We had no alternative but to follow. There was nothing else we could do; they were senior officers. We walked alongside them, Gertie next to the American officer, Wendell Gibbs, and I beside the British officer, John Nieland, knowing that they would interrogate us.

Our conversation was casual as we walked toward their quarters. What part of the States were we from, where had we been, what we had seen, how we were bearing up with the war. We reached their headquarters, which was just a short distance beyond where the GIs had dropped us. They probably heard and saw the jeep in this quiet, forsaken place and decided to investigate.

The building was a solid stone structure with steps leading into a large, high-ceilinged room filled with many shelves stacked with newspapers, pamphlets, and magazines, and all kinds of printed material lining the walls, stacked on tables, chairs, and even the stairs. We realized we were in what had just recently been the German intelligence headquarters, now in Allied possession. When the officers first asked us where our headquarters was stationed, we casually lied. "Oh, just up the road."

We had told enough about ourselves so they knew we were army nurses and not Mata Hari's. They told us to look around while they cleared a table and disappeared into the kitchen to fix something to eat. We were relieved and grateful, for it had been several hours since breakfast; besides we were always hungry. After a lunch of scrambled eggs (which was a real treat), hot tea and hard biscuit, they let us peruse the printed news that German people were being deceived into believing. "Germany was winning the war, and to devote all their energy toward the victory".

The afternoon passed quickly as we exchanged stories and looked at pictures in the various magazines. In time, Gert and I began to be concerned about getting back to base before dark, but we were wondering about the lie we had told them about our base being "just up the road." Gert asked, "What time do you have, Rad? I believe I forgot to wind my watch." I looked at my wristwatch and said, "Oh, we'd better get going. It's four-thirty."

We picked up our helmets and purses and announced that we had better head back for camp. We also gathered the pamphlets, newspapers, and a magazine they said we could have.

Both officers immediately stood up, and the American said, "Oh, we'll drive you back. We wouldn't think of letting you go by yourselves. This territory is not safe. The Germans were here just yesterday. You never know about stragglers."

As we climbed into the Reconnaissance car, Gert and I looked at each other dubiously. When we neared the Medical Unit with the Red Cross, they didn't slow down but continued right on. We both breathed a sigh of relief when the American said, "That is a clearing station, in bivouac. We know there are no nurses there."

It was nearly a two-hour drive to our camp. They knew all along that we had come from near Versailles. Unfortunately, we had not mentioned that we had set out to see the Chartres Cathedral while perpetuating our deception of coming from "just up the road." They would probably have taken us there had we but mentioned it.

The next day as we moved eastward toward Paris, I was surprised to see American Sherman tanks lumbering up the road behind us, their big gun pointed in our direction. We thought Major Harry P. Harper, in command of our 51st Field Hospital, really outdid himself by putting us ahead of the tanks, until I spotted berets on the soldier's heads. Our drivers, noticing the tanks closing in on our truck, edged off the road to let them pass. I got out my camera when I first saw the tanks advancing and snapped a picture. It was the first time we had seen the French army since landing on the continent.

Major General Jaques P. Leclerc's 2nd Armored Division waved the V for victory sign with hands raised, and shouted greetings as they passed us. It was characteristic of diligent Major Harper to sometimes intersperse us with the Infantry to be sure we would be close by when they needed us—but tanks? Tanks were usually ahead of the infantry. Our trucks diverted south of Paris where we bivouacked.

Ernie Pyle

25 August 1944

Among other Americans who were also diverted from Paris were the news correspondents anxious to be the first to enter Paris, the world-famous city that had been occupied by the Germans since June 14, 1940. As the correspondents drove by our camp and saw us in the field, they stopped to invite us to celebrate with them that evening. They were billeted in a house in Rambouillet, several miles beyond our camp. Although many of the women were tired from the months of harshness of travel, work, and little sleep due to the thunder of bombs, mortar and artillery, quite a few accepted the invitation. It was the first time such an opportunity had presented itself since we landed on the continent, and perhaps we might not have another opportunity for a party. It was also a reason to get our Class A's out of the bedroll and air them out in anticipation of going to Paris. Our uniforms, buried in the bottom of the bedroll, would be full of wrinkles, but tonight it would not matter. Our C.O. arranged transportation, and after supper we climbed into the truck and were off to Rambouillet.

It was cool in the evening, but our olive drab uniforms were wool and we were warm enough in the back of the truck. When we reached the correspondents' quarters, we were greeted by a group of exuberant men who with outstretched arms helped support us as we jumped off the rear of the truck. They escorted us up the few steps of the dwelling into a large room that they had cleared except for chairs and a table set against the wall. The correspondents were civilians, but they also wore olive drab uniforms. They were considerably older than the young officers we had partied with in the air force while in Africa. However, the music heard from a record player had the same familiar strains. We intuitively began singing and soon were dancing in the arms of our new acquaintances.

These men represented world-wide newspapers including *The New York Times, Chicago Tribune,* and *London News,* and magazines *Look* and *Time,* and the *Pathe News* newsreels viewed in the theaters in the States. They, like we, were waiting on the outskirts of Paris for the French army to have the honor of liberating Paris. As we mingled in the crowded living room, a slightly built man greeted me with a kiss on both cheeks while asking me to dance. One might not have noticed him in the crowded room except for the dark beret he wore tilted over the side of his forehead. A fringe of drab sandy hair stuck out on the opposite side of the beret. In spite of his slight build, he hardly looked like a Frenchman.

"I'm Ernie Pyle," he said. "It's a French custom, kissing like that." As he said that, he was tagged and I found myself dancing with another correspondent. However, Ernie kept coming back, and we continued to get acquainted. He held me close as we danced between interruptions of being tagged. The Victrola played music that we all knew and loved: "Stardust," "Red Sails in the Sunset," "Isle of Capri." He hummed the tunes in my ear as he held me close.

There were bottles of cognac, calvados, wine, cheeses, and French bread spread on the table along the wall. Ernie said, "We did a bit of scrounging, as you can see along the wall. Shall we check it out?"

We found delicious French bread sliced and spread with butter, along with hard-boiled eggs cut in half, tomato slices, and clusters of grapes. I suspect the newsmen cut the eggs so they would go around. We placed the tomato on the bread and the egg in hand and enjoyed the treat. Everyone was in high spirits, anxiously looking forward to going to Paris.

We compared the correspondents' living conditions with high army headquarters officials and Red Cross personnel who lived in capital cities far from the front with all the comforts of home, making occasional jaunts to the front to see how things looked. They didn't live in the mud, in tents, on rations, with artillery flying overhead. Since they were near large port cities, they had access to food from refrigerated ships that supplied meat, milk, and delicacies that never reached us, as there was no refrigeration.

I had heard about Ernie Pyle, but had not read any of his stories since we did not have access to news media up front.

Ernie had no qualms about tagging the tall correspondents and kept coming back to me. He was the Scripps Howard News Correspondent and had been following the Infantry and telling their stories through the news media since the war began in Africa. His fame as a correspondent was that he lived in the mud of winter, slept in the pup tents with the Infantry, and wrote about how GI Joe lived and died in the war. It was his personal contact with the GIs in fox holes exposed to gunfire, artillery, and tank warfare that brought the war news home. He told it the way it really was. Ernie Pyle made a point of writing the names of the GIs and where they hailed from that made his stories personal and interesting.

We exchanged news of where we had been while as we danced looking eye to eye. His eyes were blue edged by upturned wrinkles at the temple, suggesting a sense of humor. His brow below the beret was lined with wrinkles. His thin lips spread into frequent hints of a smile as we exchanged small talk. His manner seemed shy yet friendly as he questioned me about my experience in the war. He was curious. We discovered that we had traveled much the same paths of war across North Africa, Sicily, and now France. We laughed at the "A-rab" antics we both recalled in Africa. Our hospitals were quite distant from the front line in Africa in the early phase of that war. However, our Third Auxiliary Surgical teams were sent to Tebessa, the 16th Medical Regiment and the 48th Surgical Hospital at Tabarka, and operated with British units at Souk El Khemis close to the front where Ernie had been. Our entire unit also served on D.S. earlier at the 7th Station Hospital in Oran, the 61st Hospital near Constantine, and the 38th Evacuation near Beja and the 3rd General near Matuer. Ernie nodded as I mentioned familiar places and events of our parallel journey in the past nearly two years. He noticed a group of his comrades heading toward the kitchen and took my hand as we followed. Several men had obtained champagne from some hidden source and poured it into glasses and tumblers and offered each a container half filled with the sparkling fluid. We all raised our glass as someone suggested: "To Paris and Victory!" We repeated the toast in unison.

As I sipped my champagne, I could not help notice a certain indefinable longing in Ernie's expression as we reminisced. I wondered why he chose to be away from the States and home for such a long time, as he was not in the army and was free to do as he pleased. Most of us could hardly wait for the war to end so we could go home. He had been away three years. He was stationed in London in 1941, and wrote about the "Blitz," when England was bombed nightly by the Luftwaffe, then went to North Africa in 1942, Sicily, and Italy in 1943 and now, in 1944, in France.

Our party came to a sudden end when we heard our truck backing into the driveway. As we parted, Ernie kissed both cheeks again, saying, "It's been great to be with an American girl. Seems like home. Perhaps we will meet in Paris."

Pyle won the Pulitzer Prize along with many other awards for his eyewitness accounts about the ordinary GIs fighting the war. After a short time in France, Ernie Pyle visited the States and continued on to the Pacific Theater of war where he followed the assaults on Iwo Jima and Okinawa. He was killed in a foxhole on Ie Shima by Japanese machine gun fire. A white stone marker on his grave has the following inscription:

AT THIS SPOT THE 77TH INFANTRY DIVISION LOST A
BUDDY, ERNIE PYLE, ON APRIL 18, 1945

Paris

25 August 1944

Brigadier General Jacques LeClerc's 4th Armored
Division, with the aid of the American First Army, was
given the honor of liberating Paris. There were several
outbreaks of fighting in the buildings leading to the Arc
de Triomphe and on avenues leading to the Arc, which
were occupied by Germans that had to be captured before
Paris was free. The French shouted, sang, laughed,
kissed, embraced and threw flowers at the troops as
they marched past. Despite Hitler's order to fight for
the city, the surrender was signed by General Dietrich
von Choltitz on the 25th of August 1944, at the railroad
station at Mont Parnasse.

On the 26th, French General Charles de Gaulle
entered Paris to head the greatest parade in history, led
by the French Liberation Forces. Americans in khaki
and steel helmets marched up the Champs Elysees
while the bands played the "Star Spangled Banner,"
the "Marseillaise," and "God Save the King." At the
Arc de Triomphe, General de Gaulle placed a wreath of
gladioli and a cross of roses on the Tomb of the Unknown
Soldier with its eternal light. The American First Army
stopped, turned to face the tomb of the Unknown Soldier,
and saluted. In the stillness of that poignant moment a
bugler blew taps, and all the grief seemed to pour forth in
those liquid, pathetic tones. For a moment no one stirred.
Then the American army faced eastward and continued
to march toward the front. The millions gathered at the
site broke out in singing and celebration. The French
had survived the occupation by the Nazis since June 14,
1940.

Pandemonium reigned in Paris, as more Americans

Nurses Radawiec and M. Johnson in Paris

entered the city on August 26, 1944. A group of us nurses got a ride with an officer friend of one of the girls. The streets were lined with citizens exhilarated with joy. They tossed flowers as we rode past and made the "V" sign of victory with hands raised high, threw kisses, waved, hugged and patted us on the shoulder. There was much hand clasping and expressions of joy radiating on everyone's face when we reached a second-story restaurant. We celebrated by sipping poor tasting, weak ale as we watched the parade from a balcony. There was no food, since the Germans had expropriated everything into Germany during the occupation. Paris residents, we were told, were on the verge of starvation. After the day

Team surgeons: Major Charles A. Serbst is third from left.

of celebration in Paris, we returned to camp to hear that we were to move in the morning.

We began packing our gear, since the army always got an early start in the dark. The bedroll would be

Commandeered German vehicle. Enlisted Man Thibault, Dr. Dashe, E.M. Maravick and Scolett, Dr. Meyers.

In French town in Normandy, a cow is being used as a draft horse. Germans had commandeered most of the peasants' horses. (Photo by 3rd Aux Group Dr. A. M. Mery)

rolled up last thing in the morning. I crawled into my sleeping bag and soon was sound asleep, but not for long, as the noise of truck motors and voices jarred us awake. My tent mates and I splashed cold water on our faces out of helmets, combed our hair, put on some lipstick, and slipped into our fatigues. With a mess kit in one hand and steadying the helmet on our heads with the other we dashed to the mess tent for breakfast. It was a warm breakfast, hot oatmeal, for a change, bread with marmalade, and coffee. I never could stomach the tart canned grapefruit juice at that early hour. We knew that when traveling there would not be much lunch and often a very late supper, depending on where we bivouacked, so we ate heartily. We hurried back to brush our teeth and roll up our bedrolls. It took two of us to roll one, one from each side, to get it snug and strapped tightly so it would not fall apart when the GIs tossed it into the truck. We wore our wool coats now, as it was chilly at night, accompanied by the usual paraphernalia. After climbing into the trucks that were parked on the road, we sat on the hard benches and waited.

At 4:00 o'clock it was dark and chilly. Drowsiness was a problem after the few hours sleep. Our drivers started up the motors while Major Harry Harper, standing beside the road, determined to keep us close to the infantry, interspersed our trucks between those of the infantry division commanded by General Courtney Hodges. We drove past many cities along the way, including Soissons, Laon, Dinant, and Namur, and crossed the Meuse River, then came to a stop at a small village where our trucks turned into an empty field. We got off the trucks and stood around not knowing if we would continue or stay there. Nobody seemed to know what was going to happen next, so we sat on the ground and waited. It was as always, "Hurry up and wait."

Chapter 7:
Belgium

9 September 1944

Liege fell on the 8th of September. We bivouacked in Petit Rechain, a small village north of Verviers, which had been liberated by the First Army earlier in the day. This was in advance of the infantry division clearing station. The field had just been swept for possible mines by the engineers, as was the custom, since the enemy always planted mines as they retreated unless they were followed too closely by the Allies. As we turned off the road into the field I saw a woman come out of a house across the street to sweep the porch steps as if nothing had happened. Shortly, the streets filled with civilians, old men, women and children, at first cautiously, then with flags waving and singing their national anthem. They welcomed the Americans with open arms, and as more people gathered, they formed into a parade that soon jammed the main road. A group of our officers who had ventured out to explore were caught up in the celebration. They came back to camp decorated with garlands of flowers and carrying bouquets of roses. They told about being hugged and kissed on both cheeks.

Directly across the field from our bivouac area the homes looked intact without any indication of war. As we waited in the field, a straggly dog came over to one of the nurses who was eating a piece of Limburger cheese that she had procured earlier and raised up on his hind legs to sniff it. Thinking he was hungry, she gave him a piece. He ate it, then ran off howling as if he had been shot. After sitting on the ground waiting to see whether the tents would go up or whether we would continue, several of us decided to do a bit of exploring as was our practice when we were idle.

As we walked along the road, a thin, sprightly old

man standing on the porch of a house greeted us saying, "Bon jour Mademoiselles." A plump, somewhat younger woman stood in the doorway, wiping her hands on a white apron tied about her thick waist nodded her head in a friendly manner.

"Bon jour, monsieur, Madame," we replied in unison. I added, "Comment telle vous?" We had acquired a few phrases in French from our stay in Africa the year before.

They motioned us into their home. The little man, bowing nervously, anxious to be friendly, chattered French phrases, some of which we understood and the rest we guessed at the meaning. This being borderline territory, we realized his wife was a German hausfrau. Her legs were wrapped in white elastic bandages indicating she had circulatory problems. They led us into a cozy kitchen and put a teakettle on the wood-burning stove. We sat down at the table, introduced ourselves, and began chatting in broken French phrases with many gesticulations while waiting for the teakettle to boil.

As Frau Blanchy poured our tea, our eyes took in the surroundings and fastened on the hand-operated wringer-type stand and washtubs standing in the adjoining room. Simultaneously, our thoughts turned to bathing. We pointed to the tubs and made our desire clear with motions of washing ourselves. Monsieur Bodson Blanchy, went into the pantry and came out with a copper boiler and invited us to return when the water would be heated. That evening we had our second bath since landing on the continent. Frau Blanchy kept adding more water to the boiler as we took turns bathing in the washtub on the kitchen floor. It felt good to be sitting immersed in warm water instead of the usual cold sponge bath from a helmet in a cold tent. We visited them the next day and brought chocolate and soap in exchange for their hospitality.

They led us into their parlor and pointed to the shell holes in their windows and china cupboard. With difficulty they explained how the Germans had deceived

The E. Bodson Blanchy family,
our Belgian hosts

the Americans by waving white flags of surrender. Earlier, the Germans had strung steel wires across the road, and when the first Americans came speeding past in their jeeps with windshields down, they were decapitated. The Germans had concealed themselves in the homes and shot at the Americans during the melee that followed.

We began to understand why the villagers were so anxious to be friendly. Clearly, they were afraid of being accused of being collaborators. They were familiar with Hitler's method of dealing with saboteurs.

Hitler had picked the village of Lidice for revenge after Czech President Edouard Benes, exiled in England, sent two Czech paratroopers to assassinate the vicious terrorist SS Reinhard Heydrich. Heydrich, the German governor of Bohemia and Moravia (now in the Czech Republic) was killed on May 27, 1942. This act provoked the Nazis to a savage reprisal against the entire village. All the people in the village of Lidice were gathered into a large building, around which petrol was poured and set on fire. Anyone attempting to escape through the windows was shot. Those few people who had been away on holiday returned to a completely desolate village.

They saw children's tricycles, toys and dolls strewn on the pathway to the town square where the people had been murdered.

This scene was repeated ten days later in Lezaky, a village near Prague. And again in August 1944 in a French village, when the 2nd SS Panzer Division massacred the entire population of Oradour-sur-Glane near Limoges, after hearing that explosives were stored there by the French maquisards, a roving band of FFI. The SS locked all the males in barns, the women and children in the church, and set fire to the entire village. Anyone attempting to escape was shot. All 642 villagers perished. We began to realize how helpless people were as the Nazis captured one country after another.

This thin, kindly looking little Frenchman and his frau could do nothing when the Germans took over their home. We sympathized with them in their apprehension as we Americans arrived. They told us they were worried about their young son who was interned in Germany, as were all young men in occupied countries. They were forced to either work in munitions factories or serve in the army. Their son had just turned seventeen when he was taken away, and they had not heard from him in over a year. They were very anxious because they knew the Allies were bombing strategic areas all over Germany.

While we were bivouacked at Petite Rechain, the rumor spread that the First Army had crossed the German border at Trier (Treves) on the 12th of September, advancing five miles into the Reich. It was the first German city to fall to the Americans,.

However, because supplies were beginning to slow down all along the line for all the Allied forces, we were still in bivouac in the field. I was pleasantly surprised to see a familiar figure coming toward where we nurses were gathered. It was Major Bayne, a fellow I had met when much had been blocked out of my mind. Casualties were so devastating, the hours in surgery endless, and the exhaustion so severe, that little is recalled of those months.

However, I remembered that we had had instant rapport when we first met, and I was happy to see him again. He was attached to the Ninth Air Force and I assumed he was working in headquarters, since he did not fly on missions. He seemed to have a lot of freedom and always had transportation available. I don't remember that we questioned what anyone did in their organizations since we were all part of the army and did whatever was expected of us without inquiring about specifics. As he approached my side he said, "Hello, Rad."

I rose from among my nurse comrades where we sat waiting for orders for our next move. I joined the Major, a bit embarrassed at being somewhat disheveled, as we all were, and as we walked toward his jeep parked near the road, he continued, "That's a hell of a way to spend your time, you all sitting on that damp ground. Would you like to ask someone to come along and we'll go into Liege and see what we can find to do, something better than this, certainly."

I went back and motioned to Gertie Trainer to come to me, because she and I had been on adventures before. After Bayne greeted Gertie, she and I got into the back seat of the jeep. Major Bayne started the motor and we were on our way.

It wasn't long before we were in the center of town facing a tall building with a tapered facade, shaped like an electric iron, with roads running in five directions at its point. As we neared it we saw "Hotel Cosmopolite" above the entrance. Bayne stopped and said, "I'll see what goes on here."

He jumped out to inquire, while Gertie and I waited in the jeep. He was back in a few minutes saying, "We can *manger* here, but the concierge says it will take time to cook up something."

I don't know how Bayne's Texas accent registered to the Frenchman; besides, he was the fastest talking Texan I'd ever met. It seemed to me that there were more

Texans in the army than men from anywhere else. Gertie and I got out of the jeep and we entered as Bayne held the heavy carved wooden door entrance to the lobby. I was surprised as we entered to see a group of men occupying one of the tables near the rear wall. We chose one close to the concierge's desk.

We hardly got seated when the concierge said that since we had to wait for the food to be prepared, it might be better for us to go upstairs and wait in the rooms. He led us up the stairs and opened a door at the top of the stairway. Gert and I entered a bright, sunny corner room with curtained windows on two walls and a double bed covered with a brightly quilted spread. Bowing, he closed the door behind us and led Major Bayne down the hall. When Gert and I opened the door to the bathroom and saw the bathtub, we were ecstatic. In no time she and I had our clothes off and in turn took a hot bath in the large white tub. The bed looked like sheer luxury, compared to the hard canvas cots in the big tent in a damp field. We couldn't resist lying down to feel the softness of the mattress and look up to see a white painted ceiling instead of dark tarpaulin. We decided this was paradise.

Before long there was a knock on the door, and Bayne announced that dinner was ready. We followed him down the stairs into the dining room, where we saw that we were the only guests. The chef brought platters filled with beef au jus, mashed real potatoes, fresh green beans, and a salad of sliced tomatoes, French bread with real butter and dessert, a sweet pudding topped with whipped cream. There was wine in several varieties with each course. It was a feast fit for a king. While we ate, Bayne said, "I parked the jeep around the bend of the building as it would not do to have it set in front of the hotel." He added that the concierge explained that he didn't want us downstairs earlier because of the possibility that a stray German might come into the hotel and it might have created an unpleasant situation. He also had bolted the door.

Leisurely, we enjoyed our good fortune and talked about our recent experiences and our last bath in the Frenchman's kitchen. After the long, pleasant dinner, we went upstairs, where Gert and I could hardly wait to get undressed and into the soft bed with white sheets and down-filled pillows. Gertie said, "Where did you meet this guy, Rad? Are we ever lucky to get out of that damp field!"

"I don't remember where, but I sure am glad he found the Third Aux."

We were grateful to Major Bayne for his thoughtfulness and knew that he, too, was enjoying the same comfort. We would not be missed at the bivouac field, as there was no roll call and the girls knew we might be late coming back.

In the morning, the smell of coffee reminded us that we had better get back to reality in case our camp got orders to move. There was a knock on the door, and the Major announced, "Breakfast will be ready in a half hour."

It didn't take us long to slip into our fatigues and go downstairs to find, on the same table where we had had dinner last night, a pot of steaming coffee along with cups and saucers. As Bayne poured the coffee, the waiter brought plates with fried eggs, fried potatoes, French bread, butter and cream for our coffee. After we finished eating, Major Bayne went to the concierge's desk, and I noticed him laying a wad of wrinkled bills on the counter. We expressed our thanks to the man and were on our way.

When we got back to camp, Gert and I felt sheepish about our good fortune, but when we discovered that we hadn't even been missed, we decided not to mention it to the others.

Our respite was cut short; that afternoon we were on the road and setting up operation a few miles north of Petit Rechain. With fall coming, the rains began, and soon ambulances and trucks bringing wounded from the battlefield churned the ground into a sea of mud. Trucks, jeeps, weapons carriers—all vehicles—sank up to the middle of their hub caps in the quagmire, and became immobilized. The high-top boots we now wore again became heavy with mud. The mud slowed the army almost to a stop.

On several occasions, Belgian doctors dressed in bright blue uniforms with gold braid on epaulets, gold cord hanging across their chest, and their visored caps trimmed with gold braid, visited our operation tents, anxious to observe our surgeons operating. I helped them into sterile gowns and directed them to stand behind the surgeons. They asked questions about procedures and remarked on our generous use of the antibiotic penicillin, which was just becoming available to us. We poured 100,000 units into open bellies, chests, and other massive wounds as a precautionary procedure. These older Belgian doctors seemed impressed as they observed the skillful hands of our young surgeons while they probed for shrapnel, tied bleeders, cut into organs and intestines and removed damaged tissue. These young surgeons had had more experience in the past two years than they might have had in many years of peacetime surgery. The Belgians were profuse in thanking the surgeons for allowing them to observe them while they operated.

12 September 1944

The 51st Field Hospital was first in receiving wounded after the First Army penetrated German territory. In the eighty-six hours since we had set up, we operated on 1004 severely wounded. It was the heaviest surgical stand for the hospital during this period. As the army advanced and wounded were collected from the battlefield, the three platoons that comprised the field hospital followed close behind.

Unfortunately, the service of supply headquarters was not able to keep the entire front line supplied with vital materials to continue the advance. As the weather worsened, the infantry were running out of ammunition, the supply of gasoline was running low, and even rations were getting scarce. Our major port in Cherbourg was still the only port where ships could dock to unload supplies. Cherbourg, on the northwestern peninsula of France, was some six hundred miles to the rear, farther than the initial invasion beaches of Utah and Omaha in June.

Trucks bringing supplies from Cherbourg to the front, called the "Red Ball Express," were failing to deliver the necessary equipment fast enough to keep the front line equipped. The army slowed, held the line and stopped to reorganize. When the Red Ball Express was investigated, it was found that some truck drivers were not "on the ball." They detoured off the given route, stopped in undesignated areas where their freight was sold or stolen and never reached the front where it was so desperately needed. Court-martial proceedings sent the guilty men to prison. The problem would remain with the Allies until depots and a major port could be opened up closer to the front. Although the British captured Antwerp on the 4th of September 1944, the Germans held on to its sea approaches until late in November. The race across the continent now brought us almost to a halt just inside the German border.

Enlisted men Houston, Rogers, Wm. Thomas and Levy

Chapter 8:
Germany

14 September 1944

The roar of thousands of bombers flying high above assured us that the air force was carrying on with the war and those airstrips that now were established in France were getting fuel that flowed through pipelines beneath the English Channel from England to the western shore of France. This ingenious scheme came into operation just in time. However, to get the fuel and the thousands of tons of supplies to the German border, many hands were required to load it onto trucks. Trains and railways in France lay in ruins because of the Allied bombings. Looking up, I could barely distinguish the B-25s, B-26s, and B-17s, and the many fighter plane escorts. Later, we heard that five thousand planes were involved in bombing Germany, from the Siegfried Line all the way to Berlin.

The Third Auxiliary Surgical Group, my organization when I was not on detached service at a field hospital, had moved up to the outskirts of Eupen, and we were back with our own people while we waited for supplies to catch up. Eupen had been annexed by the Germans from Belgium and had been resettled by German people along the border. There were no flags or welcoming throngs when we arrived into this area. The people were sullen. One Sunday, a group of us decided we would attend church services in the city not far from our camp. The local citizenry, old men, women and very few children, tolerated our presence with equanimity, but when a sudden swish of an artillery shell exploded some distance away vibrating the church, we weren't comfortable in their midst. My comrades eyed each other wondering if we were safe. Our artillery guns were softening Aachen's resistance while we waited for the Red Ball Express to bring up supplies so the war could continue.

A Surprise

I was in my tent reading a book when a corpsman came to the opening and said, "You're wanted on the telephone, Lieutenant."

"Telephone? Me? In Germany?" I was bewildered! What could it mean? I hardly realized that there were telephones up front. I had never heard of anyone having a telephone call while overseas. As a matter of fact, I never had reason to think about such a happening. Of course, there was communication between various units for war purposes, but this was a call for me.

I got up and followed the corpsman to the headquarters tent, my mind in a state of perplexity. "Who, what could it possibly mean?"

When I reached headquarters tent, Corporal Jenkins informed me that it was long distance. I picked of the receiver wondering who could be calling, and tremulously spoke into the portable field telephone. "Hello, this is Lieutenant Radawiec."

"Rad? Brunson here. How are you sweetheart?" I was speechless. "Are you there, Rad? Listen, I just arrived in France a few days ago. I want desperately to see you. Trouble is, I fly every day, weather permitting, and can't get away. But I want very much to see you."

"Brunson?" I was still speechless.

"Can you get away honey? You can get a ride with our observation plane. Can you come? Will you?"

"Well, what a surprise! How did you ever find me, Brunson? I hardly know myself where I am from day to day. Where are you? Did you say Cambrai?"

"Yes, darling. I had to come back to see you before the war finished. I've missed you so. Just tell the Cub pilot to bring you to the B-26 bomber field in France. He will know. Try to come, sweetheart."

"I'll try, but I have never heard of such a possibility. It will have to be tomorrow or the next day, as we never stay long in one place. It's good to hear your voice again Brunson."

"Try, try hard, darling. I'll be looking for you. It's great to hear your voice, my love. Good-by, sweetheart."

"Good-by, Bruns, I'll see what I can do. Good-by, dear."

I was elated! Brunson had been the light of my life in those long months spent in Africa. I had figured he had forgotten me after he returned to the States. He had been entertained by Hollywood stars—among them, Alexis Smith. He was celebrated because of his decorations, among them the Distinguished Flying Cross on two occasions, for performance over and above the call of duty, and outstanding marksmanship on bomb runs. He was a hero. He had flown fifty missions as a bombardier with the Fortresses based in North Africa. He had an outstanding record for hitting the target. He had bombed the Brenner Pass, a 4,495-foot pass where a railroad connected Austria to Italy, and where Hitler and Mussolini met to discuss the war. He was a celebrated guest at USO shows with movie stars in publicity attempts to recruit "Flying Boys" to replace the great losses suffered in the bombing runs over enemy territory. He was indeed a hero.

I was thrilled to hear his voice again. I had allowed myself only casual friendships after he was sent back to the States. I remembered how desolate I felt after he was gone, how alone, when I heard he had flown away without one more time together, a last good-bye. I had grown accustomed to looking skyward at the familiar sound of the Fortress, to see its wings tilt as he passed over our tent area, and know in a short time he would be at our recreation tent calling, "Hey, Rad."

I was beginning to learn that I would need to control my emotions as the war raged. War does not abide any enduring relationship. You move with the army never knowing when or where. Besides, since landing in France in June, there had been no respite from work or to think of the past. I was thrilled and anxious to see my lover again.

Since we were idle, Marcelle, my tent mate, went

with me to inquire at the nearby airfield about flying to the 585th Bomb Squadron, 394 Bomb Group base near Cambrai, the B-26 airfield. "Sure, glad for the company," the young lieutenant said. "We reconnoiter back and forth all the time. This trip will be a nice change."

Without much ado we arranged to take off the following day. Because our group was scattered at various field hospitals and our chief nurse was at headquarters in another area, we had free reign, within reason, to do as we saw fit when we were not operating. Besides, the Third Aux was a civilian group of professionals, and the army seemed to tolerate its difficulty to adjust to army protocol, I thought.

I got the Scarab ring that Brunson had placed on my finger a year ago out of its small box, and put it on my third finger of my left hand. I had not worn any rings while working since the invasion, as they would puncture the sterile rubber gloves I wore in surgery. Early the next morning Corporal James drove Marcelle, who had a friend at the Cambrai base, and me to the small airfield near Eupen. We girls never traveled alone in these times. In fact, we did no traveling at all except as the army moved. We strapped ourselves into the small plane with the help of the pilot, Lieutenant Young. The ground crew spun the prop and we were off in a cloud of dust. As we looked below, we could trace the path of the war in recent days. Wide tracks made by tank treads, and ruts due to the heavy traffic that had so recently torn up the roads curved below us. Occasionally a huge bomb crater caught our eyes. The pilot scanned the sky for possible enemy planes, since the Luftwaffe flew low and fast. Now and then we saw a Swastika on a disabled tank tilted on its side at the edge of the road. The trees were beginning to change into shades of gold, yellows and reds in the woodlands below.

As we approached the airfield landing strip in France, a jeep raced across the field and stopped short of our plane's wing tip. It was Brunson in dress up pinks, his air force visor cap crushed, as was the custom, to the familiar jaunty angle that I remembered so well. He approached the cockpit and helped Marcelle as she jumped to the ground. Lifting me under my arms, his heavenly blue eyes met mine as he set me on the ground. He put his arms around me, pressing me close as he whispered, "My dearest, I've missed you so very much." Our lips met in a kiss.

I introduced Marcelle, and Brunson said, "Welcome back to France. I trust you didn't see any Messerschmitts." His arms around me, holding me close, we kissed again and he said, "Honey, it's almost a year since we said good-by in Tunis. Remember?"

How well I remembered. I had led an unattached kind of existence after he was gone. With the end of the African campaign and after a month in Sicily, we had returned to England. Then, following six months of preparing for the invasion, we had finally landed in France in June. Since then my days had been filled with work in the field hospitals as the infantry fought desperately to gain a foothold on the Continent. We followed close behind the infantry at Omaha, Coutances, and Cherbourg, and saw the slaughter at St. Lo. The stalemate at Avranches and Mortain followed by the Falaise disaster—those were long periods of disastrous casualties. I don't remember much about those days. We hardly had time to think, no time for anything other than operating on those terrible wounds, and the sleep of exhaustion. No time to reflect on any other type of existence other than war. We had become like robots.

Brunson held me close, and we kissed. As he looked toward Marcelle he said, "Excuse me, but I have been waiting a year for this." Then looking into my eyes he said, "How lucky can a guy be? First, to find you in the field in Eupen, and your being able to come to me. It's a miracle, especially since it was impossible for me to get away. We fly everyday day that weather permits. Besides that we are restricted to camp because of certain plans that are now in progress.

I learned later that "Clarion," a code name for secret bombing missions, was being developed at the time. The object was carpet bombing over all of Germany and included the B-26 "Bridge Busters."

Brunson continued, "We aren't to trust anyone, and no one is allowed to leave the post. There is no time for socializing."

"Socializing? What is that? I thought. Then, looking at my returned lover, I said, "Oh, Bruns, I can't believe this is true, that we're together once more. I've missed you so very much."

Then I said, "Oh, I didn't tell you. Marcelle made it a lot easier for me to come. She has a friend in your squadron she would like to see. And we were lucky to get the Cub plane. Everything turned out just perfectly."

We climbed into the jeep. Marcelle insisted on my sitting up front beside Brunson as he drove to his headquarters. I looked at him as we rode, his face tan, contrasting with his blonde wavy hair just barely visible on the one side of that floppy cap.

He turned toward me, his deep blue eyes tantalizing, and whispered. "I love you."

It was good to hear those words after the barren existence of the past year, exciting to be near him again. "Tell me Bruns, how is it that you are back? Surely, after fifty missions . . ."

"No, darling, I didn't have to come back, but I had to find you, to be with you. This war was lasting too long for me to be so far away. I had to know how you felt before you departed for the States. I wanted to find out if I stood a chance. It took a bit of doing to get to this place however, instead of the Pacific."

We headed toward headquarters where Marcelle, after a few minutes, located her friend, and they escorted us to the quarters where Marcelle and I would share in our overnight stay. I dropped my musette bag and helmet on the bed, then opened my make-up case and reached for my comb and mirror. Marcelle's friend, clasping her arm said," Come, I want to show you my quarters. See you both at lunch, Bruns."

Standing in front of me, his hands on my shoulders, Bruns said, "You're as beautiful as ever, but, honey you are so pale and thin. Where is that golden girl I left in Africa?"

"There's no sun in the operating tents," I said. "Besides, we've had nothing but rain except for the few weeks in August. Now it's back to the rainy season again. No, I haven't been lying in the sun as we did back in Africa, my sweet."

"You look so fragile dear, your eyes—are you O.K.?"

"Oh, I'm all right. As for my eyes, they have seen a great deal of destruction and death since June. By the way, you're not the best correspondent in the world, Bruns. I thought you had forgotten me."

His letters had been spaced by rather long intervals after we parted in Africa. I recalled the times his damaged Fortress had to make emergency landings in Tunis because it would not make it to back to Telergma, when several of his crew had been seriously wounded. I remembered the chicken dinners at the French home in Ain M'Lila, along with Captain Wolfe and Edythe, realizing that our men were getting very jittery. They called it "nerves." Edythe and I, to take their minds off the pressure, told about the trivial happenings at camp; the antics of Whimpy the pup. But that was long ago.

Now Brunson put his arms around me, holding me close to his body, his eyes looking into mine, his lips close. He said, "Honey, I've loved you all the time. Remember you said you had to go back home to see your "guy" before you could make a commitment? I wanted to be fair about that. I didn't want to make it any more difficult, but I love you and had to come back to see how you still feel. I could not let you go back without our being together again. Now here we are. You are in my arms and I never want to let you go, ever."

"Bruns, it was a devastating time for me. I thought you had forgotten me. I looked for your letters, and when they were so few, I decided "out of sight, out of mind.""

"Well darling, I was still in the service and you know how busy the army can keep one. I did a considerable amount of teaching. The Army Air Force needs new recruits desperately, as so many are being lost to the Luftwaffe, their new fast fighters, those ME-109s. I taught new bombardiers how to use the Norden bombsight. It necessitated a good bit of travel. But let's not talk about that, I'm just thrilled to see you again, to hold you close, my dear. By the way you are not wearing the identification bracelet I sent you." His eyes shifted to the Scarab ring. He placed his hand over the ring and my hand, adding, "I hope it continues to bring me luck. I'm glad you are wearing it."

"About the bracelet, Bruns, I never received a bracelet."

"That's probably where some of my letters went. Down into the deep blue. As for letters, I didn't get very many letters either, my love."

"Well, I responded to yours, and if I got few, then so did you. Besides, there was no time for writing the past months, no time for anything except work."

Bruns's turned his face for a moment. "I see Captain Moore and Marcelle, heading this way." He watched them through the window, coming across the field. "He's going to bring Marcelle here. You're both going to bunk here. Let's get out of here. I want to show you my boudoir."

We entered a small room on the lower level and sat down on the only place available, a French narrow metal-framed bed. It was wonderful to be with Brunson again. He rekindled stored feelings that had lain dormant a long time as we sat close and reminisced about the happenings in the past year. He teased about other fellows I might have had. I didn't explain that there was no time for dating or that I was hurt too much with partings or that I found it much easier to be true to my lover back home.

We reminisced about the past, about our African days together. But mostly we were happy to be close again. There was so much lost time to make up.

At noon we met Marcelle and her captain at mess. Later they joined us in the officers club, where we played several rubbers of bridge. Afterwards, Brunson and I went for a walk into the woods just beyond his headquarters. It is a custom for French families to walk in the woods in an evening or Sunday afternoons. There are many well-trodden paths, but we chose a lesser, narrow one, to be alone. Holding hands, our shoes crunching the crisp, brightly colored autumn leaves; we walked until we came to a huge Chestnut tree, beneath which Brunson spread the blanket that we were accustomed to carrying. So much lost time to make up in this short visit. We sat down beneath the tree facing each other, his eyes on mine, and reminisced about our days in Africa. The time he pinned his Silver Wings on my blouse with much fanfare, and the many evenings spent watching the moon climb over the ridge of the Atlas Mountains. It was not safe to be alone after dark in the country, and our dates were always in groups of four.

Now in his arms, I found the moments together precious. We were making up for a lost year and wondered what the future held for us. We knew the war would be fierce now that we were in German territory. We had heard that Hitler had directed his army to fight to the death.

As for Brunson, his bombing missions deep into well-protected Germany were very hazardous. Now our time together was swiftly passing and the chill of the autumn evening was closing in on us. Bruns got up and held out his arms to me. I grasped his hands and he pulled me up, pressing me close to his body. We kissed passionately. As we started back to camp, arms around one another's waists, he said, "I can't believe this is really happening. I've dreamed about you, about holding you in my arms so often. I'll never let you go."

Later, at mess, the other fellows looked longingly at us. They were missing their loved ones far away. Brunson took some ribbing about being so lucky, as did Marcelle's captain. After supper we went to the officers' club and danced to music from a record player. No one danced as smoothly as Brunson. He was still wearing those cowboy boots that he wore in Africa. He reminded me of the party at Chat au Dunne, where we first met and fell in love. I was sure that it was the silver evening dress I wore that evening that attracted him.

He said, "It was you, the girl I saw in the mirror as you fluffed your red hair, the golden tan of your face, neck, and arms. You were a dream come true in the desert. I had to race like hell to get to you before you were mobbed."

He mentioned the white cathedral we visited at Carthage where I said a silent prayer for his safety on the bomb runs that he flew almost every day. We recalled the huge full moon over the Byzantine dome of the cathedral when we walked out into the night. It was an unforgettable picture, a postcard scene. Now, as the evening was drawing to a close, dancing to the strains of, "Always", Bruns said, "That was my request, Rad, that last record. Yes, I'll be loving you always, my dear."

We walked up to his tiny room, and were alone, for a long time. Brunson held me close as he pledged his love. "I hate letting you go again, Rad. I'll always want only you." We lingered a little longer, caressing, not wanting to part.

"It's getting very late, Bruns, I'd better get back to my room. Marcelle will wonder." I arose, smoothed my hair with my hand, and straightened my clothes as we headed toward the hall. My darling's arms, holding me close to his side, led me to my room. Marcelle was sound asleep. It was very late.

After breakfast, Brunson helped us into the jeep and we drove to the airfield where the Cub plane was being readied for takeoff. He put his arms around my waist, saying, "I'll try to be a better correspondent, sweetheart.

You'll see. I love you very much. Take care of yourself."

"Good-bye Brunson, I love you."

"Good-bye, my darling." Bruns helped us up into the plane, throwing a kiss as we parted. The propeller whirled as we taxied off, leaving a trail of dust obscuring my sweetheart as he waved good-bye.

When we arrived at our camp, we were told to be ready to move in the morning. Marcelle and I got busy rearranging our bedrolls, laying our class A uniforms flat on them and sorting through our belongings to have all the needed articles in our musette bags that we carried with us. We worked quickly while it was still daylight, since we always started out in the safety of the dark. Our bedrolls would be rolled up and strapped the first thing when we awakened, and placed outside the tent for our GIs to toss into the truck while we ate breakfast.

After traveling for about an hour, our trucks came to a stop in front of a stone building, an empty schoolhouse. The nurses cots and bedrolls were set up on the second level; the officers and headquarters established themselves on the first floor, while the enlisted men were billeted in the basement. Nurse's cots were crowded into several rooms, with just enough space to walk between them. Since the weather was turning cold and damp, we were pleased to be housed in a building for the first time, instead of a tent.

There were no young people about outside, nor did we see any civilians.

Northeast of us was the ancient city of Aachen, the birthplace of Emperor Charlemagne in 742. Charlemagne was crowned king of the Frankish empire by Pope Leo III in Rome in 800. Aachen was the city of the coronation of thirty-two emperors and kings, and was known for its sulfur medicinal spring waters since early Roman days.

I was sitting on my cot, which happened to be against a corner wall, when I was startled to hear the whoosh and felt the vibration of a low flying artillery shell barely clearing the top of the building, heading in the direction of

Aachen. The windows rattled as it whooshed past. Aachen was being pulverized. My roommates and I wondered if our artillery crew was aware that we had just moved in. We hoped they would aim the shells a bit higher. I knew that artillery crews did not see what they are aiming at, but this shell sounded too low for comfort, and sometimes a shell does go astray. We did not set up our field hospital here, as the front line had not yet stabilized.

As was our custom when idle, we decided to explore the surrounding area. While traveling on the paved winding road with an officer one afternoon, we drove past a deep wooded area. There was no sign of life, nor had we run into any other traffic in the past several miles. Almost simultaneously as the thought occurred to me, my friend said, "I've got an eerie feeling about that thick dark interior and I'm suspicious of possible snipers among those trees."

Usually we ran into GIs in army vehicles coming and going, but this was an area of over eighty unguarded miles. With feelings of apprehension we made a U-turn and headed back in the direction we had come.

Several weeks later while on another road, we were stopped by our M.P.s, at nearby crossroads and were asked questions such as: "Who are the Yankees, the Cardinals? What is Detroit known for manufacturing primarily?"— questions most Americans could answer.

We thought it strange, and laughingly made light of the queries, but the MPs were dead serious, and we had to answer them. Weeks later we discovered the reason for the questioning. It was a time when English-speaking German soldiers, dressed in captured American army uniforms, were stationed at outward posts directing stray American soldiers behind the German front line. Jeeps, weapons carriers, captured tanks, and downed planes all disappeared behind enemy lines. The M.P.s were checking to be sure we were really Americans and not German infiltrators. We heard that a carload of M.P.s disappeared in Rotgen, and later learned that our own Third Auxiliary

Adjutant, Lieutenant Alfred Sensenbach, along with enlisted men, Sergeants Loren R. Mullison and Luis C. Hultine, disappeared without a trace on September 21, 1944. They were on the road delivering mail to us Third Auxers who were on D.S. at the various front line field hospitals. They had been stopped by English-speaking Germans wearing American uniforms at crossroads and were directed behind enemy lines. They became prisoners of war, and were not heard from until the end of the war.

2 October 1944

After the American Eighth and Ninth Air Forces dropped 57,000 tons of bombs on the front line, First Army reached the Siegfried Line, where the cement pillboxes had been the most impregnable fortification in Europe. Major General Maurice Rose, promoted from the ranks, was in command of the 3rd Armored Division Combat Command B. He began the fighting with a reconnaissance toward the Siegfried Line. After losing three tanks to camouflaged German antitank guns, one of his armored combat commands stopped short of the "dragons' teeth," concrete pyramid-shaped obstructions with not enough space for a vehicle to pass between. At dawn, bulldozers cleared the crater ahead of General Rose's command, but the fill would not support the heavy tanks, and the engineers had to blast the dragon's teeth with explosives to provide a path for the tanks to pass through. Thus began the fierce battle that would last until the middle of December.

General Rose was to reconnoiter into the Huertgen border with his infantry. Despite his determined, brave leadership, the soldiers were reluctant when they saw the German fortifications, along with many natural obstacles. The steep rolling hills and ravines, the dark forest and rushing streams, backed by four rows of dragons teeth. Pillboxes, roadblocks, machine gun emplacements, and fields of thousands of mines also hampered advancement.

This was country easily defended but difficult to attack. It was also borderland that had been ceded to Belgium at the end of World War I. Local people no longer greeted us with open arms of gratitude, as in the past weeks. Instead, they were inscrutable, morose, with no love for the Americans, and they showed it.

To our men, the atmosphere was foreboding as they faced the towering fir trees that permitted no light even when the sun came out; now with the rain, the sky was dark with clouds, and the air filled with the smell of burning peat.

To the north were the forests of Rotgen and Huertgen above the Hohe Venne upland, with the Ardennes to the south. Another reconnaissance force was halted short of the village of Rotgen, between Aachen and Monschau, facing the dragons' teeth on one side, a precipice on the other and a huge crater ahead. German heavy mortar and artillery rounds exploded on contact with treetops, dropping shrapnel on the infantry below in the dense fir forest. Mines planted by the Germans were everywhere, along with felled trees. Tanks or tank destroyers were out of the question on the narrow trails and mined areas. The fighting was interlocked so closely that artillery and planes could not be used even if the weather permitted the planes to fly. The Germans in their bunkers, pillboxes, and log-covered foxholes were relatively safe.

German 88-mm artillery and anti-tank guns mounted on Mark IV's (Tigers) and Mark V's (Panthers) in their thick armor were superior to our Sherman tanks with their 75-mm guns in spite of their greater maneuverability. Our advantage was that we had a greater number of Shermans. However, due to the marshy terrain and thick undergrowth, the vehicles could not penetrate the forest. The infantry had to carry their supplies and ammunition bodily. The fighting dragged on through October and November with tremendous losses for the Americans as they struggled against the odds. The Germans now were fighting on their homeland, and were not going to give an inch without a life-and-death struggle. The rainy season continued, and the men were mired in mud.

Huertgen Forest

21 October 1944

Aachen fell on the 21st, after seven days of fierce fighting. The 13th Field Hospital, where I was on D.S. from the Third Auxiliary Surgical Group, moved into the area southeast of Aachen, on the northern fringe of the Huertgen Forest. We set up the operating area in a bombed factory, while the personnel were housed in an adjoining building that was strewn with wreckage from a recent bombing. The large windowed wall of our room was blown out, but the toilet was a pleasant surprise until we discovered that the water mains were blown up and we had to resort to a latrine, as usual. The weather was turning colder and the rain continued without letup. My three roommates and I covered the large opening in the wall with blankets for blackout and to keep out the rain and later snow that began to flurry. There was no heat in the building, but since we spent most of the time in the surgical building, it was of no concern. Our sleep periods were short, and we didn't undress much and had plenty of heavy wool blankets to cover up. Our helmets served our immediate needs.

While walking from my quarters to the surgical area in daylight one day I discovered that we were next to the ordnance supply headquarters. This was target area for the Luftwaffe. I never found time or opportunity to question the reason for the close proximity, but this was hard-won territory inside Germany and there was little choice. It was also Buzz Bomb alley, the V-1 and V-2 bomb route, and we could hear and see the red flares as they flew over us enroute to the port at Antwerp, which was in Allied hands since the 28th of November. We feared the Buzz Bombs more than the Luftwaffe, since they were pilotless flying bombs that dropped indiscriminately at a set distance, whereas we trusted the Luftwaffe pilot to drop his bombs on a specific target, hopefully not a hospital. I still worried that we should not have been next to an ordnance supply headquarters.

I had experienced a Buzz Bomb attack while traveling across one of the many bridges in Leige earlier. This was above a wide railroad terminal, where many rails crossed one another. Our GI driver was driving several of us people to the 13th Field Hospital when the reconnaissance car slowed down behind a horse-drawn wagon loaded with hay. An elderly farmer walking off the side of the road held the reins of the huge Percheron horse that was slowly plodding across the viaduct. All of a sudden, to our surprise the farmer dropped the reins and threw himself into a ditch beside the road. Our driver stopped abruptly behind the wagon when the horse stopped. The farmer had recognized the sound of the Buzz Bomb before we did. I looked over my shoulder toward the sound and saw the huge bomb flying low toward us. We watched, fascinated, as it continued over our heads, then saw it drop on the railroad terminal ahead and below us in a huge explosion that mushroomed smoke and flames and debris skyward. The concussion whipped our helmet-clad heads backward with a snap. It happened so quickly we never got out of the car.

We became familiar with the sounds of the V-1 and V-2 engines as well as the sounds of the various planes, artillery and guns. In September while in Verviers, we clocked the Buzz Bombs as they flew over us. They were as regular as a bus, every half-hour.

Other Third Aux Surgical teams were operating at various field hospitals at Rotgen, Elsenborn, Butgenbach, Stolberg, and Eschweiler. Later, I was dumbfounded by the destruction of Eschweiler and Duren, as we drove through in a jeep and looked down on the rubble that had once been good-sized cities. Our bombers and artillery had done a thorough job of destruction.

21 October 1944

At the 45th Field Hospital at Elsenborn, eight Third Aux nurses were in bivouac watching the Buzz-Bombs fly overhead and felt the earth tremble as our artillery shelled the Siegfried Line. One of the nurses in the 45th Field Hospital, Nurse Lieutenant Frances Slanger, was writing to the *STARS AND STRIPES*, putting into words what a lot of us felt. Here is the way she put it:

"It is two o'clock in the morning, and I have been lying awake for an hour, listening to the steady, even breathing of the other three nurses in the tent. The rain is beating down on the tent with torrential force. The wind is on a rampage. Its main objective seems to be to lift the tent off its poles and fling it about our heads. The fire is burning low, just a few live coals in the bottom. I couldn't help thinking how similar to a human being a fire is. It can run down very low, but if there is a spark of life left, it can be nursed back. So can a human being. It is slow, it is gradual, but it is done all the time in these field hospitals. We have read articles in the various magazines, praising the work of nurses in the combat areas. Praising us for what? The GIs say we rough it. True, we live in tents, sleep on cots, and are subject to the vagaries of the weather. We wade ankle-deep in mud, but they have to lie in it. We have a stove and coal. We even have a laundry line in the tent. Our drawers are at this moment doing the dance of the pants, what with the wind howling, the tent waving, the rain beating, the guns firing, and me writing with a flashlight. It all adds up to a feeling of unreality. Sure we rough it, but in comparison with the way you men are taking it, we can't complain. You, the men behind the guns, the men driving the tanks, flying the planes, sailing the ships, building the bridges, paving the way, and paying with your blood, you are the ones to whom we doff our helmets. Every GI wearing the uniform has our greatest admiration and respect.

Yes, this time we are handing out the bouquets. We are handing out the bouquets because we have seen you when you are brought in bloody, dirty with mud and so tired. We are handing out the bouquets because we have gradually seen you brought back to life. We have learned a great deal about our American soldier and the stuff he is made of. The wounded do not cry. Their buddies come first. Your patience and determination, your courage and fortitude are awesome to behold. Rough it? No! It is a privilege to be able to take care of you and it is a great joy to see you open your eyes and say with that swell American grin "Hi, Babe!"

The members of the 45th Field Hospital had read this letter and commented on how fortunate they were compared to the GIs on patrol, when the earth shook with the impact of two nearby explosions. In the nurses' tent they put on their helmets and huddled together, not knowing which way to turn. Terrified, they kneeled with their arms around each other. The third shell fell in the middle of their area. Frances Slanger collapsed. I'm hit," she said.

In another tent Major Hermon Lord, the platoon C. O. was mortally wounded. An enlisted man was killed outright. Three more nurses had been hit: Elizabeth Powers, Margaret Bowler of the 13th Field Hospital platoon, and Gladys Snyder of the Third Auxiliary Surgical Group. The casualties were brought into the operating tent.

Frances Slanger was the most serious. She had a wound of the abdomen and was already in deep shock when first seen. She knew she was dying, but her only concern was for the others. We poured blood into her as fast as we could. It was no use. Within a half hour, Frances Slanger was dead. We buried her in the military cemetery where she lies side by side with the fighting men she served.

16 November 1944

Five divisions, consisting of 80,000 men under Major General Lawton Collin's Vllth Corps, were assigned to reach the bridges west of the Roer River and to get control of various dams in the area. The attack was preceded by 2,200 Allied bombers escorted by 1000 Fighter planes dropping 10,000 tons of bombs in front of the VIIth and

XIIth Corps, who were to attack above the Ardennes, along with a barrage from 1200 artillery guns. The attack was countered by heavy German reserves, and the Americans suffered some of their heaviest losses in the war.

The surrounding villages had changed ownership many times. Tree stumps, fallen branches, and shell holes filled the forest There were many brave acts, but the GIs were getting discouraged in their cold, muddy foxholes, dodging machine gun fire from protected bunkers, pillboxes and artillery blasting 88's that rained hot shrapnel on everyone below. Men were exposed to the mines underfoot as they plodded through the fallen trees, huge branches, and the bodies of their comrades.

As the weather froze another affliction, trench foot, developed, a condition resembling frostbite, resulting from exposure to cold, moisture and circulatory problems. Soldiers fighting in the mud and snow neglected or were unable to take off their boots or change socks. Trench foot occasionally turned into gangrene. Hundreds of G I's were evacuated to the rear due to this disease.

In the forest, the GI medics and litter bearers were exposed to the same dangers as the infantry—the 88s, tree bursts, land mines, gun and mortar fire. Foxholes were no protection from the hot shrapnel falling from above. When the medics and litter bearers fell, they were replaced by a new shipment of soldiers who had just arrived from the States without any previous experience in warfare.

Many of my wounded said that they had just left the States ten days earlier. They had been transferred into new units and were unable to remember their units when they were questioned after being wounded. Many lay where they fell twenty-four to forty-eight hours before they were rescued. Weary litter bearers trudged through the mud, snow and mines, collecting the human wreckage. They loaded them on the weapons carriers, preceded by an armored tank, and guided by mine-sweeping engineers who were returning after delivering ammunition that was so vitally necessary to the men at the front. Then, with their wounded—some stacked on top of each other—they headed back through the shelling of the mortars and 88s to the field hospital. A wounded man stayed awake a day and a night to warn the litter bearer who found him that a German had placed a booby trap beneath him, that would explode when they came to move him.

When the wounded finally reached the hospital they were bled out, with a hardly perceptible blood pressure, wet, cold, and bloodied, but so grateful to be alive. They felt safe at last. Someone would take over as they fell into much-needed sleep.

I heard one soldier say to the one on the adjoining litter, "I'll take the watch Bud, while you catch some sleep." They were back on the battlefield. There was deep camaraderie among the boys. We called them boys; many were only nineteen years old. They were dying in the woods by the thousands. Medics were bringing them in by the truckload. They were dying now in the hospital because of wounds that were beyond remedying. Their concern for each other in the inferno they had traversed bound them in love and concern for one another.

I heard a litter bearer shout so he could be heard above the noisy generators, the delirious ramblings, and the artillery bursts, "Where do you want me to put these wounded, Lieutenant?"

I replied, "Right where you are, on the floor at the entrance, anyplace, just leave a space to walk between them." I had no time to look at dog tags, only to get at the wounds, sorting those who had first priority for surgery and survival.

Normally my duty was in the operating area, but with the sudden influx of many wounded it called for every doctor to report to surgery, and I replaced the doctor who was in charge of triage. I checked the new arrivals' wounds, assessed their condition for priority for surgery, and when the surgeons were ready for the next casualty,

I would suggest those I considered highest priority. They did not have time to go over the entire area, but they would make the final decision.

Often, a newly arrived wounded soldier would ask in a rasping voice, "Where am I?"

"In a hospital, in Germany," I replied.

"Oh," his voice disappointed, "it was such a long trip." Then, realizing there was a nurse beside him, asked "Where are you from, nurse?"

"Michigan, Ann Arbor," I replied as I rolled him to his side with a corpsman's help, and began cutting off clothing to get at the wound that had been hastily covered in the woods by a medic.

"Oh, home," he sighed, his breath coming in short gasps as he fought for air. His was a massive through-and-through chest wound. Quickly, I covered the wound with a dressing, front and back, and taped the entire area to prevent air from entering his chest.

A corporal called my attention to the soldier on the next litter, whose abdomen was oozing blood. His intestines were exposed and pulsating. I covered the massive wound with Vaseline gauze to keep the intestines from exposure to air and dehydration. Then I went from litter to litter, releasing and re-applying tourniquets on torn limbs to keep tissue alive and prevent hemorrhage, and gave blood transfusions, plasma and intravenous solutions. I sent the corpsman for blood when I noticed it running low in the bottle of the soldier that I stood next to. The corpsman called across the room, "There's no more blood, Lieutenant."

The wounded soldier beside me said, "Take mine, nurse, I don't need it." He knew he was dying.

"Bring the plasma, corporal," I said, disgusted with him for having said that.

We had used gallons of blood, and it just seeped out of the wounds. We began to bleed our own personnel to tide us over.

I approached the next litter and lifted the blanket.

326

Youthful German prisoners

The medics had brought in the upper torso of a young man, and he was alive! My eyes quickly shifted to his lower self. He was watching me. I tried a faint smile. His bladder was torn and genitals gone, the hipbones fragmented. The cold had coagulated the blood and sheer determination kept him from dying up to now. There was little that could be done for him, with so many others that could be saved. An injection of morphine was all that would help him.

Many wounds were caused by the "Bouncing Betty." Triggered when stepped on, the mine would spring into the air and explode crotch-high, emasculating or cutting a man in half as the steel fragments flew in all directions.

Although I did not have time to look at the dog tags of soldiers, I returned to the Ann Arbor boy's litter and jotted his name on a scrap of paper and put it in my fatigues pocket. After the war I contacted the family of Private Myrl Heusel, to let them know their son had died in a hospital on November 26, 1944 near Huertgen, Germany, and that I had cared for him. He was nineteen years old.

Now and then the medics brought in a seriously wounded German soldier. One of these, with his first words, asked, "Kaffee Schwesta? Cigaretten"?

They had had ersatz coffee for so many years it was his last wish to taste real coffee. It was difficult not to give him a sip despite the fact that it was not wise in the face of possible surgery.

I knelt on the floor to check the wounds of this blond young German and felt the same compassion I felt for our men. How could I hate him? He was paying the same price as our soldiers, his life. A soldier has to fight; he cannot turn his back on the enemy. I examined his wounds, and sadly thought the backlog was too great. His turn would probably not come in time.

There was another very young German boy that we moved to the far end of the room against the wall, and placed a bulky temporary hanging to keep him isolated as he spat at everyone who came near. He was of the Jugend Hitler Youth that had been indoctrinated in school with the notion of their racial superiority, and was filled with hatred toward us. Our wounded GIs resented our taking care of the Germans after their experience of seeing their buddies die in the Huertgen.

In the freezing rain, now turning to snow, the infantry wore everything that they could layer on top of layer: wool coats, jackets, wool shirts, pants and underwear. It was tough cutting through the heavy seams of wool clothing with my large bandage scissors that hung on a string attached to my fatigues. I had to get at the wounds quickly, evaluate and prepare them for surgery without causing further injury, bleeding, or pain.

On several occasions a grenade attached to the pants of a soldier fell to the floor as we cut them off. Fortunately the pins stayed intact. The hum of generators filled the background, along with occasional delirious shouts and mutterings as the men's minds drifted back to the battlefield. Many had lain covered with a blanket of snow for two days and more before being brought into the field hospital. Severe hemorrhage had caused brain damage for lack of blood and oxygen, resulting in irrational behavior. They shouted and tried to roll off the litters, cursing the "dirty bastards." We had to strap them securely to the canvas litters on the sawhorses to keep them from injuring themselves further.

Many of the infantry survived massive wounds, because of the cold and snow that slowed their circulation, and because they were in excellent physical condition up to the moment of injury. Now as they thawed they began to feel pain.

I went from litter to litter in the large room where the wounded were continually being brought in. I stopped at the litter of a newly arrived soldier whose eye and forehead was covered with a bloodied abdominal pad. I lifted it to find his eye and part of his temporal skull gone, leaving a mass of clotted blood and brain tissue exposed. Because his legs were contracting and extending, I drew back the blanket to find his arms and legs missing at midpoint, with sharp splinters of bones exposed, torn muscles oozing blood, contracting and twitching. A thought flashed through my mind: he must have tripped on a Bouncing Betty. I stood beside him, and touched him on his shoulder saying, "You're in a hospital soldier; I'm going to help you."

He didn't respond. The convulsing jarring of arms and leg remnants continued. I went to the supply table, poured sterile water into the spoon attached over the alcohol burning lamp, dropped the white tablet of morphine into the liquid, and drew it up into the syringe. There was nothing more anyone could do for him.

Placing my hand on his shoulder, I inserted the needle and pressed the liquid into his flesh, silently praying that this would stop the twitching, and ease his pain. I lifted the covers off his arms and legs to lessen the friction of the wool blanket, and replaced it with a sterile sheet. My heart ached and raced and skipped beats; sobs held back in my throat. I blinked away the tears. There was no time to cry.

Thoughts raced through my mind. *What a dreadful waste of lives all around me! The futility of it all! The terrible suffering and dying! Machines were tearing men to pieces. We could never keep up or undo the damage even if we had a hundred times the help. Was there no other way to solve world problems? War was destroying our finest youth! Have men not advanced in civilization and morality to be able to solve world economic and social problems by means other than killing? No amount of money or sacrifice was worth the price these men were paying in lives, suffering, crippling, and heartbreak, along with the irreparable waste of resources.* A part of me was dying!

With the arrival of more surgeons to handle the backlog, a need arose for more anesthetists. (In the 1940s, an anesthetist had to have an M.D. degree.) Because of the urgency, one doctor-anesthetist was able to anesthetize and monitor two patients at a time by placing them head to head. I was now called from the triage area to return to the operating area to administer anesthesia. When we were in England, waiting for the invasion I had had a three-week course. Although I learned a variety of methods along with spinal anesthesia, I was now giving deep inhalation drip ether, while a corpsman took my place to do triage.

16 November 1944

The First Army had reached a stalemate in the Huertgen Forest. The Ninth Division had been fighting desperately without much progress, when Major General Norman D. Cota, commanding the 28th Division, was sent to relieve them. General Cota was unhappy with the army plan, but he had no alternative except to follow orders from his superiors. When he entered the forest he saw artillery-damaged tree trunks covering the ground, mines that had been dug up piled high along with ration boxes and bloated bodies of the fallen soldiers. The men in the 9th Division were a sorry looking band of soldiers. They were discouraged, dirty and completely exhausted.

Under General Cota's command the 28th Division took over with artillery support and engineers. Because the terrain was extremely rugged, tanks were not able to get into the area, while the Germans, approaching the battle from a more favorable terrain could. The air force could not locate targets in the woods even if weather would permit them to fly. Clouds filled the sky and snow and rain pelted the men as they continued to fight. They were harassed to follow directions, and keep in contact with their platoons in the dark forest among anti-personnel mine fields, mortars and machine gun fire that mowed them down when they exposed themselves. The engineers trying to clear the minefields were driven to cover.

The Germans, behind the coils of barbed wire, booby traps, trip wires and mines, bunkers covered with foliage, fox holes protected with logs, and cement pillboxes, were safe. When the infantry started to attack, the Germans cut them down with machine gun and mortar fire. Shells fell on the assault units carrying ammunition to our men, setting off their ammunition and blowing the men to pieces. Men got separated from their squads and units and were lost. Machine gun fire ripped through the forest at anyone that moved. The men had no choice when told to continue, to get out of the foxhole, face the enemy and get gunned down.

Tanks and tank destroyers were still not able to get through to assist them, due to the thick woods, mines, and other obstacles. The men dug trenches with their bare hands. As the siege continued without progress, the shelling shattered men's nerves when the Mark IV and Mark V tanks, along with the German infantry, attacked them from both sides, as in the Schmidt village area fight.

It was a lost cause! The soldiers panicked. Brave medics stayed with their wounded. The dead lay where they fell. Demoralized, our men refused to eat, their nerves shattered. They cried. Terror stricken, they dropped their guns and raced to the rear, some helping the wounded who were still on their feet, leaving behind others crying for help. Worst of all their retreat had been started by a rumor. The Germans were not on their trail after all. It was artillery fire that had frightened them. This was the second time the men had run away.

The attack on Schmidt was the most devastating action to a division in the war. The 28th Divisions' collision with the 116th Panzer Division and two other divisions resulted in over 6000 casualties—killed, wounded, captured and missing—without much to show for the loss. The savage war continued with the 4th Infantry Division taking over after the 28th was relieved. The situation was repeated as mines, mortars, and artillery 88s exploded at tree height, killing and maiming those below.

It seemed to me that many soldiers were relieved when they were wounded. They felt they had a chance for survival in getting out of a sure death situation in the forest. To reach a hospital and look up at the face of a nurse led them to believe they were far from danger, far from the fighting. The wounded were often delirious due to loss of blood and suffered brain damage due to exposure and cold.

All those fighting in the Huertgen, the infantry, the engineers who cleared the mines, the armored divisions, tank and artillery crews who had been fighting without let up since the invasion in June, began to suffer battlefield fever. Exhaustion, lack of sleep, hard physical exertion, lose of appetite, nerve tension, hopelessness, emotionally spent at seeing the torn bodies and death of their buddies, caused many men to collapse, resulting in the *battle fatigue* classification. Some military commanders, however, viewed this as psychopathic or cowardly behavior.

Battalion commanders, company commanders, staff officers and noncoms fell alongside the GIs. Courageous wounded lay awake for hours to warn their rescuers that the Germans, after they had stripped them of their field jackets and cigarettes while they lay semi-conscious, had placed mines beneath them. Men risked their lives to save comrades. Replacements marched seven miles on muddy rocky trails with fir branches obstructing the path and cold gusts of wind and rain drenching them as they stumbled and sloshed in mud and snow, balancing their gear and rifles, heading toward hell. They stooped beneath branches of trees stripped of foliage, tripped on concrete chunks ripped from former bunkers, pill boxes and rusting steel rods that protruded dangerously. They saw our tanks and other vehicles damaged by mines, and the litter of gas masks, helmets, and blood-stained jackets.

This was how the 121st Infantry Division, coming to aid the depleted 4th Division, was greeted. Officers and platoon leaders, seeing their men shattered by mines and felled by the mortars and the 88s as they pushed forward, went berserk and had to be relieved. In the following days, three company commanders lost their commands because they failed to reach their objectives. Many other officers were relieved of their command or broke under the stress. Tanks and heavy equipment mired in the mud or knocked out by mines or mortars obstructed the narrow trail. Engineers attempting to clear a path were easy targets for the enemy. Progress was meager. Replacements kept the numbers up, but the new men could not match the veterans they had replaced. Snow and sleet added to the unrelenting punishment of guns and the explosion of shells. The acrid smell of burning flesh permeated the air, along with the gasping of the mortally wounded.

The 1st Division, known as the "Big Red One," under Major General C. Ralph Huebner's command, was attacking from the northwest, heading east toward the Roer River. General Collins thought Huebner unduly cautious and met with him, letting him know he was displeased with the slow progress. Fighting in the Huertgen Forest's eastern edge, Huebner's Big Red One, and the 2nd Battalion's 26th Infantry under Lieutenant Colonel Derrell M. Daniel, sent a platoon of tanks down the narrow cart track leading into the village. Infantry had just reached the houses, but the German artillery quickly put two tanks out of commission, letting one through. One tank had overturned, blocking the road so that no other vehicle could pass on the narrow track. Engineers had to build a bypass, but it was too late to save the infantry that had entered Merode. Germans began shelling the houses. The last message from the infantry was, "There's a Tiger coming down the road, and it's firing into every house. Here he comes!" Then the radio went dead.

Nothing but shell holes and tree stumps remained. There were many heroic acts performed in the woods, but the GIs were becoming discouraged in the cold, muddy foxholes, dodging the machine gun fire from well-protected bunkers and pill boxes. The men were hard-pressed to avoid the mines underfoot as they trekked through fallen branches, foxholes, and bodies. Frostbite and trench foot continued to plague the replacements as they fought in the mud and snow.

In two weeks, the 1st Division, along with the 47th Infantry, a regiment of the 9th Division, advanced less than four miles. The cost was 4000 casualties. The 26th Infantry lost nearly 1500. Another 500 were lost due to combat fatigue and trench foot. The 8th Division's 121st Infantry suffered 1250 casualties. There were nearly 5000 replacements in this period of fighting.

Colonel Charles T. Lanham's battalion, sweeping toward Duren, suffered over 4000 battle casualties, along with 2000 more due to other causes. The gain was a six-mile advance. Men were so physically exhausted that they discarded their heavy winter coats. Later, they were so cold they could hardly use their equipment.

Units of the 2nd Ranger Battalion were called to assist Brigadier General William G. Weaver at Castle Hill. Their losses were heavy. These men, trained for hazardous fighting, quickly captured it, but in the process only one-fourth of their men survived. Again the casualties were 4000 and 1200 more to fatigue or other reasons.

The 83rd Division under Maj. Gen. Robert C. Macon, fighting its way out of the forest toward the Roer, suffered 1000 casualties in three days, and the 5th Armored 150 more casualties. In the three months of fighting, 120,000, along with many thousands of replacements, fought in Huertgen. Over 24,000 Americans were killed, missing or wounded; 9000 lost to trench foot and other diseases, plus combat fatigue. In the months of war that began in October in the Huertgen, losses exceeded 25% of those wounded who reached the front line field hospitals during this phase.

Fighting in the forest was a costly tragedy. The advantage was to the Germans who were dug in. Little has been written about the terrible cost in suffering and lives lost in the Huertgen Forest fighting.

Court Martial

Toward the end of November, Marcelle Johnson and I were lying on our cots exhausted from the long hours and hard work of the past months, when the field hospital nurse banged into our quarters with a summons paper in hand, and announced that Marcelle and I were to report to First Army Headquarters for court-martial proceedings!

"For what?" we both exclaimed.

"For ignoring an order to report for duty on the ward!" she bellowed.

It was a forgotten incident; when nurse Glump had demanded that we go on duty in the ward after we had just got off duty following a hard eighteen-hour shift in surgery. Nurse Glump, a heavy-set woman, a cigarette dangling from the corner of her thick lips, looked adamant as she spoke. Her fatigue belt was tied tight around her bulky waist, dividing the fat above and below. She glowered at both of us.

Marcelle, not one to be easily intimidated, sat up abruptly on the cot and said, "Look here Glump, we start operating immediately when we arrive at a new destination. I don't know what you were doing while we were overwhelmed in the operating area. I've never seen hide nor hair of any of you people coming in to see what was going on in surgery. You sit on your haunches drinking coffee until you start receiving our post-operatives!"

I joined in by throwing the blanket off my face and adding, "Besides, we are under 3rd Auxiliary Surgical Group's authority, not yours. Our work is in surgery with our surgeons. Frequently we were short of help in surgery because you were incapable of running the supply area, and you took one of our Third Aux nurses to do your work. While in surgery we were doubling in triage and the operating area because of your intrusion on our personnel. Surgery is our primary assignment at the various field hospitals."

Up to then we had been too busy to complain about the loss of one of our surgical nurses working in an area other than surgery.

Nurse Glump threw the papers on the foot of the nearest cot and turned toward the exit without further word.

The following week we three nurses, Lieutenants Marcelle Johnson and Mildred Radawiec, and Nurse Glump, appeared before a group of officers seated in a semi-circle in a large, otherwise empty room. The officers ranked from First Lieutenants to Lieutenant Colonels. They perused the papers they each had in hand and looked at us in a studied manner.

We accused were not completely aware of the seriousness of the charge. We were exhausted, discouraged, and emotionally drained. We felt no guilt; we'd had enough of war, and didn't give a damn. We were tired of war and we wanted to go home.

Glump sat a short distance from us, her chin protruding customarily upward, looking defiant. She would show us who was in charge. The colonel, looking from one to the other of our three faces, asked Lieutenant Glump to rise, to raise her right hand and swear to tell the truth and nothing but the truth. Glump rose, she looked surlily in our direction as she raised her hand and swore to tell the truth.

"Lieutenant Glump, explain to the court with what

offense these officers are charged,"

"They are charged, Sir, with disobeying my order to report to duty on the ward in the hospital on the 26th of November 1944."

The Colonel, looking toward Marcelle and me said, "Lieutenant Radawiec, rise and swear to tell the truth and nothing but the truth while raising your right hand."

I arose and did as I was told.

He then asked, "Lieutenant Radawiec, are you guilty of disobeying an order given by Lieutenant Glump?"

"No sir, I am not guilty, Colonel. Lieutenant Glump has no authority over me. I am not obliged to take orders from her. My assignment to the field hospital is to assist the surgeons in my organization, the Third Auxiliary Surgical Group, in the operating area. I am under the professional control of the surgical group teams who operate at the field hospitals in the First Army."

The officers looked at each other quizzically, when one officer said, "You may sit down."

Looking at Marcelle, the Colonel ordered her to take the oath, then asked, "Lieutenant Johnson, are you guilty of not obeying an order given by Lieutenant Glump?

"Sir, I can only repeat Lieutenant Radawiec's statement that Lieutenant Glump has no authority over me. I want to add that we are on detached service from the Third Auxiliary Surgery Group to the field hospital temporarily, to assist our Third Auxiliary Surgeons in the operating room. That is the purpose for our assignment to the field hospital. Lieutenant Glump has no authority over us."

The men studied all three nurses, noting expressions, reactions and composure. They had leafed through our folders beforehand, and now they stood up and left the room where they apparently discussed the decision they would arrive at. Upon returning, they sat down and looked at each of the three women. The two accused sat with our hands clasped in our laps, unperturbed. We were too tired to care what happened. We had worked as hard as humanly possible the past six months since the invasion, and had no feelings left about anything that might happen.

The men had our folders with past records, which they had apparently studied. They would judge the record and performance of our two years of operation in the war. They apparently knew nothing of the woman who was accusing us and were not impressed with her belligerent manner.

Finally, Colonel Sullivan spoke, "I see no reason for prosecution of this situation. From the records before us, we see exemplary performance over two years of service in Africa, Sicily, the invasion of France, Belgium, and now Germany. The Third Auxiliary Surgical Group regards both officers with highest esteem. Since they are under the Third Auxiliary Surgical Group's jurisdiction and temporarily on detached service in the surgical area to assist their surgeons, we find no reason for this prosecution. Case dismissed."

12 December 1944

I was awakened to the sound of ack-ack guns outside the opening in the wall of our quarters. I pulled back the blanket and stuck my head out the opening. Below, I discovered an anti-aircraft gun emplacement. The gun crew was blasting away at an American star-marked plane that flew over as I watched.

We were not aware that anti-aircraft guns were just outside our wall since we always reported to surgery as soon as we arrived at a new destination. I was puzzled when I saw the anti-aircraft crew shooting at what looked like a low flying American observation plane. That plane made us aware of the enemy tactic of using captured American planes and vehicles, and German soldiers dressing in the uniforms of captured Americans. The anti-aircraft crew apparently had orders to shoot at any plane that flew over this area.

The German concentration of troops on the western

front in the fall of 1944 assured them that "time" would be to their advantage to produce new submarines, V-I and V-2 bombs, and even the atomic bomb. Hitler argued that these new weapons would turn the tide of the war. By recapturing the port at Antwerp, thus cutting the Allied supply line and splitting the Allied front, he could resume a new campaign in France. He began building secret armies behind the Siegfried line in the Forest. His scheme during the Huertgen Forest fighting was playing for time. Well protected behind four rows of dragons' teeth, pill boxes, bunkers, roadblocks, machine gun emplacements and mine fields, he played a cat-and-mouse game with the Americans, picking them off as they staggered about in the dense forest not knowing where to turn. He needed time to perfect and produce enough weapons to turn the war around in his favor and force the Allies into the Channel. He wanted another Dunkirk.

To be sure, Hitler did have the capability to turn about and do just that. In 1943 he had the XXI submarine capable of traveling 16 knots and remaining submerged for long periods at great depth. The XXIII was smaller but very maneuverable, and capable of doing great damage to Allied shipping. The new jet Messerschmitt 262 fighter, capable of 550 mph flying at 27,000 feet altitude, appeared in October 1944, and resulted in doubling our losses—two of our fighters to every one of theirs. It was the first jet plane ever mass produced.

At Breman, miles of railroad trains were found with prefabricated parts for the submarines, just a few months too late. Had they been available earlier, they could have cost the Allies much damage to our supply line, or worse yet prevented the Allies from landing. Despite the Allied bombings, German aircraft, along with other weapons produced in 1944, expanded three times over production in 1942. In tanks, the rate was five times that of 1942.

Allied air forces concentrated bombing on oil refineries and communications, forcing the Germans into the production of synthetic gasoline now that they no longer had access to Rumanian oil. However, they could not produce enough aviation fuel, so the thousand jet aircraft that could have scored victory over the Allied air forces were grounded for lack of fuel, as well as lack of trained Luftwaffe pilots and the necessary airfields.

The Germans stopped work on an atomic bomb in June of 1943 because they were behind in its construction due to the destruction by Allied bombing of the heavy water (deuterium oxide) factory in Norway.

They felt sure that the war would soon be over. Besides, they did not want to tie up war production in an enterprise that was uncertain. There was talk of a V-3 bomb in the making that could reach the United States. When the German counterattack on the 16th of December began, it caused some fear that this might well be true.

In November 1944, German pilots volunteered to ride the V-1 and V-2 Buzz bombs, and direct them to their targets and be destroyed with them, just as the Japanese Kamikaze practiced in the Pacific war, by flying their planes into the funnels of Allied ships. However, it was discouraged by Albert Speer, Minister for Production and Armaments. Secret weapons restored German courage and fanaticism. Later, it was admitted that these volunteers did not fully understand what the job entailed.

While the Americans were dying in the Huertgen Forest, to the south and ten miles beyond the Siegfried Line, concealed by fir trees and bad flying weather that kept our reconnaissance planes grounded, the Germans were secretly assembling twenty-nine combat divisions in the heavily wooded Eifel area. Hitler's plan was to cut the Allied supply line in Antwerp, where American supply ships first arrived on November 28, 1944.

The Ardennes Counterattack

16 December 1944

The German counterattack, also called the Battle of

the Bulge, caught the Americans by complete surprise. Orders to the 13th Field Hospital personnel stated: "Prepare to retreat! Pack your musette bag with your personal needs along with your gas mask. That is all you are allowed to carry."

Other personal items, bedrolls, duffel bags and suitcases would be left behind. All the dying, and the suffering, the exhausting work in the Huertgen Forest, and now this.

Except for a few newly operated soldiers who could not be moved and would be left behind with several surgeons and medics to care for them, the rest of us would set up our hospital farther to the rear.

We were dejected, tired physically, and emotionally exhausted. We had been rising in the morning in the cold dark with the full blast of icy wind billowing the blanket in the windowless void, working continuously, seven days a week, collapsing at shift's end into stuporous sleep day after day, night after night.

I lay down and covered myself with the olive-drab, fuzzy wool blanket up to my eyes, feeling cold chills. Marcelle, lying across the room, was covered up to her chin. Our other two teammates were scouting the premises, tracking down the latest rumor. Where would the enemy come from—the north, the south? We could be cut off in a pocket in Germany.

We had felt forlorn even before the counterattack, since mail had not come through in several months. Our headquarters at Spa, in Belgium, twenty miles south west of us, were not venturing into German territory any more than necessary since our adjutant and two enlisted men disappeared in late September.

Marcelle and I got up and hurriedly threw our most precious possessions into our musette bags, including the crumpled cookies we had received in a package that was mailed in October. Then we lay back on our cots and waited for further orders.

Our officers, still lamenting the breakage of their

precious bottles when they landed in France, leaving a trail of Scotch, this time wrapped their liquor rations carefully in towels.

As we waited, a state of apathy set in. We felt that nothing could affect us anymore. Discouraged after months of exhaustive work, we waited, our minds reeling with what might happen next. How much longer would the war last? We knew we were expendable.

There also was the possibility of our continuing on to the Pacific theater after the European war was over. We were experienced troops, and when we volunteered it was for the duration plus six months. This was our third winter overseas.

Three German armies caught the American army in its weakest unprotected area, an eighty-five-mile stretch lying between the First Army on the north and the Third Army in the south. It was the same area from which Hitler had launched his attack on France in 1940.

The counter-attack began with the Fifth Panzer Army led by the Prussian General Baron Hasso von Manteuffel. General Sepp Dietrich, a sergeant from World War I who supported Hitler in the Munich Beer Putsch, was now rewarded by von Manteuffel and put in charge of the Sixth Army. The Seventh Army was led by General Ernst Brandenberger. SS Lieutenant Colonel Jochen Peiper, who had fought in the tank war in Russia, had charge of the First Panzer Division.

SS Lieutenant Colonel Otto Skorzeny, considered by the British intelligence to be one of the most dangerous men in Europe, was listening to Hitler's orders: "I have chosen you for a very important task in my plan for the December offensive. I want you to train the Germans who speak English to go behind the American lines. German soldiers will be disguised wearing captured Americans uniforms and drive in captured American vehicles. They will confuse American soldiers with orders, spread rumors, and direct them behind our lines.

"You will seize the bridges over the Meuse River so

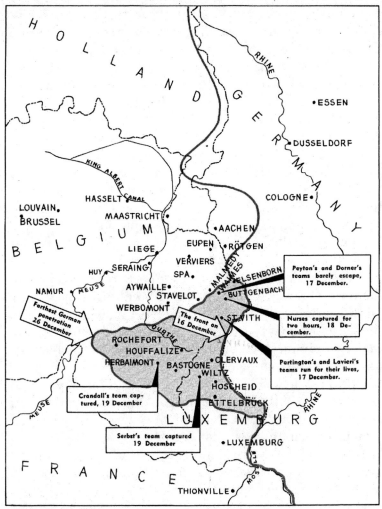

The Battle of the Bulge.

that Germany will regain the seaport at Antwerp and throw the Allies into the Channel."

These three German armies, with horse-drawn artillery, howitzers, and guns, mobilized on the southeastern edge of the Huertgen Forest while our Americans soldiers were dying in the woods. Their movement of tanks, half-tracks and infantry along with Luftwaffe plane skirmishes to the front line concealed the noise of their approach to within three miles of the Allied front. Twenty divisions, 250,000 men and machines had secretly built up to drive the Allies out of Europe. These preparations were going on while other Germans, secure in their heavily protected bunkers were killing our infantry in the heavily wooded Huertgen Forest. "Watch on the Rhine" had begun. The weather was overcast, perfect for Hitler's plan. Allied planes, the only possible drawback to Hitler's plans, would not be able to fly.

Awakened by the noise of artillery and mortar bursts, officers of the Ninth Division in the northern section of the Ardennes dashed to the Battalion Command Post. They were confused by the nearby explosions.

On an earlier reconnaissance, they had seen horses pulling German artillery, but the shelling now was close. A burst struck a mess tent farther back, tearing a hole in the tent while the cook was fixing breakfast. The enemy had also knocked out telephone lines and jammed the American radio wave length with German band music, so that Lieutenant Alan Jones was isolated as the barrage hit his area farther south.

Several miles to the west of the Roer River and beyond, the 28th Division was being hit by German artillery. The people in the town of Clervaux were afraid that the Germans were coming back. The 4th Division farther south, close to Echternach, was being hit hard by mortar and artillery, tearing up their communication wires. As the attacks continued, each group, isolated from others due to the communications failure, thought it was a local attack.

The enemy attacked across 85 miles of sparsely guarded front. Sepp Dietrich, leading the 6th Panzer Army, attacked the American 9th Division, assisted by the Luftwaffe's new jet planes roaring overhead at a speed never seen before. The Panzer crews wore white-sheeted clothes over their uniform as they approached the front line, making them hardly discernible from the snow-covered ground.

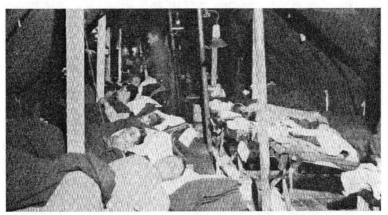

All serious surgery done at the 51st Field Hospital under Commanding Officer Major Harry P. Harper was done by the 3rd Aux. Surgical Group in three platoons.

They were met by green American troops—former cooks, bakers, musicians, clerks, truck drivers and loggers—who now stood up to the enemy and fought and held the line from Monschau to the Losheim Gap.

Here the Germans brought their tanks into play from behind the dragons' teeth via selected areas that had been softened in previous fighting, by placing planks over sections of concrete. Assault guns, armored vehicles and tanks roared past the thinly held line of the American infantry. Losheim Gap lines were cut by infiltrating Germans, isolating the Americans.

General Manteuffel's 5th Panzer Army had bypassed the American 14th Cavalry south of Losheim Gap, attempting to reach Schonberg, situated behind the Schnee Eifel. Another of Manteuffel's groups of infantry were driving a wedge on the other side of the Schnee Eifel, thus encircling and isolating General Alan Jones's 106th Division. Monteuffel was directing a tank and infantry division at the worn-out American 28th Division, and though he captured several of their kitchens, the 28th rallied and drove them back.

Young, thin German soldiers lay dead with hot dogs still in their mouths.

The 28th Division, despite its successful struggle against the assault, was in serious trouble. They were surrounded as the enemy cleared the roads to Clervaux, Bastogne, and to the Meuse River. Communication lines were disrupted along the entire front as the enemy approached. Without telephone or radio communication, each squad, platoon, and company fought on their own until capture or death.

Speeding toward Versailles, General Omar Bradley, oblivious of any problems, headed to a conference with General Eisenhower. He had left Luxembourg several hours before, unaware that the Germans had attacked. In Versailles, Eisenhower was attending the wedding of his orderly, Sergeant Mickey, who was marrying a WAC. Earlier, Eisenhower had written a letter to Field Marshall Montgomery in regard to a bet that the War would be over before Christmas, stating that he still had nine more days.

In Losheim Gap, every village was in turmoil as civilians begged to be taken along with the retreating Americans. American flags would be replaced by German flags by other smirking and nodding Germans.

As men fought their isolated battles with interrupted messages and confusion, the enemy advanced. Major General Gerow's Vth Corps in the northern sector was still attacking eastward toward the Roer dams. Now he was being attacked. He called Lieutenant General Courtney Hodges at First Army Headquarters at Spa, asking permission to halt his attack for fear of being isolated or annihilated. Hodges, having heard earlier that the 2nd Division had reached a crossroad at the Siegfried Line, was happy that the attack toward the Roer Dam was at last succeeding, and advised Gerow to continue with the attack. He felt the German action was a spoiling attack from the scant conflicting reports he was receiving.

In Versailles, while discussion was going on with

Bradley and Eisenhower's staff, a message was delivered to British intelligence officer Major General Stone, who read it to the group: "This morning Germans have counterattacked at five separate points on the First Army front."

Bradley assumed it was to distract Patton's 3rd Army from attacking the Saar further south, by drawing him north to help in the Ardennes, a spoiling attack. Eisenhower thought differently, and advised Bradley to borrow Major General Middleton's division from Patton, who objected vehemently just as he was about to attack the Saar. He had cussed and fussed. "Damn it, there's no attack, it's just a spoiling attack to stop my offensive."

Bradley also called Ninth Army headquarters to send the 7th Armored Division to help Middleton.

In the meantime, the Sixth Panzer Army led by Sepp Dietrich on the northern sector of the Ardennes, and the Fifth Panzer Army led by the Prussian General Manteuffel, had penetrated the Losheim Gap. Now Dietrich was heading west and Manteuffel south toward St. Vith. A collapsed railroad overpass stalled Dietrich, as traffic jammed for miles eastward, with tanks and infantry immobilized. SS Lieutenant Colonel Jochen Peiper reached the stalemate and, sidetracking the overpass, plowed down the embankment, his armored car skidding over the field with tanks and other vehicles following. They ran into their own mines that they set when they left this area months before.

He was ruthless in his desire to proceed even at the cost of losing tanks to explosions, but stopped for the night when advised that more mines were ahead as well as Americans troops. Meanwhile, Colonel Otto Skorzeny and his men, dressed in American uniforms, were stalled behind the damaged overpass at a time when it was important for them to be far ahead to perform their assignment.

At Versailles, reports that all hell had broken loose across the entire front were being received from the

Corpsman Jimmy Polite

commanders. The entire Allied front line was a disaster. At the First Army Headquarters at Spa, enemy parachutists and patrols were reported behind American lines. Military Police stopped Americans on the road and asked these questions: Who are the Yankees? Who is Minnie Mouse? Questions most Americans could answer. Then the MPs explained, after the correct answers were given, that Germans had parachuted into our area wearing American uniforms and riding in captured jeeps.

Now First Army Headquarters was in turmoil. All orders were in a state of confusion as the headquarters began to pack and burn its papers and set fire to equipment that was too difficult to move.

On D-Day, June 6, 1944, Jimmie Polite, a Third Aux member, crossed the Channel on HMS LSM 930, and was in the first truck off the ship. He drove a two-and-a-half-ton water truck pulling a water trailer. He said, "How I made it God only knows. There were dead soldiers floating all around and dead on the beach." Jimmie was awarded the Bronze Star.

He was a member of the Third Auxiliary, but now on D.S. in the motor pool at the 51st Field Hospital. He kept the trucks and jeeps in running condition. In the German counter-attack, when all hands were needed in the operations area, Jimmie was assisting a surgeon. He tells his experience during the "Bulge" as it was referred to more frequently. Private Jimmie Polite writes:

"I was in Malmedy on the 16th of December during the battle of the Bulge. The weather was terrible; it was snowing, sleeting and raining all at the same time. Colonel Blatt, Corpsmen Ressler, Shorty and I were all in the Colonel's car on our way to Headquarters to find out what was going on. Colonel Blatt, went in, stayed only a minute, and came out running, he yelled, "The Germans are killing everyone. They're not taking prisoners. Headquarters are burning all their records. The Germans have massacred several hundred soldiers that had surrendered at the crossroads. Everyone is to evacuate Malmedy."

There was only one road out and it was jammed, not only with trucks and vehicles but people running away. The water tank hauled by a truck was covered with humanity hanging on for life. As they joined the escapees, Jimmie Polite said, "We passed several of our surgeons walking, so they put Shorty and me out, and the officers took our place. Shorty and I went back to the hospital, which was in a schoolhouse. It looked like everyone was gone." Jimmie continued:

"One soldier on a litter on the X-ray table asked me for a drink of water. I told him he couldn't have any water." He said, 'You might as well give me some water, since everyone has gone and left us here.'
"I got a 4x4 (a gauze square), wet it and put it in his mouth." (Jimmie knew that a pre-operative was not to have fluids, and he was following the rules.) "I found Major Penterman was still here so we put all the wounded on the litters and on the trucks. Some were walking wounded. I remember one soldier saying, 'I have no pants.' I told him to get in the truck. If the Germans get here, you won't need any pants. I wrapped him in a blanket and he got on. It was getting dark by the time we got everyone loaded. We were about the last ones to leave Malmedy. The Engineers had set the bridges to blow up; I guess we were the last to cross. It took me a few days to find and get back to my unit. I knew they would come to get mail so I went to the APO and waited.
You would be proud of the nurses. They all cried because they wanted to stay with their patients, but they were ordered out.

The285th Field Artillery Observation Battalion, a defenseless one hundred and fifty men from Battery B traveling in jeeps and trucks, having left Malmedy, stopped at a roadside cafe to ask direction to Vielsalm going southward. This being Alsace territory, the French proprietress welcomed and directed them.

Having observed the Americans on the winding road minutes before, SS Peiper's half-tracks and tanks stopped the Americans and ordered them into the field next to the cafe. The men dropped their weapons and raised their hands while talking among themselves without any fear when a shot rang out followed by machine gun blast. The few who tried to crawl away were shot. The Germans raided the cafe and set it on fire as they drove away.

Peiper's column moved on and, as the following troops passed the fallen bodies, they continued to shoot at the mounds of dead. However, some were still alive. They were waiting for the troop carriers to pass. They began to whisper to see if there were others alive. About twenty thought they could get up and escape. They hated to leave those wounded that could not get up, but they knew that other Germans would come to take their boots and watches and then they would all be killed. They began to run through the field toward the woods. However, another group of Germans caught sight of them as they ran, and shots were fired.

Three men reached the woods and survived to tell about the Malmedy Massacre where 147 men perished.

As Peiper continued toward the west, a small liaison plane spotted the column through a break in the clouds. In a short time the IX Tactical Air Command sent fighter-bombers to the area. They destroyed ten half-tracks and tanks. Unconcerned, Peiper decided to strike out for the Meuse River the following day, then on to Antwerp. The German soldier's spirits lifted as they began to anticipate seeing Paris and winning the war on the western front.

Manteuffel's 2nd Panzer Division drove toward Bastogne, where many railroads crossed and roads led to the west. The natives were anxious to escape from Wiltz, east of Bastogne, but they were ordered instead to seek safety in underground shelters and cellars instead of taking to the roads to escape.

The 28th Division, after leaving the Huertgen fighting at the end of November, set up their command post in Wiltz. Major General Rose and his task force of the 9th Division, after a hard-fought battle had been defeated at Clervaux northeast of Wiltz.

More German forces were coming up from the south. Among them was Commander General Heinrich van Luttwitz, who by chance learned that the 82nd and 101st Airborne Divisions were being flown to the battle in Ardennes. He decided that the Americans were in trouble, since they had to call the parachute troops. The 101st Paratroops landed in Bastogne, while the 82nd Paratroops were ordered by General Hodges to stop SS Peiper on his way to the Meuse.

The 10th Armored Division Commander of Combat B, Colonel William Roberts, heading up from the south toward Bastogne, reported to Major General Troy Middleton. Middleton, VIIIth Corps Commander, showing him a map, directed Roberts to divide his command into three sections: one directed east on the St. Vith road, one southeast to the Wiltz road, and the third five miles north to form a half circle around Bastogne to protect the city. However, the Panzers had reached Bastogne from all directions, and the city was surrounded. Utter confusion developed as panic and fear seized the people. They remembered Hitler's blitzkrieg in 1940 and were terrified.

Colonel Descheneaux, seeing huge Tiger Tanks clamoring toward his troops, decided to surrender rather than see his men slaughtered. He said "I don't care if I'm court-martialed, I'm going to save as many lives as possible." He ordered his men to break up their guns and pistols. His men looked at him with surprise. He was a courageous man who had always followed orders from

351

his superiors and they respected him highly. Colonel Descheneaux repeated, "Break up your guns!" He then broke down and sobbed as he went below into his trench. When the Germans began relieving his men of their watches and cigarettes, he spoke up saying, "Let my men keep a pack." As the troops passed down the hill, they saw well-armed Grenadiers with many mortars and guns along with hordes of Germans surrounding his hill. Colonel T. Paine, who had objected to the surrender earlier said, "You were right." One regiment after another without food or water and ammunition running out, had no choice but to surrender, as the Germans came over the hill rounding up the Americans. At Schnee Eifel, over eight thousand men surrendered; the largest group to hold out this long. The enemy relieved them of their watches, rings, and coats. It was bitter cold.

At Verdun, Eisenhower, having been warned that Otto Skorzeny had sent special troops dressed in American uniforms to kill him, met with his generals. They were a serious group of men. The Germans must not reach the Meuse. First Army General Hodges' position had to be protected. Eisenhower asked General Patton how soon he could get to Luxembourg, and take charge. Patton replied, "I'll be in Bastogne before Christmas." Eisenhower assigned Lieutenant General Jacob L. Devers to cover the void left by Patton, also instructing him to retreat if necessary. Patton turned his Third Army north to the Ardennes, having telephoned his chief of staff, General Hobart Gray, to begin preparations for the attack.

Eisenhower was worried about the crisis. Bastogne would fall in a short time, he knew. General Bradley in Luxembourg was cut off from General Hodges in Belgium. Communication between north and south was not possible. There was but one solution. Bradley would command the southern section, and the logical man for the northern would be British Field Marshall Montgomery. It would stir up a lot of dissension among his generals who had no love for the man, but it had to be done! Bradley accepted the suggestion after the surprise of the idea dissolved. It would bring more help to the troubled area,

Montgomery headed the 21st Army Group, and had wished that the Americans had listened to him before. He had wanted them to attack from the northern sector with his own 21st Group. He instructed his young officers to contact the various American units and meet the next afternoon at 1:00 o'clock. Then he went to bed. He was an older soldier and needed his rest. Attacks and counter-attacks continued. Wounded fell, and American soldiers taken prisoner were sent to the east by the hundreds as the Germans gained headway. Bastogne was already surrounded. Vielsalm, except for a narrow corridor facing west, was isolated. St Vith was captured by the enemy. Three Commanders of 27th Battalion had to be replaced because of heart attacks, battle fatigue, and the strain of battle. Barton's Third Army, turning from its planned attack on the Saar in the East, now headed north. Montgomery, in his paratroopers' jacket and red beret, rode past the GIs in their foxholes in the northern part of the battle. They were inspired, but American generals were dubious about him and his wanting to tidy up the straggling line.

20 December 1944

When the Germans turned southward, toward the Ardennes, our 13th Field Hospital, just north of the Germans' position, retreated westward to the outskirts of Aywaille, in Belgium. We set up operation in a French chateau in the woods. We nurses slept on the floor above. A guard was posted at the front door entrance. While fumbling with his gun, he accidentally pressed the trigger and the bullet went through the ceiling, through the foot of my cot, just missing my foot. He came running up the stairs, frightened at what he had done. I sat up and pointed to the hole above me in the ceiling where the bullet lodged. He breathed a sigh of relief. That was the fourth time I had nearly been a casualty in the war, and mostly by accident.

While fierce fighting continued in the Ardennes farther south, we operated on casualties of the sporadic fighting in the near area that kept us occupied. During idle periods we explored the large estate and discovered a barricaded room, where furniture and perhaps treasures were stored. Tall wooden barriers kept us out.

The chateau was surrounded by steep hills and tall pine trees. Someone found some skis in an adjoining building, which several of us put to good use. It was a change from work, and outdoor exercise. Marcelle and I skied down some of the gentler slopes. The operating room in the chateau was the first time we had ever set up operations in a house rather than a tent. We continued operating in the area until the Bastogne fight was over.

During the German Counterattack that began on the 16th of December, the Third Auxiliary Surgical Group (who did all the seriously wounded—those who would not survive any delay) operated at the following field hospitals that were in the path of the German counterattack.

Incidents that I include here tell of their personal experiences, and originally appeared in the book *Front Line Surgeons*, authored by Major Clifford L. Graves, who was my comrade in arms.

All field hospitals comprised three platoons, which leapfrogged each other as the front line advanced.

The First Platoon of the 47th Field Hospital at Waymes comprised Majors Alfred Hurwitz and James M. Higgenbotham, one surgical Lieutenant Nurse and two enlisted men. The Third Platoon of the 47th Field Hospital at Butgenbach was staffed by the following team: Major John B. Peyton, Captain Ralph A. Dorner, Captain Claude M. Warren, Captain Hollis H. Brainard, a Lieutenant Nurse and two enlisted men.

The Third Platoon of the 42nd Field Hospital at St. Vith was staffed by Major Philip F. Partington and Captain Frank J. Lavieri, a Lieutenant Nurse and two enlisted men. The Second platoon of the 42nd Field

Hospital at Wiltz was staffed by Majors Charles A. Serbst and Duncan A. Cameron, a Lieutenant Nurse and two enlisted men. Other hospitals that were also in the path of the German counter-attack were the 13th, 45th and 51st Field Hospitals on the northern sector.

Captain Claude M. Warren tells his experience during the German counter-attack:

All during the night of 16 December we heard tanks and trucks going past our building, a battered schoolhouse without light or heat. But to our surprise they were heading away from the front. We knew that a battle was going on but we could not understand why the tanks were running away from it. Some of our men became greatly worried. After all, we were only a few miles from the front line. But to most of us it was a joke. If the Jerry's did come through, we could get out in a hurry, and our troops would chase them back in a hurry.

At midnight we admitted a soldier with traumatic amputation of both legs. He was in profound shock, and we spent the rest of the night working over him. At seven in the morning, he was just beginning to respond. I was dead tired. I went down to eat a cold breakfast and got ready to go to bed. Captain Dorner's team was taking over. At this moment we heard small arms fire down the road and we all ran out. Jeeps were racing by all loaded to the gills. A wave of excitement gripped us. The battle was coming to our door! I was thrilled. This was the stuff we were waiting for these many months.

There was a temporary lull in the traffic. The next vehicle to come down the road was a bicycle, propelled by a Belgian boy. He was yelling bloody murder and pointing at his foot. Captain Peckins was the one who knew German and he questioned the boy in the middle of the street. The boy said he had been shot by a German soldier five hundred yards down the road. The bullet had lodged in his boot but did not penetrate the skin.

Some of us became panicky, but I thought, "What the hell? If they capture us, we may be exchanged and actually get home earlier." I did not get much time to pursue this pleasant trend of thought. A radar truck came speeding down the road. There was a sharp bend where our building was. The truck was going too fast, careened off the road, and came to rest in a ditch. I ran out through the slush. The driver was already out of his cab, surveying the damage. "How does it look up front, Captain?" I tried to be casual.

He looked up, annoyed. "Rough. Got out just in time." Then noticing my unsoldierly appearance, he added, "What are you doing here?"

"We are running the hospital."

"The hospital? You mean you are running a hospital out here? You better get yourself some guns or you will be operating on Heinies. Bullangen is full of them."

"I knew that Bullangen was only a mile away and I swallowed hard."

At this point Major Henderson, the platoon commander, came over. Before he could open his mouth the captain spoke up. "Better step back, Major. I'm going to set this truck on fire."

"On fire? What do you mean? That truck is worth money, isn't it?"

"I don't care, as long as the Jerry's don't lay a hand on it." The captain and his men placed thermite charges and the truck started smoldering.

Major Henderson still could not believe the captain. But at least he decided to get the nurses out. Our surgical nurses Peggy Baker, Marge Harvey, Shirley Ralph, and Ida Marsh left without anything but the clothes on their backs. Everyone had to go in one ambulance. No room for baggage. They went to the 2nd Division Clearing Station at Elsenborn, and later they were evacuated from there. I still did not think that the Germans would reach us; so, like a fool, I did not pack a thing. I did not even pick up my watch and pen or a ring that I had pulled off while operating. At eight o'clock Lieutenant Colonel Cook, 2nd Division Surgeon, came in. He was so out of breath that he could hardly talk. He yelled at Henderson: "Get everybody out of here and damn quick. The Germans are down the road!"

We now had only two vehicles left and they were supposed to be for the patients. I ran upstairs in a fog, half scared, half thrilled. I was sure that we would be back by nightfall. I grabbed my movie camera and some film but left the rest. The panic was contagious. Everybody ran out on the road. The first people to get there were Major Peyton and Captain Brainard. They hadn't even bothered to pick up their belongings. They looked down the road and saw a truck coming at them.

"There's our chance!" shouted Peyton. "Let's flag him." The

driver stopped. Peyton and Brainard jumped on. There was no room in the cab so they crouched low in the body. Down the road they went, slithering and swaying. The shooting seemed to get closer all the time. Peyton scrambled to his feet and raised his voice above the tumult and shouted:

"Hey driver! Where are you taking us?"

"Bulangen. I want to get my buddies out!"

"Hell's bells! Let me out. We are just Medics!"

Payton and Brainard got out of that truck so fast they completely forgot about their overcoats. They hid in a ditch, dodged bullets all morning, and managed to hitch a ride later. Meanwhile the rest of us were straggling down the road toward Waymes. We clambered aboard any vehicle that was going our way. Within an hour we had all gathered at Waymes. Our patients had preceded us. The fellow with both legs shot off was in poor shape again, and I started blood on him. Our teams were ordered to the 44th Evacuation Hospital at Malmedy. The hospital was sending fifteen of its men to the same point. That made a total of thirty-one, and all we had was one ambulance and a water truck! I still don't know how we did it. We were jammed closer than sardines. The water truck had twenty men clinging to its sides. The Third Aux was in retreat all right.

From Waynes to Malmedy is only a few miles. At the halfway point we passed the spot where the road to St. Vith turns off. It was now about noon and the area was deserted. Two hours later, Battery B of the 285th Field Artillery Observation Battalion passed the same spot. This was where the notorious Malmedy massacre took place two hours later.

Rifle and machine gun fire could be heard everywhere. We learned that the German bombers had been over and that the road to Eupen had been cut by enemy paratroopers. Everyone was in a dither. No one knew what to do or where to go. A tank commander stopped me and asked me which way he should go! I told him to keep right on going and he would see plenty of Germans.

At the 44th Evacuation Hospital things seemed quiet at the moment and we went upstairs to take a nap. Captain Dorner and his men came in soon afterwards. But Dorner was disgusted. He was sweating out orders to report to Oxford where his hospital was located, and he had enough of war. "Call me if the krauts come down the street," he said as he let himself down on the cot dressed in nothing but his shorts. A moment later, he was fast asleep.

We did not have to wake him up. The noise was terrific. Word spread like wild fire: 'The Germans are on the way! Everybody get out on their own power! That was about two o'clock, the time of the Malmedy massacre. We all sat up and looked at one another. There was no longer any desire to be a hero. We had lost every piece of property we owned and we knew that the stuff was gone for good. We were in a tight spot.

The entire 44th Evac Hospital poured out into the street, Bud Dorner at the head. He didn't even take time to put on his shirt and was running at a dogtrot in his shorts. At any other time we would have laughed ourselves silly because Dorner was a big fellow and was struggling to get into his pants as he ran. Pretty soon, Colonel Blatt raced by, shouting at the top of his voice: "Hurry up! They are coming down the road!" I'll never forget the scene.

The 44th Evac group made its way to Spa on foot and by truck. Our team was instructed to proceed to Luxembourg without delay. That was a little too far to walk, so the 134th Medical Group (an administrative outfit functioning under Corps) supplied us with a truck. We loaded quickly and headed out. Our road lay through Stavelot. We were going like a bat out of hell and I thought that our driver was doing a bang-up job. I congratulated him on his dexterity. "Thanks Captain," he said. "This is the first time I have driven one of these!"

About halfway to Stavelot, we were stopped by an American tank. We inquired. "Get back where you came from," was his advice. "The Germans have a road block up ahead."

We raced back. Again we missed disaster by inches. Later that afternoon, a convoy carrying the 13th Medical Group was bombed and two doctors, one of whom I knew well were killed. We reached Spa again at about four o'clock and listened to Headquarters for a while. They laughed at the idea that they might have to retreat. The next day they damn well did, all the way to Huy! I had some mail and Christmas packages waiting for me and grabbed them on the run. Then Colonel Crisler our Third Auxiliary Commanding Officer called us in, and said we were to go to Bastogne forthwith. "The Germans are everywhere," he said. "Use your own judgment." Bastogne? The name did not mean anything to us.

We left late in the afternoon. It was almost dark. We could have gone all the way to Liege but we decided to take the direct route through Malmedy and St.Vith. This was the day that the 7th Armored was trying to get through to St.Vith. The traffic congestion was unbelievable. Everywhere the tanks of the 7th Armored ran head-on into the fleeing troops of the 106th. At one point a major, fighting mad, told his tank drivers to keep on going, even if it meant pushing the oncoming vehicles off the road. It was no use. The tanks were stalled.

South of St. Vith, the roads were strangely deserted. We did not know what to make of it but kept on going as fast as we dared in the blackout. Suddenly we saw a bright glow ahead. It was a farmhouse that had been set on fire. I figured that we'd better turn around and get back to St.Vith. The road was narrow here and, to help our inexperienced driver, I got out. There was a side road, and I motioned the driver to back into it. Then, just as I told him to turn his wheels, there was a roar of engines and three dark shapes loomed up out of the darkness. Tanks! The situation was such that the tank drivers were blinded by the fire in the distance whereas I had the advantage of looking at them with the light in my back. Even so, I saw no more than a faint outline. The lead tank was advancing at a pretty good clip. I thought that he could crowd our truck off the road and so I ran towards him, swinging my arms and shouting at the top of my voice. He could not hear me but he saw me and he throttled his engine. He said something that did not make sense. Then I got a terrific shock. He was talking German!

Suddenly the whole situation dawned on me. These were German tanks and the only reason they had not opened fire was that they took us to be Germans too! They were not more than twenty yards away and I had to think fast. If I said something in English, we would be discovered and we never would have gotten out alive. I had to continue with the deception. But how? The only word I knew was "Ja." I had no choice. Mustering my last bit of strength, I shouted back "Ja, ja, ja!" Then without waiting for an answer, I ran back toward our truck and told the driver to step on it. He exerted himself. We shot out of the side road, caromed around the corner, and beat it. We didn't even look back. Quickly we outdistanced the tanks. When we arrived at Bastogne, it was midnight, just twenty-four hours since we received the first alarm! Brother, we had had it."

(End of Captain Claude M Warren's quote.)

The earth was covered with snow on December 23 in

Bastogne. Food was being rationed, fuel and ammunition were running out, when men of the 327th Glider Infantry saw some Germans, one carrying a white sheet on a pole, coming down the road. They notified their command post, saying, "There are some krauts coming down the road with a white flag. Looks like they want to surrender." Two infantry sergeants went to meet the krauts. Two were Panzer Lehr Division officers, the other two were enlisted men. One of the officers who spoke English, Hellmuth Henke, said "We want to meet with your commander." The two German officers were blindfolded by strips of cloth torn off the sheet and were led to the command post. The message was that unless the U.S. Army Commander of the encircled Bastogne surrenders, they would all be annihilated, including all the people in the city.

Brigadier General Anthony McAuliffe was sleeping when he heard his chief of staff, Lieutenant Colonel Ned Moore, enter with a paper in his hand. He asked, "What's the news Ned?

"The commander of the krauts demands that we surrender" replied Colonel Moore.

McAuliffe, picking up the paper and rubbing his eyes trying to figure what he should do, said, "Aw Nuts!" Then he asked, 'What shall I say?"

An enlisted GI said, "That first crack you made would be hard to beat." McAuliffe asked, "What did I say?" The GI replied,"You said 'Nuts!' "

Colonel Joseph P. Harper, having heard about the German demand, said he would take the reply back to the German officers himself The German lieutenant Henke, who had been in business and spoke excellent English, asked, "What does it mean?"

The American officer replied, "It means, 'Go to hell.'"

With the sky clearing on the 23rd of December, the Allied Strategic and Tactical Air Force joined in the battle, slowing the German advance. C-57 planes began dropping supplies to the besieged army in Bastogne. The tide had turned; the German advance slowed.

On Christmas day, American soldiers opened boxes of K-rations. They were hungry. A rumor was spread that our turkeys had been captured by the Germans.

On the 12th of January the 90th Division drove toward the northwest between Wiltz and Bastogne. At the same time, the 35th Division and the 6th Armored approached from the opposite side, capturing the German 5th Parachute Division and 15,000 prisoners. The battle of Bastogne was over.

On the northern sector, Montgomery and Hodges's attack was making headway. Patton, despite some difficulties, met with the First Army at Houffalize on January 17. The Germans were retreating, leaving 75,000 dead, along with burned villages and devastation. Dietrich's 6th Panzers and Manteuffels army were escaping eastward.

Hitler's attempt to cross the Meuse to reach Antwerp cost a heavy price in lives. He drove a sixty-mile wedge between Liege and Namur in the American zone, the eighty-five miles in Luxembourg that were protected by three newly arrived American divisions and the three decimated divisions that were waiting to be outfitted after having fought in the futile Huertgen Forest battle. In thirty-eight days of the Ardennes counterattack, the Germans lost 220,000 men, of which 110,000 were wounded or killed. The Americans suffered 115,000 casualties, of whom 19,000 were killed, 62,000 wounded and 15,000 captured. The British who fought on the northern edge of the Bulge suffered 1,400 casualties. Wounded soldiers lay where they fell and froze to death due to the difficulty to rescue them. The Ardennes counterattack was over on January 17, 1945.

Voices of Other Nurses

On December 16, four nurses from the Third Auxiliary Surgical Group were on duty in the first platoon of the 47th Field Hospital at Waymes when the Germans counter-attacked.

They were Lieutenants Norine Webster, Reba Green, Mary Murphy and Mabel Jessop. Nurse Lieutenant Mabel Jessop wrote:

When we went to breakfast on the morning of 17 December, we all knew that there was a push on. But even our commanding officer was completely in the dark about the seriousness of the situation. The only source of news we had was from the battle casualty. His words carry a weight and authority of the eyewitness but they are distorted by personal emotions. It is a worm's eye view. Nevertheless, we all eagerly questioned the soldiers that were brought to us during the early hours of that day.

They were men from the 2nd Division, and they were in a state of acute jitters. Most of them had been forced to retreat before an overwhelming force of tanks on the Elsenborn moors. At about nine o'clock there was a sudden influx of patients and personnel from the platoon at Butgenbach (this was the flight that has been related by Captain Warren.)

Then we knew that things looked bad. We made a half-hearted attempt to be cheerful, and started looking after the new arrivals as best we could. Very soon orders came to transfer all patients to the 67th Evacuation Hospital at Malmedy. Yet, we ourselves were to stay and operate the hospital! Evidently we were considered expendable.

Next, Majors Peyton and Dorner, our surgeons, were ordered out. This only heightened our anxiety. The noon hour came and went, but nobody could eat. The food was the usual cold, tasteless mixture of canned rations and dehydrated potatoes. Why eat when you might have to run for your life? It is better not to be encumbered by a full stomach.

At one o'clock, the bomb burst. Evacuate immediately! Patient's first, nurses next, personnel last. I never saw such a quick job of loading. Within ten minutes, all our patients were on their way, and the surgical teams went with them. This convoy reached Malmedy without incident. About ten minutes after they had left, it was our turn. There were ten of us (six platoon nurses and four of us surgical nurses). We all piled into one ambulance. We left everything behind except for a few toilet articles.

At half past one we approached the intersection where half an hour later the Malmedy massacre took place. The tank battalion responsible for this atrocity was coming up from the south at the very time we approached from the east. If the weather had been a little clearer, we would actually have seen them. As it was, we did not see them, but we certainly heard the shelling with which they announced their arrival. This shelling began at half past one and was aimed at our convoy. Our driver drove off the road and sought protection in a wooded area. Here, we found ourselves in the company of half a dozen trucks in the same predicament. The shells were still coming in.

Sister, were we scared! How could we ever get out again? When shells land so close that you can see the explosions right in front of you, you think that the enemy must know exactly where you are and you expect to be blown up with the next blast. We will never know if the Germans did see us, but it doesn't make much difference. We all agreed that it would be folly to try to get back in the trucks. Our only chance was to crawl back towards Waymes. And that is what we did.

Did you ever try to make yourself inconspicuous when you are wearing dark clothes and everything else is white? Before I had gone a hundred yards, I was covered with mud and slush and melting snow and the others looked even worse.

Soon we saw more American trucks coming our way and we signaled them to stop. The shelling had stopped now and it seemed safe for the oncoming vehicles to turn around. We clambered on and were back in Waymes a few minutes later. But Whew! That half hour in the ditch! I think I lost ten pounds there.

In Waymes we found the hospital completely dismantled. Only a skeleton crew remained. We surveyed the situation. Obviously our retreat to the west had been cut off. Retreat to the east would take us right back into Butgenbach which we knew to be in enemy hands. Retreat to the south would have taken us to St Vith, which was already surrounded. Retreat to the north would have been possible except that this road junction was located a mile to the east, the very direction that we most wished to avoid. We were surrounded. There was nothing to do but await capture.

Our building had been shorn of what little comfort it had offered up until this time. No stove, no lights, no warmth. We felt as if we were already in prison. In our dismay, we retreated to the basement, which seemed about the safest place. Some of us had not opened yesterday's mail and started reading it. There was a letter from Michigan for me. It started, "Dear Mabel! You lucky devil. How I wish that I were with you now."

I managed a wry smile. Then Mary Murphy spoke up. "Listen to this, kids." Her letter described in extravagant detail a party that was to be held in her hometown on 17 December. The letter ended: "Hurry back here!"

Shells fell all afternoon, some within a few hundred yards. Our building was not hit in this barrage. We divided our time between the basement and the upstairs. At six o'clock, two ambulances arrived with casualties from the fight at Butgenbach. They were in severe shock and in need of immediate attention. Thankful for a chance to get busy once more and to forget our troubles, we unloaded equipment and set to work. More ambulances arrived. We did the best we could. At two o'clock in the morning, somebody said that a German half-track had passed our building. We had not been aware of any particular fight in the vicinity and assumed that the town had passed into enemy hands without a struggle. So we were prisoners.

All during the night, American soldiers who had been cut off came straggling in. Some were from service units and others from combat units. That posed a problem. The combat soldiers were fully armed. If we allowed them to stay, the Germans would accuse us of violating the rules of the Geneva Convention. So we made them deposit their weapons in a distant part of the building. The commanding officer of the platoon destroyed the records. The rest of us tried to remember that lecture on the rights of prisoners of war. All I could think of was, name, rank, and serial number. But what if they asked all sorts of trick questions? The Germans were supposed to be darn clever at that.

At ten, I left my ward to go into the corridor and grab a smoke. The corridor ran along a courtyard, which in turn emptied, on the street by means of a gate. I was looking at this gate when I saw two men approach. One was dressed in a German captain's uniform. The other wore an American uniform with a sergeant's stripes and a 5th Armored shoulder patch. They had their rifles in the ready. The one in the American uniform shouted to our truck drivers in English: "Your hospital is under arrest. Everybody line up in the yard!"

I stood thunderstruck. Was this how it felt to be captured? Although we had plenty of weapons to overpower our would-be captors, nobody dared move for fear of violating the Red Cross rules. We marched out into the courtyard and lined up. While the German captain kept his gun pointed at us, his sergeant went through the lines, telling everybody to surrender personal equipment. In a short time he had a dandy collection of pocketknives, bandage scissors, and fountain pens. I'll never forget those moments.

The thought that was going through my head was: What if they capture my diary? Diaries were forbidden in the combat zone but most of us kept them anyway. Mine was tucked away in my bedding roll, down at the other end of the building. I was just debating whether I should even make an effort to find it when the sergeant announced that the entire hospital staff, including all our patients, was to get loaded immediately. We had ten minutes to gather our belongings. That finished all chance of retrieving the diary.

Major Laird, our platoon commander, played skillfully for time. "What about all our seriously wounded?" he asked. "It is contrary to the laws of the Geneva Convention to move them."

The SS captain delivered a long tirade, which was in turn translated into English by the accomplice for the benefit of Major Laird. There followed an interchange of questions and answers, arguments and counter-arguments, until finally the SS man relented. Non-transportable were to be left behind in the care of four medical officers. All the nurses, and a dozen technicians—everybody else—was to get on the trucks right away. It looked bad. Getting several hundred men on trucks under those conditions is no small matter. It involves lots of pushing and pulling, shouting and shoving. Men broke ranks, made noise, and dropped equipment. The lone SS captain could not be everywhere.

In the confusion, one of our drivers slipped away. Luck was with him. Although the street filled with excited civilians, none of them paid any attention to the scurrying American. Combat troops were nowhere to be seen, but an anti-aircraft unit had just pulled up the road and our driver gave them the word. In a moment, three American half-tracks started towards the school.

Throughout all this I was startled to see the citizens of Waymes welcome the Germans with open arms. These were the people that we had entertained at our mess. And given our candy to! The German sergeant in American uniform was evidently a nephew of the woman who ran the tavern where we had our quarters. We had given her lots of our things and she was always a model of hospitality and graciousness. But on this day, she had the crust to come out on the street, embrace her nephew, and point at us in a gesture of contempt! It was galling in the extreme.

Things now happened so fast that nobody could keep track of them. Evidently, our captors were warned about the approaching half-tracks, and they started running even before we knew what was going on. Halfway across the street they were caught in the fire from the anti-aircraft men. The Germans fired back, but their bullets went wild. We ducked. That was one thing we had learned well the day before. All our combat men dived for their guns and joined in the melee. It was like the hounds chasing the hare and, in this case, the hounds suffered more than the hare. Several Americans were wounded, but the Germans, to the best of my knowledge, escaped. At least we never saw them again.

At eleven, just one hour after we were captured, a lieutenant colonel of the First Division entered our courtyard, gun in hand. In stentorian tones, he announced that the situation was under control. We all came outside, ready to sing the praises of our liberators. Before we could burst into song, machine gun fire broke out again, and not very far away either. Anxiously, we looked around, "Don't worry," said the colonel. "Those are my men chasing the Jerrys. You are now enjoying the protection of the famous First Division!" We could have hugged him.

Major Laird decided that this was a good time to get away. He ordered all the patients loaded on the trucks. Then we got on, and after that there was very little room for anything else. All our belongings stayed behind, never to be seen again. When Major Laid went back a week later, he found the place literally ripped apart from stem to stern. Our friends, the civilians, took everything that they could use and scattered the rest to the far corners. They did the most thorough job of looting that he had ever seen. Even our poor African Arabs could not have improved on it.

We pulled out amid the din of battle. Where could we go? Malmedy was a ghost town. Spa was being evacuated. Liege was supposedly safe. And yet, when we arrived there that evening and found a temporary refuge at the 15th General Hospital, we heard that fifteen Americans had just lost their lives in a Buzz-bomb explosion there. No place was safe from Hitler's rage. We felt like hunted animals.

The 47th Field Hospital was eventually reunited at Spa a week later. Practically everybody of the first and third platoons had lost all they had. We were indeed a chastened bunch, but we sang our Christmas carols with solemn gratitude that our lives had been spared. They were spared because of the magnificent stand of our American fighting soldiers. It was to them that we owed our safety. Never shall we forget it.

(End of quote by Lieutenant Nurse Mabel Jessop.)

Major Charles A. Serbst writes:

18 December 1944

Today was a day of crisis. The Germans were staking everything on a quick success. They had landed parachute troops in American uniform along the Eupen, Malmedy road and these men roamed the countryside for days, wreaking havoc wherever they went. Butgenbach was in German hands; Malmedy was under heavy pressure; Stavelot had fallen. An armored spearhead had continued beyond Stavelot to La Gleize, at which point it was only five miles from Spa. Spa was important to the Germans. They sent their tanks forward under cover of the murky sky. There was very little to stop them.

At First Army Headquarters at Spa, General Hodges knew of the danger that threatened him but he did not know from which side the Germans would come. Everybody on the "palace guard" was pressed into service. Cooks, clerks, bakers, censors, quartermaster squads, truck drivers, ordnance crews, and intelligence teams, everybody who could tote a gun was in arms.

Third Auxiliary Surgical Group Headquarters was also based at Spa. Colonel Crisler alerted his surgeons, nurses and enlisted personnel. None of them had any idea of the proximity of the enemy. They congregated in the yard, scanned the skies, and made the usual wisecracks. Then they saw something that made then quiet. The battle for Spa was fought on the ridge between the town and the valley of the Ambleve, directly to the south. The first thing the Third Auxers saw was a strafing attack by American P-47's. Those P-47s saved Spa. How they did it was a story in itself.

The tanks coming towards Spa were spotted quite by accident. The air artillery liaison officer of First Army Headquarters had taken to the air in a Cub plane, even though the weather limited visibility to less than a mile. As he wandered around through the low overcast, he happened on the German tanks that were just coming out of the valley at Andrimont. The Major reached for his intercom. "Come down here, if you want to see something." He was talking to a flight of P-47's up above. That was all the fighters needed. Down they came and caught the German task force in the most vulnerable position, on a narrow, hollow road without avenue of escape. Never was there a more one-sided battle.

Even though Spa was saved, it was no longer a desirable headquarters location. At five o'clock, word was passed to vacate. Major Harold Hansen was in charge of loading and he used his head. He ditched all the circulars, all the reports, all the inventories, and he took along all the blankets, all the heaters, all the radios. "I really ought to booby-trap this place," he commented fiendishly as he made his last check.

"Well why don't you throw life-savers on the floor?" suggested, Foregger. "The krauts might trip on them!"

"Hell, no," said Hansen. "If they can trip over them, they can eat them. But I'll blow up the generators right now." And he made off in the direction of the garage.

The Third Aux was not the only unit abandoning Spa. A regular exodus took place. The townspeople gathered in the streets to see the trucks pull out, and it was obvious that they were expecting to see the Germans pull around the corner.

To be in a retreat of that sort is the most demoralizing experience a soldier can suffer. Darkness settled. The convoys stalled a hundred times. Rain began to fall. Captain Brattesani said, "Let's keep on going until we are home!" He spoke for many. The trucks kept going only as far as Huy, a little town on the Meuse. Before long, Huy was bulging at the seams because hundreds of units converged on it that night. The Aigle Noir, the only presentable hotel in town, was full of generals and colonels. With such competition, Third Auxers had to take a back seat. All the schools, convents, and ware houses were jammed to the gills and when Third Aux Colonel Francis scouted around for a place the choice was quickly narrowed down to the opera house, the conservatory, and a boarding school for girls! For a few days, officers and men lived amid the faded glories of the opera house. Later, they set themselves up in the conservatory and cooked their meals in the shadow of two grand pianos. One place was as bad as another. Only the Aigle Noir provided warmth and comfort, and this was where Third Auxers drowned their sorrows for the rest of the Bulge.

Another Third Aux team with the second platoon of the 42nd Field Hospital came under fire on December 18 when the enemy surrounded them at Wiltz. Major Hubert, the platoon commander and a Third Auxer Major Serbst discussed their problem. What to do with the non-transportable casualties? Huber wanted to abide by army regulations, which said that such casualties should not travel. Serbst argued that a truck ride could not possibly hurt these men as much as the treatment they would receive at the hands of the Germans. Serbst was right but Huber prevailed.

The hospital was divided into two sections: those to go and those to stay. There were 26 non-transportable. Major Cameron and Serbst flipped a coin. Cameron won. Serbst lost. Serbst's teammates who would stay were: Captain Evan Tansley, Captain Harry Fisher, and Captain Eugene F. Galvin. The platoon commander, Major Huber, and one other medical officer would also remain at Wiltz to face the music. The trucks took off a little after nine p.m. They carried all the transportable patients, most of the platoon personnel, the Third Aux nurses and Cameron's men.

On the outskirts of Wiltz, other trucks joined the procession. Two half-tracks led the way. For those who stayed behind at Wiltz, the prospects were grim. During the night the Germans shelled the bridge across the Wiltz and the concussions blew out all the windows. Huber and Serbst moved the patients to the basement. It was an anxious and haggard group of men that worked through the long hours of darkness, fearful of what the morning would bring.

At seven o'clock the men ate a cold breakfast. At eight they heard machine-gun fire in the village. The sounds of battle crept closer and closer. Huber seized a bed sheet, fashioned it into a white flag, and went outside. He could see German paratroopers on the road and tried to attract their attention. At first, the Germans kept firing but Huber escaped the bullets.

Finally, the Germans saw that they were dealing with a

hospital. They approached Huber and told him to line up his men in the courtyard. Worn from their vigil and glad that the uncertainty was over, the Third Auxers emerged. The first thing the paratrooper did was to search their prisoners. They seemed to be mainly interested in cigarettes. When they came to Harry Fisher, they stopped. "Jude!"

Fisher cringed. He was taken out of the line and marched off. The intent was clear. It was a moment of agony for the rest of the men. "The bastards," muttered Serbst. "They are going to shoot him."

Prisoners

A German captain addressed himself to the small group of Americans that remained in the courtyard. "You are prisoners of the Fifth Panzer Army. We will establish a Hauptverbandplatz in this building. You will remain here and take care of your own wounded."

Back in the basement the Third Auxers tried to look cheerful in front of their patients but they did a poor job of it. Fisher was going to be executed! It couldn't be worse. The curtain was ringing down on team number eleven. The Hauptverbandplatz moved in shortly. It was the German version of a clearing station, and consisted of five officers and fifty enlisted men. The officers tried to be friendly but they did not hesitate to expropriate all the hospital supplies. And no wonder. Their own equipment consisted of paper bandages, crude instruments, and makeshift sterilizers.

The only instrument that was new and shiny was an amputation saw. The German surgeons wielded it with uncanny dispatch. They would take off an arm or a leg as readily as the American would incise a boil. When Serbst registered his amazement, they said, "We do not have the time or the money to undertake tedious and expensive reparative surgery. A man with a stump can be discharged in a few weeks. A man with a plaster cast uses up a hospital bed for months."

During the next few days, scores of American casualties were brought to Wiltz. Many of them died for lack of blood. Conditions grew steadily worse. There was no heat. Supplies were giving out. The news from the front was disheartening. Shells landed sporadically. The Third Auxers worked in a spirit of utter dejection.

On Christmas Eve, the German officers sent several bottles of wine to the basement. Serbst ordered the wine passed around to the casualties, but before this could be done, four shells landed in rapid succession in the courtyard. Four Americans were injured by falling beams and flying glass. The Germans suffered even worse. It was a sad Christmas Eve.

On Christmas Day, Germans and Americans had a joint dinner. The corps surgeon dropped in. He was a jolly sort of fellow and promised the American a quick return to their own troops. As the day wore on, it was obvious that the Germans were getting worried. Third Army tanks were beginning to bite into the southern shoulder of the Bulge. American planes came over and plastered Wiltz. The building shook to its very foundation.

On December 27, the Germans decided to evacuate. They loaded their own patients first, starting in the morning. At noon it was the Americans' turn. Officers and men were separated. There were over eighty casualties, at least half of them non-transportable. Serbst could hardly conceal his bitterness when the wounded had to be placed on open trucks for the long journey. And a long journey it was. The retreat was now general. Roads were jammed. It took all day to get to Bitburg, just beyond the Siegfried Line. At this point, the convoy spilt up. The wounded were moved to the hospital on the Rhine. The medical personal were detained in Bitburg.

Bitburg had no facilities for prisoners of war. In fact it had no facilities for anything. The driver was completely at a loss. Finally, after diving around in the blackout for the better of an hour he dumped his load at the city jail, a ramshackle structure that had only two cells. The jailer was overwhelmed with this sudden influx. He did his best. Nuns brought soup. It was thin stuff but it was warm. Third Auxers ate like hungry dogs. Then they unrolled their blankets and bedded down on the concrete floor. They were dead tired. They remained in the Bitburg jail for two days. The nuns ran out of soup, and the jailer was busy with other chores. The prisoners took another hitch in their belts.

"I always thought that the oubliettes[2] went out with the Inquisition," said Tansley. "Guess I was wrong."

The next morning, December 30, the journey was resumed. The Third Auxers, including some of the hospital personnel, were marched to a railroad siding. A train was waiting. It was a welcome sight to the men who had been dragging their blankets and bedding rolls over the wet and muddy road. The train took off. It chugged for hours along the winding valley of the Moselle. At Winningen it came to a halt. Third Auxers heard that the bridge was blown and that they would be marched into Coblenz the following day.

Again the prisoners were led to the town jail. Again they spread their blankets on the concrete floor. Again they tried to kill the hunger pains by hitching up their belts. The day had gone without any food.

That evening it started to snow. It snowed all night and part of the next morning. Then the weather cleared up and the men were lined up for the march.

"I wonder how far it is," said Serbst, eyeing his sleeping bag, his blanket, his musette bag and his duffel bag with misgiving.

"Too far," said Galvin. "We'll never make it."

The bridge at Winningen had been bombed. A ferryman had strung a cable across the river and took the Third Auxers across. They began the march, weak with hunger and numb with cold. "Look at those planes coming down this way," said Serbst. "I bet they are after the bridge."

Serbst was right. It was a flight of American bombers. The men dropped their burdens and crouched low. Concussions rocked the countryside. Waterspouts dotted the river. Mud and debris flew sky-high. What was left of the bridge disintegrated.

The men picked themselves up. They were covered with slush from head to foot. It was several minutes before they regained their composure.

The German guards decided that the main road was too dangerous. They switched to a trail. This trail led to the hills, rising precipitously to an altitude of eight hundred feet. It was partly frozen, partly rock-strewn. Footing was precarious. The paraboots caused painful blisters. The baggage, an awkward burden at best, now became a threat to progress. One misstep could spell disaster. Gradually the precious articles went down the steep ravine—first the sleeping bags, next the blankets, finally the duffel bags. At the top, only musette bags remained.

From Winningen to Coblenz by main road is barely ten miles but across the hills the distance grew to twice that much. And the German guards did not tarry. They knew that American planes would come over again and they wanted to be in a Coblenz air-raid shelter when it happened. On and on they went, every step a strain, every hill a hazard, and every mile a misadventure. Even the sky turned hostile. Fresh snow began to fall. White with fatigue, Galvin turned to his fellows. "I don't know if I'll ever get to Coblenz," he said. "Maybe Harry Fisher's way out was the easiest."

At this moment, the Third Auxers were already in the foothills overlooking the Rhine valley. Soon they could see the city itself. Coblenz was in a strategic location. Situated at the confluence of the Moselle and the Rhine, it had for years been the traditional home of the *Wacht am Rhein* (Watch on the Rhine). A previous generation of Germans had erected a huge statue of Kaiser Wihelm I where the two rivers come together, and this spot had been proudly call the *Deutsche Ecke* (German Corner). But there was nothing proud about it when the Third Auxers appeared on the scene. Kaiser Wilhelm was hanging head-down in a most ignominious position and his horse had erupted all sorts of hardware through a gaping hole in its side. The scene seemed to be symbolic of the fate threatening all of Germany in the winter of 1945.

The streets of Coblenz were deserted. It was a ghost city. Suddenly the air-raid alarm sounded and the streets became filled with scurrying civilians on their way to the shelters. The Americans were swept along in the maelstrom. Once inside, they sank to the floor. They were exhausted. The Coblenz shelters were unique. They had been dug into the side of the hills facing the Rhine and they were indestructible. At the moment the Third Auxers entered they were jammed. Thousands of Germans milled about. Soon these people began to realize that Americans were in their midst and they gave vent to their feelings in no uncertain terms. "*Heraus mit den verdammten Amerikaner!*" (Out with the damned Americans!) The Third Auxers could not understand the words but the accompanying gestures were unmistakable. Many an American bomber crew had been brutally murdered under such circumstances. Even the guards assumed a threatening attitude. It was a moment fraught with peril. The Third Auxers picked themselves up and retreated. They had no desire to stay in these sinister surroundings. One by one they slipped out, their ears still ringing with deprecations. Bombs were falling; Serbst led his men to a tarpaper shack. "May I sweat this one out with you?" quipped Tansley.

"You are welcome," was the reply.

The raid continued for half an hour, and destroyed the last remaining bridge over the Rhine. It was getting dark. The guards had instructions to take the prisoners across the river. They pressed a rowboat into service. It was a treacherous crossing, made more so by the blackout. On the far side, hills loomed again. The guards started for Ehrenbreitstein along a steep road. Higher and higher it went. Galvin was near collapse. Tansley's feet were frozen. Serbst was staggering. Only superhuman efforts kept these men going. The ancient walls of Ehrenbreitstein had seen Americans before. In 1918 occupation troops had swarmed over these same ramparts, and the Germans were a friendly people. But in 1944 this had changed. The atmosphere was charged with resentment, and when another air raid sounded, the Germans went to their shelters and the Americans stayed outside. "It's New Year's Eve, boys." These are the best fireworks I have seen since I left the States," said Galvin.

The march continued into the night. It did not end until the guards themselves were overcome with fatigue. Then they locked their prisoners in a bunker. Here the eleven Americans were crowded together in a space of twenty feet square. The slit-like windows allowed the frigid air to blow back and forth, and the men would have frozen, had they not huddled close together. Such was New Year's Eve for team number eleven.

The next day was one of the coldest of the entire winter. The skies were clear and the sun shed its light over a landscape scintillating in its whiteness. The hills of the Taunus were covered with a blanket of snow. The road stood out in sharp relief, stretching away to the east as far as the eye could see.

"I wonder where these Krauts are taking us," mused Tansley.

"To Limburg," said Huber, who had been talking to one of the guards. Limburg was thirty miles. Thirty miles of painful progress in freezing weather, through snowbound country. It was a grim prospect.

The march started early in the morning. Presently, the Third Auxers heard the rumblings of a truck. The vehicle approached at breakneck speed. And as luck would have it, there was an empty trailer behind the truck. The guard held up his hand. The truck stopped. The men climbed on the trailer.

The truck driver seemed to be in a great hurry. He paid no heed to the slippery road, and many curves, the steep declivities. Faster and faster he went. The men in the trailer held on for dear life. Their vehicle bounced from one side of the road to the other, traveling on two wheels more than on four. Crazily, it scraped trees, poles, and fences. Desperately, the Third Auxers hung on. "We've had it, boys," gasped Tansley.

The truck headed down towards the bottom of a small valley. Going more than fifty miles an hour, the trailer did not have a chance. It skidded sideways, side-swiped a cement abutment, broke loose from the truck, and landed upside down in the ditch. In this accident that could easily have killed every occupant, only one man was seriously injured and that was the German guard! He smashed his leg. The others landed in soft snow and came off with nothing worse that cuts and bruises.

The truck driver summoned aid. The Third Auxers fashioned a crude splint for the casualty and carried him to a nearby German farmhouse.

Then they continued on their journey. Footsore as they were, they still preferred walking to riding. That night they reached Montebaur. The guards moved their prisoners into a youth hostel. The housemother took pity on the starved Americans and gave them their first hot meal in three days. The meal was a watered-down version of mulligan stew but it tasted like the juiciest steak. The Third Auxers relaxed. This was more comfort than they had had since they left Wiltz on December 18,

On the next day, January 2, The Americans reached Limburg, site of the notorious Stalag XII A. Misery, want, and disease stalked the prison population. The men slept in barracks of about the same size as U.S. Army barracks, with the difference that, while an American barracks houses twenty men, the German barracks housed four hundred! Bunks were stacked in tiers. Nobody ever took his clothes off and nobody ever took a bath. Sanitary facilities consisted of one washbasin and one latrine for four hundred men.

Rations were shaved down to a bowl of soup a day. Besides this, each group of six men received a loaf of bread. The loaves were the same size. And yet, the man who brought back a loaf that was only a fraction of an inch undersize was castigated as if he had committed a major crime. The wooden soup bowls were never washed. Dysentery, typhus, and tuberculosis were rampant.

Shortly after their arrival, the Third Auxers were separated. Tansley went to work in the camp hospital. The hospital was a disgrace. When Tansley arrived, there were almost three hundred American casualties, mostly from the Battle of the Bulge but also from the frequent air raids. With two other medical officers, Tansley had to look after the ills and wounds of men who had been neglected for months. Every wound was infected, every illness complicated.

On the first day, Tansley changed the bandages so enthusiastically that he used up a week's supply. Then he made a rule: only when the pus was dripping through the bandages did the wound get dressed. "Ambrose Pare' did better in the 15th century!"

On the January 13, Serbst and Galvin were sitting disconsolately on their bunks when there was a commotion outside. "Looks like another bunch of Krieges," said Serbst, munching a piece of stale bread. His chief interest was now centered on food.

"Maybe there is somebody we know in there," said Galvin, and he looked inquiringly at the handful of pitiful prisoners who had lined up outside. "I think they're coming in here. You indoctrinate them, Gene."

"You mean I have to show them how to cut a loaf of bread into six pieces? Hell they'll learn that quickly enough."

The new prisoners were coming in. Serbst lifted a weary eye. The usual motley crew. Hungry men. Ragged men. Dejected men. Then Serbst saw something that made his eyes pop. A big smile parted his lips. He jumped to his feet. "Harry Fisher—we thought that the Germans had shot you!"

"Hell, no! I fought the battle of Bastogne."

"Well, give us the dope Harry."

(End of quote by Major Charles A. Serbst.)

Captain Harry Fisher continues the story:

"You remember how the Krauts picked me out of the line at Wiltz? They took me to the motor pool and asked me if I knew how to drive an ambulance. I said that I was a medical officer, but the Feldwebel made a threatening gesture and I

Third Aux members taken prisoner in the "Battle of the Bulge," the German counterattack of December 17, 1944: Evan Tansley, Eugene Galvin, Charles Serbst and Harry Fisher. (photo taken after the war)

knew damn well that old Harry didn't have a chance. We started for the front right away. I had one German orderly with me. When we got to the bottom of the hill, we hitched up with a Verbandplatz detachment of the Panzer Lehr Division. It was a regular convoy. I turned the heater up and was just beginning to enjoy myself when bang! A shell hit directly in front of me. Blew out my radiator. The truck ahead of me was demolished. Dead Krauts everywhere. It didn't stop them, though. We switched to a German ambulance and away we went. We drove several miles 'till we got to Bras, not very far from Bastogne. There was a heavy battle going on at Wardin. The Krauts decided that they wanted a first-aid station at Bras. That was about noon. We picked the only undamaged house in the place and set up. All we had was two German medical officers and a handful of enlisted men."

Fisher had been pitched into one of the greatest battles of the war. It was a battle between hastily gathered American troops and a whole German Panzer Army. The defenders of Bastogne were made up of the 101st Airborne, one combat command of the 10th Armored, and the 705th Tank Destroyer Battalion. The 10th got there first. Its combat command arrived at four o'clock in the afternoon of December 18. The first units of the 101st arrived at midnight. The tank destroyers arrived on the evening of the 19th. The skirmish took place on the evening of December 18 at Longvilly, six miles to the east. Here the 10th Armored fought off an overwhelming force of German armor for several hours before withdrawing to Neffe.

On the morning of December 19, when Fisher became a willy-nilly member of the Panzer Lehr, the Germans launched an all-out attack on Wardin, just off the Bastogne-Wiltz road. They wiped out Company I of the 10th Parachute Infantry and created a gap that was not plugged until the next day. It was this engagement that provided many anxious hours for Fisher in the first-aid post at Bras.

Fisher continues:

"It was rugged. Bras is located on high ground and Wardin on low ground. Whenever the fog lifted, we could see German tanks engaging American infantry. The Germans had seven Tiger tanks and a whole battalion of armored infantry. The Americans had just one company of infantry and no anti-tank weapons at all. The German tanks moved up, each one with a platoon of infantry in support. It was murder. I don't see how our boys took it as long as they did. The Krauts shot up every house in the village and every basement too. By nightfall, there wasn't a wall standing. Then the wounded started coming in. The first one was a paratrooper who had been shot in the abdomen. He told me that the attack had come as a complete surprise. The German armor was upon them before they could even ask for artillery support. Fog swirled in and out. Long-range firing was out of the question. The first thing this fellow saw was a Tiger tank and a bunch of Krauts, and all he had was a machine gun! He could have held his fire and retreated to the basement. Not him. He blazed away with all he had. He wiped the Krauts out in about thirty seconds. Then the Tiger swung around and let him have it. Can you imagine getting hit with an 88 at fifty yards? That fellow had what it takes. He lived twelve hours.

Company I was practically destroyed. There were a

hundred casualties that I saw myself. There were many more that I never saw at all. I'll never forget that night. I was trying to take care of a hundred casualties in one of those two-by-four Belgian basements. Most of the casualties had to stay outside in the rain. American shells started coming at us and we decided to get out as quickly as we could. We left most of the casualties behind. The next day, 20 December, we moved to Wardin. This was a couple of miles closer to Bastogne. I could see the town plainly, and it looked like open country to me. But, instead of moving along the main road, the Krauts advanced on Marvie. From Marvie to Bastogne is only a little over a mile. I guess they figured that they had us if they could take Marvie.

We arrived towards noon and set up in the usual location: a bombed-out basement. That's all that was left of Wardin, just basements. I could see four Tiger tanks and six half-tracks closing in on Marvie. The answering fire didn't seem to hurt them in the least. Later I heard that we only had a couple of light tanks there. They tried to get out but were shot up in the process.

Then something happened. Tigers tanks were beginning to get into trouble. Two of them were hit in a matter of seconds. The fire came from the north. The third tank made a dash for the village and ran smack into a bazooka man who finished it in short order. The fourth one turned chicken and ran off. Meanwhile, the half-tracks had reached Marvie and deposited the infantry. They slugged it out with our boys for a full two hours. The half-tracks cruised up and down, but the fighting was done indoors. You could only guess at it.

Later in the afternoon, the Germans put smoke on Marvie. After that, nobody knew who was where. Night closed in. That was when the snow began. Wounded men didn't have a chance. They either bled to death or froze to death. I saw one man who had been firing a machine gun at the Germans. A Kraut crawled up and heaved a grenade at him. You know what those German grenades do. Well, this fellow lay next to his machine gun all night, literally splattered with lead. Then the Germans brought him in. I counted over a hundred wounds. The poor fellow was so cold he couldn't move a muscle. He couldn't even talk. All he could do was move his head. He died in a couple of hours. What a miserable way to die."

To Fisher, the battle of Marvie seemed a debacle

but to the Germans it was a major setback. Marvie remained in American hands even though German half-tracks ranged the streets. The Germans could not enter Bastogne but kept on pushing around it. On December 20 they cut the road to Neufchateau and completed the encirclement of Bastogne. On December 21, there were several engagements west of the town but these lacked the strength and persistence of the previous two days. On the 23rd of December the Germans demanded that the Americans surrender, to which General McAuliffe had replied, "Nuts!"

On December 23, a fleet of C-47's dropped supplies and reinforcements to the defenders. The drop-zone was just west of the town. Fisher in his post at Wardin could see the whole spectacle.

All through the day, we could see the flights. It was the most thrilling thing I have ever seen. Late in the afternoon, gunfire started up again. The poor fellows at Marvie were taking it on the chin. The Krauts had put snowsuits on and they sneaked up on Marvie behind their tanks. At one point, they flushed an American half-track out of the woods just south of Marvie. I saw the driver hightailing it for the village. The Americans in Marvie thought he was German and let him have it. That was the end of him. His vehicle blocked the road all the rest of the night and kept the German tanks away.

The next thing I saw was an old-fashioned whoop-and-holler attack by the Germans. I could hear them yell. Their flares lighted the entire area. A hayloft was hit and started to burn. The bright light of the flames against the background of snow was fantastic. It beat any show I ever saw. But I was too damned cold to be impressed. That fire killed the German chances. It showed them up as plain as the nose on your face, and the Americans picked them off one by one. At eight o'clock, two American tanks moved into Marvie from the north. They raised plenty of hell. Gradually, the fire died down. Then, they started bringing us casualties. One of them was a Lieutenant Morrison who had been shot in the chest. He told me that Marvie was being defended by the 327th Glider Infantry and that they were giving the Heinies a hell of a time. I did what I could for Morrison and evacuated him. We sent all our wounded as quickly as possible to the Hauptverbandplatz at Wiltz. I don't know what became of Morrison."

"I remember him," said Serbst. He got along all right."

Fisher continued his narrative:

"The night attack of 23 December carried Germans past Marvie. Two of their tanks actually entered Bastogne. They were quickly knocked out, however. The Germans were never again able to exploit their advantage. All through the siege, they made the same mistake of putting pressure on a limited front only. By the time they had created a break-through, the 101st was waiting for them with reinforcements.

The next day, 24 December, six P-47s flew over and bombed the hell out of Marvie. They also attacked German positions at Wardin. Brother, I never want any part of that again. Fortunately, the 4th Armored was coming up from the south now. The 4th Armored had licked the Krauts at Avranches, and the Krauts knew it. But the worst thing for the Krauts was the artillery fire from Bastogne. They never knew where they would be hit next.

On Christmas Day we pulled out and moved to Oberwampach. No blood, no plasma, no instruments, no decent bandages. And a steady stream of casualties. It was killing. I never worked so hard in my life. Oberwampach was a one-day stand. The Krauts folded just as quickly as they had rushed in. Our next stop was Hoscheid. That was a big jump to the rear, and we knew darn well that the Germans were getting kicked in the teeth. At Hoscheid we set up in the village inn. The conditions were dreadful but I was so tired that it made little difference to me. I hadn't slept for days.

The hardest thing was seeing our boys die without being able to do more than pat them on the back. On Christmas Day, the Americans drew a bead on us. Shells came in from all directions. The first ones landed just outside the village. Then they got the range and the whole place began to disintegrate. One shell blew in the front door. That was enough for the Krauts. They got out of there in a hurry. All the time I kept hoping that we would get some protection from our Red Cross that marked our hospital, but the sign was so small that nobody could see it. We got out of Hoscheid late that night, Christmas night. We traveled all night and covered five miles. Then we set up in a church near Vianden. This was the day the 4th Armored got through to Bastogne. I heard about it from our own boys, but the Germans wouldn't admit it. I never saw such overbearing fat heads. On the first of January, Patton's tanks were catching up with us again. We got out of Vianden and moved to Bitburg. Here we set up in a school, and I saw at least a hundred American casualties. I wasn't able to do much for them though.

The next day, a flight of B-26's came over. Six bombs landed near our hospital. When we picked ourselves up, we counted eight dead and twenty-five wounded. There was a kid from the 101st Airborne with a cast on his leg. He was blown forty feet and did not have a scratch! Bitburg became uninhabitable overnight. We packed and moved to Kochem on the Moselle. There we got a train and went to Winningen."

"Winningen?" interrupted Serbst. "I know that place. Perish the memory."

Fisher added, "They put me to work in a hospital there. Even gave me some soup. But how can you work in a place that is bombed every day? They put me in a truck and shipped me here. Now, what has gone on with you?"

"We have had a rugged time, thank you." Serbst told Fisher the whole dreary business ending with, "And as far as this camp is concerned, it is worse than the Black Hole of Calcutta. Look around. Did you ever see a bunch of sad sacks like this?"

Fisher had to admit that Limburg was disgraceful. In a way, he was lucky, because he was the last member of the team to arrive there and the first to leave. On January 20 he was marched with hundreds of others to a railroad siding. The train was made up of boxcars, and each car was divided into three compartments with chicken wire. During the First War, Americans had marveled at the French who packed forty soldiers and eight horses into their boxcars. But the Germans went them one better. They jammed seventy-five prisoners into each car, slammed the door shut, and drew a bolt across. There was no room to sit. The air was foul. The close confinement was maddening. A prisoner in Fisher's compartment went berserk and had to be restrained. Everyone was desperate.

Suddenly, the air-raid sirens sounded. The German guards ran without bothering to unlock the doors. A standing train is a juicy target for any bomber. The men knew the fate that awaited them. Explosions started in various parts of the yard. Fisher was sure that his end had come. At the last moment, somebody unbolted the door. Frantically, the men squeezed through. Fisher jumped and started running. He did not look where he was going. He just ran. A gigantic crater loomed ahead of him. He lost his footing and rolled towards the bottom of the pit. A terrific explosion rent the air and a piece of sheet metal was blown across the crater in such a way as to form a perfect roof for it! Fisher was stunned. He examined himself. Not a scratch! Third Aux luck held out.

In that Holocaust forty men were killed and many more were injured. Fisher worked over his comrades till he dropped in his tracks. Eventually, ambulances and trucks arrived and the wounded were taken to the camp hospital. Here Tansley and Fisher joined efforts, crushed by the thought that American bombs were killing American soldiers. During the night the Germans brought up fresh cars, and in the morning the loading started over again. Fisher seethed when the guards again bolted the doors but there was nothing he could do. This time, there were no bombs, just endless hours of harrowing confinement in the dark, locked cars.

The hours grew to days and the prisoners lived on bread and water. The only sanitary facility was a one-gallon bucket, which added its effusions to the general pollution. Bitter cold, starvation rations, cramped positions, gnawing fear, noisome air—these were the mental and physical hazards besetting the prisoners on their journey. When it was time to detrain, many men were too weak to walk.

At Hammelburg, Fisher was joined by Serbst and Galvin. Lieutenant Sensenback came later. On March 13 still another Third Auxer showed up: Captain Saul Dworkin. Thus, the Hammelburg camp became a gathering point. Even as liberation was just around the corner, two more Third Auxers appeared on the scene. They were enlisted men George F. Broerman and Louis Turi. They had been separated from the officers, stripped of their possessions, and marched to Hammelburg. Broerman almost died of pneumonia on this march.

General Patton Attacks Prison Camp

The abortive liberation of Hammelburg by "Task Force Baum" is a saga of the 4th Armored Division. On March 26, this division was camped south of Frankfurt. Hammelburg was sixty miles away. General Patton thought that a small task force could beat a path across this territory, seize the camp, and bring the prisoners back. Although he never admitted it, he was probably moved by his desire to free his son-in-law, Lieutenant Colonel Waters, who had been captured in Tunisia two years before. The order was issued on March 26. Captain Baum was in charge. His force was long on speed but short on strength. It consisted of 10 medium tanks, 6 light tanks, 3 assault guns (105mm), 27 half tracks, and 6 jeeps, a total of 42 vehicles and 293 men.

They jumped off from Schweinheim at half past one in the morning on March 27. The town had been softened up by a preparatory artillery barrage, but not enough to allow clear passage. There was a fierce fight in the streets of the town, and one of Baum's medium tanks came to grief. It was but a taste of things to come. Baum piloted his party with skill. Light tanks ahead, mediums in the center, half-tracks in the rear. The route lay along the line of Aschaffenburg-Lohr-Gemunden.

At first the Germans were puzzled. In the darkness they could do little more than level an occasional rifle shot at the marauders. Gradually, however, they began to realize that they were dealing not with the redoubtable 4th Armored but with a task force of modest proportions. Here and there, anti-tank units began to harass the Americans. Baum pushed on.

At Gemunden the bridge was out. The tanks turned north, and at Burgsinn they found a bridge and crossed. On the far side, German tanks laid down interdictory fire. The task force began to suffer losses in materiel as well as in personnel. The only hope lay in speed. Baum called his men together. "Hammelburg is fifteen miles away," he said. "Drive like hell. Keep maneuvering. Use natural cover. Keep them guessing."

The Germans had prepared an ambush at Pfaffenhausen. A sharp fight ensued, and Baum lost many of his half-tracks as well as several light tanks. The only way to get to Hammelburg was to strike out cross-country. Charging through woods and pastures, the force out-smarted the Germans and caught sight of its objective at half past four in the afternoon. Hammelburg was guarded by a battalion of German infantry. Baum's job was to subdue the garrison, liberate the prisoners, and beat a retreat before the Germans could bring up their tanks. The odds were against him.

The medium tanks and assault guns laid a covering fire; the light tanks and half-tracks, with following infantry, advanced on the camp. German counter-fire knocked out five of the half-tracks, but the 105's overpowered the opposition, and when the tanks arrived at the camp gates, they found the Germans on the run.

Third Auxers had their first inkling of what was going on when the shelling started. Most of the shells landed in the Serbian sector of the camp. One of the Serbs made his way to the American sector to explain that the Serbs had suffered casualties and to find out if the Americans could establish contact with the attackers. Colonel Waters volunteered.

He improvised a white flag from a bed sheet and started for the main gate. A German guard shot him in cold blood, and Colonel Waters collapsed with a serious wound in the groin. He was carried back to the barracks.

A short time later, American tanks poked their noses through the gate. Pandemonium broke loose. The prisoners poured out, surrounded the tanks, shouted their joy, and shook hands with their liberators. It was a moment of unbounded enthusiasm.

Then came disillusionment. The prisoners learned that this was only a small task force, and only fifteen hundred of them had a ride on the few available vehicles! Baum was appalled, as it was manifestly impossible to accommodate all the prisoners. Major Serbst and a few others found room in the jeeps and half-tracks. Some climbed on the tank turrets. But the vast majority had to walk. Everybody grabbed his belongings and streamed for the exits. Within fifteen minutes, the entire prison population had vanished in the rapidly gathering darkness. It was the quickest mass-evacuation of the war.

That evening, German radio announcers talked gleefully of the tremendous losses suffered by the Americans in the tank attack on Hammelburg. The announcers were right. Baum's force had been cut to half its original size, even before it entered Hammelburg. Soon, it was to be dissipated altogether. The Germans concentrated an entire armored division outside the camp gates. The jig was up.

Baum decided to make his break in a northerly direction. He sent one of his light tanks as an advance patrol. This was followed by a half-track and then by a jeep carrying Colonel Goode and Serbst. Goode was the senior American officer in the camp. There was a distance of several hundred yards between the scout-tank and the jeep. Almost immediately, the tank was hit by a Panzer Faust. The explosion killed many of the prisoners on the tank turret, and the entire column was thrown into confusion. Small-arms fire raked the road. Serbst went foreword to see what he could do. When he came to the tank, he found dead and dying everywhere. One man was bleeding severely from a deep wound of the arm. Serbst took the man's belt and made an emergency tourniquet. Then he turned to the others. He had his hands full.

Meanwhile, Baum made an about-face with his remaining vehicles. In the resulting withdrawal, Serbst lost all contact with Task Force Baum. In fact, he suddenly was entirely by himself. As he was debating what to do, two other Americans stumbled across his path. They were Major Saunders of the 9th Armored and Major Fischer of the 106th. The three men made an estimate of the situation. Obviously, their escape lay west. But where was west? Serbst looked up. Quickly, he oriented himself. "Task Force Serbst" set out. The star class at Fort Sam was paying off.

In the early morning, the three men came upon the remainder of Baum's tanks. They had drawn up in the woods, hoping to evade the withering fire of the German anti-tank weapons. Of the original 293 men in the task force, less than a hundred were left. Baum could see that he did not have a chance. His mission now was to save as many of his men as possible. With a fine eye for the drama of the moment, he addressed his decimated contingent: "Officers, non-coms and men! We have come to the end of the road. Every man is on his own. As nearly as I can tell you, our lines are still at Aschaffenburg. Disable your tanks and try to find your way back. Good luck. The 4th Armored is proud of you."

Thus came the end of Task Force Baum. The men scattered and were rounded up later in the day by heavily armed German search parties. Baum himself was wounded. Of the entire task force and prison population, only a handful made good their escape. Serbst was among them. The rest were apprehended and taken back to Hammelburg. Serbst's break for freedom is a saga of its own.

For thirty-six hours, the three men hid in the woods. There were too many Germans to risk a getaway. Moreover, the searchers were jittery and shot at everything that looked only faintly suspicious. After the firing subsided somewhat, the Americans struck out. They marched at night and hid during the day. They avoided the roads and fled to the woods at the slightest sign of trouble. The nights were the worst. The weather was miserable, cold, and the men had only their tattered combat jackets and threadbare trousers. Often, they would have to make long detours to stay away from farms and villages. They forded several small streams and stole a rowboat to cross the river Sinn. They went without food for three days.

On the fourth day they became so hungry that they devoured a stack of raw potatoes. The next day, they did the same thing with a stack of raw beets and became violently ill as a result. And all the time, Serbst was navigating by the stars. On April 4, after they had marched for eight days, the men were so desperate that they decided to enter a village. It was broad daylight but nobody paid any attention to the three beggars. "What is this, anyway?" complained Serbst. "Do we look that bad?" Finally, a farmer approached the trio.

"*Amerikaner*"?

"*Ja, ja.*"

"*Hammelburg*"?

"*Ja, ja.*"

"*Kommen Sie herein.*"

The farmer called to his wife and led the Americans into the parlor. Presently, the wife brought hot soup, fried potatoes, and liverwurst. It tasted like manna to the starved men. The farmer offered them a place in his barn, provided they would keep under cover. "We still have plenty of SS men around here," he warned. The footsore men stretched out for their first real rest in a week. On April 6 an American patrol approached: two jeeps and a half-track. Serbst could hardly contain himself. He ran to the middle of the road, waved his arms like mad and shouted at the top of his voice.

Within a minute, he was talking to a captain of the 14th Armored Division. The three men jumped on the jeep and raced back to the division command post at Gemunden. From there they were taken to the 27th Evacuation Hospital in Aschaffenburg, where they had their first bath in months.

When Serbst looked at himself in a mirror, he could hardly believe his eyes. Who was this gaunt looking man? Hollow eyes, scraggly beard, scrawny neck, flabby arms, and sagging stomach! It wasn't even a reasonable facsimile. Serbst smiled wanly. "Look here, fellow," he said to his image. "There isn't a thing wrong with you that a little good food won't fix up."

He was right. When he arrived in New York a few weeks later, he was already well on the road to recovery. Major Serbst is a Third Aux legend. He was the premier front line surgeon. Wherever his comrades gather, they drink a toast to the man who blazed a trail on Omaha beach, stood by his guns at Wiltz, and defied the Germans at Hammelburg.

Of the Third Auxers who were recaptured at Hammelburg, only Galvin stayed until the liberation on April 6. He was flown to Bad Orb on the same day and arrived home before any of the others. He, too, has much to be proud of. The other Third Auxers were evacuated from Hammelburg a few days before the Americans arrived. Those who were unable to walk were loaded on a train. Fisher became train surgeon and Sensenbach his assistant. POW men whose normal weight was 160 pounds dropped down to 85 on rations that consisted of dry bread and water at the end of the war.

The Battle of the Bulge that began on the 16th of December and was obliterated on January 23, 1945 has been called the greatest battle the American army ever fought in ferocity, casualties, and the numbers engaged in it. During those thirty-eight days the German army lost 150,000 men, and the American army 136,000.

The Third Aux led a hard life during the weeks of the Bulge. The situation was so confusing that some of the field hospitals ceased operation. Everybody was running for his life. The severe weather wrought havoc everywhere. The isolation, the military reverses, the uncertainty of the captured surgical teams and other personnel marked a low point not only in performance but in morale.

On December 18, the 13th Field Hospital retreated from Huertgen area and set up in a chateau in Aywaille, Belgium. We discovered later that we had been part of the Ninth Army under the command of Field Marshall Bernard Montgomery who commanded the Ninth and the First Armies north of the Ardennes. At the end of the Battle of the Bulge on the 23rd of January, we continued following the First Army eastward toward Duren, Eschweiler and on to Bonn. In February, I (the writer, Lieutenant Mildred Radawiec) was transferred from the 13th Field Hospital to the 45th Evacuation Hospital, and now we headed southward toward Luxembourg.

Dresden

February 13, 14, 15, 1945

Bombing this beautiful city had been scarcely mentioned in recollections of the war until the 1960s. Rumor, our main source of information, was that after two night attacks on the 13th and 14th of February by 773 Lancasters, (the British Air Force preferred night bombings) the air raid sirens no longer functioned. The daylight raids by the American Eighth Air Force on the 14th and 15th involved 600 planes. They were loaded with tons of incendiaries that were dropped on railroads junctions, factories, and main arteries of roads.

People were still entombed in the rubble when I was in Dresden weeks later. They were trapped and burned in cellars, in homes, in collapsed stone buildings and in the streets. The underground shelters dug under factories on the outskirts of the city accommodated only the workers. The public had been advised to go to the parks, the zoo and schools for safety. Most went into the cellars of the tall buildings where they lived and where the bombs started the firestorms that collapsed the stone buildings on those who sought shelter in the basements.

I recall later hearing reasons to justify the bombing of this ancient city. One, perhaps, was because ceramic parts needed for the intricate parts of fuses for mines and the V-1 and V-2 missiles were manufactured in Dresden. Another reason was that Prime Minister Churchill wanted to impress the Russians, who were finally making headway toward the Elbe River.

Dresden was world renown for its production of fine china and porcelain, where porcelain was invented in 1707 by J.F. Bottger. The City was also famous for its tall spires, its bridges, sculptures and museums. Germany's majestic 18th century church, the Frauenkirche, was bombed flat. For centuries, Dresden had been the cultural center of Europe. Its architecture, theaters, libraries and art were world renown. Her galleries included famous works by old masters such as: Rembrandt, Vermeer, Botticelli, Holbein, van Dyck, Rubens, Hals, Canaletto, and Granach, among others. Many paintings, Greek sculptures and objects too large to move remained in the galleries. Those that could be moved were stored in the countryside far from towns, in various homes of the aristocracy and castles. The movers were sworn to secrecy.

It was the center of some of the world's greatest treasures. Porcelain, gold, silver, jeweled collection of Grunes Gewolbe; for famous watches, geometrical instruments, and chronometers. Its buildings were decorated with sculptures, and reliefs from the classical period of Greece. It was the center for music where Handel, Wagner, Bach, Strauss and many others entertained Europeans. Theaters, Libraries and the Zoo at Grosser Garten, where tigers, apes, monkeys, elephants and many other species had been preserved, assuming that the city was not a military target, and that they would be safe.

With the Russian westward advance in January 1945, Martin Mutschmann, the Gauleiter, of Dresden, decided to move the treasures from east of the River Elbe to west of the river, while refugees in packed trains, in horse drawn carts and on foot, along with freed concentration camp prisoners all heading westward, clogged the roads. There were not many places found to store all the treasures, and many were relegated into damp mines and quarries.

These masses of people were on the roads when the British RAF bombers appeared on the night of February 13. Dresden had no protection from the bombers. The anti-tank and anti-aircraft 88s, along with the searchlights that had been here in the past had all been sent to the various fronts. Schoolboys manned the light flak that could attack low-flying aircraft, but there was no defense against the high-altitude British Lancasters and American Fortresses.

Having seen the destruction of St. Lo, Aachen, Cologne, Eschweiler and Duren, I was not interested in going into Dresden to see more of the same. However, we were deeply concerned about the fate of the civilians, and prison camp refugees who were now turned loose, all fleeing from the advancing Russian army. It was estimated that a million, mostly women and children, had crowded into Dresden seeking refuge. They came by the trainloads, on bicycles, by horse drawn carts, and on foot. The refugees, along with the local citizens, were unaware that the roar of approaching bombers on the night of February 13 meant death for thousands.

The firestorm that developed compared to the later atomic bombing of Hiroshima. Dresden's tall buildings, built close together, created a horrendous windstorm. Sandstone buildings that might withstand 1200 degrees of heat collapsed, while those built of stone remained burnt out shells. Bombers flying at 20,000 feet flew through the red glow that rose above them, felt the vibration and turbulence of their aircraft. The tremendous column of hot air from the burning city and the cold winter wind at ground level on the fringes of the fires created a suction that sucked people into the inferno.

The few survivors told of the heat, of their feet burning as they raced over the hot ash and charred bodies of the fallen victims, the hot rubble of collapsed buildings. The victims' lungs burst from the heat that reached 3000 degrees. Patients in hospitals simply died in their beds if they were unable to get out on their own. The bombers came in relays, night and day, of the 13th, 14th and 15th of February. The firestorm was seen a hundred miles away.

Animals in the zoo asphyxiated; those that escaped were shot by the few men that were in the area, men too old to fight, the sick, or soldiers recuperating from wounds. Dazed animals wandered in the inferno. Because of the countless number of refugees that sought refuge in Dresden, the estimated dead were around 130,000. Bodies completely disintegrated in the intense heat.

Responsibility for this needless disaster was placed on, Air Chief Marshal Sir Arthur Harris, who opposed precision attacks, dismissing them as impractical "panacea" and demanded area bombing. In choosing Dresden, a city not bombed before, he hoped it would cause the collapse of German morale, and with Prime Minister Winston Churchill's approval, it might even benefit the Russians. The USAAF Strategic Air Force preferred daylight precision bombing of military targets and did not approve of the bombing of civilians. They knew there were mostly women and children left in Dresden, as most men were at the various war fronts. The air force crews had no voice in the decisions made by the leading authorities.

26 February 1945

After the disruption of the German Ardennes

counterattack on December 16, 1944, the capturing of several of our Third Auxiliary Surgical teams, our mail, and the escape of our headquarters from Spa, leaving behind or burning what could not be taken along, things were in a state of confusion.

As the war turned in our favor, my letter to Brunson, sent early in December, was returned with the envelope marked "MIA" (missing in action). I wrote his organization inquiring for information about him. I got a reply in June 1945, stating that Brunson's plane was shot down, with but one parachute opening. A sergeant had survived, but could not account for any other survivors. I prayed that he was a POW.

Confirmation

In 1985, I sent an inquiry to a bombardiers' reunion in California, and received a response from Captain E. Craig Amspoker, who was in the same flight as Brunson on February 21, 1945. This was the massive raid on Eastern Germany code named "Clarion," by the combined U.S. and British Air Forces. He said that Captain Brunson, of the 585th Squadron, was the lead bombardier in the first "box" of the seven thousand planes. After dropping his bombs on Munster, Germany (his accuracy was later rated "superior"), Brunson's plane was shot down by a German fighter plane.

Ludendorff Bridge in Remagen, Germany

7 March 1945

The Ludendorff Railroad Bridge across the Rhine River was an unexpected prize on the 7th of March when First Army's 9th Armored Division reached the Rhine at Remagen and found it intact. Lieutenant Karl Timmerman, of Able Company, 27th Armored Infantry

Battalion, had just replaced an officer who had been wounded in an attack on Mechenheim a few hours before. He was about to lead his platoon across the bridge when he saw a German soldier, covered by his troop's automatic guns and tanks, make a dash to set off the demolition charges. The end of the bridge erupted in a sheet of flame followed by the roar of explosives and debris. Emerging from the smoke, the German soldier was ready to dash back across the bridge when an explosion shook the earth, and parts of the bridge flew into the air. As the smoke cleared, the bridge, except for some surface damage, was intact.

Lieutenant Timmerman headed toward the bridge urging his men to follow, but they were reluctant. They were afraid the bridge would explode while they were on it. With some urging from the lieutenant, one infantryman after another gathered up courage and followed Timmerman across. The Germans made a desperate effort to contain the rapidly expanding beachhead across the Rhine. They kept their guns trained on the Ludendorff Bridge for many days, and they even sent a suicide squad down the river to blow it up, but to no avail.

The Germans fought desperately to push the GIs back. They even fired V-2 buzz bombs at the bridge. The bridge finally collapsed due to heavy bomb damage on the 17th of March, but by this time the U.S. Army Engineers had built other bridges.It was a tremendous achievement for the Americans to get across the Rhine with the bridge intact. Not since Napoleon had any conqueror ever crossed the Rhine.

Hitler raged at the German failure to demolish the Bridge. He recalled the responsible officer, and sentenced him to death. Hitler also used it as an excuse to replace Field Marshal Rundstedt of the German armies in the west with Field Marshal Kesselring, who was called from the war in Italy.

I was on duty with the 45th Evacuation Hospital, and we were situated northwest of Remagen, when news reached us that the Ludendorff Railroad Bridge had been crossed and was intact. It was exciting news, which meant our infantry would be able to cross the Rhine River without the Engineers having to build a bridge under fire from the Germans, who were secure on the far side of the river with their guns and tanks pointed at them.

However, even before the Americans secured the eastern side of the Rhine, refugees began to inundate us at the 45th Evacuation Hospital, where I was in charge of the large holding tent. These were forced labor exiles from various countries of Europe who had worked in the German factories. They were excited with their newfound freedom from the work camps. Some bragged that they had occasionally sabotaged work in the factories. There were Russians, Czechs, Polish, Austrians, and Frenchmen who had been interned since the invasions of their respective countries.

They were a straggly, half-starved motley crew, unshaven, haggard, and cold in their tattered jackets and sweaters, their heads covered with a variety of caps and scarves. Their worn boots were wrapped in rags to keep their feet covered. Many had old festering sores that needed treatment. All were dirty, unkempt, and weak from starvation and disease. In a short time the huge tent was full of transient refugees telling their stories of abuse, cruelty, starvation, and no medical care.

Out of the midst two wily Russians approached me in a patronizing manner. They were sly, suspicious-looking Tartars who had heard me speak their language to another Russian. They wanted me to intercede for them as a special favor to get to a certain destination. They wanted to get as far away from the Germans as they could. I explained that I was a nurse in the army hospital and could do nothing special, but assured them they would be as safe as anyone else here.

They were unaware that I was but one member of sixteen million troops in the United States Army. Besides, I was not sure that I could trust these two out of my sight.

We discovered contraband weapons and knives that the refugees left in the latrine and other inconspicuous places along the edge of the tent flaps. Refugees had been frisked, but not thoroughly because of the great numbers that were now descending on us. Some had passed by the checkpoint without having been caught with the contraband.

I heard stories of reprisal by fleeing refugees for past mistreatment by Germans. I also heard about a soldier from the Bronx who had captured a small group of Germans but could not handle the group by himself, so for his own safety machine-gunned the five prisoners. He probably remembered the Malmedy massacre or was afraid of his prisoners, and one can hardly blame him since he was outnumbered. That incident disturbed me, however, for we had not yet learned to hate the enemy.

The refugees would have to be placed in a controlled situation where they would be contained and fed. The army had to quickly establish a camp for the thousands that were escaping from east of the Rhine. In the meantime they wandered through the big tent asking about the war's progress, since all they had heard was that Germany was winning the war. They were ignorant of the fighting even in the vicinity.

I was amused when I caught sight of the company dog passing my desk with a slice of bread held loosely in his mouth. He was going to bury it somewhere in the far corner of the tent. The refugees would probably dig it up as fast as the dog returned to my desk. Bread was a precious commodity.

Allied planes bombed factories and trains carrying supplies. Our hospitals followed close behind as the troops advanced toward the east. Giessen and Marburg were captured on the 28th of March. Next the Third Army sliced through fifty miles of enemy territory and sealed the southern boundary of the Ruhr pocket. Simultaneously, the Ninth Army expanded along the northern boundary. The two armies met at Lippstadt on the 1st of April and completed the encirclement.

This was the crowning disaster for the Germans. Out of approximately sixty divisions on the western front, twenty-one were trapped! The yield was even greater than at Stalingrad, hitherto the largest operation of its kind. The Ruhr pocket was rapidly liquidated. On April 11, Essen fell. Three days later, the pocket was split in two by the junction of American spearheads at Hagen. On April 19, all resistance ceased in the area.

When the First and Third Armies met at Lippstadt, the 45th Evacuation Hospital, where I was on duty since February, became part of the Third Army.

Buchenwald Concentration Camp

On April 10, the United States Third Army stormed the gates of the Buchenwald Concentration Camp at Weimar, on the heels of the SS Schutzstaffel and his staff, who had been in charge of the camp. The soldiers were shocked to discover the horror and brutality of the Nazi regime. The 45th Evacuation Hospital, following close behind, was assigned the job of sorting the dying from those who might live, the delousing, fumigating, and sending the starving sick to the local hospitals. Barracks were cleaned, and the army brought in food and necessary supplies to continue giving care to the remaining prisoners who were now under the care of their own people but supervised by our hospital personnel, doctors and corpsmen. Typhus, a prevalent communicable disease carried by lice on rats, led to violent death and reached epidemic proportions in the crowded unsanitary conditions in concentration camps, along with tuberculosis, pellagra, diarrhea, malnutrition and other diseases.

It was a dismal cold gray day when we nurses went into the camp after it was fumigated, and saw the devastation at Buchenwald. Rain pelted the hard ground that had been tread into cement-like hardness by the feet of thousands of prisoners enclosed by a high electrically charged barbed wire fence. The shrieking wind furiously whipped my wool coat. The dampness permeated to my bones as I approached the naked, emaciated bodies stacked like cordwood against the outside wall of the wooden barracks. Piled one on top of the other, they stacked five feet high and extended along the wall of the barracks. They were staggered to balance the load, heads hanging heavily among the feet that loomed large by comparison to the sticks that were their shinbones. Arms dangled in all directions. Their gaunt hollow cheeks, with teeth protruding from slack jaws, were covered with the last days' growth of beards. Half-open eyes stared upward. Death had at last released the starved corpses, who once were vital, cherished human beings.

Near the gate, a short distance from the barracks, a flat-bed wagon, with a heaping load of naked bodies, stood abandoned. As the American Third Army entered Weimar, it had been enroute to the huge excavation dug by those inmates still able to work, when the camp commandant and the SS guards unhitched the horses and galloped away. I had my Argus camera with me and took pictures. The sky darkened ominously, the rain turned

Buchenwald

to hard pellets of hail and snow, and the wind shrieked fiercely as I leaned forward to brace myself against its force. Chilled, my body began to shiver and my teeth to chatter uncontrollably as we followed the prison inmate who led us nurses into one of the many barracks. He spoke English, as did many Europeans, since it was taught in grammar schools. I wondered why anyone would remain in this morbid place, and I said to the guide, "You are free now. Why are you staying here?"

He replied, "Where would I go? How could I get there? The war is not finished. My home is in Czechoslovakia. They are fighting there still. I don't know where my family is. All communication is disrupted."

The inmates continued to live in their usual day-to-day routine. Order and discipline had to be maintained and the weak cared for. Burying of the dead continued as before. The ravages of starvation and disease had progressed beyond the point of return for many, despite the arrival of the Americans.

Our guide, whose home had been in Prague, speaking with a clipped English accent, led us nurses and the doctors who had joined us, and told us about life in the

Buchenwald

camp. "When this camp was built here on the outskirts of Weimar, women, children and men were housed in the various barracks. The children were our greatest source of joy in those early days. Adults saved crusts of bread so the children could have more, as they were growing and needed the extra nourishment. Then one day, all the small children were rounded up into a truck and were taken away to the sound of heartbreaking cries of mothers, fathers, and all the others, young and old. Eventually, as the place filled with new prisoners, the women were sent away, and the camp became a depressing, foreboding chamber of horrors for men only."

He continued as we walked toward the next barracks. "Our day began at four o'clock. Breakfast consisted of a tin cup of ersatz coffee and a piece of dry black bread. Then the men were herded together in the compound and marched to the adjoining aircraft factory, where they worked fourteen hours a day, interrupted only for a bowl of potato peel soup and another crust of bread at noon. Supper was ersatz coffee and a ration of dry bread. The bread was weighed so that they all had an equal amount, to avoid bickering and fighting among themselves. The end crust was disputed about. Some felt they were deprived because of the added weight of the crust."

We entered a typical barracks. On entering, we faced a central narrow aisle dividing wooden shelves on both sides of the room. On each wall before going down the aisle, I noticed two spigots for water with a tiny tin catchall type of sink below, with a pipe that ran underneath into a trough for drainage. This was the sole water supply for drinking and washing. Needless to say the one faucet did not serve the seven hundred men who slept here. The building was one that normally could hold forty or perhaps fifty. Toilets were open trenches outside, dug by the inmates.

The shelves were continuous three-tiered bunk beds, broad enough so that two rows of men slept head to foot. Those next to the outside walls froze in the unheated enclosure. The shelves were spaced so the men could just barely crawl through. They slept so crowded that they had to tilt sideways on the boards to accommodate the hundreds of men, like sardines in a can. They slept on the bare wooden shelves with scarcely enough blankets to cover them as the cold wind blew through the cracks in the walls and windows.

As we walked down the now-empty boards, we came upon a half dozen occupants lying on one shelf at about eye level. They looked comatose. Several, whose faces were turned in our direction as we stopped, expressed no sign of perception. They were too feeble, only days away from the stacked bodies outside. Vacant eyes stared at us without comprehension. We were too late. The ravages of starvation, disease, and lost hope had progressed beyond return.

Our Czech guide said that when a prisoner became too weak to work or sick, he was admitted to the medical clinic in the camp. His service was not yet finished. Now he became a guinea pig at the clinic, where typhus serums were experimented with and other research conducted. The prisoners were injected with various experimental drugs, bacteria, diseases, and transplants, along with lethal drugs whose course was followed to observe how quickly they would kill. Our guide added, "They seemed to derive pleasure in watching the death struggle."

We walked across the compound and entered the hospital clinic on the far side of the camp. From all outward appearances it had the same look that most army post clinics have, the laboratories, officers' cubicles, and furnishings. Now, the place was deserted. Everyone had abandoned it. Upon entering the hospital ward, we were told that most of the sick had been transferred to the local hospitals in the city. However, those with tuberculosis were still here. We were stunned to see two patients sharing each bed. The hollow-cheeked faces, with sunken dark eyes turning in our direction, resembled wizened little men. Their thin, small bodies looked as if they were children six or seven years old. The boys said they were twelve and fourteen. There had been no attempt at isolation of contagious or infectious diseases. These youngsters had failed to develop normal growth due to a deficient diet and the normal childhood life activities.

Our guide added that when the clinic staff ran short of human guinea pigs, they made rounds at the barracks. The SS officers, on entering the building, would shout: *"Achtung! Achtung!"* The inmates staggered into lines and stood at attention as the staff goose-stepped, pointing out the victims with their riding crop and shouting, *"Du! du! du!"* Those selected stepped foreword trembling with fear. An awesome silence prevailed across the barracks as friends saw comrades for the last time. They knew that their days were numbered, as no one ever returned from the clinic. They were picked at random: this one because his eyes were brown, that one because his skin was fair. The commandant's wife, Ilse Koch, fancied lampshades made of human blond skin. The inmates called her the Bitch of Buchenwald. There were no "gold bricks" here. Nobody wanted to go to the hospital as long as they could stand and drag themselves to work. Getting sick meant death one way or another.

Approximately a month before the Americans arrived, Allied planes had bombed the aircraft factory adjoining the camp and put the inmates out of work. Several who tagged along with our group bragged about committing sabotage on the job. I was curious, and asked one of the prisoners, "What did you do?"

"Oh, I threw metal fragments that jammed the precision machines. It stopped them, and we had some free time."

We didn't know whether he was telling the truth or bragging about what he would have liked to have done. After the destruction of the factory, the men were assigned to various tasks throughout the city, some as gardeners or domestics, others cleaning up bomb damage and various other maintenance odd jobs. They were identified by their black and white striped pajama-like clothes, and the tattoo number each one had on his forearm. They returned to the electrically charged barbed wire enclosure at night and were counted before supper.

Next we entered the kitchen barracks. This was the most sought-out job in the entire camp. Here, if one was lucky, was a chance to survive starvation. A few extra crumbs or a crust of bread might be stolen if one was cautious. However, the job was hard to get, as the kitchen workers did survive, and there were no openings. In the center of the room stood a huge cauldron bolted to the cement floor. It was in this pot were boiled the potato peels that were collected in the neighborhood. Occasionally a carrot was dropped in, but never, ever reached beyond the kitchen crew. Three-foot-long ladles lay on the bare counter beside it, ready to fill the tin bowls held by the inmates as they filed past. The ersatz coffee was brewed here and the black bread metered out. Our guide told of the intrigue that flourished. Favors, bribes and bits of news exchanged for bread. A crust of bread held great barter possibilities.

We went down into the basement of a solidly built cement structure where we saw meat hooks imbedded in the four walls at about nine foot heights. It was here that discipline was invoked, where inmates were punished for any infraction, no matter how trivial—for example, fighting over a crust of bread that a dying comrade could no longer hang on to. The SS trooper tied a rope around the wrists of the inmates, then hung them on the hooks and beat them with a rawhide whip that I saw lying on a bench. They were punished for any triviality, or for punishment's own sake, no reason except to show the Nazis' superiority and control.

The next building was tiled in large squares that had once been white, but now smudged with gray ash. The room was lined with thick metal oven doors spaced at intervals. Our guide opened a door and pulled out the sliding rack. On it was a skeleton, his rib cage still intact. Cremation was incomplete because the fuel supply had run out. Our guide added that the victims were sometimes still alive when placed in the oven. The shortage of fuel was the reason for the bodies we saw stacked up against the outside wall of the barracks and those bodies on the wagon. The inmates now had to dig huge pits for the burials.

Next we entered the gas chambers, where thousands of Russian officers had been herded and gassed with cyanide pellets dropped on them from openings in the ceiling above. Another type of execution, of a large group of Polish officers, was by crowding them into a large room, then shooting them through narrow apertures that opened in the walls.

Finally we entered a room that resembled an office. Several chairs and filing cabinets lined the walls. Behind a large desk sat a pallid-faced, hollow-cheeked man who greeted us. He had a wide forehead, thin receding hair, pale eyes and an inscrutable yet compassionate appearance. His bearing was dignified—or was it a stoic air? I wondered. He was in civilian clothes, unlike the rest of the inmates, and wore black pants with a thin white stripe and a white shirt. He was now in charge of the concentration camp since the commandant and the SS guards had fled. He greeted us in a professional manner as he rose from his chair, saying, "I am Doctor Skodeck. (I don't remember real names). I see you have already met my countryman, Mr. Letorek," he nodded to our guide.

He then sat down and continued, "Mr. Letorek was a barrister before he became a prisoner. He is a Czechoslovakian political prisoner, just as I am. We were arrested for expressing our political views seven years ago when Germany invaded Czechoslovakia, and have been in various prisons ever since."

His face enigmatic, he expressed no emotion as he talked. The years of confinement had erased all feelings. Doctor Skodeck was permitted to practice medicine in the camp, but with few medical supplies, he could do little for the starving men. His was a conflicting life. He was one of the masses, but not quite, since he served the Nazis. He was both the confidant of the masses and exploiter, at the will of the SS guards. His eyes expressed sadness, his expression tranquil; we sensed he was deeply concerned about the inmates. There were prisoners from many nations along with Jews from all of Europe. Dr. Skodeck's survival these many years was perhaps due to his profession, that even under the dire circumstances his work gave him cause for living. I could not help but wonder at his composure and serenity. Surely he had found some inner resource that gave him strength, and courage to endure all the years of imprisonment. He was in the process of clearing his desk when our guide led us into the room, and was holding a letter in his hand.

"I have just finished writing this letter. It is addressed to Pope Pius XII, the Vatican, in Rome, Italy. You may be interested in its content."

He handed it to me, as I was closest to the desk. I began to read:

"I wish to inform your Highness that Princess Mafalda, King Victor Emmanuel's sister, was a patient of mine here at Buchenwald Concentration Camp. She was en route to Rome for an audience with your Highness, when her car was intercepted by the Fascists."

I stopped reading to hear what Doctor Skodeck said. "The princess's presence at camp was kept a secret from the rest of the inmates. Her compound was isolated by a trench to make it inaccessible to the rest of the inmates. However, an Italian digger got a glimpse of her and soon the presence of the distinguished prisoner was whispered about in camp. When bombs were dropped on the aircraft factory adjoining the camp, a stray bomb demolished her hut, and she was severely wounded. We did all that we could to save her, amputating her arm, which was badly crushed. We gave blood transfusions and provided her with German sisters who cared for her around the clock. In spite of all our efforts, complications set in and she died."

That explained one individual's life and death in camp. Inmates attempted to count them as they disappeared or when they buried them. There were well over 51,000 deaths at Buchenwald.

Now, with new freedom, those whose imprisonment was more recent and were reasonably well, decided to repay past grudges. One went to Herr Kluch's house. He took a knife off the shelf and hacked off his finger to retrieve a ring he claimed was his when he entered camp. There were many incidents of reprisals.

Our 45th Evacuation Hospital doctors and corpsmen were assigned to fumigate and delouse the inmates. We nurses were not involved in the operation except as observers. The sick were transferred to local hospitals. Refugee camps were being established as a holding place until the war ended, and inmates could then return to their various countries.

There were nationals from all the countries of Europe: French, Russians, Yugoslaves, Poles, Czechs, Greeks, Belgians, Dutch, Magyars, Slovenes, Lithuanians, Ukrainians, Hungarians, Romanians, Norwegians, and Danish, along with Australians, New Zealanders, and others who served as slave laborers, or were prisoners of war. Jews outnumbered the others, because in many countries they owned much of the property and were rich. Hitler hated them. He confiscated their property, sent them to work as slave laborers in various concentration camps, where they starved to death or were eliminated. Young men in occupied countries were conscripted either into the German army or into forced labor in the industries. When we questioned the local citizenry of Weimar about Buchenwald, they denied any knowledge of what was going on in the camp enclosure. However, the prisoners told us that the German citizens drove by on Sundays and spat at them as they passed the wire enclosure.

I was shocked at the evidence of cruelty we had seen. We would not have believed it had we not seen and talked with the survivors. One very thin man told us of the thousands that he had seen die here. We now understood why our infantry hated the "Krauts" as they called them, as they had seen the brutal acts committed on their buddies in war. We began to look at the Germans with trepidation. Our tour of the torture chambers completed, we went outside and found the sun bursting forth in full splendor, spreading bright rays from behind soaring clouds. Nature had shown many faces of its dimensions today.

When I got back to our own camp, I wrote a letter to my parents, telling them what I had seen. It was difficult to believe that Germans, with all their scientific technology, academic and theological knowledge, had allowed this to happen in a civilized country. I heard later that my family was so shocked that they let others see my letter and it reached the local newspaper. It was published in the *Detroit Free Press* along with my photograph on May 19, 1945.

I took pictures during my tour of Buchenwald while the inmates were being cared for by their own fellow inmates. When a major in the army, who had control of the sector, heard that I had taken pictures, he offered to develop my film. Normally I would send my film home with other items, but being naive and trusting I gave the film to him to develop, and though I got the pictures, he kept my film. Many of the pictures shown in museums are much like my original shots.

April 1945

We remained in Weimar for several weeks while waiting for the Russians to reach Berlin, as had been agreed at Yalta on 7th of February 1945, by the big three: Churchill, Roosevelt, and Stalin. We heard rumors that the Russians were nearing the capital city, but it was taking them a long time, we thought, since Americans had reached the agreed-upon stopping point west of the Elbe River. North of, us the Ninth Army might have taken Berlin a month ago, but was stopped at the Elbe even though they had crossed it. The Elbe had been selected as a natural barrier between Russian and Western Allies. Idle American troops were becoming impatient as they waited, and fraternization with Germans was not permitted. To lessen tension, troops were sent to the Riviera, Paris, Brussels and Partenkirchen in the Garmisch Alps for R&R (Rest and Recouperation).

In the meantime Germans, interned forced labor workers, and freed concentration victims were fleeing from the East as the Russian army approached Berlin. German residents deserted their homes knowing what was in store for them when the Russian army arrived. Elderly women, heavyset German fraus, pulled carts and wagons filled with their possessions and all they were able to carry on their backs, fled to the American sector. There were no men or horses to help them. We heard that German women were throwing themselves into the river to escape the fate that awaited them as the Russians approached the Elbe. Rape and murder, the soldiers' prize in war since the beginning of all wars.

In the Ruhr pocket in the west, 325,000 Germans began to surrender to the Americans, where Field Marshal Walther Model, because he felt it was a disgrace to surrender, committed suicide on April 21. The American Army disregarded, or were unaware of the German scientists who were left behind as we departed Weimar and other areas that were turned over to the Russians for occupation. This resulted in Russia gaining the technology the German scientists developed in the pilot-less V-1 and V-2 bombs. It also won for Russia the distinction of being first in orbit with the space satellite "Sputnik," launched in 1957, and spurred the dormant USA into action in the space race.

In 1945, the German scientist Wernher von Braun

surrendered himself, his staff, and his research to the Americans. His expertise contributed to the United States in the development of intercontinental ballistic missiles and its space program later. Dr. Richard W. Porter, an an American electrical engineer, who began work on developing guided missiles while working for General Motors in 1944, was chosen to head the American space program. He helped to recruit the German scientists who developed Explorer 1. Launching the satellite in 1958 calmed our nation, whose nerves were frayed because the Soviets had launched the world's first orbital satellite.

25 April 1945

Driving along the Elbe River, Lieutenant Albert Kotzebue, in company G, 273rd Infantry Regiment, 69th Division, along with his small group of men had orders that if they came across any Russians to try to arrange a meeting between the Russians and Colonel C. M. Adams, whose regiment captured Leipzig the day before. Kotzebue's patrol had started out on the 24th with orders not to go any farther than seven miles eastward. The next day they spotted a Russian cavalry man surrounded by a group of laborers in the distance. Kotzebue selected a man in his group who spoke Russian to join him in asking the Russian where they could meet his commander.

The Russian, being suspicious, suggested that one of the laborers, a Pole, could lead them better than he, and galloped away. The Pole led them on to Strehla, on the Elbe, where with his binoculars Kotzebue saw many Russians on the far bank. Against all orders, he fired two green flares, an agreed-upon signal; then seeing several boats tied together, he and five companions, one who spoke Russian and another who spoke German, crossed the river. On the east bank they met a Russian major and two Russian soldiers. Kotzebue and his companions were the first to link up with the Russians. The linkup was credited to General Hodges's First Army.

Lieutenant William Robertson, with a small group of

soldiers, reached Torgau that same day, just twenty miles north of Lieutenant Kotzebue's crossing of the Elbe. When rifle shots crossed the river Robertson drew an American flag on a white sheet he found in a house nearby, then climbed up the city's high castle and draped the flag over a wall. Waving his arms he shouted. "*Amerikanski*, stop firing!"

A green flare, the recognition signal, came from the east bank. He had no flares to return but called out asking the Russians to cross over. When no one did, he had a Russian prisoner from among his laborers shout in Russian to come across. Then they began to cross the collapsed bridge on hands and knees. When Robertson and his translator came face to face with the Russian soldiers creeping toward him, after a few words exchanged among the Russians, Robertson couldn't find any words to express his feelings. He grinned and patted the Russians knees in greeting: a comrade in arms.

Marshall Ivan Konev and his First Ukrainian Army, after reaching Berlin, continued to the Elbe where he joined the American Forces. Thousands of frightened Germans in the past few days were gathering at the Elbe River bank hoping to be ferried across as the Russians closed in on them from the east. Many wounded German soldiers, their heads wrapped in soiled bloodied bandages, were among the civilians. Women carrying pitiful bundles, along with black bread and hanging on to small children crying, were begging to get across. The soldiers who were fortunate enough to get across wanted to surrender to the Allies, as they were fearful of the treatment they knew they would receive from the Russians.

Torgau, on the Elbe River

27 April 1945

Our work began to slow down as the war was diminishing. On a bright clear day, Lieutenants Craig and Hardy stopped by to see if Gertrude M. Trainor and I would like to go for a ride. They decided to drive to the Autobahn, a smooth macadam divided double highway that was built wide enough to permit planes to take off and land. We were surprised to find miles of undamaged wide, paved highways. This was many years before American roads compared with the Autobahn. We drove for miles without seeing any traffic coming or going until we reached an outpost at Torgau where we were stopped at a telephone booth-like structure at the Elbe River.

Three Russians were crowded in the small space. A soldier in a long flared wool coat, wearing a Persian fur tope on his head came out of the booth. We got out of the jeep and saluted our new comrade. On the far side of the Elbe River we saw hundreds of horses that we assumed were once the property of German officers now in the hands of the Russian army troops that were milling about.

Twenty feet beyond the Russian post, an American captain at a similar post, recognizing our uniforms,

Third Aux surgeons meeting with Russians.
Major Marion E. Black (third from left) and Major Douw S.
Myers (far right)

came to us and saluted. After a return salute and introductions, we explained where we were stationed and our organizations. We asked him if we could go across the Elbe to meet the Russians. The captain, glad to have someone to talk with replied, "It's all right with me, but you'd better ask the Russian officer here for permission." I could speak some Russian, so with my companions I turned to the Russian. The other Russians were huddled together eating sausages that gave off a strong odor of garlic, along with thick slices of black bread and drinking a dark fluid that looked like very strong tea. I understood the Russian soldiers as they spoke between bites, but I had difficulty in expressing our wish to cross the river. However, selecting my words and pointing I made clear that we wished to meet with the Russian army on the other side of the Elbe.

The three Russians looked at each other quizzically, then the officer looking at me directly, said, *"Nyet,"* along with other words that meant they wouldn't dare let us cross the River. The officer explained that his soldiers were enjoying the spoils of war, and it would be dangerous for women. He said he did not wish to create an international situation just as peace was about to be reached. Since we could go no further we returned to the Autobahn and home.

Chapter 9:
The Riviera and R&R

28 April 1945

The War in Europe was coming to an end. Idle American troops, waiting for the Russian army to reach Berlin, were becoming restless. The army began sending officers to various R & R (rest and recuperation) centers. Toward the end of April, I was among a group of nurses who were allotted a seven-day leave to the Riviera.

We flew from Germany to Nice, France in a C-47 transport plane, the old workhorse that had flown so many paratroopers into areas of combat. At Nice we were met by the familiar two-and-a-half-ton truck that carried us over winding mountainous roads to Cannes, where we thought we would be billeted.

Instead, the truck continued on and on. Needless to say, we were disappointed as we passed the beautiful azure-blue Mediterranean and luxurious hotels facing the sea beyond the beach. We had not seen soldiers dressed in their pinks since we left London, before the invasion of France. Instead, the truck gathered speed as the men waved and whistled. We had heard that Cannes was reserved for men officers. The town was alive and radiating excitement, with hundreds of men in a holiday spirit.

Our spirits sagged as the truck continued on for what seemed endless miles. It finally came to a halt in front of a quiet, deserted hotel, small in comparison to the Ritz Carlton, where the officers we passed were quartered. Our driver helped us as we jumped off the rear end of the truck and collected our bags. We entered the quiet atmosphere of the lobby with uncertainty. We would stay in Juan les Pins, and for a good reason. As we discovered later, this was to our benefit. We would need to get away from the pandemonium of Cannes and get some rest. A local bus reserved for army personnel commuted between the two cities all day long. Parties and dancing continued from teatime to far into the night. Swimming, sunning on the sandy beach, sitting under the umbrella-protected patio along the promenade sipping *vin blanc*, or just idling, filled the rest of the day. A French orchestra played our favorite romantic tunes as we danced with new acquaintances to music that brought back sentimental memories. The days were filled with excitement as we celebrated the closing days of the war.

The concierge of the hotel, when I stopped for my key after having spent the morning lying on the beach, asked, "Would you like to go to a dinner party that Princess Antionette de Monaco is planning tomorrow?"

He had a single invitation, and was offering it to me. The Frenchman and his wife had greeted me on the many occasions when I passed the lobby coming and going from the beach and into Cannes. We exchanged the few French phrases I had become familiar with, and now they honored me with this invitation. Of course, I was delighted to have the opportunity to visit Monaco!

"Oui, Monsieur, Merci."

I could not think of any new phrases, but he could see

At the Riviera, 1945. Nurse Radawiec, foreground

415

that I was happy to accept. As he gave me my room key, he said that someone would pick me up at eleven the next morning. I could hardly believe my luck.

The following day a lieutenant at the wheel of a reconnaissance car came by to pick me up. I was impressed. Perhaps, I thought, we were an official party representing the United States government.

Seated in the back seat were two captains and a Red Cross woman. I climbed into the front seat with the lieutenant, who introduced me to the rest of the party. I was still curious and excited at my good fortune for this invitation and how it came about.

We traveled along the winding road with hairpin turns, sometimes within view of the ever-changing shades of blue of the Mediterranean, other times obscured by the heavy growth of trees and vegetation. We passed purple bougainvillea and feathery yellow mimosa, along with ripe oranges and grapefruit growing along the roadside. The fragrance of wisteria filled the air. Everyone commented on our good luck for the opportunity to see Monaco.

As always, it was easy to be with new acquaintances in the service. The feeling of camaraderie was always felt, like being part of the same family. Everybody was excited about what lay in store for us.

Turning a very sharp bend, we suddenly saw in the distance the royal palace perched atop a green expanse of lawn, surrounded by trimmed hedges and palm trees. As we neared the buildings, we saw beds of bright red cyclamen and bird-of-paradise plants. Two royal guards in bright colored, seventeenth-century-era attire were standing on either side of the iron grill gate. They wore tall bushy headgear attached to straps across their chins. I suddenly felt transported into an ancient fairyland with the castle in the background. The gate was opened, and we entered the palace grounds and proceeded to a gazebo overlooking the sea.

Princes Antoinette de Monaco, dressed in a long full-skirted summery sheer green print dress greeted

416

us with open arms. She was attractive due more to her savoir-faire than to any special feature. Her light brown wavy hair outlined a wide forehead; her pleasant smile and sparkling eyes made us feel at ease. There were five more guests from different branches of the service who had arrived shortly ahead of us. We followed her as she led the way into the wood-latticed gazebo. Wicker chairs and settees placed in small groups allowed for easy conversation and camaraderie.

Navy Lieutenant Bressler, from the nearby navy club that had once been the residence of the American actress Maxine Elliot, was seated next to me. I had met him earlier at the navy club and was told that Maxine was a paramour of a sea captain in the early 1900s. Her greater than life-size oil portrait hung at the curve of the winding stair leading from the great hall. This same villa was later occupied by the Aga Khan and named "la Horizon." It was here that Aly Khan, son of the Aga, and Rita Hayward, an American Hollywood screen star, spent their honeymoon, many years later. Other guests included a Special Service Officer, another Red Crosser, and a WAC: ten altogether. I was the only nurse.

Cocktails and hors d'oeuvres, passed by palace servants, lent a spirit of gaiety as we loosened and intermingled with one another. We discovered that each one had been picked randomly at the various hotels just as I had been. The navy lieutenant and I paired off and strolled along the paths of the flower garden high above the sea and commented on our luck in having been chosen to attend such a pleasant party.

Antoinette apologized for being alone to greet and entertain us. She explained that her father, Prince Alphonso, was not well and confined to his bed. Her brother, Prince Rainier, was on an undersea expedition hunting octopi and would not be back for several days. However, she would like us to return for an octopus luncheon when he returned. The afternoon passed quickly and pleasantly with many diverse topics discussed by the heterogeneous group. Antoinette explained that her mother was visiting in Scotland. However, we learned later that her parents were not living together; in fact, had separated.

Toward evening we were led to a round table set on the lawn on a ridge overlooking the brilliant blue sea in the background. The white damask linen cloth draped the grass. The table was set with silver and gleaming crystal. A bowl of spring flowers in a low silver bowl decorated the center of the table. Sparkling red and pale wine was poured into the crystal goblets by waiters dressed in black tuxedos and black ties. Dinner was served course after course and with each a special wine. We ate leisurely for hours, enjoying the camaraderie and the delicious food. Ice cream, a delicacy we had not seen in all the years at war, was molded into the image of the palace. It was the *piece-de-resistance.*

Coffee was served demitasse as we completed an unforgettable dinner. The fairytale experience vanished as if by magic, as our reconnaissance car arrived to drive us back to our hotels in Cannes and Juin le Pins, and reality. The next day I flew back to my tent along the Neckar River in war torn Germany, to the 45th Evacuation Hospital, to resume my duties.

Work began to taper off as time passed, and we were allowed time off. In May, while I was in Paris, a French woman who had heard that I had been at Buchenwald Concentration Camp approached me at the Normandy Hotel where the nurses were billeted. She was concerned about people who had been inmates of the concentration camp, and hoped that I could help her find out if they were alive or any news of them. She wrote several names and addresses on a piece of paper. One was her son; the others were sons of close friends who had been conscripted into forced labor. She printed their names along with their former addresses: Her son: Pierre Piveteau, 318423, 15 Weimar, and Paul Corbin de Mangoux, were of great concern to Madame Paul Vois, who lived at 63 Avenue

Raymond Poincare in Paris XV1. Madame Piveteau, whose son was missing, lived on 21 rue Charles Despeaux, Chaton Seine, France.

I took the paper, but knew there was nothing I could do to alleviate her anxiety. I doubted that any records survived as the Allied Armies reached the camps. Besides, I was in no position to pursue the matter, since I was on duty far away, camped along the Neckar River, across from Heidelberg. However, I have kept the list and as I look at it now, I wonder if the young men survived.

May 1945

It had been two weeks since American troops were stopped west of the Elbe River that separated us from Marshal Ivan Konev's First Ukrainian Army. The U.S. Army began sending GIs to R&R to keep them occupied and to keep them from fraternizing with the Germans, particularly frauleins, as the war began to wind down. They were being sent to Paris, Partenkirchen, and the French Riviera while we waited for the Russians to reach Berlin.

This was a political decision, that Russia should have the honor of taking Berlin, made against the wishes of the military minds. As work at the forward hospitals began to diminish, I had the good fortune to get a second LOA (leave of absence) to go to the Riviera. This time I was more familiar with the area and more adventurous. I was billeted at a hotel in Juan le Pins as before. Army provided a bus to take us into Cannes on a regular basis, where we swam, sunbathed in the Mediterranean with new acquaintances and attended afternoon tea parties with officers dressed in pinks with wide Sam Brown belts snug around their slim waists. We joined the pianist at the grand piano in the lobby and sang our hearts out.

Our army rations were disguised by French chefs, with cheese sauces and wine added to powdered eggs and spam, served in a spacious dining room with tables for four draped with glossy linen and flowers in crystal vases. Dinners were followed with dancing far into the night to orchestras that appeared suddenly from some mysterious source. Officers tagged one another so that we danced with new partners continually, and reveled in the flattery poured on us. At midnight, like Cinderella's chariot, the bus waited at the entrance to take us back to our hotel, to the quiet restful resort at Antibes.

The hotels along the Mediterranean were overflowing with army, navy, marines, and air force officers all celebrating the near end of war. Dinner dances were planned every evening at the hotels in Cannes.

I decided to wear the silver lamé dress that I had purchased in 1942 on the spur of the moment while in New York City. The gown had been rolled it up in my bedding roll since Africa, when I met Brunson. Now the occasion had arrived to shake out the wrinkles again and celebrate. In the war, we had learned without being aware of the fact, that we lived only in the present. There was no past or future. The bouffant gray net double flared skirt below the slim-waist silver lamé sleeveless top with the long stemmed pink velvet rose, was still worth the price I had paid at a reckless moment. Silver sandals completed my attire. The tan I had acquired from spending days on the beach contrasted with the silver of the gown.

Our new acquaintances called for us in a jeep. Nurse Kay C. Watry, her lieutenant and my Captain Russel, whom I had met earlier in the week, were dressed in their pinks. The men whistled at the sight of my formal dress. Captain Russel sighed, "I can see I'm going to have a rough time, Rad. I can pull rank only up to captain, but that isn't going to be much good tonight."

"Oh I wouldn't worry too much Russ," I answered. "If they tag me, you can tag back."

We went to the Ritz Carlton Hotel for dinner, where we ate army rations so expertly disguised that they were unrecognizable. The Spam was covered with breadcrumbs with spices and sauces added. The legumes were swimming in butter, the hot bread covered with a white napkin to keep it warm. Wine was served in crystal goblets. The huge chandelier sparkled, illuminating the dining room to its full grandeur. A rose in a crystal vase with a sprig of fern adorned each table. A string quartette playing our favorite sentimental songs created a romantic atmosphere as we enjoyed a leisurely dinner.

After dinner, a jazz band began with the "Saint Louis Blues" as the lights dimmed and the rotating floodlight changed colors, highlighting the dancing partners. Couples floated past to the rhythm of jazz.

"Shall we dance?" Russel asked. He put his arm around my waist as we joined the couples on the highly waxed floor. He danced holding me firmly with confidence as though defying anyone to cut in on us.

Champagne and wine served by catering waiters between dances lent a festive air to the party. Hilarity filled the atmosphere as men tagged one after another. Generals and colonels tagged majors and those of lesser rank. Captains waited for the breaks in the music to get back to their girls. We danced and sang along with the music far into the night. Toasts were made and repeated to the various celebrities in the ballroom. Captains did not mind if a senior officer in their own unit cut in to dance with their dates. My silver gown was a success.

I excused myself to go to the powder room, where nurses in uniform looked at me with envy. My deep tan and the dress deceived them into thinking I was a French woman. They sized me up and made several caustic comments.

"Wonder who the hell *she* is. She must be some general's woman. It doesn't look like the war has hurt her much. Look at the tan, spends all her time on the beach in those next-to-nothing bathing suits, flirting with the troops." I powdered my nose and left the room.

The celebration continued far into the night, and as we were leaving the dance hall I saw men sliding down the rail of the winding staircase with their champagne glasses in hand. They threw the glass into the wall, sending thousands of splinters sparkling through the air. Hilarious joy, laughter, and singing filled the air as the war in Europe came to end on May 8, 1945, V-E (Victory in Europe) Day.

The next day, while I was sitting on the patio of the Ritz Carlton under the shade of a bright multi-colored umbrella, a British "leftenant" (as the British say it) with a cheery greeting asked, "May I join you Miss?" Then, he added, "My name is Morley."

His Eisenhower-type jacket was pinned with ribbons and decorated with medals. He was taller than the usual Englishmen, and his positive, amiable manner impressed me. Since I had not had occasion to meet a British officer socially, I was glad to have him join me. He raised his hand to attract the waiter and asked me what I wished to order. Since beer was what I had seen others drink, it was what I requested. After the waiter poured our ginger beer, we lifted our glasses to touch and toasted to "the end of the war."

As we sipped our beer while watching the sunbathers on the beach across the promenade, a sudden bustling among the occupants of the surrounding tables alerted us to the emergence of a voluptuous French *madame* walking past on the avenue in front of us. The men at the adjoining table gawked at the curvaceous figure as she swayed seductively, her chin held high, pretending to be unaware of the whistles, the yoo hoo's and sighs.

As for myself, I was fascinated by the unusual dog prancing at "heel" just a pace behind her. His brown tight curly fur was full at the chest, but from the chest down his abdomen was clipped short, down to the skin. He had fur cuffs on his thighs and ankles, and his prancing paws were clipped bare of fur. He strutted on them like a ballerina as he followed the madame, close to her side. A pom-pom on the end of a cigar like tail swayed gently, as though he were waving a baton. He knew everyone was looking at him. He was on show, just as the madame knew all eyes were on her. I arose from my chair saying,

"Excuse me Leftenant, but I've got to find out about that dog," and started after the dog and his mistress.

As I approached her side, I said, "*Excuse, moi Madame, on vous charmont Caniche . . .*, when my French gave out and I resorted to English. "Is it possible to purchase such a dog?"

"*Ah oui, Mamselle.* It so happens that he has sired a litter that is now three weeks old. I will take you there, to show you, *oui?*" she asked.

By this time my lieutenant paid the tab and joined us; I believe he felt I needed protection. Besides, his French was considerably more articulate than mine. We turned back in the direction she had come from, and walked several blocks along the promenade, then turned into a narrow side street where she stopped and told us to wait at the entrance of a modest hotel.

It was a small, unpretentious walk-up hotel, a far contrast to the Ritz. We waited at the door while she climbed the stairs. I wondered about what kind of life she led. The lieutenant probably knew, as he stood protectively beside me. In a few minutes she came down with a beautiful small, caracul curled brown ball of fur with bright blue eyes, and placed it on the floor. His sire strutted about, proud of his progeny, nudging the little one, as though he ought to show his best self. I fell in love immediately with the cuddly creature, and knew I had to have him. Besides, what better souvenir could I bring home? The war was nearly finished, and I would soon be going home. I could just slip him into my pocket; he was so very small.

The financial arrangement began. Francs were of not much value, but products were. This is typical in war. Money cannot be eaten or smoked, and nothing else had much value. "Where could I get cigarettes? American dollars?"

"How much?" asked my leftenant. He was afraid I would settle for some ridiculous amount, I thought.

"One hundred dollars," came the reply, without

hesitation.

In cigarettes, that meant five cartons, the current price being twenty dollars a carton. An onion sandwich and a bottle of wine for four cost sixty dollars for lunch a day earlier. The French Franc was practically worthless.

"I will have to see where I can get cigarettes." Since I didn't buy my quota regularly, except some to have on hand to give away (I rarely smoked), I hadn't more than a carton with me at my hotel. "I will come tomorrow, Madame, if I can procure the cigarettes. I will see what I can do." And with an *"Au revoir Madame"* we all shook hands and parted.

As the leftenant and I strolled along the narrow side street, he said, "That's a pretty stiff price for a pup, don't you think?"

"But what a lovely souvenir he will be. I wonder where I can get four cartons of cigarettes. I have American dollars, but I hate parting with them at face value. She will get five times their value." I looked at the leftenant for assurance.

"Quite a bit of responsibility too, I'd think," he added.

"The war is just about finished. Surely we'll be going home soon. It would be easy to take a small puppy back. He can fit in my pocket."

The leftenant smiled knowingly. He must have known something I wasn't aware of.

We ambled back to the Ritz Carlton, where we parted and I boarded the bus that took me to my hotel at Juan les Pins. I had to scurry about to get cartons of cigarettes. Since there was so little to purchase in the shops, I was able to beg, borrow and procure three cartons, but that was all. The rest would be in American dollars and Francs. I was not sure if that would buy my puppy.

The next day I boarded the bus for Cannes and to the little hotel down the promenade and around the corner. I asked for Madame Morey, and in a few moments she came down the stairs with the little puppy cuddled in her arms. The concierge must have told her on the phone that an American woman wanted to see her.

The hundred dollars was paid in various denominations and cigarettes. She took my name and address and would send me his registration with the Paris Caniche Club and his pedigree. I hadn't thought about that, but when the papers arrived a year later, I was surprised and delighted with the fancy names in my dog's ancestry. There were five generations of champions with names I could hardly pronounce.

The puppy's sire was Guichotte de Etchegoya and because he was born in 1945, his name had to begin with the letter T, as this was the procedure with the Caniche Club for pedigreed poodles. He was Teddy de Etchegoya. However, there was a nurse in my outfit whose name was Teddy, and I did not wish to offend her so I called him Pepé. It fitted him since he was full of pep.

Now, I realized why the Lieutenant looked so quizzically yesterday when I said I wanted the dog. Suddenly I had the full-time responsibility for the feeding and mopping of a yelping baby on my hands. He had just been weaned and needed milk and housing.

"Pepé"

My bathroom at the hotel provided the house, but where to find the milk? After I conferred with my waiter at the hotel, he came back with a bottle of milk the chef provided, along with a saucer. To keep the yelping from disturbing the other guests I had to close the windows and plug all the openings. It wasn't as much of a problem as it might have been, since the guests were all nurses, and fortunately most were at Cannes far into the night.

At the end of my seven-day leave, I flew back on the C-47 to my camp in Germany with Pepé in the hood of my trench coat that I detached, and carried him looped over my arm. His head stuck out above the gathered cord. My tent was his home, leashed to the leg of my cot. Powdered milk, then cooked cereal, was his fare until he could eat the same food as I from the mess kitchen. I got him his own mess kit, and lined up with two at chow. He raised a big fuss and whined when I had to leave him, in spite of the fact that there were five girls in the tent. He howled and yelped until he learned I would return with his food when he saw the mess kit in my hand. Thereafter, when I left my tent for other reasons, I would rattle the mess kit, then deposit it outside the tent and take off without his loud protests.

My hospital, the 45th Evacuation, moved into what had once been a German barracks, and we nurses were quartered on the third floor. In the lavatory, the row of washbowls drained into an open trough in the tile floor below and carried the water away. I knew I could not run down three flights of stairs to take Pepé to toilet around the clock, so I tried to teach him to use the trough below the wash bowls in the lavatory. We had some success with the trial and error method, and because the floor was tile there was no damage done. I mopped it up. However, later, when I took him outdoors to play, and he needed to toilet, he would race as fast as his little legs would go into the building to make a puddle in the lobby of the building.

My Pepé had acquired a playmate; a puppy called Buchenwald that our corpsmen got attached to when we cleared out the concentration camp. He had a pathetic, furtive, timid personality, and whined when I talked to him. The two dogs romped and fought playfully and occasionally stole candy even though it was in a thick-waxed wrapper on the bedside box of the nurse's cots. When Pepé got fleas, probably from his playmate, and worms, I had to find a veterinarian. The fleas were different than any I had ever seen, they were like tiny crabs. The vet eliminated both problems in short order. The days passed quickly into weeks, then months, and Pepé thrived and grew until he was a full-grown Poodle. I had to guard him closely, as in the army everything is "ours," and he might have disappeared as the troops moved.

Chapter 10:
Germany Surrenders

8 May 1945

Hitler's former U-boat Commander, Karl Doenitz, was now in command of the Third Reich and had sent Admiral Friedeburg and General Jodl to Reimes to sign the unconditional surrender to the Allies. General Eisenhower, along with British, French, Soviet and American representatives, were all present. The surrender was on May 8, 1945. British and Americans celebrated V-E (Victory in Europe) Day. The German surrender was ratified in Berlin, where Field Marshall Keitel, Admiral Freideburg, and General Stumpf signed for Germany. General Spaatz, Air Chief Marshall Tedder, Marshall Zhukov, and General de Lattre, signed for the Allies. The Soviets celebrated V-E Day on May 9, 1945.

A Pleasant Surprise

June 1945

My hospital moved frequently, and because our APO kept changing our mail was long in transit. At the end of the war I discovered I had been attached to the First Army, the 12th Army Group, the 9th, the 3rd, the 15th and now the 7th. I had been in the Fifth Army in Africa, so that covered all the armies in the European Theater of Operations.

I was surprised when Major B.T. Bayne, who had escorted me on a weekend in Liege, appeared at my hospital on another free weekend. He was on his way to Paris and wanted to know if I could get away. I had not seen him in months and was delighted to see a familiar face. I was also surprised that he had found me, since I had transferred from the Third Aux., to the 45th Evacuation

Hospital and we had moved a half-dozen times since then. My work was routine nursing in this hospital. I assigned corpsmen their work, gave bed baths to the sick, alcohol back rubs, passed food trays, and kept the ward ready for the sudden inspections. I changed dressings on the wounded, made rounds with the doctors, passed medications, gave injections, and charted. My daily life consisted of work, sleep, and an occasional movie, with little other diversion.

Many members of my former organization, the Third Auxiliary Group, had been dispersed to various organizations depending on the number of points they had, a gage for determining length of service or campaigns, I never knew which. I had 104 points and would be sent to the States soon. At least that's what we were led to believe. Many would be sent to the Pacific Theater of War because of their experience. I missed my former comrades, and I was pleased to see Major Bayne in the lobby. His arrival was timed perfectly, when I was free, with no plans, bored and lonely. One can be lonesome in spite of being surrounded by hordes of people, lonely for a familiar face, a loved one far away, or a comrade with whom one could communicate or confide in.

Bayne embraced me, as I exclaimed, "Oh, what a surprise! I thought our paths would never cross after the war ended. I'm glad to see you."

"I don't give up easily Rad; you must know that by now. I'm on my way to Paris. Do you think you can get away?"

"Paris! Wonderful! This is my weekend off duty. Wait here while I go see my chief nurse. She is great, always concerned about our needs, and quite tender hearted. Make yourself comfortable. It should take only a few minutes."

I was right about my chief nurse. She probably had wondered if I was contented with my assignment here and was aware I had not been going out much or dating. "Yes," she said, "and have a good time, Lieutenant."

I packed my musette bag with the few overnight articles I would need, and arranged for Pepé to be cared for by my roommate. Bayne helped me into the jeep and we were on the way to Paris. The weather was warm, with a gentle spring breeze in the air. I was delighted to have an entire weekend in Paris with my friend. A carefree feeling engulfed us as we drove past small country villages, stone houses with smoke rising out the chimneys, children playing in the streets once more. Old men in the fields working their horses, cultivating the black soil. Driving on the winding roads past quaint villages was a peaceful change from the devastation of the German cities we had left. "Do you remember the last time we were together?" Bayne asked.

"I sure do," I replied. "It was a 'banquet' before the Battle of the Bulge. It was about the middle of December, and what a meal that was! It was like the last supper a prisoner can request before he goes to the electric chair."

We had come by the restaurant quite by accident while driving through Spa, in Belgium, just days before the German counterattack.

"That's a dinner I will never forget. We ate for hours and hours. And the wine, remember? We finally stopped emptying our goblets to keep the waiter from refilling them," Bayne added.

"As I remember it, we ate a long time, just as the French did before Hitler invaded France. Now they hardly have anything to sit down to."

"Yes, and afterwards we drove through Duren and looked down on the ashes of what had once been a thriving city. That was on December 14. It was the first German city I saw that was completely demolished. There was nothing standing above eye level, only chimneys, boulders and stones."

As we reminisced, the time passed quickly and we arrived in Paris about noon. We drove to the Normandy Hotel where I registered. It was the hotel reserved for women officers. I wanted to be sure I would have a place to stay the two nights. The Normandy is in the center of Paris, accessible to all the sights.

Our first stop was lunch at a small café, where we sat at an umbrella-shaded outdoor table. A wandering accordionist provided an exhilarating atmosphere for us. GIs, their arms around the waists of *mademoiselles,* promenading past us with grins on their faces as their eyes met mine. Our lunch was meager, only a sandwich with a spread of probably spam disguised with spices, and a bottle of wine.

"Well that wasn't much; I hope we have better luck for dinner tonight, Rad."

"But the surroundings and music are pleasant; besides, I wasn't hungry," I replied.

After lunch we visited the Sacre Coeur Cathedral and marveled at the beautiful multi-colored leaded windows and were glad they had been spared from damage in the war. Paris, except for the skirmish on the street facing in front of Notre Dame, where several shops were damaged when grenades were tossed at a truck full of Germans, was free from destruction. The Napoleonic period architecture had survived. We looked down on Napoleon's tomb at the Hotel des Invalides and its twirled marble columns.

We walked to the Tuileries Garden on the right bank of the Seine, sat on a bench to watch children playing, nurse maids wheeling babies in prams, and elderly Frenchmen feeding pigeons scraps of bread. A restful scene, peace at last, free after nearly five years of war. Many varieties of colored spring flowers filled the Tuileries Garden, as they have since Catherine de Medici built the palace in the sixteenth century. There was an array of beautiful contrasting colors among rows of bright red and yellow tulips and daffodils. Perennials and many varieties of annuals created a lovely panorama. The new growth of lacy green leaves on trees lent a fairyland setting to the garden. French, British, and Americans in uniform wandered among the lanes, seemingly enjoying its beauty.

We sauntered along the shop-lined streets with their scant display of merchandise and mediocre jewelry. The French had buried their valuable possessions in caves in the country during the Nazi occupation, and hadn't brought them out yet. As we passed women's fashion shops displaying beautiful gowns, we paused at Lanvin's couture shop window. Noticing my interest as I examined the fine details of the gowns, Bayne suggested we go inside and pretend we were couturiers, interested in fashions, prospective buyers.

"Great! I'll be out of uniform soon, and I will need to catch up on style. I gave all my clothes away before I joined the army except for some furs. I had a pair of silver fox stoles and a mouton jacket that I had stored.

"I'll have to start my wardrobe from scratch," I said. "This will give me ideas of what the latest fashions are."

We entered the shop and were guided up the stairs by an elderly Frenchman. He opened a door into a large room where chairs were set up in a semi-circle, then bowed to us to enter. The chairs faced an elevated platform, and we found two seats in the midst of a dozen people, chattering in French. They did not question us, and we surmised that the guide simply assumed we were part of the gathering crowd coming to view the new season's fashions.

As we got seated, models began displaying the latest creations. They promenaded in the semi-circle while chattering French men and women gestured and nodded among themselves. We enjoyed looking at the beautiful models in long colorful satins and sheer gowns as they gracefully swayed and pirouetted in front of the buyers. After we watched the show a few minutes, Bayne asked, "Which one would you like Rad?"

"These are just models, Bayne. They have to be custom-made to order. They will cost hundreds of dollars."

"I know, I'll have it sent to you," he responded.

"You're very generous, my dear, but no thanks. It may be a long time before we get home. The war in the

Pacific is yet to be fought, and we're in for the duration, remember?"

The Fashion show finished and we decided to stroll down the Avenue Des Champs-Elysees, and bought perfume at the Guerlain Shoppe. I bought two bottles of Shalimar (cost, 918 Francs), two Miltouko (316 Francs), and one Rouge (52 Francs). The total came to 1390 Francs. The perfumes were gifts to be sent home.

An ancient Egyptian obelisk, discovered in the 19th century by a French archeologist, stood in the center of the perfume square where many other famous perfume houses are situated.

In the evening, restaurants were crowded with hungry GIs looking for a change from rations, but food was very scarce. We were lucky to find a small restaurant on an off-the-beaten-track street, where we enjoyed a delicious dinner. A candle set inside a glass bowl on the table provided a romantic glow in the semi-darkened room. The flickering light brought out Bayne's lean carved features, his firm chin, his engrossed attention, eyes searching mine. He asked, "Who was it that wrote, 'Oh to be in England now that April is here?' Do you remember?"

I tried to recall. "No, that was somewhere in my past, now forgotten. Or is it the *vin blanc?*"

"I don't think there's much alcoholic content in the wine. As for the author, it'll probably come to me tomorrow. Right now, I'm enjoying just being with you. Let's go for a walk. There's so much to see."

Overlooking the entire city, the Eiffel Tower stood like unfinished steel works in the distance waiting to be completed. Someone said there was a restaurant at an upper level, but the elevator was not running and nobody seemed to venture up the stairs. The tower had been built in 1889 to celebrate the one hundredth anniversary of the French Revolution and the International Fair. It is a symbol similar to the Washington monument, the Kremlin in Moscow, and the statue of Liberty that Gustave Eiffel also took part in designing its skeletal framework.

We walked by the Notre Dame Cathedral, the Louvre, the bridges spanning the Seine, the opera house where we joined the queue for tickets to see *"Samson et Delilah."* Bayne held my hand during the performance, pressing it now and again as the performance struck him. I felt at ease when with him, and had confidence in his ability to handle every situation that arose with composure.

Because I had always taken a serious view of life and work, I enjoyed the freedom from responsibility when with him. There was a mysterious force that drew us together, like his ability to locate me wherever I was stationed.

On the stage, the biblical characters performed beautifully. We both enjoyed the scene when Samson with his mighty arms tore down the pillars of the temple. It was late and dark when it was over, and since we had walked most of the day, we went directly toward the Normandy Hotel where I was billeted. In the lobby we embraced and he kissed me on my cheek. His lips close to my ear, in a low voice, because the room was noisy with nurses and their dates chattering, he said, "It's been great being with you, Rad. See you for breakfast at nine, here, O.K.?"

That was what I liked about him. He was a congenial dear friend. I enjoyed being with him, and he never became possessive. He always made being together exciting. The Normandy was noisy with nurses dashing about from room to room, talking about their dates and where they had been. Several were trying to figure out the purpose of the strange fixture in the middle of their rooms. It was a ceramic pedestal with a waterspout in the center of a large bowl. Was it a Sitz bath or a sort of douche contraption? Nobody knew how it was supposed to function. I wondered about its sanitation, but *"c'est la guerre"* was a phrase used by the French to blame or pass on anything and everything. We too soon adopted the expression.

I walked up the flight of stairs to my room, kicked off my shoes and undressed. I removed my makeup, washed, and was soon asleep on clean white sheets with a soft lightweight blanket and a bedspread, asleep on heavenly billowing clouds with a soft feather pillow instead of a narrow canvas cot with a heavy wool khaki blanket.

The next morning on the way to the dining room, I spotted Bayne before he saw me in the lobby. He looked sharp in his Eisenhower jacket, pressed olive-drab pants, clean-shaven, his crew-cut hair brushed, and his shoes polished. As I approached him, he greeted me saying, "Hi, gorgeous! Ready for another day of sight seeing?"

"Good morning. Yes, I'm ready. It's amazing what a soft bed can do for one. What's your hotel like?"

"Well, the guys were trying to figure out a piece of equipment in practically the center of the room. It looks like a toilet. Damnedest thing. Didn't know how to use it. Couldn't sit on it. Pressed the lever and it spattered all over the place. The bed was great, except . . ."

I interrupted, "It's a Sitz bath. Hemorrhoids must be a national affliction."

"You're kidding, Rad. You know Paris better than that. By the way, it came to me in the night. It was Robert Browning who wrote "Oh, to be in England now that April is here. I was confusing it with "Paris in the Spring."

We entered the dining area and were greeted by a waiter dressed in a dark suit, a white shirt, and black tie. It seemed strange to see men dressed in civilian clothing again.

"*Bonjour Mademoiselle, Monsieur.*" Nodding, he led the way to a table for two near the window. Breakfast was served with a flair, waiters with napkins draped over arms, graciously bending, greeting patrons. The sunny-side-up eggs were a treat. Coffee? Mediocre. Nobody in the world makes coffee Americans are satisfied with. Warm milk instead of cream didn't add much, but the dining room with chandeliers glistening and flowers in crystal vases on each table covered with a white linen cloth made everything splendid, beautiful. It was good to be alive.

We were filled with enthusiasm as we went outside into the warm spring air. Bayne decided we should ride today. The jeep was parked in front of the hotel. We were on our way to the Louvre this morning. We drove along the Seine past many bridges and ancient buildings, admiring the architecture of the famous architects of past generations. As we entered the huge former palace, we were faced with the Winged Victory of Samathrace in the entrance. There were no guides, so we roamed the halls leisurely, from alcove to alcove. The famous paintings of Cezanne, Rembrandt, Titian, Raphael, da Vinci, and many many others were all viewed within arm's length. We spent hours marveling at the intricate detail of these world-famous masterpieces.

After several hours we decided we could never see all that we wanted in one trip; besides, we were getting hungry. It was time to start a reconnaissance for food, not an easy task in crowded Paris. We settled for an omelet at a small restaurant, then to the Normandy for a rest. We would have dinner in the evening after we had seen as much as we could in the light of day.

In the afternoon we rode to the Champs Elysee to the Arc de Triomphe where the eternal flame burns in memory of France's unknown soldier of World War I, who lies buried beneath the arch. We drove up and down the various avenues of central Paris, parked the jeep, and walked in the circle of avenues.

At one of the avenues leading off the circle of the Arc we discovered Maxime's Restaurant, world famous for its cuisine. We tried the door, and to our surprise it opened into an exquisite room, with oil paintings hung on the walls that looked much like the Louvre. A waiter in tuxedo ushered us to a table alongside a small dance floor. Bayne and I looked at each other in amazement. We could hardly believe it to be true. We ordered our dinner, which began with an aperitif followed by course after leisurely course of food that we had forgotten still existed, served with a different wine with each course, and continued on and on for hours.

We danced between the courses to waltzes, fox trots, and tangos played by the string orchestra. Now and then a wandering violinist stopped at our table to play a request. The waiter refilled our wine glasses from the bottle of champagne in the ice-filled silver bucket on our table. A vase of tall red roses beside it added to the festive occasion. Crystal chandeliers dimly lit the room. All the tables were occupied with French couples in groups of four. We saw no one leave as the hours passed. Finally, we decided it was time to return to our hotels, and Bayne asked for the bill. He placed a handful of French paper on the plate the waiter held out to him and with *beaucoup merci's* and bowing, we departed into the dawn. The dew in the grass reflected diamonds. Paris in the spring!

The next afternoon we retraced our route back to the hospital and work.

Berchtesgaden

August 1945

The 45th Evacuation Hospital was set up in Schweinfurt on the Main River, Germany. As our work lessened, a tour to the Bavarian Alps was arranged for a group of us officers. We were going to see Hitler's Eagle's Nest, in Berchtesgaden, in the Obersulzberg mountains in Bavaria. Berchtesgaden is located on the left bank of Ache River, several miles from the Austrian border. The *Fuehrer's* country home was nestled on top of the mountain nearby.

It was here that an important event took place on September 13, 1938, when the Prime Minister of Great Britain, Neville Chamberlain, flew to Berchtesgaden to meet with Hitler. The meeting resulted in the Munich Conference, which was an attempt to appease Hitler as he began to conquer surrounding countries. Hitler had annexed Austria in March 1938. Chamberlain, on departing, had Hitler sign a friendship note that he felt would secure "PEACE for our time."

A crisis developed in Czechoslovakia, with a population of 14,000,000, of whom 3,000,000 were German-speaking people living in an area known as the Sudetenland, resulting in political disputes, and German troops moved in on October 1938. Czechoslovakia was forced to cede one-fifth of her country. The land ceded contained most of its industries and fortifications, along with 800,000 of its people. In March 1939 Germany completed the occupation of the rest of Czechoslovakia. When Germany invaded Poland on September 1, 1939, France and Britain declared war on Germany on the 3rd of September, resulting in the outbreak of World War II.

Our group consisted of twelve men and women who staffed the hospital, which now was becoming slowly deactivated. We traveled in the usual truck heading south through the Brenner Pass, a passage through the Tyrol area of the Alps about 5000 feet above sea level, and among the lowest valleys in the mountains.

This has been a main road since Roman times, when Druses, Emperor Augustus's stepson, traveled over this pass to conquer the Barbarians when his armies traveled

Nurse Radawiec at Berchtesgaden

north. One of these tribes was called Breuni, or Breones, from whom the pass derived its name. A carriage road was built in 1772, and much later a railroad in 1867. It became the boundary between Italy and Austria after World War I. Hitler and Mussolini met here to form an alliance in 1940, and later joined forces to fight the Allies.

We stopped and I took some pictures of the Brenner Pass for sentimental reasons. My now MIA (missing in action) lover, Captain Brunson, a bombardier in the Fortress Group in North Africa, spoke of having dropped bombs on the Pass while he was with the 2nd Bomb Squadron (H), 2nd Bomb Group, in the Fall of 1943. I kept hoping he was a prisoner of war. In July, the last response to my inquiry was that his plane crashed over Germany on February 22, 1945.

After many hours of mountain travel over treacherous hairpin turns, we reached Berchtesgaden, where Hitler had laid plans to invade all the surrounding countries. It was here also that he wrote the book, *Mien Kamph*. As the Russian army neared his Berlin bunker, Hitler intended

Entrance to the "Eagle's Nest"

to leave Berlin on his fifty-sixth birthday on April 20, 1945, and to continue the fight from Berchtesgaden, but it was too late. Wade H. Haislip's XV Corps captured Salzburg and Hitler's hideaway the week following the bombing by the R.A.F. Lancasters. The R.A.F. had dropped bombs called "Tallboys" (12,000 pound bombs) along with incendiary bombs on the SS (Storm Troops) who guarded the entrance to the mountain leading to the Eagles Nest, where Hitler lived. The SS were cruel fanatical troops who fought viciously to remain in the Fuehrer's favor. Haislip's men found smoldering ruins at the entrance to the SS quarters at the base of the mountain that lead to the tunnel entrance.

We rode the elevator, which was dug into the center of the mountain, to the top. We could have climbed the stairs carved into the rock on the outside of the mountain, but after our long trip we took the easier route. Standing on top of the mountain, looking into the horizon, I could see Austria, Czechoslovakia, Italy, Germany and Switzerland by merely turning my head.

It was no wonder that Hitler began thinking himself undefeatable when standing on top of this mountain. He was another Caesar, indestructible, omnipotent, dominating every country that he had set out to conquer. Inside the large map room where he had planned his strategy, I took snapshots of the round table that held the maps on which he planned future logistics. His living quarters were extensive, with large, comfortably furnished rooms. They connected with the underground shelter that housed hundreds of his SS henchmen. It was a vast, tunneled city with quarters for a small army and enough supplies to withstand a siege.

We were billeted at the Berchtesgadener Hof, the hotel that was frequented by the Nazi party. Where Hitler, Goebbels, Goering and other party members drank ale and danced with their women, accompanied by German music. We sat in the same booths and drank similar ale. The present management continued business as usual in the luxurious hotel. Several of us nurses rode the elevator to the roof and sat at umbrella-shaded tables that protected us from the bright sun's rays. On every table a vase with fresh flowers decorated the white linen tablecloths. Now and then a cloud enveloped us as it soared over us. The panorama of the Alps peaks in varies shades of mauve, purple and pink contrasted with the green woodland below, creating a beautiful picture.

While I lay on my bed resting before dinner, a nurse in the adjoining room entered mine and excitedly announced that an atomic bomb had been dropped on Hiroshima on the 6th of August 1945, and on Nagasaki on the 9th, and that the Japanese wanted to surrender.

We were thrilled with the news. It meant we would be going home instead of to the far Pacific to continue with the war. We knew nothing about atomic bombs, nor were we concerned. The war was finished and that was all that mattered. We had heard of the brutality of the Japanese in their treatment of American prisoners and civilians. We discovered that the Japanese did not place the same value on life when we heard that their pilots committed "Kamikaze," by riding their bombers into the funnels of our ships in the Pacific.

We blamed the Japanese for our becoming involved in the war, although Chief of Staff General George Catlett Marshall had already laid necessary plans for rescuing our allies as we saw Hitler's Nazi army occupying and bombing Europe in the prior two years.

General Eisenhower said that it would cost over a million American lives if Japan had to be invaded. Japan surrendered on September 2, 1945 on the battleship USS Missouri in Tokyo Bay. General MacArthur accepted the surrender on behalf of the Allies.

Chapter 11:
Return to France—and Home

October 1945

My orders finally arrived to leave Germany. With Pepé on a leash in my right hand and my large suitcase in the other hand, we boarded the train to Paris. From Paris I was driven to an army station in Vincennes, where I was billeted for a short time. By now Pepé's curly hair grew long, covering his face, his eyes, nose, and his body, making him look like a plump bear. I realized that he couldn't see when we played "catch ball," or me when I called him, and discovered that he would have to have a hair cut as is customary with poodles.

After I inquired about pet grooming and where I could find a shop, Pepé got his first haircut. When I went to call for him later in the day, I didn't recognize him. If he hadn't jumped all over me, kissing and licking me, I would not have known that this was the same dog that I parted with earlier. He probably thought I had forsaken him, or perhaps he sensed all along my concern for his future. He was clipped in the puppy style, with a mustache and a beard, his face smooth, a fez on the top of his head and cowboy chaps on his hips down to his paws, which were clipped close to the skin. His body fur was clipped short, and on the end of his cigar-length tail perched a pom pom. He caught everyone's attention in the area, since few GIs had seen a clipped French Poodle. He pranced like a ballerina and felt much cooler. He could now see the ball when we played.

Before I left Germany, I took him to a German veterinarian to get his "shots" as I knew I could not leave the country without a certificate indicating that he did not have rabies. When I moved to France, I began calling army headquarters and port commanders about taking a dog back to the States. Of course, I did not reveal who I was, as I wanted to remain incognito.

One does not realize what a wonderful telephone system we have in the States until you tried calling long distance in a foreign country. The French operator tried to make the connection with, *"allo, allo,"* the only distinguishable sound, that ended in long periods of waiting without success. After many days and repeated attempts I finally reached the commander at the port at Le Havre. I started saying, "This is Lieutenant Hall (not my name, of course) in the Army Nurse Corps. I have a dog and want to get permission to take it home when I leave France."

There was a long silence before the commander answered. Then he said, "You know that if I gave you permission to take a dog back to the States there would be as many dogs as troops on board ship going back. No, I cannot give you permission to take your dog to the States, Lieutenant."

I hung up the receiver, my heart heavy. I knew I couldn't abandon my Pepé here. I loved my dog. He knew only me. Perhaps, I would try to stay until such a time when I could bring him back with me, in spite of wanting desperately to go home. But it might be difficult to arrange with the army; they might not be sympathetic with my feelings. Or perhaps I could arrange to leave him with a French family and have them send him to me later. No, that was no good, since Pepe did not understand French. He would be very confused with the change from living with troops who made a big fuss over him to

Pepe with Nurse M. Huntington and German child

a small French home. I would be haunted by those large brown soul-searching eyes. He was accustomed to eating army rations and the French could hardly be expected to provide the kind of food he was accustomed to. I was in a quandary. It took away the joy of looking foreword to going home.

The Port of Embarkation

At last my orders arrived to move to Camp Lucky Strike at Le Havre. I boarded the train with my suitcase and Pepé on a green leather leash that I had purchased in Paris. I had no problem with the trains because dogs are permitted to ride with the French when they travel. Besides, the trains were filled with army personnel and run by the U.S Army. I arrived at camp to find hundreds of tents and thousands of khaki-clad men and women waiting for a ship to take them home. I was assigned a cot in a tent with nineteen other nurses. Now Pepé's place was tied to the leg of my cot again. I went to mess with two mess kits once more, and had no problems, as all the nurses grew fond of Pepé. So too were the men who were stationed across the road some distance away. Once again I had to guard him, as he might have been dognapped and lost to me forever, since troops were pulling out daily.

At Le Havre, going home with Pepe

I went to the commander in charge of boarding ships to see what I could do about Pepé. He was sympathetic, and said he would see if there was a French family in the near area that would take him until some future time when they could send him to me. Of course I could not accept that advice for the same reasons as

444

before. That left me with only one recourse: I would have to smuggle him aboard ship.

I took my suitcase to a workshop on the post and had the friendly GI drill several holes in the base of my large case. I would suspend Pepé with a scarf around his belly, then snap it to the top of the latch so he could breathe and carry him on aboard ship. It meant I had to leave most of my possessions behind, except my musette bag that held my personal needs. I would have to put him to sleep with a capsule that I had ready for such an occasion.

We girls had a similar experience trying to get Whimpy, our enlisted men's dog into Sicily in 1943. I was prepared this time. When my ship came in, I had a lot of moral support from the nurses who were boarding ship with me. I gave Pepe a small dose of seconal when I thought the time was right, and shoved him into my suitcase when he got drowsy. I clamped the scarf in the top so he was suspended and could breathe through the holes I had drilled in the base. We climbed into the back of the two-and-a-half-ton truck that drove us to the port for embarkation. As is customary in the army, you hurry up, and then you wait and wait for hours and hours. Well Pepé wasn't about to stay in the suitcase forever. He began to whine; I had to let him out. With the nurses encircling us, no one noticed one dog.

However, six hours later when I tried to get Pepé back into the case as we were about to walk up the gangplank, he would not cooperate. Besides, the pill I gave him when I anticipated we might go aboard had a negative effect. It made him very hyperactive. We were moving, there was nothing to do except pick him up in my arms and carry him. A nurse placed my overcoat over him and I climbed up the gangplank, leaving my suitcase behind. Someone thoughtfully carried the empty suitcase aboard. Pepé seemed to understand our predicament, for he lay motionless in my arms as I followed along with the nurses.

As we passed the ship's officers standing at attention

along the passageway, they scrutinized us nurses rather thoroughly. Out of the corner of my eye I saw the captain of the ship The Thomas H. Berry break from the line and come in my direction. He stopped in front of me, lifted the edge of the coat to see two big dark brown eyes look back at him. Pepé did not move. It was as if he knew what we were about. He lay relaxed in my arms, as the captain let the coat drop back over his face. Earlier we had been assigned a number to the cabin we would occupy. Looking at my plaintive face, on the verge of tears, the captain asked,

"What is your cabin number, Lieutenant?

"Two twenty," I replied with a tremulous voice.

"I'll be there shortly to see about the dog."

I felt sick as I entered my cabin and collapsed on my bunk with Pepé, who was suffering from the effects of the sleeper, lying at my feet. I agonized while reflecting on the rumors I had heard at camp Lucky Strike that dogs found aboard ship were thrown overboard. I felt the vibration of the ship's engines start up as I lay on the bunk and fretted.

Soon after the engines started there was a rapping on the cabin door. One of my cabin mates opened it.

"We've come to take your dog."

I saw another officer standing next to the captain as they approached my bunk. I thought to myself, Why two? Is one going to hold me while the other takes Pepé away? "Oh, no, I can't go back without him." I was on the verge of tears.

"We're going to keep him in the steward's cabin during the voyage. You can visit him anytime you like."

"Oh thank you, thank you, sir. I just couldn't go home without him."

I put Pepé's leash on him and said, "Pepé going for a walk." He loved to hear that phrase. I watched as the steward led him out the door. At the first corner Pepé raised his leg. It was the first time; he had always squatted before.

The steward was a friendly young man, and I enjoyed many dinners in his cabin when I visited Pepé. However, I was shocked to see him open the porthole and throw the tray full of dishes, including the shiny metal cover that kept the food hot, into the ocean. But, as the French blamed everything on *"Cest la Guerre,"* so did I. It was such small wastage.

Upon reaching New York Harbor, and as we were about to debark, I tucked Pepé into my suitcase after the sleeper had taken effect and we debarked without any complications. On the army bus that met us at the port, I let him out of the case and we both stared out the window at New York City, at the honking, beautiful, colorful cars, at the masses of people in bright colored clothes, red, blue, green; at the tall buildings standing erect. It was a great contrast to the olive-drab khaki world of demolition we had come from. The driver passed through the bus and handed each of us a pint of milk, the first in over three years!

I decided to stay in New York for a day or two, and registered at a near hotel, since I had to buy a carrier for Pepé. I could not board the train with him as I had in Europe. I found a kennel in the neighborhood and left him there, because he could not stay in the hotel with me. As I walked up the avenue in my Class A uniform passing crowds of people; no one noticed me nor my two rows of ribbons on my jacket, the Meritorious Service Plaque on one sleeve and the six gold stripes for having been overseas three years on the other.

I stopped to look at a jewelry shop window, at something that caught my eye, and went inside to inquire about it. The salesman's attention was drawn to the Scarab ring that Brunson had given me. He was interested in it and its antiquity, but on looking at it closely remarked that the setting was fragile as it spun around so the hieroglyphs could be seen on the underside of the Scarab. He suggested that I should think about having it stabilized. I decided to have it done there, and the next day it was fixed with a firm gold ring with seashells on each side of the green beetle. It was much firmer and quite attractive.

While walking past the Charles of the Ritz Beauty Shoppe I decided to get a permanent wave. The shops in Europe had never been very satisfactory. It turned out the same as all my perms, far too curly. After inquiring about the train schedule, I telephoned my family to tell them I would be in Detroit at three o'clock the next day.

The following morning I checked out of the hotel and went to the kennel to pick up Pepé. I placed him inside the wicker carrier that I had purchased and took a cab to the New York Grand Central Station, where we boarded. When we arrived in Detroit, my sister Julia was parked at the Michigan Avenue entrance to the station. I had already let Pepé out of the carrier and led him into her car.

As we embraced, she said, "You're so thin. Didn't they feed you in the army? And your eyes, they're changed. Oh, but I'm so glad you are back safe."

"Oh, we had enough to eat. It was just that it was always pretty much the same."

Mentioning "eyes" suddenly brought to mind that Brunson had mentioned my eyes the last time I saw him in Cambrai, France. Yes, my eyes had seen the destruction of war, the loss of our youth, the broken hearts. It would take awhile to adjust to normalcy. The memories of the war are indelible. My experience in that terrible conflict had given me a lasting respect for life and for those who had fought to preserve it. We drove home.

Home at last!

Epilogue

Forty years later in 1985, I read in a newsletter that a group of bombardiers were planning a reunion in California. I wrote to the organizer, asking him if he would put an inquiry about Captain Herbert P. Brunson on the bulletin board. Within weeks I received a letter from Captain E. Amspoker USAAF, who wrote saying that he was in the same flight over Germany when Captain Brunson's ship went down on the 21st of February 1945. Brunson's bombs had proved superior on the run. However, his plane veered out of formation, trailed off to the right and rolled over into a spin. This was on the "Clarion" the secret carpet-bombing strategy that was in the planning process when I last was with Brunson in France in October 1944. The description of the flight is in the book *Bridge Busters*, the story of the 394th Bomb Group. At last I knew!

In retrospect, I believe that we who were there suffered a great deal from amnesia. We block out the destruction of war, the suffering, the cruelty, and we remember the pleasurable experiences. In reading my diary I find it filled with happy events, the fellowship of new friends, dancing to the music of a record player with those I loved, the instant rapport with some, the variety, the unity, the pleasure of an egg, an orange, the mistique of Coke. These were the simple things that gave us gratification.

Now I write within the clutter that one surrounds oneself with, things one *must* have—the computer, all the papers and books scattered about, television, radio, a full house, and children.

Yes, I married my long time sweetheart, Dr. Robert K. MacGregor.

Mildred A. MacGregor
(ex. 1st Lt. Mildred A. Radawiec, Army Nurse Corp.)

Acknowledgements

I want to thank the following people for making this book possible by keeping in touch over the many years.

Doctor Clifford L. Graves kept members of the Third Auxiliary Surgical Group together after the war ended, with letters. He had been a central figure in the Third Aux organization. After some years he developed a tradition of sending newsletters every five years to keep the "family" together, and kept this up the rest of his life. Members sent him their vital experiences in the war, which he included in his letters.

In 1950, Doctor Graves published the book *Front Line Surgeons*, retelling many of their World War II experiences. After his death in 1985, his wife, Catherina, sent me a box full of his communications from over the years. In 1990, I began to continue Cliff's tradition, except that I decided to write every year, as many of the members did not have five more years, and I included in the mailing some "lost" nurses and enlisted men. I sent a hundred and seventy letters, but that number dropped to about a hundred and fifty as letters began to be returned. Today there are about 45 members left; most are enlisted men who were eighteen years old when they were drafted into the army.

I asked members to send me interesting memories of their war experiences that I could pass on in my letters. Over the years many doctors have sent me brief diaries of the highlights of their careers, as did some nurses and enlisted personnel. Among them were John Chobanian, Emile Natelle, Lionel J. Thibault (a most loyal correspondent over the years, along with Chobanian), and Claude W. Thomas. Natelle became a POW (prisoner) captured in the Battle of the Bulge on December 16, 1944, along with a group of our surgeons, and walked from Belgium across Europe all the way to the Polish border in the coldest of winters, freezing and starving nearly to death, along with thousands of others who died.

I also want to thank lan Davidson, in Devan, United Kingdom, for the many years he has spent on Exercise Tiger, in an effort to establish a proper memorial for the 1200 men who died on the night of April 27, 1944 in a practice run on how to invade a beach in the English Channel, when German U-Boats sank two LSTs and damaged a third. The disaster was hushed up so that the Germans would not know about their success, and was all but forgotten until 1987, when war debris washed up on the beach at Slapton Sands.

I especially want to thank my weekly writing group for their support and friendship. The group was begun in the late Seventies by Ruth Campbell, Director of Social Work and Community Programs for the Geriatric Center at the University of Michigan Health System. Members of the group share thoughts, memoirs, reminiscences, happiness and sorrow. They encourage rather than correct. Our love and respect for each other creates joy for us all. They have listened to my reading of this entire book over many years.

Lastly, I thank Don Skiff, a member of this group, for his work in preparing the manuscript for printing.

Statistics

World War II was the most disastrous event in human history.

World War II Deaths

Approximately 62,000,000 lives—civilian and military—were lost in World War Two.

Soviet Union (pop. 168,500,000)	about 23,200,000
China (pop. 517,568,000)	10,000,000
Germany (pop. 69,623,000)	7,500,000
Poland (pop. 34,775,000)	5,600,000
Indonesia (pop. 69,435,000)	4,000,000
Japan (pop. 71,380,000)	2,600,000
India (pop. 378,000,000)	1,587,000
Yugoslavia (pop.15,400,000)	1,027,000
French Indo-China (pop. 24,600,000)	1,000,000
Romania (pop. 19,934,000)	841,000
Hungary (pop. 9,129,000)	580,000
France (pop. 41,700,000)	562,000
Italy (pop. 44,394,000)	459,500
United Kingdom (pop. 47,760,000)	450,400
United States (pop. 131,028,000)	418,500
Czechoslovakia (pop. 15,300,000)	365,000
Lithuania (pop. 2,575,000)	353,000
Greece (pop. 7,222,000)	300,000
Latvia (pop. 1,995,000)	227,000
Netherlands (pop. 8,729,000)	205,900
Ethiopia (pop. 17,700,000)	205,000
Philippines (pop. 16,000,000)	147,000
Austria (pop. 6,653,000)	110,000
Malaya (pop. 4,391,000)	100,000
Finland (pop. 3,700,000)	97,000
Belgium (pop. 8,387,000)	88,100
Burma (pop. 16,119,000)	60,000

Korea (pop. 23,400,000)	60,000
Pacific Islands (pop. 1,900,000)	57,000
Portuguese Timor (pop. 500,000	55,000
Singapore (pop. 728,000)	50,000
Canada (pop. 11,267,000)	45,300
Other (pop. 172,047,000)	187,100

In Nazi Concentration Camps, about 6,000,000 Jews, plus many other European nationals.

(Source: Wikipedia.org, as of 1/20/2007)

(Footnotes)
[1] This description first appeared in *Front Line Surgeons.*
[2] Ed. Note: An oubliette was a form of dungeon which was accessible only from a hatch in a high ceiling. To exit an oubliette was impossible under any circumstances, without outside help. The word comes from the French *oublier*, "to forget," as it was used for prisoners whom it was desired to forget.